COMPILATION OF SELECTED AEROSPACE LAWS

VOLUME 3: MISCELLANEOUS MEASURES AND INDEX

Updated through the 118th Congress

Includes provisions of:

Homeland Security Act of 2002 • Federal Aviation Act of 1958 • Airport and Airway Improvement Act of 1982 • Federal Airport Act • International Air Transportation Competition Act of 1979 • General Aviation Revitalization Act of 1994 • Clean Air Act • Title 10 U.S.C. • Aviation Medical Assistance Act of 1998 • Death on the High Seas • Title 18 U.S.C. • Airport Security Improvement Act of 2000 • National Transportation Safety Board Amendments Act of 2000 • Consolidated Appropriations Act, 2004 • Transportation, Treasury, Housing and Urban Development, the Judiciary, and Independent Agencies Appropriations Act, 2006 • Cape Town Treaty Implementation Act of 2004 • Implementing Recommendations of the 9/11 Commission Act • National Transportation Safety Board Reauthorization Act of 2006 • National Transportation Safety Board Reauthorization Act of 2003 • Public Law 109-87 • Safe, Accountable, Flexible, Efficient Transportation Equity Act: A Legacy for Users (SAFETEA-LU) • Department of Transportation and Related Agencies Appropriations Act, 2000 • National Defense Authorization Act for Fiscal Year 2016 • National Defense Authorization Act for Fiscal Year 2017 • John S. McCain National Defense Authorization Act for Fiscal Year 2007 • Aircraft Certification, Safety, and Accountability Act • American Security Drone Act • Pilots Bill of Rights • FAA Reauthorization Act of 2024

Prepared By M. TWINCHEK

2025

Forward

T his Compilation of Selected Laws is a resource for those interested in laws governing civil aerospace. This compilation includes laws governing civil aviation, aviation safety, airport improvement, the Federal Aviation Administration(FAA), the National Transportation Safety Board, aviation security, essential air service, commercial airlines, general aviation, unmanned aircraft systems, aviation labor, international aviation, commercial space transportation, air traffic management, and general FAA operations.

The materials included comes from publicly available, open source information, prepared for the public by the Office of the Legislative Counsel of the U.S. House of Representatives and the Office of the Law Revision Counsel.

Items listed as a Statute Compilation do not appear in the U.S. Code or that have been classified to a title of the U.S. Code that has not been enacted into positive law. Each Statute Compilation incorporates the amendments made to the underlying statute since it was originally enacted and are current as of the date noted.

This compilation is not an official document and should not be cited as evidence of any law. The official version of Federal law is found in the United States Statutes at Large and in the U.S. Code, the legal effect of which is established in sections 112 and 204, respectively, of title 1, United States Code.

A special thanks is extended to the Office of Law Revision Counsel and the House Office of the Legislative Counsel for providing the U.S. Code and statute compilations; and to the Government Publications Office for hosting and making these available for use to the public. An additional thank you is offered to the staff of the House and Senate Committees who were gracious in responding to inquiries and providing background information to the legislation included.

Questions and comments may be directed to:
M. Twinchek
Email: mtwinchek@outlook.com

Contents

MISCELLANEOUS PROVISIONS

SELECTED PROVISIONS OF THE HOMELAND SECURITY ACT OF 2002

PUBLIC LAW 107-296

HOMELAND SECURITY ACT OF 2002

[Public Law 107–296; Approved November 25, 2002]

[As Amended Through P.L. 118–103, Enacted October 1, 2024]

AN ACT To establish the Department of Homeland Security, and for other purposes.

Be it enacted by the Senate and House of Representatives of the United States of America in Congress assembled,

SECTION 1. SHORT TITLE; TABLE OF CONTENTS.

(a) [6 U.S.C. 101 note] SHORT TITLE.—This Act may be cited as the "Homeland Security Act of 2002".

(b) TABLE OF CONTENTS.—The table of contents for this Act is as follows:

* * * * * * *

TITLE XV—TRANSITION

* * * * * * *

Subtitle B— Transitional Provisions

Sec. 1511.   Transitional authorities.

* * * * * * *

TITLE IV—BORDER, MARITIME, AND TRANSPORTATION SECURITY

* * * * * * *

Subtitle C—Miscellaneous Provisions

* * * * * * *

SEC. 423. [6 U.S.C. 233] FUNCTIONS OF TRANSPORTATION SECURITY ADMINISTRATION.

(a) CONSULTATION WITH FEDERAL AVIATION ADMINISTRATION.—The Secretary and other officials in the Department shall consult with the Administrator of the Federal Aviation Administration before taking any action that might affect aviation safety, air carrier operations, aircraft airworthiness, or the use of airspace. The Secretary shall establish a liaison office within the Department for the purpose of consulting with the Administrator of the Federal Aviation Administration.

(b) REPORT TO CONGRESS.—Not later than 60 days after the date of enactment of this Act, the Secretary of Transportation shall transmit to Congress a report containing a plan for complying with the requirements of section 44901(d) of title 49, United States Code, as amended by section 425 of this Act.

(c) LIMITATIONS ON STATUTORY CONSTRUCTION.—

(1) GRANT OF AUTHORITY.—Nothing in this Act may be construed to vest in the Secretary or any other official in the Department any authority over transportation security that is not vested in the Under Secretary of Transportation for Security, or in the Secretary of Transportation under chapter 449 of title 49, United States Code, on the day before the date

of enactment of this Act.

(2) OBLIGATION OF AIP FUNDS.—Nothing in this Act may be construed to authorize the Secretary or any other official in the Department to obligate amounts made available under section 48103 of title 49, United States Code.

SEC. 424. [6 U.S.C. 234] PRESERVATION OF TRANSPORTATION SECURITY ADMINISTRATION AS A DISTINCT ENTITY.

Notwithstanding any other provision of this Act, the Transportation Security Administration shall be maintained as a distinct entity within the Department.

* * * * * * *

TITLE VI—TREATMENT OF CHARITABLE TRUSTS FOR MEMBERS OF THE ARMED FORCES OF THE UNITED STATES AND OTHER GOVERNMENTAL ORGANIZATIONS

SEC. 601. [6 U.S.C. 331] TREATMENT OF CHARITABLE TRUSTS FOR MEMBERS OF THE ARMED FORCES OF THE UNITED STATES AND OTHER GOVERNMENTAL ORGANIZATIONS.

(a) FINDINGS.—Congress finds the following:

(1) Members of the Armed Forces of the United States defend the freedom and security of our Nation.

(2) Members of the Armed Forces of the United States have lost their lives while battling the evils of terrorism around the world.

(3) Personnel of the Central Intelligence Agency (CIA) charged with the responsibility of covert observation of terrorists around the world are often put in harm's way during their service to the United States.

(4) Personnel of the Central Intelligence Agency have also lost their lives while battling the evils of terrorism around the world.

(5) Employees of the Federal Bureau of Investigation (FBI) and other Federal agencies charged with domestic protection of

the United States put their lives at risk on a daily basis for the freedom and security of our Nation.

(6) United States military personnel, CIA personnel, FBI personnel, and other Federal agents in the service of the United States are patriots of the highest order.

(7) CIA officer Johnny Micheal Spann became the first American to give his life for his country in the War on Terrorism declared by President George W. Bush following the terrorist attacks of September 11, 2001.

(8) Johnny Micheal Spann left behind a wife and children who are very proud of the heroic actions of their patriot father.

(9) Surviving dependents of members of the Armed Forces of the United States who lose their lives as a result of terrorist attacks or military operations abroad receive a $6,000 death benefit, plus a small monthly benefit.

(10) The current system of compensating spouses and children of American patriots is inequitable and needs improvement.

(b) DESIGNATION OF JOHNNY MICHEAL SPANN PATRIOT TRUSTS.—Any charitable corporation, fund, foundation, or trust (or separate fund or account thereof) which otherwise meets all applicable requirements under law with respect to charitable entities and meets the requirements described in subsection (c) shall be eligible to characterize itself as a "Johnny Micheal Spann Patriot Trust".

(c) REQUIREMENTS FOR THE DESIGNATION OF JOHNNY MICHEAL SPANN PATRIOT TRUSTS.—The requirements described in this subsection are as follows:

(1) Not taking into account funds or donations reasonably necessary to establish a trust, at least 85 percent of all funds or donations (including any earnings on the investment of such funds or donations) received or collected by any Johnny Micheal Spann Patriot Trust must be distributed to (or, if placed in a private foundation, held in trust for) surviving spouses, children, or dependent parents, grandparents, or siblings of 1 or more of the following:

(A) members of the Armed Forces of the United States;

(B) personnel, including contractors, of elements of the intelligence community, as defined in section 3(4) of the

National Security Act of 1947;

(C) employees of the Federal Bureau of Investigation;
and

(D) officers, employees, or contract employees of the
United States Government,

whose deaths occur in the line of duty and arise out of terrorist
attacks, military operations, intelligence operations, or law
enforcement operations or accidents connected with activities
occurring after September 11, 2001, and related to domestic
or foreign efforts to curb international terrorism, including the
Authorization for Use of Military Force (Public Law 107–40;
115 Stat. 224).

(2) Other than funds or donations reasonably necessary
to establish a trust, not more than 15 percent of all funds or
donations (or 15 percent of annual earnings on funds invested
in a private foundation) may be used for administrative
purposes.

(3) No part of the net earnings of any Johnny Micheal
Spann Patriot Trust may inure to the benefit of any individual
based solely on the position of such individual as a shareholder,
an officer or employee of such Trust.

(4) None of the activities of any Johnny Micheal Spann
Patriot Trust shall be conducted in a manner inconsistent with
any law that prohibits attempting to influence legislation.

(5) No Johnny Micheal Spann Patriot Trust may
participate in or intervene in any political campaign on behalf
of (or in opposition to) any candidate for public office, including
by publication or distribution of statements.

(6) Each Johnny Micheal Spann Patriot Trust shall comply
with the instructions and directions of the Director of Central
Intelligence, the Attorney General, or the Secretary of Defense
relating to the protection of intelligence sources and methods,
sensitive law enforcement information, or other sensitive
national security information, including methods for
confidentially disbursing funds.

(7) Each Johnny Micheal Spann Patriot Trust that receives
annual contributions totaling more than $1,000,000 must be
audited annually by an independent certified public accounting
firm. Such audits shall be filed with the Internal Revenue

Service, and shall be open to public inspection, except that the conduct, filing, and availability of the audit shall be consistent with the protection of intelligence sources and methods, of sensitive law enforcement information, and of other sensitive national security information.

(8) Each Johnny Micheal Spann Patriot Trust shall make distributions to beneficiaries described in paragraph (1) at least once every calendar year, beginning not later than 12 months after the formation of such Trust, and all funds and donations received and earnings not placed in a private foundation dedicated to such beneficiaries must be distributed within 36 months after the end of the fiscal year in which such funds, donations, and earnings are received.

(9)(A) When determining the amount of a distribution to any beneficiary described in paragraph (1), a Johnny Micheal Spann Patriot Trust should take into account the amount of any collateral source compensation that the beneficiary has received or is entitled to receive as a result of the death of an individual described in paragraph (1).

(B) Collateral source compensation includes all compensation from collateral sources, including life insurance, pension funds, death benefit programs, and payments by Federal, State, or local governments related to the death of an individual described in paragraph (1).

(d) TREATMENT OF JOHNNY MICHEAL SPANN PATRIOT TRUSTS.—Each Johnny Micheal Spann Patriot Trust shall refrain from conducting the activities described in clauses (i) and (ii) of section 301(20)(A) of the Federal Election Campaign Act of 1971 so that a general solicitation of funds by an individual described in paragraph (1) of section 323(e) of such Act will be permissible if such solicitation meets the requirements of paragraph (4)(A) of such section.

(e) NOTIFICATION OF TRUST BENEFICIARIES.—Notwithstanding any other provision of law, and in a manner consistent with the protection of intelligence sources and methods and sensitive law enforcement information, and other sensitive national security information, the Secretary of Defense, the Director of the Federal Bureau of Investigation, or the Director of Central Intelligence, or their designees, as applicable, may forward information received from an executor, administrator, or other legal representative of the estate of a decedent described in subparagraph (A), (B), (C), or (D) of subsection (c)(1), to a Johnny Micheal Spann Patriot Trust on how to contact individuals eligible for a distribution under subsection (c)(1) for the purpose of providing assistance from such Trust: *Provided,* That, neither forwarding nor failing to forward any information under this subsection shall create any cause of action against any Federal department, agency, officer, agent, or employee.

(f) REGULATIONS.—Not later than 90 days after the date of enactment of this Act, the Secretary of Defense, in coordination with the Attorney General, the Director of the Federal Bureau of Investigation, and the Director of Central Intelligence, shall prescribe regulations to carry out this section.

* * * * * * *

TITLE XV—TRANSITION

* * * * * * *

Subtitle B—Transitional Provisions

SEC. 1511. [6 U.S.C. 551] TRANSITIONAL AUTHORITIES.

(a) PROVISION OF ASSISTANCE BY OFFICIALS.—Until the transfer of an agency to the Department, any official having authority over or functions relating to the agency immediately before the effective date of this Act shall provide to the Secretary such assistance, including the use of personnel and assets, as the Secretary may request in preparing for the transfer and integration of the agency into the Department.

(b) SERVICES AND PERSONNEL.—During the transition period, upon the request of the Secretary, the head of any executive agency may, on a reimbursable basis, provide services or detail personnel to assist with the transition.

(c) ACTING OFFICIALS.—(1) During the transition period, pending the advice and consent of the Senate to the appointment of an officer required by this Act to be appointed by and with such advice and consent, the President may designate any officer whose appointment was required to be made by and with such advice and consent and who was such an officer immediately before the effective date of this Act (and who continues in office) or immediately before such designation, to act in such office until the same is filled as provided in this Act. While so acting, such officers shall receive compensation at the higher of—

(A) the rates provided by this Act for the respective offices in which they act; or

(B) the rates provided for the offices held at the time of designation.

(2) Nothing in this Act shall be understood to require the advice and consent of the Senate to the appointment by the President to a position in the Department of any officer whose agency is transferred to the Department pursuant to this Act and whose duties following such transfer are germane to those performed before such transfer.

(d) TRANSFER OF PERSONNEL, ASSETS, OBLIGATIONS, AND FUNCTIONS.—Upon the transfer of an agency to the Department—

(1) the personnel, assets, and obligations held by or available in connection with the agency shall be transferred to the Secretary for appropriate allocation, subject to the approval of the Director of the Office of Management and Budget and in accordance with the provisions of section 1531(a)(2) of title 31, United States Code; and

(2) the Secretary shall have all functions relating to the agency that any other official could by law exercise in relation to the agency immediately before such transfer, and shall have in addition all functions vested in the Secretary by this Act or other law.

(e) PROHIBITION ON USE OF TRANSPORTATION TRUST FUNDS.—

(1) IN GENERAL.—Notwithstanding any other provision of this Act, no funds derived from the Highway Trust Fund, Airport and Airway Trust Fund, Inland Waterway Trust Fund, or Harbor Maintenance Trust Fund, may be transferred to, made available to, or obligated by the Secretary or any other official in the Department.

(2) LIMITATION.—This subsection shall not apply to security-related funds provided to the Federal Aviation Administration for fiscal years preceding fiscal year 2003 for (A) operations, (B) facilities and equipment, or (C) research, engineering, and development, and to any funds provided to

the Coast Guard from the Sport Fish Restoration and Boating
Trust Fund for boating safety programs.

FEDERAL AVIATION ACT OF 1958

PUBLIC LAW 85-726

FEDERAL AVIATION ACT OF 1958 - SEC. 613

[Repealed by P.L. 103–272, Enacted July 7, 1994, except for the following section.]

AN ACT To continue the Civil Aeronautics Board as an agency of the United States, to create a Federal Aviation Agency, to provide for the regulation and promotion of civil aviation in such manner as to best foster its development and safety, and to provide for the safe and efficient use of the airspace by both civil and military aircraft, and for other purposes.

Be it enacted by the Senate and House of Representatives of the United States of America in Congress assembled,

* * * * * * *

SEC. 613. [49 U.S.C. 40103n] REGULATIONS.

(a) NATIONAL DISASTER AREAS.— Before the 180th day following the date of the enactment of this section [Nov. 5, 1990], the Administrator, for safety and humanitarian reasons, shall issue such regulations as may be necessary to prohibit or otherwise restrict aircraft overflights of any inhabited area which has been declared a national disaster area in the State of Hawaii.

(b) EXCEPTIONS.— Regulations issued pursuant to subsection (a) shall not be applicable in the case of aircraft overflights involving an emergency or a ligitimate [sic] scientific purpose.

AIRPORT AND AIRWAY IMPROVEMENT ACT OF 1982

PUBLIC LAW 97-248

PUBLIC LAW 97-248

[Titles V and VI of Public Law 97–248; 96 Stat. 671]

* * * * * * *

TITLE V—AIRPORT AND AIRWAY IMPROVEMENT[1]

---

[1] The Airport and Airway Improvement Act of 1982 was repealed by Public Law 103–272 except for the following.

SEC. 530. RELEASE OF CERTAIN CONDITIONS.

(a) CRYSTAL CITY, TEXAS.—(1) Notwithstanding section 16 of the Federal Airport Act (as in effect on January 3, 1949), the Secretary of Transportation is authorized, subject to the provisions of section 4 of the Act of October 1, 1949 (50 App. U.S.C. 1622c), and the provisions of paragraph (2) of this subsection, to grant releases from any of the terms, conditions, reservations, and restrictions contained in the deed of conveyance dated January 3, 1949, or any other deed of conveyance dated after such date and before the date of enactment of this section, under which the United States conveyed certain property to Crystal City, Texas, for airport purposes.

(2) Any release granted by the Secretary of Transportation under paragraph (1) of this subsection shall be subject to the following conditions:

(A) Crystal City, Texas, shall agree that in conveying any interest in the property which the United States conveyed to the city by a deed described in paragraph (1) the city will receive an amount for such interest which is equal to the fair market value (as determined pursuant to regulations issued by such Secretary).

(B) Any such amount so received by the city shall be used by the city for the development, improvement, operation, or maintenance of a public airport.

(b) BROWNWOOD, TEXAS.—(1) Notwithstanding section 16 of the Federal Airport Act (as in effect on June 26, 1950), the Secretary of Transportation is authorized, subject to the provisions of section 4 of the Act of October 1, 1949 (50 App. U.S.C. 1622c), and the provisions of paragraph (2) of this subsection, to grant releases from any of the terms, conditions, reservations, and restrictions contained in the deeds of conveyance dated June 26, 1950, and April 1, 1963, under which the United States conveyed certain property to the city of Brownwood, Texas, for airport purposes.

(2) Any release granted by the Secretary of Transportation under paragraph (1) of this subsection shall be subject to the following conditions:

(A) The city of Brownwood, Texas, shall agree that in conveying any interest in the property which the United States conveyed to the city by the deeds dated June 26, 1950, and April 1, 1963, the city will receive an amount for such interest which is equal to the fair market value (as determined pursuant to regulations issued by such Secretary).

(B) Any such amount so received by the city shall be used by the city for the development, improvement, operation, or maintenance of a public airport.

(c) GRAND JUNCTION, COLORADO.—(1) Notwithstanding section 16 of the Federal Airport Act (as in effect on September 14, 1951), the Secretary of Transportation is authorized, subject to the provisions of section 4 of the Act of October 1, 1949 (50 App. U.S.C. 1622c), and the provisions of paragraph (2) of this subsection, to grant releases from any of the terms, conditions, reservations, and restrictions contained in the deed of conveyance dated September 14, 1951, under which the United States conveyed certain property to the city of Grand Junction, Colorado, for airport purposes and the deed of conveyance dated March 24, 1975, under which the city of Grand Junction, Colorado, conveyed such property to the Walker Field Public Airport Authority.

(2) Any release granted by the Secretary of Transportation under paragraph (1) of this subsection shall be subject to the following conditions:

(A) The property for which releases are granted under this section shall not exceed a total of eighteen acres.

(B) The Walker Field Public Airport Authority shall agree that in leasing, or conveying any interest in, the property for which releases are granted under this section, such Authority will receive an amount which is equal to the fair lease value or the fair market value, as the case may be (as determined pursuant to regulations issued by such Secretary).

(C) Any such amount so received by the Walker Field Public Airport Authority, shall be used by such Authority for the development, improvement, operation, or maintenance of the Walker Field Public Airport.

(d) NEWPORT, ARKANSAS.—(1) Notwithstanding section 16 of the Federal Airport Act (as in effect on December 17, 1947), the Secretary of Transportation is authorized, subject to the provisions of section 4 of the Act of October 1, 1949 (50 App. U.S.C. 1622c), and the provisions of paragraph (2) of this subsection, to grant releases from any of the terms, conditions, reservations, and restrictions contained in the deed of conveyance dated December 17, 1947, or any other deed of conveyance dated after such date and before the date of enactment of this section, under which the United States conveyed certain property to Newport, Arkansas, for airport purposes.

(2) Any release granted by the Secretary of Transportation under paragraph (1) of this subsection shall be subject to the following conditions:

(A) Newport, Arkansas, shall agree that in conveying any interest in the property which the United States conveyed to the city by a deed described in paragraph (1) the city will receive an amount for such interest which is equal to the fair market value (as determined pursuant to regulations issued by such Secretary).

(B) Any such amount so received by the city shall be used by the city for the development, improvement, operation, or maintenance of a public airport.

* * * * * * *

Section 16 of the Federal Airport Act, as in effect on December 17, 1947

Public Law 79-377

FEDERAL AIRPORT ACT

(AS IN EFFECT ON DECEMBER 17, 1947)

[Public Law 79–377]

[As Amended Through P.L. 89-647, Enacted October 13, 1966]

* * * * * * *

USE OF GOVERNMENT-OWNED LANDS

SEC. 16. (a) REQUESTS FOR USE.— Whenever the Administrator determines that use of any lands owned or controlled by the United States is reasonably necessary for carrying out a project under this Act, or for the operation of any public airport, he shall file with the head of the department or agency having control of such lands a request that such property interest therein as he may deem necessary be conveyed to the public agency sponsoring the project in question or owning or controlling the airport. Such property interest may consist of the title to or any other interest in land or any easement through or other interest in air space.

(b) MAKING OF CONVEYANCES—Upon receipt of a request from the Administrator. under this section, the head of the department or agency having control of the lands in question shall determine whether the requested conveyance is inconsistent with the needs of the department or agency, and shall notify the Administrator of his determination within a period of four months after receipt of the Administrator's request. If such department or agency head determines that the requested conveyance is not inconsistent with the needs of that department or agency, such department or agency head is hereby authorized and directed, with the approval of the President and the Attorney General of the United States, and without any expense to the United States, to perform any acts and to execute any instruments necessary to make the conveyance requested; but each such conveyance shall be made on the condition that the property interest conveyed shall automatically revert to the United States in the event that the lands in question are not developed, or cease to be used, for airport purposes.

* * * * * * *

INTERNATIONAL AIR TRANSPORTATION COMPETITION ACT OF 1979

PUBLIC LAW 96-192

INTERNATIONAL AIR TRANSPORTATION COMPETITION ACT OF 1979[1]

[Public Law 96–192; 94 Stat. 35]

---

[1] Public Law 103–272 repealed the International Air Transportation Competition Act of 1979 except for section 29.

AN ACT To amend the Federal Aviation Act of 1958 in order to promote competition in international air transportation, provide greater opportunities for United States air carriers, establish goals for developing United States international aviation negotiating policy, and for other purposes.

* * * * * * *

SEC. 29. (a) Except as provided in subsection (c), notwithstanding any other provision of law, neither the Secretary of Transportation, the Civil Aeronautics Board, nor any other officer or employee of the United States shall issue, reissue, amend, revise, or otherwise modify (either by action or inaction) any certificate or other authority to permit or otherwise authorize any person to provide the transportation of individuals, by air, as a common carrier for compensation or hire between Love Field, Texas, and one or more points outside the State of Texas, except (1) charter air transportation not to exceed ten flights per month, and (2) air transportation provided by commuter airlines operating aircraft with a passenger capacity of 56 passengers or less.[2]

---

[2] Section 337(a) of P.L. 105–66 (111 Stat. 1447) reads as follows:

Sec. 337. (a) In General.—For purposes of the exception set forth in section 29(a)(2) of the International Air Transportation Competition Act of 1979 (Public Law 96–192; 94 Stat. 48), the term "passenger capacity of 56 passengers or less" includes any aircraft, except aircraft exceeding gross aircraft weight of 300,000 pounds, reconfigured to accommodate 56 or fewer passengers if the total number of passenger seats installed on the aircraft does

---

not exceed 56.

(b) Except as provided in subsections (a) and (c), notwithstanding any other provision of law, or any certificate or other authority heretofore or hereafter issued thereunder, no person shall provide or offer to provide the transportation of individuals, by air, for compensation or hire as a common carrier between Love Field, Texas, and one or more points outside the State of Texas, except that a person providing service to a point outside of Texas from Love Field on November 1, 1979, may continue to provide service to such a point.

(c) Subsections (a) and (b) shall not apply with respect to, and it is found consistent with the public convenience and necessity to authorize, transportation of individuals, by air, on a flight between Love Field, Texas, and one or more points within the States of Louisiana, Arkansas, Oklahoma, New Mexico, Kansas, Alabama, Mississippi, Missouri, and Texas by an air carrier, if (1) such air carrier does not offer or provide any through service or ticketing with another air carrier or foreign air carrier, and (2) such air carrier does not offer for sale transportation to or from, and the flight or aircraft does not serve, any point which is outside any such State. Nothing in this subsection shall be construed to give authority not otherwise provided by law to the Secretary of Transportation, the Civil Aeronautics Board, any other officer or employee of the United States, or any other person.

(d) This section shall not take effect if enacted after the enactment of the Aviation Safety and Noise Abatement Act of 1979.

GENERAL AVIATION REVITALIZATION ACT OF 1994

PUBLIC LAW 103-298

GENERAL AVIATION REVITALIZATION ACT OF 1994

[Public Law 103–298; 108 Stat. 1552; 49 U.S.C. 40101 note]

[This Act has not been amended]

AN ACT To amend the Federal Aviation Act of 1958 to establish time limitations on certain civil actions against aircraft manufacturers, and for other purposes.

Be it enacted by the Senate and House of Representatives of the United States of America in Congress assembled,

SECTION 1. SHORT TITLE.

This Act may be cited as the "General Aviation Revitalization Act of 1994".

SEC. 2. TIME LIMITATIONS ON CIVIL ACTIONS AGAINST AIRCRAFT MANUFACTURERS.

(a) IN GENERAL.—Except as provided in subsection (b), no civil action for damages for death or injury to persons or damage to property arising out of an accident involving a general aviation aircraft may be brought against the manufacturer of the aircraft or the manufacturer of any new component, system, subassembly, or other part of the aircraft, in its capacity as a manufacturer if the accident occurred—

(1) after the applicable limitation period beginning on—

(A) the date of delivery of the aircraft to its first purchaser or lessee, if delivered directly from the manufacturer; or

(B) the date of first delivery of the aircraft to a person engaged in the business of selling or leasing such aircraft; or

(2) with respect to any new component, system,

subassembly, or other part which replaced another component, system, subassembly, or other part originally in, or which was added to, the aircraft, and which is alleged to have caused such death, injury, or damage, after the applicable limitation period beginning on the date of completion of the replacement or addition.

(b) EXCEPTIONS.—Subsection (a) does not apply—

(1) if the claimant pleads with specificity the facts necessary to prove, and proves, that the manufacturer with respect to a type certificate or airworthiness certificate for, or obligations with respect to continuing airworthiness of, an aircraft or a component, system, subassembly, or other part of an aircraft knowingly misrepresented to the Federal Aviation Administration, or concealed or withheld from the Federal Aviation Administration, required information that is material and relevant to the performance or the maintenance or operation of such aircraft, or the component, system, subassembly, or other part, that is causally related to the harm which the claimant allegedly suffered;

(2) if the person for whose injury or death the claim is being made is a passenger for purposes of receiving treatment for a medical or other emergency;

(3) if the person for whose injury or death the claim is being made was not aboard the aircraft at the time of the accident; or

(4) to an action brought under a written warranty enforceable under law but for the operation of this Act.

(c) GENERAL AVIATION AIRCRAFT DEFINED.—For the purposes of this Act, the term "general aviation aircraft" means any aircraft for which a type certificate or an airworthiness certificate has been issued by the Administrator of the Federal Aviation Administration, which, at the time such certificate was originally issued, had a maximum seating capacity of fewer than 20 passengers, and which was not, at the time of the accident, engaged in scheduled passenger-carrying operations as defined under regulations in effect under part A of subtitle VII of title 49, United States Code, at the time of the accident.

(d) RELATIONSHIP TO OTHER LAWS.—This section supersedes any State law to the extent that such law permits a civil action described in subsection (a) to be brought after the applicable limitation period for such civil action established by subsection (a).

SEC. 3. OTHER DEFINITIONS.

For purposes of this Act—

(1) the term "aircraft" has the meaning given such term in section 40102(a)(6) of title 49, United States Code;

(2) the term "airworthiness certificate" means an airworthiness certificate issued under section 44704(c)(1) of title 49, United States Code, or under any predecessor Federal statute;

(3) the term "limitation period" means 18 years with respect to general aviation aircraft and the components, systems, subassemblies, and other parts of such aircraft; and

(4) the term "type certificate" means a type certificate issued under section 44704(a) of title 49, United States Code, or under any predecessor Federal statute.

SEC. 4. EFFECTIVE DATE; APPLICATION OF ACT.

(a) EFFECTIVE DATE.—Except as provided in subsection (b), this Act shall take effect on the date of the enactment of this Act.

(b) APPLICATION OF ACT.—This Act shall not apply with respect to civil actions commenced before the date of the enactment of this Act.

Section 231(a)(2) of the Clean Air Act

July 14, 1955, ch. 360

CLEAN AIR ACT[1]

[1] The Clean Air Act (42 U.S.C. 7401–7626) consists of Public Law 159 (July 14. 1955; 69 Stat. 322) and the amendments made by subsequent enactments.

[As Amended Through P.L. 117–286, Enacted December 27, 2022]

* * * * * * *

TITLE II—EMISSION STANDARDS FOR MOVING SOURCES

SHORT TITLE

SEC. 201. This title may be cited as the "National Emission Standards Act."

[42 U.S.C. 7401 nt]

* * * * * * *

Part B— Aircraft Emission Standards

ESTABLISHMENT OF STANDARDS

SEC. 231. (a)

(2) (A) The Administrator shall, from time to time, issue proposed emission standards applicable to the emission of any air pollutant from any class or classes of aircraft engines which in his judgment causes, or contributes to, air pollution which may reasonably be anticipated to endanger public health or welfare.

(B) (i) The Administrator shall consult with the Administrator of the Federal Aviation Administration on aircraft engine emission standards.

       (ii) The Administrator shall not change the aircraft engine emission standards if such change would significantly increase noise and adversely affect safety.

* * * * * * *

[42 U.S.C. 7571]

* * * * * * *

SECTIONS 2274 AND 9514 OF TITLE 10 U.S.C.

TITLE 10—ARMED FORCES

This title was enacted by act Aug. 10, 1956, ch. 1041, §1, 70A Stat. 1

Subtitle A—General Military Law

* * * * * * *

PART IV—SERVICE, SUPPLY, AND PROPERTY

* * * * * * *

§2274. SPACE SITUATIONAL AWARENESS SERVICES AND INFORMATION: PROVISION TO NON-UNITED STATES GOVERNMENT ENTITIES

(a) AUTHORITY.—(1) Except as provided by paragraph (2), the Secretary of Defense may provide space situational awareness services and information to, and may obtain space situational awareness data and information from, non-United States Government entities in accordance with this section. Any such action may be taken only if the Secretary determines that such action is consistent with the national security interests of the United States.

(2) Beginning January 1, 2024, the Secretary may provide space situational awareness services and information to, and may obtain space situational awareness data and information from, non-United States Government entities under paragraph (1) only to the extent that the Secretary determines such actions are necessary to meet the national security interests of the United States.

(b) ELIGIBLE ENTITIES.—The Secretary may provide services and information under subsection (a) to, and may obtain data and information under subsection (a) from, any non-United States Government entity, including any of the following:

(1) A State.

(2) A political subdivision of a State.

(3) A United States commercial entity.

(4) The government of a foreign country.

(5) A foreign commercial entity.

(c) AGREEMENT.—The Secretary may not provide space situational awareness services and information under subsection (a) to a non-United States Government entity unless that entity enters into an agreement with the Secretary under which the entity—

(1) agrees to pay an amount that may be charged by the Secretary under subsection

(d):

    (2) agrees not to transfer any data or technical information received under the agreement, including the analysis of data, to any other entity without the express approval of the Secretary; and

    (3) agrees to any other terms and conditions considered necessary by the Secretary.

    (d) CHARGES.—(1) As a condition of an agreement under subsection (c), the Secretary may (except as provided in paragraph (2)) require the non-United States Government entity entering into the agreement to pay to the Department of Defense such amounts as the Secretary determines appropriate to reimburse the Department for the costs to the Department of providing space situational awareness services or information under the agreement.

    (2) The Secretary may not require the government of a State, or of a political subdivision of a State, to pay any amount under paragraph (1).

    (e) CREDITING OF FUNDS RECEIVED.—(1) Funds received for the provision of space situational awareness services or information pursuant to an agreement under this section shall be credited, at the election of the Secretary, to the following:

    (A) The appropriation, fund, or account used in incurring the obligation.

    (B) An appropriate appropriation, fund, or account currently available for the purposes for which the expenditures were made.

    (2) Funds credited under paragraph (1) shall be merged with, and remain available for obligation with, the funds in the appropriation, fund, or account to which credited.

    (f) PROCEDURES.—The Secretary shall establish procedures by which the authority under this section shall be carried out. As part of those procedures, the Secretary may allow space situational awareness services or information to be provided through a contractor of the Department of Defense.

    (g) IMMUNITY.—The United States, any agencies and instrumentalities thereof, and any individuals, firms, corporations, and other persons acting for the United States, shall be immune from any suit in any court for any cause of action arising from the provision or receipt of space situational awareness services or information, whether or not provided in accordance with this section, or any related action or omission.

    (h) NOTICE OF CONCERNS OF DISCLOSURE OF INFORMATION.—If the Secretary determines that a commercial or foreign entity has declined or is reluctant to provide data or information to the Secretary in accordance with this section due to the concerns of such entity about the potential disclosure of such data or information, the Secretary shall, not later than 60 days after the Secretary makes that determination, provide notice to the congressional defense committees of the declination or reluctance of such entity.

(Added Pub. L. 108–136, div. A, title IX, §913(a), Nov. 24, 2003, 117 Stat. 1565; amended Pub. L. 109–364, div. A, title IX, §912, Oct. 17, 2006, 120 Stat. 2355; Pub. L. 110–417, [div. A], title IX, §911, Oct. 14, 2008, 122 Stat. 4571; Pub. L. 111–84, div. A, title IX, §912(a), Oct. 28, 2009, 123 Stat. 2429; Pub. L. 115–232, div. A, title XVI, §1604(a), Aug. 13, 2018, 132 Stat. 2106.)

* * * * * * *

Subtitle D—Air Force and Space Force

* * * * * * *

PART IV—SERVICE, SUPPLY, AND PROCUREMENT

* * * * * * *

CHAPTER 961—CIVIL RESERVE AIR FLEET

Sec.

* * * * * * *

9514. Indemnification of Department of Transportation for losses covered by defense-related aviation insurance.

* * * * * * *

§9514. INDEMNIFICATION OF DEPARTMENT OF TRANSPORTATION FOR LOSSES COVERED BY DEFENSE-RELATED AVIATION INSURANCE

(a) PROMPT INDEMNIFICATION REQUIRED.—(1) In the event of a loss that is covered by defense-related aviation insurance, the Secretary of Defense shall promptly indemnify the Secretary of Transportation for the amount of the loss consistent with the indemnification agreement between the two Secretaries that underlies such insurance. The Secretary of Defense shall make such indemnification—

(A) in the case of a claim for the loss of an aircraft hull, not later than 30 days after the date on which the Secretary of Transportation determines the claim to be payable or that amounts are due under the policy that provided the defense-related aviation insurance; and

(B) in the case of any other claim, not later than 180 days after the date on which the Secretary of Transportation determines the claim to be payable.

(2) When there is a loss of an aircraft hull that is (or may be) covered by defense-related aviation insurance, the Secretary of Transportation may make, during the period when a claim for such loss is pending with the Secretary of Transportation, any required periodic payments owed by the insured party to a lessor or mortgagee of such aircraft. Such payments shall commence not later than 30 days following the date of the presentment of the claim for the loss of the aircraft hull to the Secretary of Transportation. If the Secretary of Transportation determines that the claim is payable, any amount paid under this paragraph arising from such claim shall be credited against the amount payable under the aviation insurance. If the Secretary of Transportation determines that the claim is not payable, any amount paid under this paragraph arising from such claim shall constitute a debt to the United States, payable to the insurance fund. Any such amounts so returned

to the United States shall be promptly credited to the fund or account from which the payments were made under this paragraph.

(b) SOURCE OF FUNDS FOR PAYMENT OF INDEMNITY.—The Secretary of Defense may pay an indemnity described in subsection (a) from any funds available to the Department of Defense for operation and maintenance, and such sums as may be necessary for payment of such indemnity are hereby authorized to be transferred to the Secretary of Transportation for such purpose.

(c) NOTICE TO CONGRESS.—In the event of a loss that is covered by defense-related aviation insurance in the case of an incident in which the covered loss is (or is expected to be) in an amount in excess of $10,000,000, the Secretary of Defense shall submit to Congress notification of the loss as soon after the occurrence of the loss as possible and in no event more than 30 days after the date of the loss.

(d) IMPLEMENTING MATTERS.—(1) Payment of indemnification under this section is not subject to section 2214 or 2215 of this title or any other provision of law requiring notification to Congress before funds may be transferred.

(2) Consolidation of claims arising from the same incident is not required before indemnification of the Secretary of Transportation for payment of a claim may be made under this section.

(e) CONSTRUCTION WITH OTHER TRANSFER AUTHORITY.—Authority to transfer funds under this section is in addition to any other authority provided by law to transfer funds (whether enacted before, on, or after the date of the enactment of this section) and is not subject to any dollar limitation or notification requirement contained in any other such authority to transfer funds.

(f) DEFINITIONS.—In this section:

(1) DEFENSE-RELATED AVIATION INSURANCE.—The term "defense-related aviation insurance" means aviation insurance and reinsurance provided through policies issued by the Secretary of Transportation under chapter 443 of title 49 that pursuant to section 44305(b) of that title is provided by that Secretary without premium at the request of the Secretary of Defense and is covered by an indemnity agreement between the Secretary of Transportation and the Secretary of Defense.

(2) LOSS.—The term "loss" includes damage to or destruction of property, personal injury or death, and other liabilities and expenses covered by the defense-related aviation insurance.

(Added Pub. L. 104–201, div. A, title X, §1079(a)(1), Sept. 23, 1996, 110 Stat. 2667; amended Pub. L. 108–136, div. A, title X, §1031(a)(60), Nov. 24, 2003, 117 Stat. 1603; Pub. L. 112–81, div. A, title X, §1064(10), Dec. 31, 2011, 125 Stat. 1587; Pub. L. 117–81, div. A, title X, §1083(c)(1)(C), Dec. 27, 2021, 135 Stat. 1923.)

SELECTED PROVISIONS OF THE AVIATION MEDICAL ASSISTANCE ACT OF 1998

PUBLIC LAW 105-170

AVIATION MEDICAL ASSISTANCE ACT OF 1998

[Public Law 105–170; 112 Stat. 47; 49 U.S.C. 44701 note]

[This Act has not been amended]

AN ACT To direct the Administrator of the Federal Aviation Administration to reevaluate the equipment in medical kits carried on, and to make a decision regarding requiring automatic external defibrillators to be carried on, aircraft operated by air carriers, and for other purposes.

Be it enacted by the Senate and House of Representatives of the United States of America in Congress assembled,

SECTION 1. SHORT TITLE.

This Act may be cited as the "Aviation Medical Assistance Act of 1998".

* * * * * * *

SEC. 5. LIMITATIONS ON LIABILITY.

(a) LIABILITY OF AIR CARRIERS.—An air carrier shall not be liable for damages in any action brought in a Federal or State court arising out of the performance of the air carrier in obtaining or attempting to obtain the assistance of a passenger in an in-flight medical emergency, or out of the acts or omissions of the passenger rendering the assistance, if the passenger is not an employee or agent of the carrier and the carrier in good faith believes that the passenger is a medically qualified individual.

(b) LIABILITY OF INDIVIDUALS.—An individual shall not be liable for damages in any action brought in a Federal or State court arising out of the acts or omissions of the individual in providing or attempting to provide assistance in the case of an in-flight medical emergency unless the individual, while rendering such assistance, is guilty of gross negligence or willful misconduct.

SEC. 6. DEFINITIONS.

In this Act—

(1)

* * *

* * * * * * *

(3) the term "medically qualified individual" includes any person who is licensed, certified, or otherwise qualified to provide medical care in a State, including a physician, nurse, physician assistant, paramedic, and emergency medical technician.

DEATH ON THE HIGH SEAS

CHAPTER 303 OF TITLE 46 U.S.C.

TITLE 46—SHIPPING

This title was enacted by Pub. L. 98–89, §1, Aug. 26, 1983, 97 Stat. 500; Pub. L. 99–509, title V, subtitle B, §5101, Oct. 21, 1986, 100 Stat. 1913; Pub. L. 100–424, §6, Sept. 9, 1988, 102 Stat. 1591; Pub. L. 100–710, title I, §102, Nov. 23, 1988, 102 Stat. 4738; Pub. L. 109–304, Oct. 6, 2006, 120 Stat. 1485

CHAPTER 303—DEATH ON THE HIGH SEAS

§30301. Short title

This chapter may be cited as the "Death on the High Seas Act".

(Pub. L. 109–304, §6(c), Oct. 6, 2006, 120 Stat. 1511.)

§30302. Cause of action

When the death of an individual is caused by wrongful act, neglect, or default occurring on the high seas beyond 3 nautical miles from the shore of the United States, the personal representative of the decedent may bring a civil action in admiralty against the person or vessel responsible. The action shall be for the exclusive benefit of the decedent's spouse, parent, child, or dependent relative.

(Pub. L. 109–304, §6(c), Oct. 6, 2006, 120 Stat. 1511.)

§30303. Amount and apportionment of recovery

The recovery in an action under this chapter shall be a fair compensation for the pecuniary loss sustained by the individuals for whose benefit the action is brought. The court shall apportion the recovery among those individuals in proportion to the loss each has sustained.

(Pub. L. 109–304, §6(c), Oct. 6, 2006, 120 Stat. 1511.)

§30304. Contributory negligence

In an action under this chapter, contributory negligence of the decedent is not a bar to recovery. The court shall consider the degree of negligence of the decedent and reduce the recovery accordingly.

(Pub. L. 109–304, §6(c), Oct. 6, 2006, 120 Stat. 1511.)

§30305. Death of plaintiff in pending action

If a civil action in admiralty is pending in a court of the United States to recover for personal injury caused by wrongful act, neglect, or default described in section 30302 of this title, and the individual dies during the action as a result of the wrongful act, neglect, or default, the personal representative of the decedent may be substituted as the plaintiff and the action may proceed under this chapter for the recovery authorized by this chapter.

(Pub. L. 109–304, §6(c), Oct. 6, 2006, 120 Stat. 1511.)

§30306. Foreign cause of action

When a cause of action exists under the law of a foreign country for death by wrongful act, neglect, or default on the high seas, a civil action in admiralty may be brought in a court of the United States based on the foreign cause of action, without abatement of the amount for which recovery is authorized.

(Pub. L. 109–304, §6(c), Oct. 6, 2006, 120 Stat. 1511.)

§30307. Commercial aviation accidents

(a) Definition.—In this section, the term "nonpecuniary damages" means damages for loss of care, comfort, and companionship.

(b) Beyond 12 Nautical Miles.—In an action under this chapter, if the death resulted from a commercial aviation accident occurring on the high seas beyond 12 nautical miles from the shore of the United States, additional compensation is recoverable for nonpecuniary damages, but punitive damages are not recoverable.

(c) Within 12 Nautical Miles.—This chapter does not apply if the death resulted from a commercial aviation accident occurring on the high seas 12 nautical miles or less from the shore of the United States.

(Pub. L. 109–304, §6(c), Oct. 6, 2006, 120 Stat. 1512.)

§30308. Nonapplication

(a) State Law.—This chapter does not affect the law of a State regulating the right to recover for death.

(b) Internal Waters.—This chapter does not apply to the Great Lakes or waters within the territorial limits of a State.

(Pub. L. 109–304, §6(c), Oct. 6, 2006, 120 Stat. 1512.)

Selected Provisions of Title 18 U.S.C.

TITLE 18—CRIMES AND CRIMINAL PROCEDURE

This title was enacted by act June 25, 1948, ch. 645, §1, 62 Stat. 683

PartSec.
I.Crimes

* * * * * * *

PART I—CRIMES

* * * * * * *

CHAPTER 1—GENERAL PROVISIONS

* * * * * * *

CHAPTER 2—AIRCRAFT AND MOTOR VEHICLES

* * * * * * *

§31. Definitions

(a) Definitions.—In this chapter, the following definitions apply:

(1) Aircraft.—The term "aircraft" means a civil, military, or public contrivance invented, used, or designed to navigate, fly, or travel in the air.

(2) Aviation quality.—The term "aviation quality", with respect to a part of an

aircraft or space vehicle, means the quality of having been manufactured, constructed, produced, maintained, repaired, overhauled, rebuilt, reconditioned, or restored in conformity with applicable standards specified by law (including applicable regulations).

(3) DESTRUCTIVE SUBSTANCE.—The term "destructive substance" means an explosive substance, flammable material, infernal machine, or other chemical, mechanical, or radioactive device or matter of a combustible, contaminative, corrosive, or explosive nature.

(4) IN FLIGHT.—The term "in flight" means—

(A) any time from the moment at which all the external doors of an aircraft are closed following embarkation until the moment when any such door is opened for disembarkation; and

(B) in the case of a forced landing, until competent authorities take over the responsibility for the aircraft and the persons and property on board.

(5) IN SERVICE.—The term "in service" means—

(A) any time from the beginning of preflight preparation of an aircraft by ground personnel or by the crew for a specific flight until 24 hours after any landing; and

(B) in any event includes the entire period during which the aircraft is in flight.

(6) MOTOR VEHICLE.—The term "motor vehicle" means every description of carriage or other contrivance propelled or drawn by mechanical power and used for commercial purposes on the highways in the transportation of passengers, passengers and property, or property or cargo.

(7) PART.—The term "part" means a frame, assembly, component, appliance, engine, propeller, material, part, spare part, piece, section, or related integral or auxiliary equipment.

(8) SPACE VEHICLE.—The term "space vehicle" means a man-made device, either manned or unmanned, designed for operation beyond the Earth's atmosphere.

(9) STATE.—The term "State" means a State of the United States, the District of Columbia, and any commonwealth, territory, or possession of the United States.

(10) USED FOR COMMERCIAL PURPOSES.—The term "used for commercial purposes" means the carriage of persons or property for any fare, fee, rate, charge or other consideration, or directly or indirectly in connection with any business, or other undertaking intended for profit.

(b) TERMS DEFINED IN OTHER LAW.—In this chapter, the terms "aircraft engine", "air navigation facility", "appliance", "civil aircraft", "foreign air commerce", "interstate air commerce", "landing area", "overseas air commerce", "propeller", "spare part", and "special aircraft jurisdiction of the United States" have the meanings given those terms in sections 40102(a) and 46501 of title 49.

(Added July 14, 1956, ch. 595, §1, 70 Stat. 538; amended Pub. L. 98–473, title II, §§1010, 2013(a), Oct. 12, 1984, 98 Stat. 2141, 2187; Pub. L. 100–690, title VII, §7015, Nov. 18, 1988, 102 Stat. 4395; Pub. L. 103–272, §5(e)(1), July 5, 1994, 108 Stat. 1373; Pub. L. 106–181, title V, §506(b), Apr. 5, 2000, 114 Stat. 136.)

* * * * * * *

§38. FRAUD INVOLVING AIRCRAFT OR SPACE VEHICLE PARTS IN INTERSTATE

OR FOREIGN COMMERCE

(a) OFFENSES.—Whoever, in or affecting interstate or foreign commerce, knowingly and with the intent to defraud—

(1)(A) falsifies or conceals a material fact concerning any aircraft or space vehicle part;

(B) makes any materially fraudulent representation concerning any aircraft or space vehicle part; or

(C) makes or uses any materially false writing, entry, certification, document, record, data plate, label, or electronic communication concerning any aircraft or space vehicle part;

(2) exports from or imports or introduces into the United States, sells, trades, installs on or in any aircraft or space vehicle any aircraft or space vehicle part using or by means of a fraudulent representation, document, record, certification, depiction, data plate, label, or electronic communication; or

(3) attempts or conspires to commit an offense described in paragraph (1) or (2),

shall be punished as provided in subsection (b).

(b) PENALTIES.—The punishment for an offense under subsection (a) is as follows:

(1) AVIATION QUALITY.—If the offense relates to the aviation quality of a part and the part is installed in an aircraft or space vehicle, a fine of not more than $500,000, imprisonment for not more than 15 years, or both.

(2) FAILURE TO OPERATE AS REPRESENTED.—If, by reason of the failure of the part to operate as represented, the part to which the offense is related is the proximate cause of a malfunction or failure that results in serious bodily injury (as defined in section 1365), a fine of not more than $1,000,000, imprisonment for not more than 20 years, or both.

(3) FAILURE RESULTING IN DEATH.—If, by reason of the failure of the part to operate as represented, the part to which the offense is related is the proximate cause of a malfunction or failure that results in the death of any person, a fine of not more than $1,000,000, imprisonment for any term of years or life, or both.

(4) OTHER CIRCUMSTANCES.—In the case of an offense under subsection (a) not described in paragraph (1), (2), or (3) of this subsection, a fine under this title, imprisonment for not more than 10 years, or both.

(5) ORGANIZATIONS.—If the offense is committed by an organization, a fine of not more than—

(A) $10,000,000 in the case of an offense described in paragraph (1) or (4); and

(B) $20,000,000 in the case of an offense described in paragraph (2) or (3).

(c) CIVIL REMEDIES.—

(1) IN GENERAL.—The district courts of the United States shall have jurisdiction to prevent and restrain violations of this section by issuing appropriate orders, including—

(A) ordering a person (convicted of an offense under this section) to divest any interest, direct or indirect, in any enterprise used to commit or facilitate the commission of the offense, or to destroy, or to mutilate and sell as scrap, aircraft material or part inventories or stocks;

(B) imposing reasonable restrictions on the future activities or investments of any such person, including prohibiting engagement in the same type of endeavor as used to commit the offense; and

(C) ordering the dissolution or reorganization of any enterprise knowingly used to commit or facilitate the commission of an offense under this section making due provisions for the rights and interests of innocent persons.

(2) RESTRAINING ORDERS AND PROHIBITION.—Pending final determination of a proceeding brought under this section, the court may enter such restraining orders or prohibitions, or take such other actions (including the acceptance of satisfactory performance bonds) as the court deems proper.

(3) ESTOPPEL.—A final judgment rendered in favor of the United States in any criminal proceeding brought under this section shall stop the defendant from denying the essential allegations of the criminal offense in any subsequent civil proceeding brought by the United States.

(d) CRIMINAL FORFEITURE.—

(1) IN GENERAL.—The court, in imposing sentence on any person convicted of an offense under this section, shall order, in addition to any other sentence and irrespective of any provision of State law, that the person forfeit to the United States—

(A) any property constituting, or derived from, any proceeds that the person obtained, directly or indirectly, as a result of the offense; and

(B) any property used, or intended to be used in any manner, to commit or facilitate the commission of the offense, if the court in its discretion so determines, taking into consideration the nature, scope, and proportionality of the use of the property on the offense.

(2) APPLICATION OF OTHER LAW.—The forfeiture of property under this section, including any seizure and disposition of the property, and any proceedings relating to the property, shall be governed by section 413 of the Comprehensive Drug Abuse and Prevention Act of 1970 (21 U.S.C. 853) (not including subsection (d) of that section).

(e) CONSTRUCTION WITH OTHER LAW.—This section does not preempt or displace any other remedy, civil or criminal, provided by Federal or State law for the fraudulent importation, sale, trade, installation, or introduction into commerce of an aircraft or space vehicle part.

(f) TERRITORIAL SCOPE.—This section also applies to conduct occurring outside the United States if—

(1) the offender is a natural person who is a citizen or permanent resident alien of the United States, or an organization organized under the laws of the United States or political subdivision thereof;

(2) the aircraft or spacecraft part as to which the violation relates was installed in an aircraft or space vehicle owned or operated at the time of the offense by a citizen or permanent resident alien of the United States, or by an organization thereof; or

(3) an act in furtherance of the offense was committed in the United States.

(Added Pub. L. 106–181, title V, §506(c)(1), Apr. 5, 2000, 114 Stat. 137.)

* * * * * * *

§39A. AIMING A LASER POINTER AT AN AIRCRAFT

(a) OFFENSE.—Whoever knowingly aims the beam of a laser pointer at an aircraft in the special aircraft jurisdiction of the United States, or at the flight path of such an aircraft, shall be fined under this title or imprisoned not more than 5 years, or both.

(b) LASER POINTER DEFINED.—As used in this section, the term "laser pointer" means any device designed or used to amplify electromagnetic radiation by stimulated emission that emits a beam designed to be used by the operator as a pointer or highlighter to indicate, mark, or identify a specific position, place, item, or object.

(c) EXCEPTIONS.—This section does not prohibit aiming a beam of a laser pointer at an aircraft, or the flight path of such an aircraft, by—

(1) an authorized individual in the conduct of research and development or flight test operations conducted by an aircraft manufacturer, the Federal Aviation Administration, or any other person authorized by the Federal Aviation Administration to conduct such research and development or flight test operations;

(2) members or elements of the Department of Defense or Department of Homeland Security acting in an official capacity for the purpose of research, development, operations, testing, or training; or

(3) by an individual using a laser emergency signaling device to send an emergency distress signal.

(d) AUTHORITY TO ESTABLISH ADDITIONAL EXCEPTIONS BY REGULATION.—The Attorney General, in consultation with the Secretary of Transportation, may provide by regulation, after public notice and comment, such additional exceptions to this section as may be necessary and appropriate. The Attorney General shall provide written notification of any proposed regulations under this section to the Committees on the Judiciary of the Senate and the House of Representatives, the Committee on Commerce, Science, and Transportation of the Senate, and the Committee on Transportation and Infrastructure of the House of Representatives, not less than 90 days before such regulations become final.

(Added Pub. L. 112–95, title III, §311(a), Feb. 14, 2012, 126 Stat. 65.)

§39B. UNSAFE OPERATION OF UNMANNED AIRCRAFT

(a) OFFENSE.—Any person who operates an unmanned aircraft and:

(1) Knowingly interferes with, or disrupts the operation of, an aircraft carrying 1 or more occupants operating in the special aircraft jurisdiction of the United States, in a manner that poses an imminent safety hazard to such occupants, shall be punished as provided in subsection (c).

(2) Recklessly interferes with, or disrupts the operation of, an aircraft carrying 1 or more occupants operating in the special aircraft jurisdiction of the United States, in a manner that poses an imminent safety hazard to such occupants, shall be punished as provided in subsection (c).

(b) OPERATION OF UNMANNED AIRCRAFT IN CLOSE PROXIMITY TO AIRPORTS.—

(1) IN GENERAL.—Any person who, without authorization, knowingly operates an unmanned aircraft within a runway exclusion zone shall be punished as provided in subsection (c).

(2) RUNWAY EXCLUSION ZONE DEFINED.—In this subsection, the term "runway exclusion zone" means a rectangular area—

(A) centered on the centerline of an active runway of an airport immediately around which the airspace is designated as class B, class C, or class D airspace at the surface under part 71 of title 14, Code of Federal Regulations; and

(B) the length of which extends parallel to the runway's centerline to points that are 1 statute mile from each end of the runway and the width of which is ½ statute mile.

(c) PENALTY.—

(1) IN GENERAL.—Except as provided in paragraph (2), the punishment for an offense under subsections [1] (a) or (b) shall be a fine under this title, imprisonment for not more than 1 year, or both.

(2) SERIOUS BODILY INJURY OR DEATH.—Any person who:

(A) Causes serious bodily injury or death during the commission of an offense under subsection (a)(2) shall be fined under this title, imprisoned for a term of up to 10 years, or both.

(B) Causes, or attempts or conspires to cause, serious bodily injury or death during the commission of an offense under subsections (a)(1) and (b) shall be fined under this title, imprisoned for any term of years or for life, or both.

(Added Pub. L. 115–254, div. B, title III, §384(a), Oct. 5, 2018, 132 Stat. 3322.)

[1] *So in original. Probably should be "subsection".*

* * * * * * *

§40A. OPERATION OF UNAUTHORIZED UNMANNED AIRCRAFT OVER WILDFIRES

(a) IN GENERAL.—Except as provided in subsection (b), an individual who operates an unmanned aircraft and knowingly or recklessly interferes with a wildfire suppression, or law enforcement or emergency response efforts [1] related to a wildfire suppression, shall be fined under this title, imprisoned for not more than 2 years, or both.

(b) EXCEPTIONS.—This section does not apply to the operation of an unmanned aircraft conducted by a unit or agency of the United States Government or of a State, tribal, or local government (including any individual conducting such operation pursuant to a contract or other agreement entered into with the unit or agency) for the purpose of protecting the public safety and welfare, including firefighting, law enforcement, or emergency response.

(c) DEFINITIONS.—In this section, the following definitions apply:

(1) UNMANNED AIRCRAFT.—The term "unmanned aircraft" has the meaning given the term in section 44801 of title 49, United States Code.

(2) WILDFIRE.—The term "wildfire" has the meaning given that term in section 2 of the Emergency Wildfire Suppression Act (42 U.S.C. 1856m).

(3) WILDFIRE SUPPRESSION.—The term "wildfire suppression" means an effort to contain, extinguish, or suppress a wildfire.

(Added Pub. L. 115–254, div. B, title III, §382(a), Oct. 5, 2018, 132 Stat. 3320.)

[1] *So in original. Probably should be "effort".*

AIRPORT SECURITY IMPROVEMENT ACT OF 2000

PUBLIC LAW 106-528

AIRPORT SECURITY IMPROVEMENT ACT OF 2000

[Public Law 106–528; 114 Stat. 2521; 49 U.S.C. 44903 note]

[This Act has not been amended]

AN ACT To amend title 49, United States Code, to improve airport security.

Be it enacted by the Senate and House of Representatives of the United States of America in Congress assembled,

SECTION 1. SHORT TITLE.

This Act may be cited as the "Airport Security Improvement Act of 2000".

* * * * * * *

SEC. 5. PHYSICAL SECURITY FOR ATC FACILITIES.

(a) IN GENERAL.—In order to ensure physical security at Federal Aviation Administration staffed facilities that house air traffic control systems, the Administrator of the Federal Aviation Administration shall act immediately to—

(1) correct physical security weaknesses at air traffic control facilities so the facilities can be granted physical security accreditation not later than April 30, 2004; and

(2) ensure that follow-up inspections are conducted, deficiencies are promptly corrected, and accreditation is kept current for all air traffic control facilities.

(b) REPORTS.—Not later than April 30, 2001, and annually thereafter through April 30, 2004, the Administrator shall transmit to the Committee on Commerce, Science, and Transportation of the Senate and the Committee on Transportation and Infrastructure of the House of Representatives a report on the progress being made in improving the physical security of air traffic control facilities, including the percentage of such facilities that have been granted physical security accreditation.

* * * * * * *

NATIONAL TRANSPORTATION SAFETY BOARD AMENDMENTS ACT OF 2000

PUBLIC LAW 106-424

NATIONAL TRANSPORTATION SAFETY BOARD AMENDMENTS ACT OF 2000

[Public Law 106–424; 114 Stat. 1886; 49 U.S.C. 1113 note]

[This Act has not been amended]

AN ACT To amend title 49, United States Code, to authorize appropriations for the National Transportation Safety Board for fiscal years 2000, 2001, 2002, and 2003, and for other purposes.

Be it enacted by the Senate and House of Representatives of the United States of America in Congress assembled,

* * * * * * *

SEC. 9. TRAVEL BUDGETS.

The Chairman of the National Transportation Safety Board shall establish annual fiscal year budgets for non-accident-related travel expenditures for Board members which shall be approved by the Board and submitted to the Senate Committee on Commerce, Science, and Transportation and to the House of Representatives Committee on Transportation and Infrastructure together with an annual report detailing the non-accident-related travel of each Board member. The report shall include separate accounting for foreign and domestic travel, including any personnel or other expenses associated with that travel.

* * * * * * *

SECTION 521 OF DIVISION F OF THE CONSOLIDATED APPROPRIATIONS ACT, 2004

PUBLIC LAW 108-199

Section 521 of DIVISION F OF THE CONSOLIDATED APPROPRIATIONS ACT, 2004

[P.L. 108-199; enacted January 23, 2004 as amended by Pub. L. 118-63, title XI, sec. 1115(b), May 16, 2024, 138 Stat. 1421]

AN ACT Making appropriations for Agriculture, Rural Development, Food and Drug Administration, and Related Agencies for the fiscal year ending September 30, 2004, and for other purposes.

Be it enacted by the Senate and House of Representatives of the United States of America in Congress assembled,

* * * * * * *

DIVISION F— TRANSPORTATION, TREASURY, AND INDEPENDENT AGENCIES APPROPRIATIONS, 2004

* * * * * * *

SEC. 521. [49 U.S.C. 40103n]

(a) IN GENERAL. The Secretary of Transportation—

(1) shall, without regard to any fiscal year limitation, maintain in full force and effect the restrictions imposed under Federal Aviation Administration Notices to Airmen FDC 3/2122, FDC 3/2123, and FDC 2/0199; and

(2) may not grant any waivers or exemptions from such restrictions, except—

(A) as authorized by air traffic control for operational or safety purposes;

(B) with respect to an event, stadium, or other venue—

(i) for operational purposes;

(ii) for the transport of team members, officials of

the governing body, and immediate family members and guests of (or attendees approved by) such team members and officials to and from such event, stadium, or venue;

(iii) in the case of a sporting event, for the transport of equipment or parts to and from such sporting event;

(iv) to permit a broadcast rights holder to provide broadcast coverage of such event, stadium, or venue;

(v) for safety and security purposes related to such event, stadium, or venue; and

(vi) to permit the safe operation of an aircraft that is operated by an airshow performer in connection with an airshow, provided such aircraft is not permitted to operate directly over the stadium (or adjacent parking facilities) during the sporting event; and

(C) to allow the operation of an aircraft in restricted airspace to the extent necessary to arrive at or depart from an airport using standard air traffic control procedures.

(b) LIMITATIONS ON USE OF FUNDS. None of the funds appropriated or otherwise made available by title I of this Act [div. F of Pub. L. 108-199, see Tables for classification] may be obligated or expended to terminate or limit the restrictions imposed under the Federal Aviation Administration Notices to Airmen referred to in subsection (a), or to grant waivers of, or exemptions from, such restrictions except as provided under subsection (a)(2).

(c) BROADCAST CONTRACTS NOT AFFECTED. Nothing in this section shall be construed to affect contractual rights pertaining to any broadcasting agreement.

* * * * * * *

SECTIONS 175 AND 180 OF DIVISION A OF THE TRANSPORTATION, TREASURY, HOUSING AND URBAN DEVELOPMENT, THE JUDICIARY, AND INDEPENDENT AGENCIES APPROPRIATIONS ACT, 2006

PUBLIC LAW 109-115

SECTIONS 175 AND 180 OF DIVISION A OF THE TRANSPORTATION, TREASURY, HOUSING AND URBAN DEVELOPMENT, THE JUDICIARY, THE DISTRICT OF COLUMBIA, AND INDEPENDENT AGENCIES APPROPRIATIONS ACT, 2006

[(Public Law 109-115)]

AN ACT Making appropriations for the Departments of Transportation, Treasury, and Housing and Urban Development, the Judiciary, District of Columbia, and independent agencies for the fiscal year ending September 30, 2006, and for other purposes.

Be it enacted by the Senate and House of Representatives of the United States of America in Congress assembled,

* * * * * * *

DIVISION A—TRANSPORTATION, TREASURY, HOUSING AND URBAN DEVELOPMENT, THE JUDICIARY, AND INDEPENDENT AGENCIES APPROPRIATIONS ACT, 2006

* * * * * * *

TITLE I—DEPARTMENT OF TRANSPORTATION

* * * * * * *

SEC. 175.

Notwithstanding any provision of law, the Secretary of Transportation is authorized and directed to make project grants under chapter 471 of title 49, United States Code, from funds available for fiscal year 2006 and thereafter under 49 U.S.C. 48103, for the cost of acquisition of land, or reimbursement of the cost of land if purchased prior to enactment of this provision and prior to a grant agreement, for non-exclusive use aeronautical purposes on an airport layout plan that section 49 U.S.C. 47107(a)(16), for any small hub airport as defined in 49 U.S.C. 47102, and had scheduled or chartered direct international flights totaling at least 200 million pounds gross aircraft landed weight for calendar year 2002.

* * * * * * *

SEC. 180.

(a) In this section:

(1) The term ``Conservation Area" means the Sloan Canyon National Conservation Area established by section 604(a) of the Clark County Conservation of Public Land and Natural Resources Act of 2002 (116 Stat. 2010).

(2) The term ``County" means Clark County, Nevada.

(3) (A) The term ``helicopter tour" means a commercial helicopter tour operated for profit.

(B) The term ``helicopter tour" does not include a helicopter tour that is carried out to assist a Federal, State, or local agency.

(4) The term ``Secretary" means the Secretary of the Interior.

(5) The term ``Wilderness" means the North McCullough Mountains Wilderness established by section 202(a)(13) of the Clark County Conservation of Public Land and Natural Resources Act of 2002 (116 Stat. 2000).

(b) As soon as practicable after the date of enactment of this Act, the Secretary shall convey to the County, subject to valid existing rights, for no consideration, all right, title, and interest of the United States in and to the parcel of land described in subsection (c).

(c) The parcel of land to be conveyed under subsection (b) is the parcel of approximately 229 acres of land depicted as tract A on the map entitled ``Clark County Public Heliport Facility" and dated May 3, 2004.

(d) (1) The parcel of land conveyed under subsection (b)—

(A) hall be used by the County for the operation of a heliport facility under the conditions stated in paragraphs (2),

(3), and (4); and

(B) shall not be disposed of by the County.

(2) (A) Any operator of a helicopter tour originating from or concluding at the parcel of land described in subsection (c) shall pay to the Clark County Department of Aviation a $3 conservation fee for each passenger on the helicopter tour if any portion of the helicopter tour occurs over the Conservation Area.

(B) (i) Not earlier than 10 years after the date of enactment of this Act and every 10 years thereafter, the Secretary shall conduct a review to determine whether to raise the amount of the conservation fee.

(ii) After conducting a review under clause (i) and providing an opportunity for public comment, the Secretary may raise the amount of the conservation fee in an amount determined to be appropriate by the Secretary, but by not more than 50 percent of the amount of the conservation fee in effect on the day before the date of the increase.

(3) (A) The amounts collected under paragraph (2) shall be deposited in a special account in the Treasury of the United States.

(B) Of the amounts deposited under subparagraph (A)—

(i) ⅔ of the amounts shall be available to the Secretary, without further appropriation, for the management of cultural, wildlife, and wilderness resources on public land in the State of Nevada; and

(ii) ⅓ of the amounts shall be available to the Director of the Bureau of Land Management, without further appropriation, for the conduct of Bureau of Land Management operations for the Conservation Area and the Red Rock Canyon National Conservation Area.

(4) (A) Except for safety reasons, any helicopter tour originating or concluding at the parcel of land described in subsection (c) that flies over the Conservation Area shall not fly—

(i) over any area in the Conservation Area except the

area that is between 3 and 5 miles north of the latitude of the southernmost boundary of the Conservation Area;

(ii) lower than 1,000 feet over the eastern segments of the boundary of the Conservation Area; or

(iii) lower than 500 feet over the western segments of the boundary of the Conservation Area.

(B) The Administrator of the Federal Aviation Administration shall establish a special flight rules area and any operating procedures that the Administrator determines to be necessary to implement subparagraph (A).

(5) If the County ceases to use any of the land described in subsection (c) for the purpose described in paragraph (1)(A) and under the conditions stated in paragraph (2)—

(A) title to the parcel shall revert to the United States, at the option of the United States; and

(B) the County shall be responsible for any reclamation necessary to revert the parcel to the United States.

(e) The Secretary shall require, as a condition of the conveyance under subsection (b), that the County pay the administrative costs of the conveyance, including survey costs and any other costs associated with the transfer of title.

* * * * * * *

SELECTED PROVISIONS OF THE CAPE TOWN TREATY IMPLEMENTATION ACT OF 2004

PUBLIC LAW 108297

CAPE TOWN TREATY IMPLEMENTATION ACT OF 2004

SHORT TITLE OF 2004 AMENDMENT [49 USC 44101 NOTE]

Pub. L. 108–297, §1, Aug. 9, 2004, 118 Stat. 1095, provided that: "This Act [enacting section 44113 of this title, amending sections 44107 and 44108 of this title, and enacting provisions set out as notes under section 44101 of this title] may be cited as 'Cape Town Treaty Implementation Act of 2004'."

CAPE TOWN TREATY; FINDINGS AND PURPOSE [49 USC 44101 NOTE]

Pub. L. 108–297, §1, Aug. 9, 2004, 118 Stat. 1095, provided that:

"(a) FINDINGS.—Congress finds the following:

"(1) The Cape Town Treaty (as defined in section 44113 of title 49, United States Code) extends modern commercial laws for the sale, finance, and lease of aircraft and aircraft engines to the international arena in a manner consistent with United States law and practice.

"(2) The Cape Town Treaty provides for internationally established and recognized financing and leasing rights that will provide greater security and commercial predictability in connection with the financing and leasing of highly mobile assets, such as aircraft and aircraft engines.

"(3) The legal and financing framework of the Cape Town Treaty will provide substantial economic benefits to the aviation and aerospace sectors, including the promotion of exports, and will facilitate the acquisition of newer, safer aircraft around the world.

"(4) Only technical changes to United States law and regulations are required since the asset-based financing and leasing concepts embodied in the Cape Town Treaty are already reflected in the United States in the Uniform Commercial Code.

"(5) The new electronic registry system established under the Cape Town Treaty will work in tandem with current aircraft document recordation systems of the Federal Aviation Administration, which have served United States industry well.

"(6) The United States Government was a leader in the development of the Cape Town Treaty.

"(b) PURPOSE.—Accordingly, the purpose of this Act [see Short Title of 2004 Amendment note set out under section 40101 of this title] is to provide for the implementation of the Cape Town Treaty in the United States by making certain technical amendments to the provisions of chapter 441 of title 49, United States Code, directing the Federal Aviation Administration to complete the necessary rulemaking processes as expeditiously as possible, and clarifying the applicability of the Treaty during the rulemaking process."

* * * * * * *

REGULATIONS [49 USC 44101 NOTE]

Pub. L. 108–297, §1, Aug. 9, 2004, 118 Stat. 1095, provided that:

"(a) IN GENERAL.—The Administrator of the Federal Aviation Administration shall issue regulations necessary to carry out this Act [see Short Title of 2004 Amendment note set out under section 40101 of this title], including any amendments made by this Act.

"(b) CONTENTS OF REGULATIONS.—Regulations to be issued under this Act shall specify, at a minimum, the requirements for—

"(1) the registration of aircraft previously registered in a country in which the Cape Town Treaty is in effect; and

"(2) the cancellation of registration of a civil aircraft of the United States based on a request made in accordance with the Cape Town Treaty.

"(c) EXPEDITED RULEMAKING PROCESS.—

"(1) FINAL RULE.—The Administrator shall issue regulations under this section by publishing a final rule by December 31, 2004.

"(2) EFFECTIVE DATE.—The final rule shall not be effective before the date the Cape Town Treaty enters into force with respect to the United States [Mar. 1, 2006, see Effective Date of 2004 Amendment note above].

"(3) ECONOMIC ANALYSIS.—The Administrator shall not be required to prepare an economic analysis of the cost and benefits of the final rule.

"(d) APPLICABILITY OF TREATY.—Notwithstanding parts 47.37(a)(3)(ii) and 47.47(a)(2) of title 14, of the Code of Federal Regulations, Articles IX(5) and XIII of the Cape Town Treaty shall apply to the matters described in subsection (b) until the earlier of the effective date of the final rule under this section or December 31, 2004."

* * * * * * *

EFFECTIVE DATE OF 2004 AMENDMENT [49 USC 44101 NOTE]

Pub. L. 108–297, §1, Aug. 9, 2004, 118 Stat. 1095, provided that: "This Act [see Short Title of 2004 Amendment note set out under section 40101 of this title], including any amendments made by this Act, shall take effect on the date the Cape Town Treaty (as defined in section 44113 of title 49, United States Code) enters into force with respect to the United States and shall not apply to any registration or recordation that was made before such effective date under chapter 441 of such title or any legal rights relating to such registration or recordation." [The Cape Town Treaty entered into force with respect to the United States on Mar. 1, 2006. See 71 F.R. 8457.]

SELECTED PROVISIONS OF THE IMPLEMENTING RECOMMENDATIONS OF THE 9/11 COMMISSION ACT OF 2007

PUBLIC LAW 110-53

IMPLEMENTING RECOMMENDATIONS OF THE 9/11 COMMISSION ACT OF 2007

[Public Law 110–53; Approved August 3, 2007]

[As Amended Through P.L. 117–81, Enacted December 27, 2021]

AN ACT To provide for the implementation of the recommendations of the National Commission on Terrorist Attacks Upon the United States.

Be it enacted by the Senate and House of Representatives of the United States of America in Congress assembled,

* * * * * * *

TITLE XIII—TRANSPORTATION SECURITY ENHANCEMENTS

* * * * * * *

SEC. 1310. [6 USC 1117] ROLES OF THE DEPARTMENT OF HOMELAND SECURTY AND THE DEPARTMENT OF TRANSPORTATION.

The Secretary of Homeland Security is the principal Federal official responsible for transportation security. The roles and responsibilities of the Department of Homeland Security and the Department of Transportation in carrying out this title and titles XII, XIV, and XV are the roles and responsibilities of such Departments pursuant to the Aviation and Transportation Security Act (Public Law 107–71); the Intelligence Reform and Terrorism Prevention Act of 2004 (Public Law 108–458); the National Infrastructure Protection Plan required by Homeland Security Presidential Directive–7; The Homeland Security Act of 2002; The National Response Plan; Executive Order No. 13416: Strengthening Surface Transportation Security, dated December 5, 2006; the

Memorandum of Understanding between the Department and the Department of Transportation on Roles and Responsibilities, dated September 28, 2004, and any and all subsequent annexes to this Memorandum of Understanding; and any other relevant agreements between the two Departments.

* * * * * * *

TITLE XVI—AVIATION

* * * * * * *

SEC. 1616. [49 U.S.C. 44924] REPAIR STATION SECURITY.

(a) CERTIFICATION OF FOREIGN REPAIR STATIONS SUSPENSION.— If the regulations required by section 44924(f) of title 49, United States Code, are not issued within 1 year after the date of enactment of this Act, the Administrator of the Federal Aviation Administration may not certify any foreign repair station under part 145 of title 14, Code of Federal Regulations, after such date unless the station was previously certified, or is in the process of certification by the Administration under that part.

* * * * * * *

SELECTED PROVISIONS OF THE NATIONAL TRANSPORTATION SAFETY BOARD REAUTHORIZATION ACT OF 2006

PUBLIC LAW 109-443

PUBLIC LAW 109-443

[Public Law 109-87; 119 STAT. 2059]

[This measure has not been amended.]

NATIONAL TRANSPORTATION SAFETY BOARD REAUTHORIZATION ACT OF 2006

[(Public Law 1-9-443)]

AN ACT To amend title 49, United States Code, to authorize appropriations for fiscal years 2007 and 2008, and for other purposes.

* * * * * * *

SEC. 10. SAFETY REVIEW.

(a) SAFETY AREA ALTERNATIVES.—With regard to an environmental review of a project to improve runway safety areas on Runway 8/26 at Juneau International Airport, the Secretary of Transportation may only select as the preferred alternative the least expensive runway safety area alternative that meets the standards of the Federal Aviation Administration and that maintains the length of the runway as of the date of enactment of this Act.

(b) COSTS TO BE CONSIDERED.—In determining what is the least expensive runway safety area for purposes of subsection (a), the Secretary shall consider, at a minimum, the initial development costs and life cycle costs of the project.

(c) SATISFACTION OF REQUIREMENT.—With respect to the project described in subsection (a), the requirements of section 303(c)(1) of title 49, United States Code, shall be considered to be satisfied by the selection of the least expensive safety area alternative.

SELECTED PROVISIONS OF THE NATIONAL TRANSPORTATION SAFETY BOARD REAUTHORIZATION ACT OF 2003

PUBLIC LAW 108-168

NATIONAL TRANSPORTATION SAFETY BOARD REAUTHORIZATION ACT OF 2003

[49 U.S.C. 113 note, 1135 note]

* * * * * * *

RELIEF FROM CONTRACTING REQUIREMENTS FOR INVESTIGATIONS SERVICES [49 USC 1113 NOTE]

Pub. L. 108–168, §4, Dec. 6, 2003, 117 Stat. 2033, as amended by Pub. L. 109–443, §3, Dec. 21, 2006, 120 Stat. 3298, provided that:

"(a) IN GENERAL.—The National Transportation Safety Board may enter into agreements or contracts under the authority of section 1113(b)(1)(B) of title 49, United States Code, for investigations conducted under section 1131 of that title without regard to any other provision of law requiring competition if necessary to expedite the investigation.

"(b) REPORT ON USAGE.—On July 1 of each year, as part of the annual report required by section 1117 of title 49, United States Code, the National Transportation Safety Board shall transmit a report to the House of Representatives Committee on Transportation and Infrastructure, the House of Representatives Committee on Government Reform [now Committee on Oversight and Accountability], the Senate Committee on Commerce, Science, and Transportation, and the Senate Committee on Governmental Affairs that—

"(1) describes each contract executed by the Board to which the authority provided by subsection (a) was applied; and

"(2) sets forth the rationale for dispensing with competition requirements with respect to such contract."

* * * * * * *

REPORTS ON CERTAIN OPEN SAFETY RECOMMENDATIONS [49 USC 1135 NOTE]

Pub. L. 108–168, §9, Dec. 6, 2003, 117 Stat. 2035, provided that:

"(a) INITIAL REPORT.—Within 1 year after the date of enactment of this Act [Dec. 6, 2003], the Secretary of Transportation shall submit a report to Congress and the National Transportation Safety Board containing the regulatory status of each open safety recommendation made by the Board to the Secretary concerning—

"(1) 15-passenger van safety;

"(2) railroad grade crossing safety; and

"(3) medical certifications for a commercial driver's license.

"(b) BIENNIAL UPDATES.—The Secretary shall continue to report on the regulatory status of each such recommendation (and any subsequent recommendation made by the Board to the Secretary concerning a matter described in paragraph (1), (2), or (3) of subsection (a)) at 2-year intervals until—

"(1) final regulatory action has been taken on the recommendation;

"(2) the Secretary determines, and states in the report, that no action should be taken on that recommendation; or

"(3) the report, if any, required to be submitted in 2008 is submitted.

"(c) FAILURE TO REPORT.—If the Board has not received a report required to be submitted under subsection (a) or (b) within 30 days after the date on which that report is required to be submitted, the Board shall notify the Committee on Transportation and Infrastructure of the House of Representatives and the Committee on Commerce, Science, and Transportation of the Senate."

PUBLIC LAW 109-87

PUBLIC LAW 109-87

[Public Law 109-87; 119 STAT. 2059]

[This measure has not been amended.]

AN ACT To authorize the Secretary of Transportation to make emergency airport improvement project grants-in-aid under title 49, United States Code, for repairs and costs related to damage from Hurricanes Katrina and Rita.

SEC. 1. EMERGENCY USE OF GRANTS-IN-AID FOR AIRPORT IMPROVEMENTS FOR FISCAL YEARS 2005 AND 2006.

(a) IN GENERAL.— (1) The Secretary of Transportation may make project grants under part B, subtitle VII, of title 49, United States Code, from amounts that remain unobligated after the date of enactment of this Act for fiscal years 2005 and 2006— (1) from apportioned funds under section 47114 of that title apportioned to an airport described in subsection (b)(1) or to a State in which such airport is located; or

(2) from funds available for discretionary grants to such an airport under section 47115 of such title.

(b) ELIGIBLE AIRPORTS AND USES.— The Secretary may make grants under subsection (a) for— (1) emergency capital costs incurred by a public use airport in Louisiana, Mississippi, Alabama, or Texas that is listed in the Federal Aviation Administration's National Plan of Integrated Airport Systems of repairing or replacing public use facilities that have been damaged as a result of Hurricane Katrina or Hurricane Rita; and (2) emergency operating costs incurred by an airport described in paragraph (1) as a result of Hurricane Katrina or Hurricane Rita.

(c) PRIORITIES.— In making grants authorized by subsection (a), the Secretary shall give priority to— (1) airport development within the meaning of section 47102 of title 49, United States Code; (2)

terminal development within the meaning of section 47110 of that title; (3) repair or replacement of other public use airport facilities; and (4) emergency operating costs incurred at public use airports in Louisiana, Mississippi, Alabama, and Texas.

(d) MODIFICATION OF CERTAIN OTHERWISE APPLICABLE REQUIREMENTS.— For purposes of any grant authorized by subsection (a)- (1) the Secretary may waive any otherwise applicable limitation on, or requirement for, grants under section 47102, 47107(a)(17), 47110, or 47119 of title 49, United States Code, if the Secretary determines that the waiver is necessary to respond, in as timely and efficient a manner as possible, to the urgent needs of the region damaged by Hurricane Katrina or Hurricane Rita; (2) the United States Government's share of allowable project costs shall be 100 percent, notwithstanding the provisions of section 47109 of that title; (3) any project funded by such a grant shall be deemed to be an airport development project (within the meaning of section 47102 of that title), except for the purpose of establishing priorities under subsection (c) of this section among projects to be funded by such grants; and (4) no project funded by such a grant may be considered, for the purpose of any other provision of law, to be a major Federal action significantly affecting the quality of the human environment.

SELECTED PROVISIONS OF THE SAFE, ACCOUNTABLE, FLEXIBLE, EFFICIENT TRANSPORTATION EQUITY ACT: A LEGACY FOR USERS (SAFETEA-LU)

PUBLIC LAW 109-59

SAFE, ACCOUNTABLE, FLEXIBLE, EFFICIENT TRANSPORTATION EQUITY ACT: A LEGACY FOR USERS (SAFETEA–LU)

[Public Law 109–59; August 10, 2005]

[As Amended Through P.L. 117–286, Enacted December 27, 2022]

AN ACT To authorize funds for Federal-aid highways, highway safety programs, and transit programs, and for other purposes.

Be it enacted by the Senate and House of Representatives of the United States of America in Congress assembled,

SECTION 1. SHORT TITLE; TABLE OF CONTENTS.

(a) [23 U.S.C. 101 note] SHORT TITLE.—This Act may be cited as the "Safe, Accountable, Flexible, Efficient Transportation Equity Act: A Legacy for Users" or "SAFETEA–LU".

(b) TABLE OF CONTENTS.—The table of contents for this Act is as follows:

TITLE IV—MOTOR CARRIER SAFETY
Subtitle D—Miscellaneous Provisions

* * * * * * *

SEC. 4406. AIRPORT LAND AMENDMENT.

(a) RELEASE OF REVERTER CONDITION.—The Secretary of the Interior shall execute such instruments as are necessary to release the condition on a portion of land situated adjacent to the community of Beaver, Alaska, conveyed pursuant to Patent No. 50–69–0130 and dated August 23, 1968, requiring that such land reverts to the United States if the land is not used for airport purposes. The Secretary shall ensure that the release executed pursuant to this subsection—

(1) applies only to approximately 33 acres of land identified as tracts II through VI of the Beaver Airport, a part of U.S. Survey No. 3798, Alaska (referred to in this section as the "community expansion land");

(2) is without any requirement for receipt of fair market value for the release and conveyance of the conditions otherwise applicable to the community expansion land; and

(3) is contingent on the conveyance by the State of Alaska of the community expansion land to the Beaver Kwit'chin Corporation, the Village Corporation of the village of Beaver, Alaska.

(b) RECONVEYANCE.—The Beaver Kwit'chin Corporation—

(1) shall reconvey to any individual who currently occupies a portion of the land referred to in subsection (a) or successor in interest to such an individual, all right, title, and interest of the Kwit'chin Corporation in and to such land as is currently occupied;

(2) may subsequently—

(A) convey the remaining land to other individuals or persons for community expansion purposes; or

(B) retain the remaining land in whole or in part for community uses.

* * * * * * *

SEC. 4408. RIALTO MUNICIPAL AIRPORT.

(a) FINDINGS.—Congress finds that—

(1) Rialto Municipal Airport/Art Scholl Memorial Airport (Rialto Municipal Airport) is a general aviation airport located within a 20-mile radius of 10 other general aviation airports;

(2) Rialto Municipal Airport is located approximately 8.5 nautical miles from the former Norton Air Force Base which was selected for closure by the Base Realignment and Closure Commission in 1988 and was closed in 1994;

(3) there has been a significant decline in based aircraft and aviation operations at Rialto Municipal Airport due to the unexpected impact of increased capacity in the immediate vicinity of the airport;

(4) the transfer of Rialto Municipal Airport's operations, assets and liabilities is supported by the general aviation operators at the airport and will not compromise service or safety; and

(5) the closure of Rialto Municipal Airport shall be in compliance with applicable Federal laws and regulations.

(b) IN GENERAL.—Notwithstanding any law, regulation or grant assurance, but subject to the requirements of this section, the United States shall release all restrictions, conditions, and limitations on the use, encumbrance, conveyance, or closure of the Rialto Municipal Airport, in Rialto, California, to the extent such restrictions, conditions, and limitations are enforceable by the United States.

(c) CONDITIONS.—A release under subsection (b) shall be subject to the following conditions:

(1) Upon conveyance of the land or transfer of any interest or rights of use or occupancy of the land—

(A) the City of Rialto will pay the United States 45 percent of the current fair market value of the property, and this amount shall be used for projects eligible under chapter 471 of title 49, United States Code, at a commercial airport—

(i) for which a certificate is issued under part 139 of title 14, Code of Federal Regulations;

(ii) that is located within 10 nautical miles of

Rialto Municipal Airport; and

(iii) that was included on the Department of Defense base closure list of 1988;

(B) the remaining 55 percent of the fair market value referred to in subparagraph (A) shall be retained by the City of Rialto;

(C) the city shall pay to the United States 90 percent of the unamortized portion of any Federal development grant for airport facilities other than land, amortized over a 20-year term, with interest. These funds shall be payable over a period of 5 years and deposited into the Airport and Airway Trust Fund and available for projects eligible under chapter 471 of title 49, United States Code.

(2) The United States will not be responsible for any environmental cleanup of any land with respect to which such release is made.

(3) All airport and aviation-related equipment located at Rialto Municipal Airport and owned by the City of Rialto before the date of the release will be transferred to a commercial airport referred to in paragraph (1)(A).

* * * * * * *

SECTION 332 OF THE DEPARTMENT OF TRANSPORTATION AND RELATED AGENCIES APPROPRIATIONS ACT, 2000

PUBLIC LAW 106-69

SECTION 322 OF THE DEPARTMENT OF TRANSPORTATION AND RELATED AGENCIES APPROPRIATIONS ACT, 2000

MEASUREMENT OF HIGHWAY MILES FOR PURPOSES OF DETERMINING ELIGIBILITY OF ESSENTIAL AIR SERVICE SUBSIDIES

[49 USC 41731 NOTE]

Pub. L. 108–176, title IV, §409, Dec. 12, 2003, 117 Stat. 2547, as amended by Pub. L. 110–190, §4(d)(1), Feb. 28, 2008, 122 Stat. 644; Pub. L. 110–330, §5(k), Sept. 30, 2008, 122 Stat. 3719; Pub. L. 111–69, §5(k), Oct. 1, 2009, 123 Stat. 2055; Pub. L. 111–249, §5(k), Sept. 30, 2010, 124 Stat. 2628; Pub. L. 112–30, title II, §205(k), Sept. 16, 2011, 125 Stat. 358; Pub. L. 112–91, §5(k), Jan. 31, 2012, 126 Stat. 4; Pub. L. 112–95, title IV, §431, Feb. 14, 2012, 126 Stat. 100; Pub. L. 114–55, title I, §102(g), Sept. 30, 2015, 129 Stat. 523; Pub. L. 114–141, title I, §102(f), Mar. 30, 2016, 130 Stat. 323; Pub. L. 114–190, title I, §1102(g), July 15, 2016, 130 Stat. 617; Pub. L. 115–63, title I, §102(g), Sept. 29, 2017, 131 Stat. 1169; Pub. L. 115–141, div. M, title I, §102(f), Mar. 23, 2018, 132 Stat. 1046; Pub. L. 115–254, div. B, title IV, §457, Oct. 5, 2018, 132 Stat. 3350; Pub. L. 118–15, div. B, title II, §2202(m), Sept. 30, 2023, 137 Stat. 83; Pub. L. 118–34, title I, §102(m), Dec. 26, 2023, 137 Stat. 1114; Pub. L. 118–41, title I, §102(m), Mar. 8, 2024, 138 Stat. 22, provided that:

"(a) REQUEST FOR SECRETARIAL REVIEW.—An eligible place (as defined in section 41731 of title 49, United States Code) with respect to which the Secretary has, in the 2-year period ending on the date of enactment of this Act [Dec. 12, 2003], eliminated (or tentatively eliminated) compensation for essential air service to such place, or terminated (or tentatively terminated) the compensation eligibility of such place for essential air service, under section 332 of the Department of Transportation and Related Agencies Appropriations Act, 2000 [Pub. L. 106–69] ([former] 49 U.S.C. 41731 note), section 205 of the Wendell H. Ford Aviation Investment and Reform Act for the 21st Century [Pub. L. 106–181] (49 U.S.C. 41731 note), or any prior law of similar effect based on the highway mileage of such place from the nearest hub airport (as defined in section 40102 of such title), may request the Secretary to review such action.

Section 1617 of the National Defense Authorization Act for Fiscal Year 2016

Public Law 114-92

NATIONAL DEFENSE AUTHORIZATION ACT FOR FISCAL YEAR 2016

[(Public Law 114–92)]

[As Amended Through P.L. 117–286, Enacted December 27, 2022]

AN ACT To authorize appropriations for fiscal year 2016 for military activities of the Department of Defense, for military construction, and for defense activities of the Department of Energy, to prescribe military personnel strengths for such fiscal year, and for other purposes.

Be it enacted by the Senate and House of Representatives of the United States of America in Congress assembled,

SECTION 1. SHORT TITLE.

This Act may be cited as the "National Defense Authorization Act for Fiscal Year 2016".

SEC. 2. ORGANIZATION OF ACT INTO DIVISIONS; TABLE OF CONTENTS.

(a) DIVISIONS.—This Act is organized into four divisions as follows:

(1) Division A—Department of Defense Authorizations.

* * * * * * *

(b) TABLE OF CONTENTS.—The table of contents for this Act is as follows:

* * * * * * *

TITLE XVI—STRATEGIC PROGRAMS, CYBER, AND INTELLIGENCE
MATTERS

Subtitle A—Space Activities

* * * * * * *

Sec. 1617.   Streamline of commercial space launch activities.

* * * * * * *

DIVISION A—DEPARTMENT OF DEFENSE AUTHORIZATIONS

* * * * * * *

TITLE XVI—STRATEGIC PROGRAMS, CYBER, AND INTELLIGENCE MATTERS

Subtitle A—Space Activities

* * * * * * *

Sec. 1617.   Streamline of commercial space launch activities.

* * * * * * *

Subtitle A—Space Activities

* * * * * * *

SEC. 1617. [51 U.S.C. 50918 note] STREAMLINE OF COMMERCIAL SPACE LAUNCH ACTIVITIES.

(a) SENSE OF CONGRESS.—It is the sense of Congress that eliminating duplicative requirements and approvals for commercial launch and reentry operations will promote and encourage the development of the commercial space sector.

(b) REAFFIRMATION OF POLICY.—Congress reaffirms that the Secretary of Transportation, in overseeing and coordinating commercial launch and reentry operations, should—

(1) promote commercial space launches and reentries by the private sector;

(2) facilitate Government, State, and private sector involvement in enhancing United States launch sites and facilities;

(3) protect public health and safety, safety of property, national security interests, and foreign policy interests of the United States; and

(4) consult with the head of another executive agency, including the Secretary of Defense or the Administrator of the National Aeronautics and Space Administration, as necessary to provide consistent application of licensing requirements under chapter 509 of title 51, United States Code.

(c) REQUIREMENTS.—

(1) IN GENERAL.—The Secretary of Transportation under section 50918 of title 51, United States Code, and subject to section 50905(b)(2)(C) of that title, shall consult with the Secretary of Defense, the Administrator of the National Aeronautics and Space Administration, and the heads of other executive agencies, as appropriate—

(A) to identify all requirements that are imposed to protect the public health and safety, safety of property, national security interests, and foreign policy interests of the United States relevant to any commercial launch of a launch vehicle or commercial reentry of a reentry vehicle; and

(B) to evaluate the requirements identified in subparagraph (A) and, in coordination with the licensee or transferee and the heads of the relevant executive agencies—

(i) determine whether the satisfaction of a requirement of one agency could result in the satisfaction of a requirement of another agency; and

(ii) resolve any inconsistencies and remove any outmoded or duplicative requirements or approvals of the Federal Government relevant to any commercial launch of a launch vehicle or commercial reentry of a reentry vehicle.

(2) STREAMLINING.—

(A) IN GENERAL.—With respect to any licensed activity under chapter 509 of title 51, United States Code, the Secretary of Defense may not impose any requirement on a licensee or transferee that is duplicative of, or overlaps in intent with, any requirement imposed by the Secretary of

Transportation under that chapter.

(B) WAIVER.—The Secretary of the Air Force may waive the limitation under subparagraph (A) if—

(i) the Secretary determines that imposing a requirement described in that subparagraph is necessary to avoid negative consequences for the national security space program; and

(ii) the Secretary notifies the Secretary of Transportation of such determination before making such waiver.

(3) REPORTS.—Not later than 180 days after the date of enactment of this Act, and annually thereafter until the Secretary of Transportation determines no outmoded or duplicative requirements or approvals of the Federal Government exist, the Secretary of Transportation, in consultation with the Secretary of Defense, the Administrator of the National Aeronautics and Space Administration, the commercial space sector, and the heads of other executive agencies, as appropriate, shall submit to the appropriate congressional committees a report that includes the following:

(A) A description of the process for the application for and approval of a permit or license under chapter 509 of title 51, United States Code, for the commercial launch of a launch vehicle or commercial reentry of a reentry vehicle, including the identification of—

(i) any unique requirements for operating on a United States Government launch site, reentry site, or launch property; and

(ii) any inconsistent, outmoded, or duplicative requirements or approvals.

(B) A description of current efforts, if any, to coordinate and work across executive agencies to define interagency processes and procedures for sharing information, avoiding duplication of effort, and resolving common agency requirements.

(C) Recommendations for legislation that may further—

(i) streamline requirements in order to improve efficiency, reduce unnecessary costs, resolve inconsistencies, remove duplication, and minimize unwarranted constraints; and

(ii) consolidate or modify requirements across affected agencies into a single application set that satisfies the requirements identified in paragraph (1)(A).

(4) DEFINITIONS.—For purposes of this subsection—

(A) any applicable definitions set forth in section 50902 of title 51, United States Code, shall apply;

(B) the term "appropriate congressional committees" means—

(i) the congressional defense committees;

(ii) the Committee on Commerce, Science, and Transportation of the Senate;

(iii) the Committee on Science, Space, and Technology of the House of Representatives; and

(iv) the Committee on Transportation and Infrastructure of the House of Representatives;

(C) the terms "launch", "reenter", and "reentry" include landing of a launch vehicle or reentry vehicle; and

(D) the terms "United States Government launch site" and "United States Government reentry site" include any necessary facility, at that location, that is commercially operated on United States Government property.

(d) RULE OF CONSTRUCTION.—Nothing in this section shall be construed to limit the ability of the Secretary of Defense to consult with the Secretary of Transportation with respect to requirements and approvals under chapter 509 of title 51, United States Code.

* * * * * * *

SECTION 282D OF THE NATIONAL DEFENSE AUTHORIZATION ACT FOR FISCAL YEAR 2017

PUBLIC LAW 114-328

NATIONAL DEFENSE AUTHORIZATION ACT FOR FISCAL YEAR 2017

[(Public Law 114–328)]

[As Amended Through P.L. 118–31, Enacted December 22, 2023]

AN ACT To authorize appropriations for fiscal year 2017 for military activities of the Department of Defense, for military construction, and for defense activities of the Department of Energy, to prescribe military personnel strengths for such fiscal year, and for other purposes.

Be it enacted by the Senate and House of Representatives of the United States of America in Congress assembled,

SECTION 1. SHORT TITLE.

This Act may be cited as the "National Defense Authorization Act for Fiscal Year 2017".

* * * * * * *

DIVISION B—MILITARY CONSTRUCTION AUTHORIZATIONS

* * * * * * *

TITLE XXVIII—MILITARY CONSTRUCTION GENERAL PROVISIONS

Subtitle C—Land Conveyances

* * * * * * *

* * * * * * *

Subtitle C—Land Conveyances

* * * * * * *

SEC. 2829D. CLOSURE OF ST. MARYS AIRPORT.

(a) RELEASE OF RESTRICTIONS.—Subject to subsection (b), the United States, acting through the Administrator of the Federal Aviation Administration, shall release the city of St. Marys, Georgia, from all restrictions, conditions, and limitations on the use, encumbrance, conveyance, and closure of the St. Marys Airport, to the extent such restrictions, conditions, and limitations are enforceable by the Administrator.

(b) REQUIREMENTS FOR RELEASE OF RESTRICTIONS.—The Administrator shall execute the release under subsection (a) once all of the following occurs:

(1) The Secretary of the Navy transfers to the Georgia Department of Transportation the amounts described in subsection (c) and requires as an enforceable condition on such transfer that all funds transferred shall be used only for airport development (as defined in section 47102 of title 49, United States Code) of a general aviation airport in Georgia, consistent with planning efforts conducted by the Administrator and the Georgia Department of Transportation.

(2) The city of St. Marys, for consideration as provided for in this section, grants to the United States, under the administrative jurisdiction of the Secretary, a restrictive use easement in the real property used for the St. Marys Airport, as determined acceptable by the Secretary, under such terms and conditions as the Secretary considers necessary to protect the interests of the United States and prohibiting the future use of such property for all aviation-related purposes and any other purposes deemed by the Secretary to be incompatible with the operations, functions, and missions of Naval Submarine Base, Kings Bay, Georgia.

(3) The Secretary obtains an appraisal to determine the fair market value of the real property used for the St. Marys Airport in the manner described in subsection (c)(1).

(4) The Administrator fulfills the obligations under the National Environmental Policy Act of 1969 (42 U.S.C. 4321 et

seq.) in connection with the release under subsection (a). In carrying out such obligations—

(A) the Administrator shall not assume or consider any potential or proposed future redevelopment of the current St. Marys airport property;

(B) any potential new general aviation airport in Georgia shall be deemed to be not connected with the release noted in subsection (a) nor the closure of St. Marys Airport; and

(C) any environmental review under the National Environmental Policy Act of 1969 (42 U.S.C. 4321 et seq.) for a potential general aviation airport in Georgia shall be considered through an environmental review process separate and apart from the environmental review made a condition of release by this section.

(c) TRANSFER OF AMOUNTS DESCRIBED.—The amounts described in this subsection are the following:

(1) An amount equal to the fair market value of the real property of the St. Marys Airport, as determined by the Secretary and concurred in by the Administrator, based on an appraisal report and title documentation that—

(A) is prepared or adopted by the Secretary, and concurred in by the Administrator, not more than 180 days prior to the transfer described in subsection (b)(1); and

(B) meets all requirements of Federal law and the appraisal and documentation standards applicable to the acquisition and disposal of real property interests of the United States.

(2) An amount equal to the unamortized portion of any Federal development grants (including grants available under a State block grant program established pursuant to section 47128 of title 49, United States Code), other than used for the acquisition of land, paid to the city of St. Marys for use as the St. Marys Airport.

(3) An amount equal to the airport revenues remaining in the airport account for the St. Marys Airport as of the date of the enactment of this Act and as otherwise due to or received by the city of St. Marys after such date of enactment pursuant to sections 47107(b) and 47133 of title 49, United States Code.

(d) AUTHORIZATION FOR TRANSFER OF FUNDS.—Using funds available to the Department of the Navy for operation and maintenance, the Secretary may pay the amounts described in subsection (c) to the Georgia Department of Transportation, conditioned as described in subsection (b)(1).

(e) ADDITIONAL REQUIREMENTS.—

(1) SURVEY.—The exact acreage and legal description of St. Marys Airport shall be determined by a survey satisfactory to the Secretary and concurred in by the Administrator.

(2) PLANNING OF GENERAL AVIATION AIRPORT.—Any planning effort for the development of a new general aviation airport in southeast Georgia using the amounts described in subsection (c) shall be conducted in coordination with the Secretary, and shall ensure that any such airport does not encroach on the operations, functions, and missions of Naval Submarine Base, Kings Bay, Georgia.

(f) RULE OF CONSTRUCTION.—Nothing in this section may be construed to limit the applicability of—

(1) the requirements and processes under section 46319 of title 49, United States Code;

(2) the requirements and processes under part 157 of title 14, Code of Federal Regulations; or

(3) the public notice requirements under section 47107(h)(2) of title 49, United States Code.

* * * * * * *

SECTIONS 604(B), 604(C), AND 1618 OF THE JOHN S. MCCAIN NATIONAL DEFENSE AUTHORIZATION ACT FOR FISCAL YEAR 2019

PUBLIC LAW 115-232

JOHN S. MCCAIN NATIONAL DEFENSE AUTHORIZATION ACT FOR FISCAL YEAR 2019

[(Public Law 115–232)]

[As Amended Through P.L. 118–31, Enacted December 22, 2023]

AN ACT To authorize appropriations for fiscal year 2019 for military activities of the Department of Defense, for military construction, and for defense activities of the Department of Energy, to prescribe military personnel strengths for such fiscal year, and for other purposes.

Be it enacted by the Senate and House of Representatives of the United States of America in Congress assembled,

SECTION 1. SHORT TITLE.

(a) IN GENERAL.—This Act may be cited as the "John S. McCain National Defense Authorization Act for Fiscal Year 2019".

(b) REFERENCES.—Any reference in this or any other Act to the "National Defense Authorization Act for Fiscal Year 2019" shall be deemed to be a reference to the "John S. McCain National Defense Authorization Act for Fiscal Year 2019".

* * * * * * *

DIVISION A—DEPARTMENT OF DEFENSE AUTHORIZATIONS

* * * * * * *

TITLE XVI— STRATEGIC PROGRAMS, CYBER, AND INTELLIGENCE MATTERS

* * * * * * *

Subtitle A— Space Activities

* * * * * * *

SEC. 1604. PROVISION OF SPACE SITUATIONAL AWARENESS
SERVICES AND INFORMATION.

* * * * * * *

(b) PLAN.—

(1) IN GENERAL.— Not later than 180 days after the date of
the enactment of this Act, the President shall transmit to the
appropriate congressional committees a plan for a department
or agency of the United States Government other than the
Department of Defense to provide space situational awareness
services and information to non-United States Government
entities.

(2) MATTERS INCLUDED.— The plan under paragraph (1)
shall include the following:

(A) An assessment of the existing and planned staff,
budgetary resources, and relevant institutional expertise of
the department or agency covered by the plan with respect
to providing space situational awareness services and
information.

(B) An assessment of the demonstrated ability of such
department or agency to work collaboratively with industry
and academia in developing best practices or consensus
standards.

(C) An assessment of the existing and planned capacity
of such department or agency to facilitate communication
between space object operators to avoid a collision.

(D) The ability of such department or agency to use
other transaction agreements or similar transaction
mechanisms to support space traffic management
requirements.

(E) Any additional authorities that would be required
to assume the responsibility described in paragraph (1).

(c) APPROPRIATE CONGRESSIONAL COMMITTEES DEFINED.— In
this section, the term "appropriate congressional committees"

means the following:

(1) The congressional defense committees.

(2) The Committee on Science, Space, and Technology, the Committee on Transportation and Infrastructure, the Committee on Energy and Commerce, and the Committee on Foreign Affairs of the House of Representatives.

(3) The Committee on Commerce, Science, and Transportation and the Committee on Foreign Relations of the Senate.

* * * * * * *

SEC. 1618. INDEPENDENT STUDY ON SPACE LAUNCH LOCATIONS.

(a) INDEPENDENT STUDY.— Not later than 30 days after the date of the enactment of this Act, the Secretary of Defense shall seek to enter into a contract with a federally funded research and development center to conduct a study on space launch locations, including with respect to the development and capacity of existing and new locations. The study shall, at a minimum—

(1) identify how additional locations affect the capability of the Department of Defense to rapidly reconstitute and improve resilience for defense satellite system launches;

(2) identify the capacities of current and new space launch locations, in light of the rapid increase in using commercial space services to support national security space missions and military requirements;

(3) identify partnerships within State government-owned and operated spaceports that should be developed to increase launch capacities and enhance the space resiliency of the United States;

(4) provide recommendations on strategic placement for future space launch sites; and

(5) identify costs associated with additional locations and whether such costs should be borne by the Department of Defense, State governments, or private entities.

(b) SUBMISSION TO DOD.— Not later than 240 days after the date of the enactment of this Act, the federally funded research and development center shall submit to the Secretary a report containing the study conducted under subsection (a).

(c) SUBMISSION TO CONGRESS.— Not later than 270 days after the date of the enactment of this Act, the Secretary shall submit to the appropriate congressional committees the report under subsection (a), without change.

(d) APPROPRIATE CONGRESSIONAL COMMITTEES DEFINED.— In this section, the term "appropriate congressional committees" means the following:

(1) The congressional defense committees.

(2) The Committee on Science, Space, and Technology and the Committee on Transportation and Infrastructure of the House of Representatives.

(3) The Committee on Commerce, Science, and Transportation of the Senate.

* * * * * * *

AIRCRAFT CERTIFICATION, SAFETY, AND ACCOUNTABILITY ACT

PUBLIC LAW 116-260

AIRCRAFT CERTIFICATION, SAFETY, AND ACCOUNTABILITY ACT

[(Title I of Division V of Public Law 116–260)]

[As Amended Through P.L. 118–63, Enacted May 16, 2024]

AN ACT Making consolidated appropriations for the fiscal year ending September 30, 2021, providing coronavirus emergency response and relief, and for other purposes.

Be it enacted by the Senate and House of Representatives of the United States of America in Congress assembled,

SECTION 1. SHORT TITLE.

This Act may be cited as the "Consolidated Appropriations Act, 2021".

SEC. 2. TABLE OF CONTENTS.

DIVISION V—AIRCRAFT CERTIFICATION, SAFETY, AND ACCOUNTABILITY

TITLE I—AIRCRAFT CERTIFICATION, SAFETY, AND ACCOUNTABILITY

SEC. 101. SHORT TITLE; TABLE OF CONTENTS.

(a) [49 U.S.C. 40101 note] SHORT TITLE.—This title may be cited as the "Aircraft Certification, Safety, and Accountability Act".

(b) TABLE OF CONTENTS.—The table of contents for this title is as follows:

Sec. 137.   Definitions.

SEC. 102. SAFETY MANAGEMENT SYSTEMS.

(a) [49 U.S.C. 44701 note] RULEMAKING PROCEEDING.—

(1) IN GENERAL.—Not later than 30 days after the date of enactment of this title, the Administrator shall initiate a rulemaking proceeding to require that manufacturers that hold both a type certificate and a production certificate issued pursuant to section 44704 of title 49, United States Code, where the United States is the State of Design and State of Manufacture, have in place a safety management system that is consistent with the standards and recommended practices established by ICAO and contained in annex 19 to the Convention on International Civil Aviation (61 Stat. 1180), for such systems.

(2) CONTENTS OF REGULATIONS.—The regulations issued under paragraph (1) shall, at a minimum—

(A) ensure safety management systems are consistent with, and complementary to, existing safety management systems;

(B) include provisions that would permit operational feedback from operators and pilots qualified on the manufacturers' equipment to ensure that the operational assumptions made during design and certification remain valid;

(C) include provisions for the Administrator's approval of, and regular oversight of adherence to, a certificate holder's safety management system adopted pursuant to such regulations; and

(D) require such certificate holder to adopt, not later than 4 years after the date of enactment of this title, a safety management system.

(b) FINAL RULE DEADLINE.—Not later than 24 months after initiating the rulemaking under subsection (a), the Administrator shall issue a final rule.

(c) SURVEILLANCE AND AUDIT REQUIREMENT.—The final rule issued pursuant to subsection (b) shall include a requirement for the Administrator to implement a systems approach to risk-based surveillance by defining and planning inspections, audits, and monitoring activities on a continuous basis, to ensure that design and production approval holders of aviation products meet and continue to meet safety management system requirements under the rule.

(d) ENGAGEMENT WITH ICAO.—The Administrator shall engage with ICAO and foreign civil aviation authorities to help encourage the adoption of safety management systems for manufacturers on a global basis, consistent with ICAO standards.

(e) SAFETY REPORTING PROGRAM.—The regulations issued under subsection (a) shall require a safety management system to include a confidential employee reporting system through which employees can report hazards, issues, concerns, occurrences, and incidents. A reporting system under this subsection shall include provisions for reporting, without concern for reprisal for reporting, of such items by employees in a manner consistent with confidential employee reporting systems administered by the Administrator. Such regulations shall also require a certificate holder described in subsection (a) to submit a summary of reports received under this subsection to the Administrator at least twice per year.

(f) CODE OF ETHICS.—The regulations issued under subsection (a) shall require a safety management system to include establishment of a code of ethics applicable to all appropriate employees of a certificate holder, including officers (as determined by the FAA), which clarifies that safety is the organization's highest priority.

(g) PROTECTION OF SAFETY INFORMATION.—Section 44735(a) of title 49, United States Code, is amended—

(1) by striking "title 5 if the report" and inserting the following:"title 5—

"(1) if the report"

;

(2) by striking the period at the end and inserting "; or"; and

(3) by adding at the end the following:

"(2) if the report, data, or other information is submitted to the Federal Aviation Administration pursuant to section 102(e) of the Aircraft Certification, Safety, and Accountability Act.".

SEC. 103. [49 U.S.C. 44736 note] EXPERT REVIEW OF
ORGANIZATION DESIGNATION AUTHORIZATIONS FOR TRANSPORT
AIRPLANES.

(a) EXPERT REVIEW.—

(1) ESTABLISHMENT.—Not later than 30 days after the date
of enactment of this title, the Administrator shall convene an
expert panel (in this section referred to as the "review panel") to
review and make findings and recommendations on the matters
listed in paragraph (2).

(2) CONTENTS OF REVIEW.—With respect to each holder of
an organization designation authorization for the design and
production of transport airplanes, the review panel shall review
the following:

(A) The extent to which the holder's safety
management processes promote or foster a safety culture
consistent with the principles of the International Civil
Aviation Organization Safety Management Manual,
Fourth Edition (International Civil Aviation Organization
Doc. No. 9859) or any similar successor document.

(B) The effectiveness of measures instituted by the
holder to instill, among employees and contractors of such
holder that support organization designation authorization
functions, a commitment to safety above all other
priorities.

(C) The holder's capability, based on the holder's
organizational structures, requirements applicable to
officers and employees of such holder, and safety culture,
of making reasonable and appropriate decisions regarding
functions delegated to the holder pursuant to the
organization designation authorization.

(D) Any other matter determined by the Administrator
for which inclusion in the review would be consistent with
the public interest in aviation safety.

(3) COMPOSITION OF REVIEW PANEL.—The review panel
shall consist of—

(A) 2 representatives of the National Aeronautics and
Space Administration;

(B) 2 employees of the Administration's Aircraft
Certification Service with experience conducting oversight

of persons not involved in the design or production of transport airplanes;

(C) 1 employee of the Administration's Aircraft Certification Service with experience conducting oversight of persons involved in the design or production of transport airplanes;

(D) 2 employees of the Administration's Flight Standards Service with experience in oversight of safety management systems;

(E) 1 appropriately qualified representative, designated by the applicable represented organization, of each of—

(i) a labor union representing airline pilots involved in both passenger and all-cargo operations;

(ii) a labor union, not selected under clause (i), representing airline pilots with expertise in the matters described in paragraph (2);

(iii) a labor union representing employees engaged in the assembly of transport airplanes;

(iv) the certified bargaining representative under section 7111 of title 5, United States Code, for field engineers engaged in the audit or oversight of an organization designation authorization within the Aircraft Certification Service of the Administration;

(v) the certified bargaining representative for safety inspectors of the Administration; and

(vi) a labor union representing employees engaged in the design of transport airplanes;

(F) 2 independent experts who have not served as a political appointee in the Administration and—

(i) who hold either a baccalaureate or postgraduate degree in the field of aerospace engineering or a related discipline; and

(ii) who have a minimum of 20 years of relevant applied experience;

(G) 4 air carrier employees whose job responsibilities include administration of a safety management system;

(H) 4 individuals representing 4 different holders of

organization designation authorizations, with preference given to individuals representing holders of organization designation authorizations for the design or production of aircraft other than transport airplanes or for the design or production of aircraft engines, propellers, or appliances; and

(I) 1 individual holding a law degree and who has expertise in the legal duties of a holder of an organization designation authorization and the interaction with the FAA, except that such individual may not, within the 10-year period preceding the individual's appointment, have been employed by, or provided legal services to, the holder of an organization designation authorization referenced in paragraph (2).

(4) RECOMMENDATIONS.—The review panel shall make recommendations to the Administrator regarding suggested actions to address any deficiencies found after review of the matters listed in paragraph (2).

(5) REPORT.—

(A) SUBMISSION.—Not later than 270 days after the date of the first meeting of the review panel, the review panel shall transmit to the Administrator and the congressional committees of jurisdiction a report containing the findings and recommendations of the review panel regarding the matters listed in paragraph (2), except that such report shall include—

(i) only such findings endorsed by 10 or more individual members of the review panel; and

(ii) only such recommendations described in paragraph (4) endorsed by 18 or more of the individual members of the review panel.

(B) DISSENTING VIEWS.—In submitting the report required under this paragraph, the review panel shall append to such report the dissenting views of any individual member or group of members of the review panel regarding the findings or recommendations of the review panel.

(C) PUBLICATION.—Not later than 5 days after receiving the report under subparagraph (A), the

Administrator shall publish such report, including any dissenting views appended to the report, on the website of the Administration.

(D) TERMINATION.—The review panel shall terminate upon submission of the report under subparagraph (A).

(6) ADMINISTRATIVE PROVISIONS.—

(A) ACCESS TO INFORMATION.—The review panel shall have authority to perform the following actions if a majority of the total number of review panel members consider each action necessary and appropriate:

(i) Entering onto the premises of a holder of an organization designation authorization referenced in paragraph (2) for access to and inspection of records or other purposes.

(ii) Notwithstanding any other provision of law, accessing and inspecting unredacted records directly necessary for the completion of the panel's work under this section that are in the possession of such holder of an organization designation authorization or the Administration.

(iii) Interviewing employees of such holder of an organization designation authorization or the Administration as necessary for the panel to complete its work.

(B) DISCLOSURE OF FINANCIAL INTERESTS.—Each individual serving on the review panel shall disclose to the Administrator any financial interest held by such individual, or a spouse or dependent of such individual, in a business enterprise engaged in the design or production of transport airplanes, aircraft engines designed for transport airplanes, or major systems, components, or parts thereof.

(C) PROTECTION OF PROPRIETARY INFORMATION; TRADE SECRETS.—

(i) MARKING.—The custodian of a record accessed under subparagraph (A) may mark such record as proprietary or containing a trade secret. A marking under this subparagraph shall not be dispositive with respect to whether such record contains any information subject to legal protections from public disclosure.

(ii) NONDISCLOSURE FOR NON-FEDERAL GOVERNMENT PARTICIPANTS.—

(I) NON-FEDERAL GOVERNMENT PARTICIPANTS.—Prior to participating on the review panel, each individual serving on the review panel representing a non-Federal entity, including a labor union, shall execute an agreement with the Administrator in which the individual shall be prohibited from disclosing at any time, except as required by law, to any person, foreign or domestic, any non-public information made accessible to the panel under subparagraph (A).

(II) FEDERAL EMPLOYEE PARTICIPANTS.—Federal employees serving on the review panel as representatives of the Federal Government and who are required to protect proprietary information and trade secrets under section 1905 of title 18, United States Code, shall not be required to execute agreements under this subparagraph.

(iii) PROTECTION OF VOLUNTARILY SUBMITTED SAFETY INFORMATION.—Information subject to protection from disclosure by the Administration in accordance with sections 40123 and 44735 of title 49, United States Code, is deemed voluntarily submitted to the Administration under such sections when shared with the review panel and retains its protection from disclosure (including protection under section 552(b)(3) of title 5, United States Code). The custodian of a record subject to such protection may mark such record as subject to statutory protections. A marking under this subparagraph shall not be dispositive with respect to whether such record contains any information subject to legal protections from public disclosure. Members of the review panel will protect voluntarily submitted safety information and other otherwise exempt information to the extent permitted under applicable law.

(iv) PROTECTION OF PROPRIETARY INFORMATION AND TRADE SECRETS.—Members of the review panel will protect proprietary information, trade secrets, and other otherwise exempt information to the extent permitted under applicable law.

(v) RESOLVING CLASSIFICATION OF INFORMATION.—If the review panel and a holder of an organization designation authorization subject to review under this section disagree as to the proper classification of information described in this subparagraph, then an employee of the Administration who is not a political appointee shall determine the proper classification of such information and whether such information will be withheld, in part or in full, from release to the public.

(D) APPLICABLE LAW.—Public Law 92-463 shall not apply to the panel established under this subsection.

(E) FINANCIAL INTEREST DEFINED.—In this paragraph, the term "financial interest"—

(i) excludes securities held in an index fund; and

(ii) includes—

(I) any current or contingent ownership, equity, or security interest;

(II) an indebtedness or compensated employment relationship; or

(III) any right to purchase or acquire any such interest, including a stock option or commodity future.

(b) FAA AUTHORITY.—

(1) IN GENERAL.—After reviewing the findings of the review panel submitted under subsection (a)(5), the Administrator may limit, suspend, or terminate an organization designation authorization subject to review under this section.

(2) REINSTATEMENT.—The Administrator may condition reinstatement of a limited, suspended, or terminated organization designation authorization on the holder's implementation of any corrective actions determined necessary by the Administrator.

(3) RULE OF CONSTRUCTION.—Nothing in this subsection shall be construed to limit the Administrator's authority to take any action with respect to an organization designation authorization, including limitation, suspension, or termination of such authorization.

(c) ORGANIZATION DESIGNATION AUTHORIZATION PROCESS IMPROVEMENTS.—Not later than 1 year after receipt of the recommendations submitted under subsection (a)(5), the Administrator shall report to the congressional committees of jurisdiction on—

(1) whether the Administrator has concluded that such holder is able to safely and reliably perform all delegated functions in accordance with all applicable provisions of chapter 447 of title 49, United States Code, title 14, Code of Federal Regulations, and other orders or requirements of the Administrator, and, if not, the Administrator shall outline—

(A) the risk mitigations or other corrective actions, including the implementation timelines of such mitigations or actions, the Administrator has established for or required of such holder as prerequisites for a conclusion by the Administrator under this paragraph; or

(B) the status of any ongoing investigatory actions;

(2) the status of implementation of each of the recommendations of the review panel, if any, with which the Administrator concurs;

(3) the status of procedures under which the Administrator will conduct focused oversight of such holder's processes for performing delegated functions with respect to the design of new and derivative transport airplanes and the production of such airplanes; and

(4) the Administrator's efforts, to the maximum extent practicable and subject to appropriations, to increase the number of engineers, inspectors, and other qualified technical experts, as necessary to fulfill the requirements of this section, in—

(A) each office of the Administration responsible for dedicated oversight of such holder; and

(B) the System Oversight Division, or any successor division, of the Aircraft Certification Service.

SEC. 104. [49 U.S.C. 44701 note]
CERTIFICATION OVERSIGHT STAFF.

Consolidated Appropriations Act,

(d) NON-CONCURRENCE WITH RECOMMENDATIONS.—Not later than 6 months after receipt of the recommendations submitted under subsection (a)(5), with respect to each recommendation of the review panel with which the Administrator does not concur, if any, the Administrator shall publish on the website of the Administration and submit to the congressional committees of jurisdiction a detailed explanation as to why, including if the Administrator believes implementation of such recommendation would not improve aviation safety.

SEC. 104. [49 U.S.C. 44701 note] CERTIFICATION OVERSIGHT STAFF.

(a) AUTHORIZATION OF APPROPRIATIONS.—There is authorized to be appropriated to the Administrator $27,000,000 for each of fiscal years 2021 through 2023 to recruit and retain engineers, safety inspectors, human factors specialists, chief scientific and technical advisors, software and cybersecurity experts, and other qualified technical experts who perform duties related to the certification of aircraft, aircraft engines, propellers, appliances, and new and emerging technologies, and perform other regulatory activities.

(b) IN GENERAL.—Not later than 60 days after the date of enactment of this title, and without duplicating any recently completed or ongoing reviews, the Administrator shall initiate a review of—

(1) the inspectors, human factors specialists, flight test pilots, engineers, managers, and executives in the FAA who are responsible for the certification of the design, manufacture, and operation of aircraft intended for air transportation for purposes of determining whether the FAA has the expertise and capability to adequately understand the safety implications of, and oversee the adoption of, new or innovative technologies, materials, and procedures used by designers and manufacturers of such aircraft; and

(2) the Senior Technical Experts Program to determine whether the program should be enhanced or expanded to bolster and support the programs of the FAA's Office of Aviation Safety, with particular focus placed on the Aircraft Certification Service and the Flight Standards Service (or any successor organizations), particularly with respect to

SEC. 104. [49 U.S.C. 44701 note]
CERTIFICATION OVERSIGHT STAFF.

Consolidated Appropriations Act, 2021

understanding the safety implications of new or innovative technologies, materials, aircraft operations, and procedures used by designers and manufacturers of such aircraft.

(c) DEADLINE FOR COMPLETION.—Not later than 270 days after the date of enactment of this title, the Administrator shall complete the review required by subsection (b).

(d) BRIEFING.—Not later than 30 days after the completion of the review required by subsection (b), the Administrator shall brief the congressional committees of jurisdiction on the results of the review. The briefing shall include the following:

(1) An analysis of the Administration's ability to hire safety inspectors, human factors specialists, flight test pilots, engineers, managers, executives, scientists, and technical advisors, who have the requisite expertise to oversee new developments in aerospace design and manufacturing.

(2) A plan for the Administration to improve the overall expertise of the FAA's personnel who are responsible for the oversight of the design and manufacture of aircraft.

(e) CONSULTATION REQUIREMENT.—In completing the review under subsection (b), the Administrator shall consult and collaborate with appropriate stakeholders, including labor organizations (including those representing aviation workers, FAA aviation safety engineers, human factors specialists, flight test pilots, and FAA aviation safety inspectors), and aerospace manufacturers.

(f) RECRUITMENT AND RETENTION.—

(1) BARGAINING UNITS.—Not later than 30 days after the date of enactment of this title, the Administrator shall begin collaboration with the exclusive bargaining representatives of engineers, safety inspectors, systems safety specialists, and other qualified technical experts certified under section 7111 of title 5, United States Code, to improve recruitment of employees for, and to implement retention incentives for employees holding, positions with respect to the certification of aircraft, aircraft engines, propellers, and appliances. If the Administrator and such representatives are unable to reach an agreement collaboratively, the Administrator and such representatives shall negotiate in accordance with section 40122(a) of title 49, United States Code, to improve recruitment

SEC. 105. [49 U.S.C. 44701 note]
CERTIFICATION OVERSIGHT STAFF.

Consolidated Appropriations Act,

and implement retention incentives for employees described in subsection (a) who are covered under a collective bargaining agreement.

(2) OTHER EMPLOYEES.—Notwithstanding any other provision of law, not later than 30 days after the date of enactment of this title, the Administrator shall initiate actions to improve recruitment of, and implement retention incentives for, any individual described in subsection (a) who is not covered under a collective bargaining agreement.

(3) RULE OF CONSTRUCTION.—Nothing in this section shall be construed to vest in any exclusive bargaining representative any management right of the Administrator, as such right existed on the day before the date of enactment of this title.

(4) AVAILABILITY OF APPROPRIATIONS.—Any action taken by the Administrator under this section shall be subject to the availability of appropriations authorized under subsection (a).

SEC. 105. DISCLOSURE OF SAFETY CRITICAL INFORMATION.

(a) DISCLOSURE.—Section 44704 of title 49, United States Code, is amended by striking subsection (e) and inserting the following:

"(e) DISCLOSURE OF SAFETY CRITICAL INFORMATION.—

"(1) IN GENERAL.—Notwithstanding a delegation described in section 44702(d), the Administrator shall require an applicant for, or holder of, a type certificate for a transport category airplane covered under part 25 of title 14, Code of Federal Regulations, to submit safety critical information with respect to such airplane to the Administrator in such form, manner, or time as the Administrator may require. Such safety critical information shall include—

"(A) any design and operational details, intended functions, and failure modes of any system that, without being commanded by the flight crew, commands the operation of any safety critical function or feature required for control of an airplane during flight or that otherwise changes the flight path or airspeed of an airplane;

"(B) the design and operational details, intended functions, failure modes, and mode annunciations of autopilot and autothrottle systems, if applicable;

"(C) any failure or operating condition that the

applicant or holder anticipates or has concluded would result in an outcome with a severity level of hazardous or catastrophic, as defined in the appropriate Administration airworthiness requirements and guidance applicable to transport category airplanes defining risk severity;

"(D) any adverse handling quality that fails to meet the requirements of applicable regulations without the addition of a software system to augment the flight controls of the airplane to produce compliant handling qualities; and

"(E) a system safety assessment with respect to a system described in subparagraph (A) or (B) or with respect to any component or other system for which failure or erroneous operation of such component or system could result in an outcome with a severity level of hazardous or catastrophic, as defined in the appropriate Administration airworthiness requirements and guidance applicable to transport category airplanes defining risk severity.

"(2) ONGOING COMMUNICATIONS.—

"(A) NEWLY DISCOVERED INFORMATION.—The Administrator shall require that an applicant for, or holder of, a type certificate disclose to the Administrator, in such form, manner, or time as the Administrator may require, any newly discovered information or design or analysis change that would materially alter any submission to the Administrator under paragraph (1).

"(B) SYSTEM DEVELOPMENT CHANGES.—The Administrator shall establish multiple milestones throughout the certification process at which a proposed airplane system will be assessed to determine whether any change to such system during the certification process is such that such system should be considered novel or unusual by the Administrator.

"(3) FLIGHT MANUALS.—The Administrator shall ensure that an airplane flight manual and a flight crew operating manual (as appropriate or applicable) for an airplane contains a description of the operation of a system described in paragraph (1)(A) and flight crew procedures for responding to a failure or aberrant operation of such system.

SEC. 105. [49 U.S.C. 44701 note]
CERTIFICATION OVERSIGHT STAFF.

Consolidated Appropriations Act,

"(4) CIVIL PENALTY.—

"(A) AMOUNT.—Notwithstanding section 46301, an applicant for, or holder of, a type certificate that knowingly violates paragraph (1), (2), or (3) of this subsection shall be liable to the Administrator for a civil penalty of not more than $1,000,000 for each violation.

"(B) PENALTY CONSIDERATIONS.—In determining the amount of a civil penalty under subparagraph (A), the Administrator shall consider—

"(i) the nature, circumstances, extent, and gravity of the violation, including the length of time that such safety critical information was known but not disclosed; and

"(ii) with respect to the violator, the degree of culpability, any history of prior violations, and the size of the business concern.

"(5) REVOCATION AND CIVIL PENALTY FOR INDIVIDUALS.—

"(A) IN GENERAL.—The Administrator shall revoke any airline transport pilot certificate issued under section 44703 held by any individual who, while acting on behalf of an applicant for, or holder of, a type certificate, knowingly makes a false statement with respect to any of the matters described in subparagraphs (A) through (E) of paragraph (1).

"(B) AUTHORITY TO IMPOSE CIVIL PENALTY.—The Administrator may impose a civil penalty under section 46301 for each violation described in subparagraph (A).

"(6) RULE OF CONSTRUCTION.—Nothing in this subsection shall be construed to affect or otherwise inhibit the authority of the Administrator to deny an application by an applicant for a type certificate or to revoke or amend a type certificate of a holder of such certificate.

"(7) DEFINITION OF TYPE CERTIFICATE.—In this subsection, the term 'type certificate'—

"(A) means a type certificate issued under subsection (a) or an amendment to such certificate; and

"(B) does not include a supplemental type certificate issued under subsection (b).".

(b) CIVIL PENALTY AUTHORITY.—Section 44704 of title 49, United States Code, is further amended by adding at the end the following:

"(f) HEARING REQUIREMENT.—The Administrator may find that a person has violated subsection (a)(6) or paragraph (1), (2), or (3) of subsection (e) and impose a civil penalty under the applicable subsection only after notice and an opportunity for a hearing. The Administrator shall provide a person—

"(1) written notice of the violation and the amount of penalty; and

"(2) the opportunity for a hearing under subpart G of part 13 of title 14, Code of Federal Regulations.".

(c) [49 U.S.C. 44704 note] REQUIRED SUBMISSION OF OUTLINE OF SYSTEM CHANGES AT THE BEGINNING OF THE CERTIFICATION PROCESS.—

(1) IN GENERAL.—Not later than 180 days after the date of enactment of this title, the Administrator shall initiate a process to revise procedures to require an applicant for an amendment to a type certificate for a transport category aircraft to disclose to the Administrator, in a single document submitted at the beginning of the process for amending such certificate, all new systems and intended changes to existing systems then known to such applicant. The Administrator shall finalize the revision of such procedures not later than 18 months after initiating such process.

(2) APPLICATION.—Compliance with the procedures revised pursuant to paragraph (1) shall not preclude an applicant from making additional changes to aircraft systems as the design and application process proceeds.

(3) SAVINGS PROVISION.—Nothing in this subsection may be construed to limit the obligations of an applicant for an amended type certificate for a transport category airplane under section 44704(e) of title 49, United States Code, as amended in this title.

SEC. 106. LIMITATION ON DELEGATION.

Section 44702(d) of title 49, United States Code, is amended by adding at the end the following:

"(4)(A) With respect to a critical system design feature

of a transport category airplane, the Administrator may not delegate any finding of compliance with applicable airworthiness standards or review of any system safety assessment required for the issuance of a certificate, including a type certificate, or amended or supplemental type certificate, under section 44704, until the Administrator has reviewed and validated any underlying assumptions related to human factors.

"(B) The requirement under subparagraph (A) shall not apply if the Administrator determines the matter involved is a routine task.

"(C) For purposes of subparagraph (A), the term critical system design feature includes any feature (including a novel or unusual design feature) for which the failure of such feature, either independently or in combination with other failures, could result in catastrophic or hazardous failure conditions, as those terms are defined by the Administrator.".

SEC. 107. OVERSIGHT OF ORGANIZATION DESIGNATION AUTHORIZATION UNIT MEMBERS.

(a) IN GENERAL.—Chapter 447 of title 49, United States Code, is amended by adding at the end the following:

"SEC. 44741. [49 U.S.C. 44741] Approval of organization designation authorization unit members

"(a) IN GENERAL.—Beginning January 1, 2022, each individual who is selected on or after such date to become an ODA unit member by an ODA holder engaged in the design of an aircraft, aircraft engine, propeller, or appliance and performs an authorized function pursuant to a delegation by the Administrator of the Federal Aviation Administration under section 44702(d)—

"(1) shall be—

"(A) an employee, a contractor, or a consultant of the ODA holder; or

"(B) the employee of a supplier of the ODA holder; and

"(2) may not become a member of such unit unless approved by the Administrator pursuant to this section.

"(b) PROCESS AND TIMELINE.—

"(1) IN GENERAL.—The Administrator shall maintain an efficient process for the review and approval of an individual to become an ODA unit member under this section.

"(2) PROCESS.—An ODA holder described in subsection (a) may submit to the Administrator an application for an individual to be approved to become an ODA unit member under this section. The application shall be submitted in such form and manner as the Administrator determines appropriate. The Administrator shall require an ODA holder to submit with such an application information sufficient to demonstrate an individual's qualifications under subsection (c).

"(3) TIMELINE.—The Administrator shall approve or reject an individual that is selected by an ODA holder to become an ODA unit member under this section not later than 30 days after the receipt of an application by an ODA holder.

"(4) DOCUMENTATION OF APPROVAL.—Upon approval of an individual to become an ODA unit member under this section, the Administrator shall provide such individual a letter confirming that such individual has been approved by the Administrator under this section to be an ODA unit member.

"(5) REAPPLICATION.—An ODA holder may submit an application under this subsection for an individual to become an ODA unit member under this section regardless of whether an application for such individual was previously rejected by the Administrator.

"(c) QUALIFICATIONS.—

"(1) IN GENERAL.—The Administrator shall issue minimum qualifications for an individual to become an ODA unit member under this section. In issuing such qualifications, the Administrator shall consider existing qualifications for Administration employees with similar duties and whether such individual—

"(A) is technically proficient and qualified to perform the authorized functions sought;

"(B) has no recent record of serious enforcement action, as determined by the Administrator, taken by the Administrator with respect to any certificate, approval, or authorization held by such individual;

"(C) is of good moral character (as such qualification

is applied to an applicant for an airline transport pilot certificate issued under section 44703);

"(D) possesses the knowledge of applicable design or production requirements in this chapter and in title 14, Code of Federal Regulations, necessary for performance of the authorized functions sought;

"(E) possesses a high degree of knowledge of applicable design or production principles, system safety principles, or safety risk management processes appropriate for the authorized functions sought; and

"(F) meets such testing, examination, training, or other qualification standards as the Administrator determines are necessary to ensure the individual is competent and capable of performing the authorized functions sought.

"(2) PREVIOUSLY REJECTED APPLICATION.—In reviewing an application for an individual to become an ODA unit member under this section, if an application for such individual was previously rejected, the Administrator shall ensure that the reasons for the prior rejection have been resolved or mitigated to the Administrator's satisfaction before making a determination on the individual's reapplication.

"(d) RESCISSION OF APPROVAL.—The Administrator may rescind an approval of an individual as an ODA unit member granted pursuant to this section at any time and for any reason the Administrator considers appropriate. The Administrator shall develop procedures to provide for notice and opportunity to appeal rescission decisions made by the Administrator. Such decisions by the Administrator are not subject to judicial review.

"(e) CONDITIONAL SELECTIONS.—

"(1) IN GENERAL.—Subject to the requirements of this subsection, the Administrator may authorize an ODA holder to conditionally designate an individual to perform the functions of an ODA unit member for a period of not more than 30 days (beginning on the date an application for such individual is submitted under subsection (b)(2)).

"(2) REQUIRED DETERMINATION.—The Administrator may not make an authorization under paragraph (1) unless—

"(A) the ODA holder has instituted, to the Administrator's satisfaction, systems and processes to ensure the integrity and reliability of determinations by conditionally-designated ODA unit members; and

"(B) the ODA holder has instituted a safety management system in accordance with regulations issued by the Administrator under section 102 of the Aircraft Certification, Safety, and Accountability Act.

"(3) FINAL DETERMINATION.—The Administrator shall approve or reject the application for an individual designated under paragraph (1) in accordance with the timeline and procedures described in subsection (b).

"(4) REJECTION AND REVIEW.—If the Administrator rejects the application submitted under subsection (b)(2) for an individual conditionally designated under paragraph (1), the Administrator shall review and approve or disapprove any decision pursuant to any authorized function performed by such individual during the period such individual served as a conditional designee.

"(5) PROHIBITIONS.—Notwithstanding the requirements of paragraph (2), the Administrator may prohibit an ODA holder from making conditional designations of individuals as ODA unit members under this subsection at any time for any reason the Administrator considers appropriate. The Administrator may prohibit any conditionally designated individual from performing an authorized function at any time for any reason the Administrator considers appropriate.

"(f) RECORDS AND BRIEFINGS.—

"(1) IN GENERAL.—Beginning on the date described in subsection (a), an ODA holder shall maintain, for a period to be determined by the Administrator and with proper protections to ensure the security of sensitive and personal information—

"(A) any data, applications, records, or manuals required by the ODA holder's approved procedures manual, as determined by the Administrator;

"(B) the names, responsibilities, qualifications, and example signature of each member of the ODA unit who performs an authorized function pursuant to a delegation by the Administrator under section 44702(d);

"(C) training records for ODA unit members and ODA administrators; and

"(D) any other data, applications, records, or manuals determined appropriate by the Administrator.

"(2) CONGRESSIONAL BRIEFING.—Not later than 90 days after the date of enactment of this section, and every 90 days thereafter through September 30, 2023, the Administrator shall provide a briefing to the Committee on Transportation and Infrastructure of the House of Representatives and the Committee on Commerce, Science, and Transportation of the Senate on the implementation and effects of this section, including—

"(A) the Administration's performance in completing reviews of individuals and approving or denying such individuals within the timeline required under subsection (b)(3);

"(B) for any individual rejected by the Administrator under subsection (b) during the preceding 90-day period, the reasoning or basis for such rejection; and

"(C) any resource, staffing, or other challenges within the Administration associated with implementation of this section.

"(g) SPECIAL REVIEW OF QUALIFICATIONS.—

"(1) IN GENERAL.—Not later than 30 days after the issuance of minimum qualifications under subsection (c), the Administrator shall initiate a review of the qualifications of each individual who on the date on which such minimum qualifications are issued is an ODA unit member of a holder of a type certificate for a transport airplane to ensure such individual meets the minimum qualifications issued by the Administrator under subsection (c).

"(2) UNQUALIFIED INDIVIDUAL.—For any individual who is determined by the Administrator not to meet such minimum qualifications pursuant to the review conducted under paragraph (1), the Administrator—

"(A) shall determine whether the lack of qualification may be remedied and, if so, provide such individual with an action plan or schedule for such individual to meet such qualifications; or

"(B) may, if the Administrator determines the lack of qualification may not be remedied, take appropriate action, including prohibiting such individual from performing an authorized function.

"(3) DEADLINE.—The Administrator shall complete the review required under paragraph (1) not later than 18 months after the date on which such review was initiated.

"(4) SAVINGS CLAUSE.—An individual approved to become an ODA unit member of a holder of a type certificate for a transport airplane under subsection (a) shall not be subject to the review under this subsection.

"(h) PROHIBITION.—The Administrator may not authorize an organization or ODA holder to approve an individual selected by an ODA holder to become an ODA unit member under this section.

"(i) DEFINITIONS.—

"(1) GENERAL APPLICABILITY.—The definitions contained in section 44736(c) shall apply to this section.

"(2) TRANSPORT AIRPLANE.—The term 'transport airplane' means a transport category airplane designed for operation by an air carrier or foreign air carrier type-certificated with a passenger seating capacity of 30 or more or an all-cargo or combi derivative of such an airplane.

"(j) AUTHORIZATION OF APPROPRIATIONS.—There is authorized to be appropriated to carry out this section $3,000,000 for each of fiscal years 2021 through 2023.

"SEC. 44742. [49 U.S.C. 44742] Interference with the duties of organization designation authorization unit members

"(a) IN GENERAL.—The Administrator of the Federal Aviation Administration shall continuously seek to eliminate or minimize interference by an ODA holder that affects the performance of authorized functions by ODA unit members.

"(b) PROHIBITION.—

"(1) IN GENERAL.—It shall be unlawful for any individual who is a supervisory employee of an ODA holder that manufactures a transport category airplane to commit an act of interference with an ODA unit member's performance of authorized functions.

"(2) CIVIL PENALTY.—

"(A) INDIVIDUALS.—An individual shall be subject to a civil penalty under section 46301(a)(1) for each violation under paragraph (1).

"(B) SAVINGS CLAUSE.—Nothing in this paragraph shall be construed as limiting or constricting any other authority of the Administrator to pursue an enforcement action against an individual or organization for violation of applicable Federal laws or regulations of the Administration.

"(c) REPORTING.—

"(1) REPORTS TO ODA HOLDER.—An ODA unit member of an ODA holder that manufactures a transport category airplane shall promptly report any instances of interference to the office of the ODA holder that is designated to receive such reports.

"(2) REPORTS TO THE FAA.—

"(A) IN GENERAL.—The ODA holder office described in paragraph (1) shall investigate reports and submit to the office of the Administration designated by the Administrator to accept and review such reports any instances of interference reported under paragraph (1).

"(B) CONTENTS.—The Administrator shall prescribe parameters for the submission of reports to the Administration under this paragraph, including the manner, time, and form of submission. Such report shall include the results of any investigation conducted by the ODA holder in response to a report of interference, a description of any action taken by the ODA holder as a result of the report of interference, and any other information or potentially mitigating factors the ODA holder or the Administrator deems appropriate.

"(d) DEFINITIONS.—

"(1) GENERAL APPLICABILITY.—The definitions contained in section 44736(c) shall apply to this section.

"(2) INTERFERENCE.—In this section, the term 'interference' means—

"(A) blatant or egregious statements or behavior, such as harassment, beratement, or threats, that a reasonable person would conclude was intended to improperly influence or prejudice an ODA unit member's performance of his or her duties; or

"(B) the presence of non-ODA unit duties or activities that conflict with the performance of authorized functions by ODA unit members.".

(b) ODA PROGRAM ENHANCEMENTS.—

(1) IN GENERAL.—Section 44736 of title 49, United States Code, is amended by adding at the end the following:

"(d) AUDITS.—

"(1) IN GENERAL.—The Administrator shall perform a periodic audit of each ODA unit and its procedures.

"(2) DURATION.—An audit required under paragraph (1) shall be performed with respect to an ODA holder once every 7 years (or more frequently as determined appropriate by the Administrator).

"(3) RECORDS.—The ODA holder shall maintain, for a period to be determined by the Administrator, a record of—

"(A) each audit conducted under this subsection; and

"(B) any corrective actions resulting from each such audit.

"(e) FEDERAL AVIATION SAFETY ADVISORS.—

"(1) IN GENERAL.—In the case of an ODA holder, the Administrator shall assign FAA aviation safety personnel with appropriate expertise to be advisors to the ODA unit members that are authorized to make findings of compliance on behalf of the Administrator. The advisors shall—

"(A) communicate with assigned unit members on an ongoing basis to ensure that the assigned unit members are knowledgeable of relevant FAA policies and acceptable methods of compliance; and

"(B) monitor the performance of the assigned unit members to ensure consistency with such policies.

"(2) APPLICABILITY.—Paragraph (1) shall only apply to an ODA holder that is—

"(A) a manufacturer that holds both a type and a production certificate for—

"(i) transport category airplanes with a

maximum takeoff gross weight greater than 150,000 pounds; or

"(ii) airplanes produced and delivered to operators operating under part 121 of title 14, Code of Federal Regulations, for air carrier service under such part 121; or

"(B) a manufacturer of engines for an airplane described in subparagraph (A).

"(f) COMMUNICATION WITH THE FAA.—Neither the Administrator nor an ODA holder may prohibit—

"(1) an ODA unit member from communicating with, or seeking the advice of, the Administrator or FAA staff; or

"(2) the Administrator or FAA staff from communicating with an ODA unit member.".

(2) REPORT.—Not later than September 30, 2022, the Administrator shall submit to the congressional committees of jurisdiction a report on the implementation of subsections (d) and (e) of section 44736 of title 49, United States Code, as added by subsection (b).

(c) ADDITIONAL ODA PROGRAM ENHANCEMENTS.—Section 44736 of title 49, United States Code, is amended—

(1) in subsection (a)—

(A) in paragraph (1)—

(i) in subparagraph (A) by striking the semicolon and inserting "; and";

(ii) by striking subparagraph (B);

(iii) in subparagraph (C) by striking "; and" and inserting a period;

(iv) by striking subparagraph (D); and

(v) by redesignating subparagraph (C) as subparagraph (B); and

(B) in paragraph (3) by striking "shall—" and all that follows through the end and inserting "shall conduct regular oversight activities by inspecting the ODA holder's delegated functions and taking action based on validated inspection findings."; and

(2) in subsection (b)(3)—

(A) in subparagraph (A)—

(i) by striking clause (i) and redesignating clauses (ii), (iii), and (iv) as clauses (i), (ii), and (iii), respectively;

(ii) in clause (i) as redesignated by inserting ", as appropriate," after "require";

(iii) in clause (ii) as redesignated by inserting ", as appropriate," after "require"; and

(iv) in clause (iii) as redesignated by inserting "when appropriate," before "make a reassessment";

(B) by striking subparagraph (B);

(C) in subparagraph (F) by inserting ", when appropriate," before "approve"; and

(D) by redesignating subparagraphs (C), (D), (E), and (F) as subparagraphs (B), (C), (D), and (E), respectively.

(d) TECHNICAL CORRECTIONS.—

(1) SECTION 44737.—Chapter 447 of title 49, United States Code, is further amended by redesignating the second section 44737 (as added by section 581 of the FAA Reauthorization Act of 2018) as section 44740.

(2) [49 U.S.C. 44701] ANALYSIS.—The analysis for chapter 447 of title 49, United States Code , is amended—

(A) by striking the item relating to the second section 44737 (as added by section 581 of the FAA Reauthorization Act of 2018); and

(B) by inserting after the item relating to section 44739 the following new items:

"44740.	Special rule for certain aircraft operations.
"44741.	Approval of organization designation authorization unit members.
"44742.	Interference with the duties of organization designation authorization unit members.".

(3) SPECIAL RULE FOR CERTAIN AIRCRAFT OPERATIONS.—Section 44740 of title 49, United States Code (as redesignated by paragraph (1)), is amended—

(A) in the heading by striking the period at the end;

(B) in subsection (a)(1) by striking "chapter" and

inserting "section";

(C) in subsection (b)(1) by striking "(1)" the second time it appears; and

(D) in subsection (c)(2) by adding a period at the end.

SEC. 108. [49 U.S.C. 44704 note] INTEGRATED PROJECT TEAMS.

(a) IN GENERAL.—Upon receipt of an application for a type certificate for a transport category airplane, the Administrator shall convene an interdisciplinary integrated project team responsible for coordinating review and providing advice and recommendations, as appropriate, to the Administrator on such application.

(b) MEMBERSHIP.—In convening an interdisciplinary integrated project team under subsection (a), the Administrator shall appoint employees of the Administration or other Federal agencies, such as the Air Force, Volpe National Transportation Systems Center, or the National Aeronautics and Space Administration (with the concurrence of the head of such other Federal agency), with specialized expertise and experience in the fields of engineering, systems design, human factors, and pilot training, including, at a minimum—

(1) not less than 1 designee of the Associate Administrator for Aviation Safety whose duty station is in the Administration's headquarters;

(2) representatives of the Aircraft Certification Service of the Administration;

(3) representatives of the Flight Standards Service of the Administration;

(4) experts in the fields of human factors, aerodynamics, flight controls, software, and systems design; and

(5) any other subject matter expert whom the Administrator determines appropriate.

(c) AVAILABILITY.—In order to carry out its duties with respect to the areas specified in subsection (d), a project team shall be available to the Administrator, upon request, at any time during the certification process.

(d) DUTIES.—A project team shall advise the Administrator and make written recommendations to the Administrator, to be retained in the certification project file, including recommendations for any plans, analyses, assessments, and reports required to support and document the certification project, in the following areas associated with a new technology or novel design:

(1) Initial review of design proposals proposed by the applicant and the establishment of the certification basis.

(2) Identification of new technology, novel design, or safety critical design features or systems that are potentially catastrophic, either alone or in combination with another failure.

(3) Determination of compliance findings, system safety assessments, and safety critical functions the Administration should retain in terms of new technology, novel design, or safety critical design features or systems.

(4) Evaluation of the Administration's expertise or experience necessary to support the project.

(5) Review and evaluation of an applicant's request for exceptions or exemptions from compliance with airworthiness standards codified in title 14 of the Code of Federal Regulations, as in effect on the date of application for the change.

(6) Conduct of design reviews, procedure evaluations, and training evaluations.

(7) Review of the applicant's final design documentation and other data to evaluate compliance with all relevant Administration regulations.

(e) DOCUMENTATION OF FAA RESPONSE.—The Administrator shall provide a written response to each recommendation of each project team and shall retain such response in the certification project file.

(f) REPORT.—Not later than 1 year after the date of enactment of this section, and annually thereafter through fiscal year 2028, the Administrator shall submit to the congressional committees of jurisdiction a report on the establishment of each integrated project team in accordance with this section during such fiscal year, including the role and composition of each such project team.

SEC. 109. OVERSIGHT INTEGRITY BRIEFING.

Not later than 1 year after the date of enactment of this title, the Administrator shall brief the congressional committees of jurisdiction on specific measures the Administrator has taken to reinforce that each employee of the Administration responsible for overseeing an organization designation authorization with respect to the certification of aircraft perform such responsibility in accordance with safety management principles and in the public interest of aviation safety.

SEC. 110. APPEALS OF CERTIFICATION DECISIONS.

(a) IN GENERAL.—Section 44704, of title 49, United States Code, as amended by section 105(b), is further amended by adding at the end the following:

"(g) CERTIFICATION DISPUTE RESOLUTION.—

"(1) DISPUTE RESOLUTION PROCESS AND APPEALS.—

"(A) IN GENERAL.—Not later than 60 days after the date of enactment of this subsection, the Administrator shall issue an order establishing—

"(i) an effective, timely, and milestone-based issue resolution process for type certification activities under subsection (a); and

"(ii) a process by which a decision, finding of compliance or noncompliance, or other act of the Administration, with respect to compliance with design requirements, may be appealed by a covered person directly involved with the certification activities in dispute on the basis that such decision, finding, or act is erroneous or inconsistent with this chapter, regulations, or guidance materials promulgated by the Administrator, or other requirements.

"(B) ESCALATION.—The order issued under subparagraph (A) shall provide processes for—

"(i) resolution of technical issues at pre-established stages of the certification process, as agreed to by the Administrator and the type certificate applicant;

"(ii) automatic elevation to appropriate management personnel of the Administration and the type certificate applicant of any major certification process milestone that is not completed or resolved within a specific period of time agreed to by the Administrator and the type certificate applicant;

"(iii) resolution of a major certification process milestone elevated pursuant to clause (ii) within a specific period of time agreed to by the Administrator and the type certificate applicant;

"(iv) initial review by appropriate Administration employees of any appeal described in subparagraph (A)(ii); and

"(v) subsequent review of any further appeal by appropriate management personnel of the Administration and the Associate Administrator for Aviation Safety.

"(C) DISPOSITION.—

"(i) WRITTEN DECISION.—The Associate Administrator for Aviation Safety shall issue a written decision that states the grounds for the decision of the Associate Administrator on—

"(I) each appeal submitted under subparagraph (A)(ii); and

"(II) An appeal to the Associate Administrator submitted under subparagraph (B)(v).

"(ii) REPORT TO CONGRESS.—Not later than December 31 of each calendar year through calendar year 2025, the Administrator shall submit to the Committee on Transportation and Infrastructure of the House of Representatives and the Committee on Commerce, Science, and Transportation of the Senate a report summarizing each appeal resolved under this subsection.

"(D) FINAL REVIEW.—

"(i) IN GENERAL.—A written decision of the Associate Administrator under subparagraph (C) may be appealed to the Administrator for a final review and determination.

"(ii) DECLINE TO REVIEW.—The Administrator may decline to review an appeal initiated pursuant to clause (i).

"(iii) JUDICIAL REVIEW.—No decision under this paragraph (including a decision to decline to review an appeal) shall be subject to judicial review.

"(2) PROHIBITED CONTACTS.—

"(A) PROHIBITION GENERALLY.—During the course of an appeal under this subsection, no covered official may engage in an ex parte communication (as defined in section 551 of title 5) with an individual representing or acting on behalf of an applicant for, or holder of, a certificate under this section in relation to such appeal unless such communication is disclosed pursuant to subparagraph (B).

"(B) DISCLOSURE.—If, during the course of an appeal under this subsection, a covered official engages in, receives, or is otherwise made aware of an ex parte communication, the covered official shall disclose such communication in the public record at the time of the issuance of the written decision under paragraph (1)(C), including the time and date of the communication, subject of communication, and all persons engaged in such communication.

"(3) DEFINITIONS.—In this subsection:

"(A) COVERED PERSON.—The term 'covered person' means either—

"(i) an employee of the Administration whose responsibilities relate to the certification of aircraft, engines, propellers, or appliances; or

"(ii) an applicant for, or holder of, a type certificate or amended type certificate issued under this section.

"(B) COVERED OFFICIAL.—The term 'covered official' means the following officials:

"(i) The Executive Director or any Deputy Director of the Aircraft Certification Service.

"(ii) The Deputy Executive Director for Regulatory Operations of the Aircraft Certification Service.

"(iii) The Director or Deputy Director of the Compliance and Airworthiness Division of the Aircraft Certification Service.

"(iv) The Director or Deputy Director of the

System Oversight Division of the Aircraft Certification Service.

"(v) The Director or Deputy Director of the Policy and Innovation Division of the Aircraft Certification Service.

"(vi) The Executive Director or any Deputy Executive Director of the Flight Standards Service.

"(vii) The Associate Administrator or Deputy Associate Administrator for Aviation Safety.

"(viii) The Deputy Administrator of the Federal Aviation Administration.

"(ix) The Administrator of the Federal Aviation Administration.

"(x) Any similarly situated or successor FAA management position to those described in clauses (i) through (ix), as determined by the Administrator.

"(C) MAJOR CERTIFICATION PROCESS MILESTONE.—The term 'major certification process milestone' means a milestone related to the type certification basis, type certification plan, type inspection authorization, issue paper, or other major type certification activity agreed to by the Administrator and the type certificate applicant.

"(4) RULE OF CONSTRUCTION.—Nothing in this subsection shall apply to the communication of a good-faith complaint by any individual alleging—

"(A) gross misconduct;

"(B) a violation of title 18; or

"(C) a violation of any of the provisions of part 2635 or 6001 of title 5, Code of Federal Regulations.".

(b) CONFORMING AMENDMENT.—Section 44704(a) of title 49, United States Code, is amended by striking paragraph (6).

SEC. 111. EMPLOYMENT RESTRICTIONS.

(a) [49 U.S.C. 44704 note] DISQUALIFICATION BASED ON PRIOR EMPLOYMENT.—An employee of the Administration with supervisory responsibility may not direct, conduct, or otherwise participate in oversight of a holder of a certificate issued under section 44704 of title 49, United States Code, that previously employed such employee in the preceding 1-year period.

(b) POST-EMPLOYMENT RESTRICTIONS.—Section 44711(d) of title 49, United States Code, is amended to read as follows:

"(d) POST-EMPLOYMENT RESTRICTIONS FOR INSPECTORS AND ENGINEERS.—

"(1) PROHIBITION.—A person holding a certificate issued under part 21 or 119 of title 14, Code of Federal Regulations, may not knowingly employ, or make a contractual arrangement that permits, an individual to act as an agent or representative of such person in any matter before the Administration if the individual, in the preceding 2-year period—

"(A) served as, or was responsible for oversight of—

"(i) a flight standards inspector of the Administration; or

"(ii) an employee of the Administration with responsibility for certification functions with respect to a holder of a certificate issued under section 44704(a); and

"(B) had responsibility to inspect, or oversee inspection of, the operations of such person.

"(2) WRITTEN AND ORAL COMMUNICATIONS.—For purposes of paragraph (1), an individual shall be considered to be acting as an agent or representative of a certificate holder in a matter before the Administration if the individual makes any written or oral communication on behalf of the certificate holder to the Administration (or any of its officers or employees) in connection with a particular matter, whether or not involving a specific party and without regard to whether the individual has participated in, or had responsibility for, the particular matter while serving as an individual covered under paragraph (1).".

SEC. 112. PROFESSIONAL DEVELOPMENT, SKILLS ENHANCEMENT, CONTINUING EDUCATION AND TRAINING.

(a) IN GENERAL.—Chapter 445 of title 49, United States Code, is amended by adding at the end the following:

"SEC. 44519. [49 U.S.C. 44519] Certification personnel continuing education and training

"(a) IN GENERAL.—The Administrator of the Federal Aviation

Administration shall—

"(1) develop a program for regular recurrent training of engineers, inspectors, and other subject-matter experts employed in the Aircraft Certification Service of the Administration in accordance with the training strategy developed pursuant to section 231 of the FAA Reauthorization Act of 2018 (Public Law 115-254; 132 Stat. 3256);

"(2) to the maximum extent practicable, implement measures, including assignments in multiple divisions of the Aircraft Certification Service, to ensure that such engineers and other subject-matter experts in the Aircraft Certification Service have access to diverse professional opportunities that expand their knowledge and skills;

"(3) develop a program to provide continuing education and training to Administration personnel who hold positions involving aircraft certification and flight standards, including human factors specialists, engineers, flight test pilots, inspectors, and, as determined appropriate by the Administrator, industry personnel who may be responsible for compliance activities including designees; and

"(4) in consultation with outside experts, develop—

"(A) an education and training curriculum on current and new aircraft technologies, human factors, project management, and the roles and responsibilities associated with oversight of designees; and

"(B) recommended practices for compliance with Administration regulations.

"(b) IMPLEMENTATION.—The Administrator shall, to the maximum extent practicable, ensure that actions taken pursuant to subsection (a)—

"(1) permit engineers, inspectors, and other subject matter experts to continue developing knowledge of, and expertise in, new and emerging technologies in systems design, flight controls, principles of aviation safety, system oversight, and certification project management;

"(2) minimize the likelihood of an individual developing an inappropriate bias toward a designer or manufacturer of aircraft, aircraft engines, propellers, or appliances;

"(3) are consistent with any applicable collective bargaining agreements; and

"(4) account for gaps in knowledge and skills (as identified by the Administrator in consultation with the exclusive bargaining representatives certified under section 7111 of title 5, United States Code) between Administration employees and private-sector employees for each group of Administration employees covered under this section.

"(c) AUTHORIZATION OF APPROPRIATIONS.—There is authorized to be appropriated to the Administrator, $10,000,000 for each of fiscal years 2021 through 2023 to carry out this section. Amounts appropriated under the preceding sentence for any fiscal year shall remain available until expended.".

(b) [49 U.S.C. 44501] TABLE OF CONTENTS.—The analysis for chapter 445 of title 49, United States Code, is amended by inserting after the item relating to section 44518 the following:

"44519.   Certification personnel continuing education and training.".

SEC. 113. [49 U.S.C. 44701 note] VOLUNTARY SAFETY REPORTING PROGRAM.

(a) IN GENERAL.—Not later than 1 year after the date of enactment of this title, the Administrator shall establish a voluntary safety reporting program for engineers, safety inspectors, systems safety specialists, and other subject matter experts certified under section 7111 of title 5, United States Code, to confidentially report instances where they have identified safety concerns during certification or oversight processes.

(b) SAFETY REPORTING PROGRAM REQUIREMENTS.—In establishing the safety reporting program under subsection (a), the Administrator shall ensure the following:

(1) The FAA maintains a reporting culture that encourages human factors specialists, engineers, flight test pilots, inspectors, and other appropriate FAA employees to voluntarily report safety concerns.

(2) The safety reporting program is non-punitive, confidential, and protects employees from adverse employment actions related to their participation in the program.

(3) The safety reporting program identifies exclusionary criteria for the program.

SEC. 113. [49 U.S.C. 44701 note] VOLUNTARY
SAFETY REPORTING PROGRAM.

Consolidated Appropriations Act, 2021

(4) Collaborative development of the program with bargaining representatives of employees under section 7111 of title 5, United States Code, who are employed in the Aircraft Certification Service or Flight Standards Service of the Administration (or, if unable to reach an agreement collaboratively, the Administrator shall negotiate with the representatives in accordance with section 40122(a) of title 49, United States Code, regarding the development of the program).

(5) Full and collaborative participation in the program by the bargaining representatives of employees described in paragraph (4).

(6) The Administrator thoroughly reviews safety reports to determine whether there is a safety issue, including a hazard, defect, noncompliance, nonconformance, or process error.

(7) The Administrator thoroughly reviews safety reports to determine whether any aircraft certification process contributed to the safety concern being raised.

(8) The creation of a corrective action process in order to address safety issues that are identified through the program.

(c) OUTCOMES.—Results of safety report reviews under this section may be used to—

(1) improve—

(A) safety systems, hazard control, and risk reduction;

(B) certification systems;

(C) FAA oversight;

(D) compliance and conformance; and

(E) any other matter determined necessary by the Administrator; and

(2) implement lessons learned.

(d) REPORT FILING.—The Administrator shall establish requirements for when in the certification process reports may be filed to—

(1) ensure that identified issues can be addressed in a timely manner; and

(2) foster open dialogue between applicants and FAA employees throughout the certification process.

(e) INTEGRATION WITH OTHER SAFETY REPORTING PROGRAMS.—The Administrator shall implement the safety reporting program established under subsection (a) and the reporting requirements established pursuant to subsection (d) in a manner that is consistent with other voluntary safety reporting programs administered by the Administrator.

(f) REPORT TO CONGRESS.—Not later than 2 years after the date of enactment of this title, and annually thereafter through fiscal year 2028, the Administrator shall submit to the congressional committees of jurisdiction a report on the effectiveness of the safety reporting program established under subsection (a).

SEC. 114. COMPENSATION LIMITATION.

Section 106(l) of title 49, United States Code, is amended by adding at the end the following:

"(7) PROHIBITION ON CERTAIN PERFORMANCE-BASED INCENTIVES.—No employee of the Administration shall be given an award, financial incentive, or other compensation, as a result of actions to meet performance goals related to meeting or exceeding schedules, quotas, or deadlines for certificates issued under section 44704.".

SEC. 115. [49 U.S.C. 44704 note] SYSTEM SAFETY ASSESSMENTS AND OTHER REQUIREMENTS.

(a) IN GENERAL.—Not later than 2 years after the date of enactment of this title, the Administrator shall issue such regulations as are necessary to amend part 25 of title 14, Code of Federal Regulations, and any associated advisory circular, guidance, or policy of the Administration, in accordance with this section.

(b) SYSTEM SAFETY ASSESSMENTS AND OTHER REQUIREMENTS.—In developing regulations under subsection (a), the Administrator shall—

(1) require an applicant for an amended type certificate for a transport airplane to—

(A) perform a system safety assessment with respect to each proposed design change that the Administrator determines is significant, with such assessment considering the airplane-level effects of individual errors, malfunctions, or failures and realistic pilot response times

172

to such errors, malfunctions, or failures;

(B) update such assessment to account for each subsequent proposed design change that the Administrator determines is significant;

(C) provide appropriate employees of the Administration with the data and assumptions underlying each assessment and amended assessment; and

(D) provide for document traceability and clarity of explanations for changes to aircraft type designs and system safety assessment certification documents; and

(2) work with other civil aviation authorities representing states of design to ensure such regulations remain harmonized internationally.

(c) GUIDANCE.—Guidance or an advisory circular issued under subsection (a) shall, at minimum—

(1) emphasize the importance of clear documentation of the technical details and failure modes and effects of a design change described in subsection (b)(1); and

(2) ensure appropriate review of any change that results in a functional hazard assessment classification of major or greater, as such term is defined in FAA Advisory Circular 25.1309-1A (or any successor or replacement document).

(d) FAA REVIEW.—Appropriate employees of the Aircraft Certification Service and the Flight Standards Service of the Administration shall review each system safety assessment required under subsection (b)(1)(A), updated assessment required under subsection (b)(1)(B), and supporting data and assumptions required under subsection (b)(1)(C), to ensure that each such assessment sufficiently addresses the considerations listed in subsection (b)(1)(A).

SEC. 116. [49 U.S.C. 44704 note] FLIGHT CREW ALERTING.

(a) IN GENERAL.—Not later than 1 year after the date of enactment of this title, the Administrator shall implement National Transportation Safety Board recommendations A-19-11 and A-19-12 (as contained in the safety recommendation report adopted on September 9, 2019).

(b) PROHIBITION.—Beginning on December 27, 2022, the Administrator may not issue a type certificate for a transport category aircraft unless, in the case of a transport category aircraft other than a transport airplane, the type certificate applicant provides a means acceptable to the Administrator to assist the flight crew in prioritizing corrective actions and responding to systems failures (including by cockpit or flight manual procedures).

(c) EXISTING AIRPLANE DESIGNS.—It is the sense of Congress that the FAA shall ensure that any system safety assessment with respect to the Boeing 737-7, 737-8, 737-9, and 737-10 airplanes, as described in National Transportation Safety Board recommendation A-19-10, is conducted in accordance with such recommendation.

SEC. 117. [49 U.S.C. 44704 note] CHANGED PRODUCT RULE.

(a) REVIEW AND REEVALUATION OF AMENDED TYPE CERTIFICATES.—

(1) INTERNATIONAL LEADERSHIP.—The Administrator shall exercise leadership in the creation of international policies and standards relating to the issuance of amended type certificates within the Certification Management Team.

(2) REEVALUATION OF AMENDED TYPE CERTIFICATES.—In carrying out this subsection, the Administrator shall—

(A) encourage Certification Management Team members to examine and address any relevant covered recommendations (as defined in section 121(c)) relating to the issuance of amended type certificates;

(B) reevaluate existing assumptions and practices inherent in the amended type certificate process and assess whether such assumptions and practices are valid; and

(C) ensure, to the greatest extent practicable, that Federal regulations relating to the issuance of amended type certificates are harmonized with the regulations of other international states of design.

(b) AMENDED TYPE CERTIFICATE REPORT AND RULEMAKING.—

(1) BRIEFINGS.—Not later than 12 months after the date of enactment of this title, and annually thereafter through fiscal year 2028, the Administrator shall brief the congressional committees of jurisdiction on the work and status of the development of such recommendations by the Certification Management Team.

(2) INITIATION OF ACTION.—Not later than 2 years after the

date of enactment of this title, the Administrator shall take action to revise and improve the process of issuing amended type certificates in accordance with this section. Such action shall include, at minimum—

(A) initiation of a rulemaking proceeding; and

(B) development or revision of guidance and training materials.

(3) CONTENTS.—In taking actions required under paragraph (2), the Administrator shall do the following:

(A) Ensure that proposed changes to an aircraft are evaluated from an integrated whole aircraft system perspective that examines the integration of proposed changes with existing systems and associated impacts.

(B) Define key terms used for the changed product process under sections 21.19 and 21.101 of title 14, Code of Federal Regulations.

(C) Consider—

(i) the findings and work of the Certification Management Team and other similar international harmonization efforts;

(ii) any relevant covered recommendations (as defined in section 121(c)); and

(iii) whether a fixed time beyond which a type certificate may not be amended would improve aviation safety.

(D) Establish the extent to which the following design characteristics should preclude the issuance of an amended type certificate:

(i) A new or revised flight control system.

(ii) Any substantial changes to aerodynamic stability resulting from a physical change that may require a new or modified software system or control law in order to produce positive and acceptable stability and handling qualities.

(iii) A flight control system or augmented software to maintain aerodynamic stability in any portion of the flight envelope that was not required for a previously certified derivative.

(iv) A change in structural components (other than a stretch or shrink of the fuselage) that results in a change in structural load paths or the magnitude of structural loads attributed to flight maneuvers or cabin pressurization.

(v) A novel or unusual system, component, or other feature whose failure would present a hazardous or catastrophic risk.

(E) Develop objective criteria for helping to determine what constitutes a substantial change and a significant change.

(F) Implement mandatory aircraft-level reviews throughout the certification process to validate the certification basis and assumptions.

(G) Require maintenance of relevant records of agreements between the FAA and an applicant that affect certification documentation and deliverables.

(H) Ensure appropriate documentation of any exception or exemption from airworthiness requirements codified in title 14 of the Code of Federal Regulations, as in effect on the date of application for the change.

(4) GUIDANCE MATERIALS.—The Administrator shall consider the following when developing orders and regulatory guidance, including advisory circulars, where appropriate:

(A) Early FAA involvement and feedback paths in the aircraft certification process to ensure the FAA is aware of changes to design assumptions and product design impacting a changed product assessment.

(B) Presentation to the FAA of new technology, novel design, or safety critical features or systems, initially and throughout the certification process, when development and certification prompt design or compliance method revision.

(C) Examples of key terms used for the changed product process under sections 21.19 and 21.101 of title 14, Code of Federal Regulations.

(D) Type certificate data sheet improvements to accurately state which regulations and amendment level the aircraft complies to and when compliance is limited to a subset of the aircraft.

(E) Policies to guide applicants on proper visibility, clarity, and consistency of key design and compliance information that is submitted for certification, particularly with new design features.

(F) The creation, validation, and implementation of analytical tools appropriate for the analysis of complex system for the FAA and applicants.

(G) Early coordination processes with the FAA for the functional hazard assessments validation and preliminary system safety assessments review.

(5) TRAINING MATERIALS.—The Administrator shall—

(A) develop training materials for establishing the certification basis for changed aeronautical products pursuant to section 21.101 of title 14, Code of Federal Regulations, applications for a new type certificate pursuant to section 21.19 of such title, and the regulatory guidance developed as a result of the rulemaking conducted pursuant to paragraph (2); and

(B) procedures for disseminating such materials to implementing personnel of the FAA, designees, and applicants.

(6) CERTIFICATION MANAGEMENT TEAM DEFINED.—In this section, the term "Certification Management Team" means the team framework under which the FAA, the European Aviation Safety Agency, the Transport Canada Civil Aviation, and the National Civil Aviation Agency of Brazil, manage the technical, policy, certification, manufacturing, export, and continued airworthiness issues common among the 4 authorities.

(7) DEADLINE.—The Administrator shall finalize the actions initiated under paragraph (2) not later than 3 years after the date of enactment of this title.

(c) INTERNATIONAL LEADERSHIP.—The Administrator shall exercise leadership within the ICAO and among other civil aviation regulators representing states of aircraft design to advocate for the adoption of an amended changed product rule on a global basis, consistent with ICAO standards.

SEC. 118. WHISTLEBLOWER PROTECTIONS.

Section 42121 of title 49, United States Code, is amended—

(1) by striking subsection (a) and inserting the following:

"(a) PROHIBITED DISCRIMINATION.—A holder of a certificate under section 44704 or 44705 of this title, or a contractor, subcontractor, or supplier of such holder, may not discharge an employee or otherwise discriminate against an employee with respect to compensation, terms, conditions, or privileges of employment because the employee (or any person acting pursuant to a request of the employee)—

"(1) provided, caused to be provided, or is about to provide (with any knowledge of the employer) or cause to be provided to the employer or Federal Government information relating to any violation or alleged violation of any order, regulation, or standard of the Federal Aviation Administration or any other provision of Federal law relating to aviation safety under this subtitle or any other law of the United States;

"(2) has filed, caused to be filed, or is about to file (with any knowledge of the employer) or cause to be filed a proceeding relating to any violation or alleged violation of any order, regulation, or standard of the Federal Aviation Administration or any other provision of Federal law relating to aviation safety under this subtitle or any other law of the United States;

"(3) testified or is about to testify in such a proceeding; or

"(4) assisted or participated or is about to assist or participate in such a proceeding."

;

(2) by striking subsection (d) and inserting the following:

"(d) NONAPPLICABILITY TO DELIBERATE VIOLATIONS.—Subsection (a) shall not apply with respect to an employee of a holder of a certificate issued under section 44704 or 44705, or a contractor or subcontractor thereof, who, acting without direction from such certificate-holder, contractor, or subcontractor (or such person's agent), deliberately causes a violation of any requirement relating to aviation safety under this subtitle or any other law of the United States."

; and

(3) by striking subsection (e) and inserting the following:

"(e) CONTRACTOR DEFINED.—In this section, the term 'contractor' means—

"(1) a person that performs safety-sensitive functions by contract for an air carrier or commercial operator; or

"(2) a person that performs safety-sensitive functions related to the design or production of an aircraft, aircraft engine, propeller, appliance, or component thereof by contract for a holder of a certificate issued under section 44704.".

SEC. 119. DOMESTIC AND INTERNATIONAL PILOT TRAINING.

(a) IN GENERAL.—Chapter 447 of title 49, United States Code, as amended by section 107, is further amended by adding at the end the following:

"SEC. 44743. [49 U.S.C. 44743] Pilot training requirements

"(a) IN GENERAL.—

"(1) ADMINISTRATOR'S DETERMINATION.—In establishing any pilot training requirements with respect to a new transport airplane, the Administrator of the Federal Aviation Administration shall independently review any proposal by the manufacturer of such airplane with respect to the scope, format, or minimum level of training required for operation of such airplane.

"(2) ASSURANCES AND MARKETING REPRESENTATIONS.—Before the Administrator has established applicable training requirements, an applicant for a new or amended type certificate for an airplane described in paragraph (1) may not, with respect to the scope, format, or magnitude of pilot training for such airplane—

"(A) make any assurance or other contractual commitment, whether verbal or in writing, to a potential purchaser of such airplane unless a clear and conspicuous disclaimer (as defined by the Administrator) is included regarding the status of training required for operation of such airplane; or

"(B) provide financial incentives (including rebates) to a potential purchaser of such airplane regarding the scope, format, or magnitude of pilot training for such airplane.

"(b) PILOT RESPONSE TIME.—Beginning on the day after the date on which regulations are issued under section 119(c)(6) of the Aircraft Certification, Safety, and Accountability Act, the Administrator may not issue a new or amended type certificate for an airplane described in subsection (a) unless the applicant for such certificate has demonstrated to the Administrator that the applicant has accounted for realistic assumptions regarding the time for pilot responses to non-normal conditions in designing the systems and instrumentation of such airplane. Such assumptions shall—

"(1) be based on test data, analysis, or other technical validation methods; and

"(2) account for generally accepted scientific consensus among experts in human factors regarding realistic pilot response time.

"(c) DEFINITION.—In this section, the term 'transport airplane' means a transport category airplane designed for operation by an air carrier or foreign air carrier type-certificated with a passenger seating capacity of 30 or more or an all-cargo or combi derivative of such an airplane.".

(b) [49 U.S.C. 44701] CONFORMING AMENDMENT.—The analysis for chapter 447 of title 49, United States Code, is further amended by adding at the end the following:

"44743.   Pilot training requirements.".

(c) [49 U.S.C. 44704 note] EXPERT SAFETY REVIEW.—

(1) IN GENERAL.—Not later than 30 days after the date of enactment of this title, the Administrator shall initiate an expert safety review of assumptions relied upon by the Administration and manufacturers of transport category aircraft in the design and certification of such aircraft.

(2) CONTENTS.—The expert safety review required under paragraph (1) shall include—

(A) a review of Administration regulations, guidance, and directives related to pilot response assumptions relied upon by the FAA and manufacturers of transport category aircraft in the design and certification of such aircraft, and human factors and human system integration, particularly those related to pilot and aircraft interfaces;

(B) a focused review of the assumptions relied on regarding the time for pilot responses to non-normal conditions in designing such aircraft's systems and instrumentation, including responses to safety-significant failure conditions and failure scenarios that trigger multiple, and possibly conflicting, warnings and alerts;

(C) a review of human factors assumptions with applicable operational data, human factors research and the input of human factors experts and FAA operational data, and as appropriate, recommendations for modifications to existing assumptions;

(D) a review of revisions made to the airman certification standards for certificates over the last 4 years, including any possible effects on pilot competency in basic manual flying skills;

(E) consideration of the global nature of the aviation marketplace, varying levels of pilot competency, and differences in pilot training programs worldwide;

(F) a process for aviation stakeholders, including pilots, airlines, inspectors, engineers, test pilots, human factors experts, and other aviation safety experts, to provide and discuss any observations, feedback, and best practices;

(G) a review of processes currently in place to ensure that when carrying out the certification of a new aircraft type, or an amended type, the cumulative effects that new technologies, and the interaction between new technologies and unchanged systems for an amended type certificate, may have on pilot interactions with aircraft systems are properly assessed through system safety assessments or otherwise; and

(H) a review of processes currently in place to account for any necessary adjustments to system safety assessments, pilot procedures and training requirements, or design requirements when there are changes to the assumptions relied upon by the Administration and manufacturers of transport category aircraft in the design and certification of such aircraft.

(3) REPORT AND RECOMMENDATIONS.—Not later than 30

days after the conclusion of the expert safety review pursuant to paragraph (1), the Administrator shall submit to the congressional committees of jurisdiction a report on the results of the review, including any recommendations for actions or best practices to ensure the FAA and the manufacturers of transport category aircraft have accounted for pilot response assumptions to be relied upon in the design and certification of transport category aircraft and tools or methods identified to better integrate human factors throughout the process for such certification.

(4) INTERNATIONAL ENGAGEMENT.—The Administrator shall notify other international regulators that certify transport category aircraft type designs of the expert panel report and encourage them to review the report and evaluate their regulations and processes in light of the recommendations included in the report.

(5) TERMINATION.—The expert safety review shall end upon submission of the report required pursuant to paragraph (3).

(6) REGULATIONS.—The Administrator shall issue or update such regulations as are necessary to implement the recommendations of the expert safety review that the Administrator determines are necessary to improve aviation safety.

(d) CALL TO ACTION ON AIRMAN CERTIFICATION STANDARDS.—

(1) IN GENERAL.—Not later than 60 days after the date of enactment of this title, the Administrator shall initiate a call to action safety review of pilot certification standards in order to bring stakeholders together to share lessons learned, best practices, and implement actions to address any safety issues identified.

(2) CONTENTS.—The call to action safety review required under paragraph (1) shall include—

(A) a review of Administration regulations, guidance, and directives related to the pilot certification standards, including the oversight of those processes;

(B) a review of revisions made to the pilot certification standards for certificates over the last 5 years, including any possible effects on pilot competency in manual flying skills and effectively managing automation to improve safety; and

(C) a process for aviation stakeholders, including aviation students, instructors, designated pilot examiners, pilots, airlines, labor, and aviation safety experts, to provide and discuss any observations, feedback, and best practices.

(3) REPORT AND RECOMMENDATIONS.—Not later than 90 days after the conclusion of the call to action safety review pursuant to paragraph (1), the Administrator shall submit to the congressional committees of jurisdiction a report on the results of the review, any recommendations for actions or best practices to ensure pilot competency in basic manual flying skills and in effective management of automation, and actions the Administrator will take in response to the recommendations.

(e) [49 U.S.C. 40104 note] INTERNATIONAL PILOT TRAINING.—

(1) IN GENERAL.—The Secretary of Transportation, the Administrator, and other appropriate officials of the Government shall exercise leadership in setting global standards to improve air carrier pilot training and qualifications for—

(A) monitoring and managing the behavior and performance of automated systems;

(B) controlling the flightpath of aircraft without autoflight systems engaged;

(C) effectively utilizing and managing autoflight systems, when appropriate;

(D) effectively identifying situations in which the use of autoflight systems is appropriate and when such use is not appropriate; and

(E) recognizing and responding appropriately to non-normal conditions.

(2) INTERNATIONAL LEADERSHIP.—The Secretary, the Administrator, and other appropriate officials of the Government shall exercise leadership under paragraph (1) by working with—

(A) foreign counterparts of the Administrator in the ICAO and its subsidiary organizations;

(B) other international organizations and fora; and

(C) the private sector.

(3) CONSIDERATIONS.—In exercising leadership under paragraph (1), the Secretary, the Administrator, and other appropriate officials of the Government shall consider—

(A) the latest information relating to human factors;

(B) aircraft manufacturing trends, including those relating to increased automation in the cockpit;

(C) the extent to which cockpit automation improves aviation safety and introduces novel risks;

(D) the availability of opportunities for pilots to practice manual flying skills;

(E) the need for consistency in maintaining and enhancing manual flying skills worldwide;

(F) recommended practices of other countries that enhance manual flying skills and automation management; and

(G) whether a need exists for initial and recurrent training standards for improve pilots' proficiency in manual flight and in effective management of autoflight systems.

(4) CONGRESSIONAL BRIEFING.—The Secretary, the Administrator, and other appropriate officials of the Government shall provide to the congressional committees of jurisdiction regular briefings on the status of efforts undertaken pursuant to this subsection.

(f) INTERNATIONAL AVIATION SAFETY.—Section 40104(b) of title 49, United States Code, is amended—

(1) by striking "The Administrator shall" and inserting the following:

"(1) IN GENERAL.—The Administrator shall"

; and

(2) by adding at the end the following:

"(2) BILATERAL AND MULTILATERAL ENGAGEMENT; TECHNICAL ASSISTANCE.—The Administrator shall—

"(A) in consultation with the Secretary of State, engage bilaterally and multilaterally, including with

the International Civil Aviation Organization, on an
ongoing basis to bolster international collaboration,
data sharing, and harmonization of international
aviation safety requirements including through—

"(i) sharing of continued operational safety
information;

"(ii) prioritization of pilot training
deficiencies, including manual flying skills and
flight crew training, to discourage over reliance on
automation, further bolstering the components of
airmanship;

"(iii) encouraging the consideration of the
safety advantages of appropriate Federal
regulations, which may include relevant Federal
regulations pertaining to flight crew training
requirements; and

"(iv) prioritizing any other flight crew training
areas that the Administrator believes will enhance
all international aviation safety; and

"(B) seek to expand technical assistance provided
by the Federal Aviation Administration in support of
enhancing international aviation safety, including
by—

"(i) promoting and enhancing effective
oversight systems, including operational safety
enhancements identified through data collection
and analysis;

"(ii) promoting and encouraging compliance
with international safety standards by
counterpart civil aviation authorities;

"(iii) minimizing cybersecurity threats and
vulnerabilities across the aviation ecosystem;

"(iv) supporting the sharing of safety
information, best practices, risk assessments, and
mitigations through established international
aviation safety groups; and

"(v) providing technical assistance on any
other aspect of aviation safety that the
Administrator determines is likely to enhance

international aviation safety.".".

(3) AUTHORIZATION OF APPROPRIATIONS.—There is authorized to be appropriated to the Administrator, $2,000,000 for each of fiscal years 2021 through 2028, to carry out section 40104(b)(2) of title 49, United States Code (as added by paragraph (2)).

(g) ASSISTANCE TO FOREIGN AVIATION AUTHORITIES.—

(1) IN GENERAL.—Section 40113(e)(1) of title 49, United States Code, is amended by inserting "The Administrator may also provide technical assistance related to all aviation safety-related training and operational services in connection with bilateral and multilateral agreements, including further bolstering the components of airmanship." after the first sentence.

(2) AUTHORIZATION OF APPROPRIATIONS.—Section 40113(e) of title 49, United States Code, is amended by adding at the end the following:

"(5) AUTHORIZATION OF APPROPRIATIONS.—There is authorized to be appropriated to the Administrator, $5,000,000 for each of fiscal years 2021 through 2023, to carry out this subsection. Amounts appropriated under the preceding sentence for any fiscal year shall remain available until expended.".

(h) SENSE OF CONGRESS REGARDING INTERNATIONAL PILOT TRAINING STANDARDS.—

(1) FINDINGS.—Congress makes the following findings:

(A) Increased reliance on automation in commercial aviation risks a degradation of pilot skills in flight path management using manual flight control.

(B) Manual flight skills are essential for pilot confidence and competence.

(C) During the 40th Assembly of ICAO, the United States, Canada, Peru, and Trinidad and Tobago presented a working paper titled, "Pilot Training Improvements to Address Automation Dependency".

(D) The working paper outlines recommendations for the Assembly to mitigate the consequences of automation dependency, including identifying competency requirements for flight path management using manual flight control and assessing the need for new or amended international standards or guidance.

(2) SENSE OF CONGRESS.—It is the sense of Congress that, as soon as practicable—

(A) the recommendations included in the working paper titled "Pilot Training Improvements to Address Automation Dependency" offered by the United States at the 40th Assembly of ICAO should be made a priority by the Assembly; and

(B) the United States should work with ICAO and other international aviation safety groups, further bolstering the components of airmanship.

SEC. 120. NONCONFORMITY WITH APPROVED TYPE DESIGN.

Section 44704(d) of title 49, United States Code, is amended by adding at the end the following:

"(3) NONCONFORMITY WITH APPROVED TYPE DESIGN.—

"(A) IN GENERAL.—Consistent with the requirements of paragraph (1), a holder of a production certificate for an aircraft may not present a nonconforming aircraft, either directly or through the registered owner of such aircraft or a person described in paragraph (2), to the Administrator for issuance of an initial airworthiness certificate.

"(B) CIVIL PENALTY.—Notwithstanding section 46301, a production certificate holder who knowingly violates subparagraph (A) shall be liable to the Administrator for a civil penalty of not more than $1,000,000 for each nonconforming aircraft.

"(C) PENALTY CONSIDERATIONS.—In determining the amount of a civil penalty under subparagraph (B), the Administrator shall consider—

"(i) the nature, circumstances, extent, and gravity of the violation, including the length of time the nonconformity was known by the holder of a production certificate but not disclosed; and

"(ii) with respect to the violator, the degree of culpability, any history of prior violations, and the size of the business concern.

"(D) NONCONFORMING AIRCRAFT DEFINED.—In this paragraph, the term 'nonconforming aircraft' means an aircraft that does not conform to the approved type design for such aircraft type.".

SEC. 121. IMPLEMENTATION OF RECOMMENDATIONS.

(a) IN GENERAL.—Not later than 1 year after the date of enactment of this title, the Administrator shall submit a report to the congressional committees of jurisdiction on the status of the Administration's implementation of covered recommendations.

(b) CONTENTS.—The report required under subsection (a) shall contain, at a minimum—

(1) a list and description of all covered recommendations;

(2) a determination of whether the Administrator concurs, concurs in part, or does not concur with each covered recommendation;

(3) an implementation plan and schedule for all covered recommendations the Administrator concurs or concurs in part with; and

(4) for each covered recommendation with which the Administrator does not concur (in whole or in part), a detailed explanation as to why.

(c) COVERED RECOMMENDATIONS DEFINED.—In this section, the term "covered recommendations" means recommendations made by the following entities in any review initiated in response to the accident of Lion Air flight 610 on October 29, 2018, or Ethiopian Airlines flight 302 on March 10, 2019, that recommend Administration action:

(1) The National Transportation Safety Board.

(2) The Joint Authorities Technical Review.

(3) The inspector general of the Department of Transportation.

(4) The Safety Oversight and Certification Advisory Committee, or any special committee thereof.

(5) Any other entity the Administrator may designate.

SEC. 122. OVERSIGHT OF FAA COMPLIANCE PROGRAM.

(a) IN GENERAL.—Not later than 180 days after the date of

enactment of this title, the Administrator shall establish an Executive Council within the Administration to oversee the use and effectiveness across program offices of the Administration's Compliance Program, described in Order 8000.373A dated October 31, 2018.

(b) COMPLIANCE PROGRAM OVERSIGHT.—The Executive Council established under this section shall—

(1) monitor, collect, and analyze data on the use of the Compliance Program across program offices of the Administration, including data on enforcement actions and compliance actions pursued against regulated entities by such program offices;

(2) conduct an annual agency-wide evaluation of the Compliance Program through fiscal year 2028 to assess the functioning and effectiveness of such program and to assess—

(A) the need for long-term metrics that, to the maximum extent practicable, apply to all program offices, and use such metrics to assess the effectiveness of the program;

(B) if the program ensures the highest level of compliance with safety standards;

(C) if the program has met its stated safety goals and purpose; and

(D) FAA employee confidence in the program.

(3) provide reports to the Administrator containing the results of any evaluation conducted under paragraph (2), including identifying in such report any nonconformities or deficiencies in the implementation of the program and compliance of regulated entities with safety standards of the Administration;

(4) make recommendations to the Administrator on regulations, guidance, performance standards or metrics, or other controls that should be issued by the Administrator to improve the effectiveness of the Compliance Program in meeting the stated goals and purpose of the program and to ensure the highest levels of aviation safety; and

(5) carry out any other oversight duties with respect to implementation of the Compliance Program and assigned by the Administrator.

(c) EXECUTIVE COUNCIL.—

(1) EXECUTIVE COUNCIL MEMBERSHIP.—The Executive Council shall be comprised of representatives from each program office with regulatory responsibility as provided in Order 8000.373A.

(2) CHAIRPERSON.—The Executive Council shall be chaired by a person, who shall be appointed by the Administrator and shall report directly to the Administrator.

(3) INDEPENDENCE.—The Secretary of Transportation, the Administrator, or any officer or employee of the Administration may not prevent or prohibit the chair of the Executive Council from performing the activities described in this section or from reporting to Congress on such activities.

(4) DURATION.—The Executive Council shall terminate on October 1, 2028.

(d) ANNUAL BRIEFING.—Each calendar year through 2028, the chair of the Executive Council shall provide a briefing to the congressional committees of jurisdiction on the effectiveness of the Administration's Compliance Program in meeting the stated goals and purpose of the program and the activities of the office described in subsection (b), including any reports and recommendations made by the office during the preceding calendar year.

SEC. 123. SETTLEMENT AGREEMENT.

(a) SENSE OF CONGRESS.—It is the sense of Congress that the Administrator should fully exercise all rights and pursue all remedies available to the Administrator under any settlement agreement between the Administration and the holder of a type certificate and production certificate for transport airplanes executed on December 18, 2015, including a demand for full payment of any applicable civil penalties deferred under such agreement, if the Administrator concludes that such holder has not fully performed all obligations incurred under such agreement.

(b) CONGRESSIONAL BRIEFING.—Not later than 60 days after the date of enactment of this title, and every 6 months thereafter until a certificate holder described in subsection (a) has fully performed all obligations incurred by such certificate holder under such settlement agreement, the Administrator shall brief the congressional committees of jurisdiction on action taken consistent

SEC. 124. [49 U.S.C. 44516 note] HUMAN
FACTORS EDUCATION PROGRAM.

Consolidated Appropriations Act, 2021

with subsection (a).

SEC. 124. [49 U.S.C. 44516 note] HUMAN FACTORS EDUCATION
PROGRAM.

(a) HUMAN FACTORS EDUCATION PROGRAM.—

(1) IN GENERAL.—The Administrator shall develop a
human factors education program that addresses the effects of
modern flight deck systems, including automated systems, on
human performance for transport airplanes and the approaches
for better integration of human factors in aircraft design and
certification.

(2) TARGET AUDIENCE.—The human factors education
program shall be integrated into the training protocols (as in
existence as of the date of enactment of this title) for, and be
routinely administered to, the following:

(A) Appropriate employees within the Flight
Standards Service.

(B) Appropriate employees within the Aircraft
Certification Service.

(C) Other employees or authorized representatives
determined to be necessary by the Administrator.

(b) TRANSPORT AIRPLANE MANUFACTURER INFORMATION
SHARING.—The Administrator shall—

(1) require each transport airplane manufacturer to
provide the Administrator with the information or findings
necessary for flight crew to be trained on flight deck systems;

(2) ensure the information or findings under paragraph (1)
adequately includes consideration of human factors; and

(3) ensure that each transport airplane manufacturer
identifies any technical basis, justification or rationale for the
information and findings under paragraph (1).

SEC. 125. BEST PRACTICES FOR ORGANIZATION DESIGNATION
AUTHORIZATIONS.

(a) [49 U.S.C. 44736 note] IN GENERAL.—Section 213 of the
FAA Reauthorization Act of 2018 (Public Law 115-254, 132 Stat.
3249) is amended—

(1) by striking subsection (g);

(2) by redesignating subsections (c) through (f) as subsections (d) through (g), respectively;

(3) by inserting after subsection (b), the following:

"(c) BEST PRACTICES REVIEW.—In addition to conducting the survey required under subsection (b), the Panel shall conduct a review of a sampling of ODA holders to identify and develop best practices. At a minimum, the best practices shall address preventing and deterring instances of undue pressure on or by an ODA unit member, within an ODA, or by an ODA holder, or failures to maintain independence between the FAA and an ODA holder or an ODA unit member. In carrying out such review, the Panel shall—

"(1) examine other government regulated industries to gather lessons learned, procedures, or processes that address undue pressure of employees, perceived regulatory coziness, or other failures to maintain independence;

"(2) identify ways to improve communications between an ODA Administrator, ODA unit members, and FAA engineers and inspectors, consistent with section 44736(g) of title 49, United States Code, in order to enable direct communication of technical concerns that arise during a certification project without fear of reprisal to the ODA Administrator or ODA unit member; and

"(3) examine FAA designee programs, including the assignment of FAA advisors to designees, to determine which components of the program may improve the FAA's oversight of ODA units, ODA unit members, and the ODA program."

;

(4) in subsection (d) (as redesignated by paragraph (2))—

(A) by striking paragraph (3) and redesignating paragraphs (4) through (6) as paragraphs (3) through (5), respectively;

(B) in paragraph (4) (as redesignated by subparagraph (A)), by striking "and" at the end;

(C) in paragraph (5) (as so redesignated), by striking the period at the end and inserting "; and"; and

(D) by adding at the end the following:

"(6) the results of the review conducted under subsection (c)."

; and

(5) by inserting after subsection (g) (as redesignated by paragraph (2)), the following:

"(h) BEST PRACTICES ADOPTION.—

"(1) IN GENERAL.—Not later than 180 days after the date on which the Administrator receives the report required under subsection (e), the Administrator shall establish best practices that are generally applicable to all ODA holders and require such practices to be incorporated, as appropriate, into each ODA holder's approved procedures manual.

"(2) NOTICE AND COMMENT PERIOD.—The Administrator shall publish the established best practices for public notice and comment for not fewer than 60 days prior to requiring the practices, as appropriate, be incorporated into each ODA holder's approved procedures manual.

"(i) SUNSET.—The Panel shall terminate on the earlier of—

"(1) the date of submission of the report under subsection (e); or

"(2) the date that is 2 years after the date on which the Panel is first convened under subsection (a).".

(b) PROCEDURES MANUAL.—Section 44736(b)(3) of title 49, United States Code, as amended by subsection (c)(2)(D) of section 107), is further amended—

(1) in subparagraph (D) (as redesignated by such subsection), by striking "and" after the semicolon at the end;

(2) in subparagraph (E) (as so redesignated), by striking the period at the end and inserting "; and"; and

(3) by adding at the end the following:

"(F) ensure the ODA holders procedures manual contains procedures and policies based on best practices established by the Administrator.".

SEC. 126. [49 U.S.C. 44704 note] HUMAN FACTORS RESEARCH.

(a) HUMAN FACTORS.—Not later than 180 days after the date

of enactment of this title, the Administrator, in consultation with aircraft manufacturers, operators, and pilots, and in coordination with the head of such other Federal agency that the Administrator determines appropriate, shall develop research requirements to address the integration of human factors in the design and certification of aircraft that are intended for use in air transportation.

(b) REQUIREMENTS.—In developing such research requirements, the Administrator shall—

(1) establish goals for research in areas of study relevant to advancing technology, improving design engineering and certification practices, and facilitating better understanding of human factors concepts in the context of the growing development and reliance on automated or complex flight deck systems in aircraft operations, including the development of tools to validate pilot recognition and response assumptions and diagnostic tools to improve the clarity of failure indications presented to pilots;

(2) take into consideration and leverage any existing or planned research that is conducted by, or conducted in partnership with, the FAA; and

(3) focus on—

(A) preventing a recurrence of the types of accidents that have involved transport category airplanes designed and manufactured in the United States; and

(B) increasingly complex aircraft systems and designs.

(c) IMPLEMENTATION.—In implementing the research requirements developed under this section, the Administrator shall work with appropriate organizations and authorities with expertise including, to the maximum extent practicable, the Center of Excellence for Technical Training and Human Performance and the Center of Excellence developed or expanded pursuant to section 127.

(d) AUTHORIZATION OF APPROPRIATIONS.—There is authorized to be appropriated to the Administrator $7,500,000 for each of fiscal years 2021 through 2023, out of funds made available under section 48102(a) of title 49, United States Code, to carry out this section.

SEC. 127. [49 U.S.C. 44513 note] FAA CENTER OF EXCELLENCE FOR AUTOMATED SYSTEMS AND HUMAN FACTORS IN AIRCRAFT.

(a) IN GENERAL.—The Administrator shall develop or expand a Center of Excellence focused on automated systems and human factors in transport category aircraft.

(b) DUTIES.—The Center of Excellence shall, as appropriate—

(1) facilitate collaboration among academia, the FAA, and the aircraft and airline industries, including aircraft, engine, and equipment manufacturers, air carriers, and representatives of the pilot community;

(2) establish goals for research in areas of study relevant to advancing technology, improving engineering practices, and facilitating better understanding of human factors concepts in the context of the growing development and reliance on automated or complex systems in commercial aircraft, including continuing education and training;

(3) examine issues related to human system integration and flight crew and aircraft interfaces, including tools and methods to support the integration of human factors considerations into the aircraft design and certification process; and

(4) review safety reports to identify potential human factors issues for research.

(c) AVOIDING DUPLICATION OF WORK.—In developing or expanding the Center of Excellence, the Administrator shall ensure the work of the Center of Excellence does not duplicate or overlap with the work of any other established center of excellence.

(d) MEMBER PRIORITIZATION.—

(1) IN GENERAL.—The Administrator, when developing or expanding the Center of Excellence, shall prioritize the inclusion of subject-matter experts whose professional experience enables them to be objective and impartial in their contributions to the greatest extent possible.

(2) REPRESENTATION.—The Administrator shall require that the membership of the Center of Excellence reflect a balanced viewpoint across broad disciplines in the aviation industry.

(3) DISCLOSURE.—Any member of the Center of Excellence who is a Boeing Company or FAA employee who participated in the certification of the Maneuvering Characteristics Augmentation System for the 737 MAX-8 airplane must

SEC. 128. [49 U.S.C. 44704 note] PILOT
OPERATIONAL EVALUATIONS.

Consolidated Appropriations Act,

disclose such involvement to the FAA prior to performing any work on behalf of the FAA.

(4) TRANSPARENCY.—In developing or expanding the Center of Excellence, the Administrator shall develop procedures to facilitate transparency and appropriate maintenance of records to the maximum extent practicable.

(5) COORDINATION.—Nothing in this section shall preclude coordination and collaboration between the Center of Excellence developed or expanded under this section and any other established center of excellence.

(e) AUTHORIZATION OF APPROPRIATIONS.—There is authorized to be appropriated to the Administrator $2,000,000 for each of fiscal years 2021 through 2023, out of funds made available under section 48102(a) of title 49, United States Code, to carry out this section. Amounts appropriated under the preceding sentence for any fiscal year shall remain available until expended.

SEC. 128. [49 U.S.C. 44704 note] PILOT OPERATIONAL EVALUATIONS.

(a) PILOT OPERATIONAL EVALUATIONS.—Not later than 1 year after the date of enactment of this title, the Administrator shall revise existing policies for manufacturers of transport airplanes to ensure that pilot operational evaluations for airplane types that are submitted for certification utilize pilots from air carriers that are expected to operate such airplanes.

(b) REQUIREMENT.—Such manufacturer shall ensure, to the satisfaction of the Administrator, that the air carrier and foreign air carrier pilots used for such evaluations include pilots of varying levels of experience.

SEC. 129. ENSURING APPROPRIATE RESPONSIBILITY OF AIRCRAFT CERTIFICATION AND FLIGHT STANDARDS PERFORMANCE OBJECTIVES AND METRICS.

(a) REPEALS.—Sections 211 and 221 of the FAA Reauthorization Act of 2018 (49 U.S.C. 44701 note) are repealed.

(b) CONFORMING REPEALS.—Paragraphs (8) and (9) of section 202(c) of the FAA Reauthorization Act of 2018 (49 U.S.C. 44701 note) are repealed.

SEC. 130. TRANSPORT AIRPLANE RISK ASSESSMENT

SEC. 131. [49 U.S.C. 40101 note] NATIONAL AIR
GRANT FELLOWSHIP PROGRAM.

Consolidated Appropriations Act, 2021

METHODOLOGY.

(a) DEADLINES.—

(1) AGREEMENT.—Not later than 15 days after the date of enactment of this title, the Administrator shall enter into an agreement with the National Academies of Sciences to develop a report regarding the methodology and effectiveness of the Transport Airplane Risk Assessment Methodology (TARAM) process used by the FAA.

(2) REPORT.—Not later than 180 days after the date of enactment of this title, the National Academies of Sciences shall deliver such report to the congressional committees of jurisdiction.

(b) ELEMENTS.—The report under subsection (a) shall include the following elements:

(1) An assessment of the TARAM analysis process.

(2) An assessment of the effectiveness of the TARAM for the purposes of improving aviation safety.

(3) Recommendations to improve the methodology and effectiveness of the TARAM as an element of aviation safety.

(c) REQUIRED NOTICE.—The Administrator shall provide notice to the congressional committees of jurisdiction on the findings and recommendations of a TARAM conducted following a transport airplane accident—

(1) in which a loss of life occurred; and

(2) for which the Administrator determines that the issuance of an airworthiness directive will likely be necessary to correct an unsafe condition associated with the design of the relevant aircraft type.

SEC. 131. [49 U.S.C. 40101 note] NATIONAL AIR GRANT FELLOWSHIP PROGRAM.

(a) PROGRAM.—

(1) PROGRAM MAINTENANCE.—The Administrator shall maintain within the FAA a program to be known as the "National Air Grant Fellowship Program".

(2) PROGRAM ELEMENTS.—The National Air Grant Fellowship Program shall provide support for the fellowship program under subsection (b).

SEC. 131. [49 U.S.C. 40101 note] NATIONAL AIR
GRANT FELLOWSHIP PROGRAM.

Consolidated Appropriations Act,

(3) RESPONSIBILITIES OF ADMINISTRATOR.—

(A) GUIDELINES.—The Administrator shall establish guidelines related to the activities and responsibilities of air grant fellowships under subsection (b).

(B) QUALIFICATIONS.—The Administrator shall by regulation prescribe the qualifications required for designation of air grant fellowships under subsection (b).

(C) AUTHORITY.—In order to carry out the provisions of this section, the Administrator may—

(i) appoint, assign the duties, transfer, and fix the compensation of such personnel as may be necessary, in accordance with civil service laws;

(ii) make appointments with respect to temporary and intermittent services to the extent authorized by section 3109 of title 5, United States Code;

(iii) enter into contracts, cooperative agreements, and other transactions without regard to section 6101 of title 41, United States Code;

(iv) notwithstanding section 1342 of title 31, United States Code, accept donations and voluntary and uncompensated services;

(v) accept funds from other Federal departments and agencies, including agencies within the FAA, to pay for and add to activities authorized by this section; and

(vi) promulgate such rules and regulations as may be necessary and appropriate.

(4) DIRECTOR OF NATIONAL AIR GRANT FELLOWSHIP PROGRAM.—

(A) IN GENERAL.—The Administrator shall appoint, as the Director of the National Air Grant Fellowship Program, a qualified individual who has appropriate administrative experience and knowledge or expertise in fields related to aerospace. The Director shall be appointed and compensated, without regard to the provisions of title 5 governing appointments in the competitive service, at a rate payable under section 5376 of title 5, United States Code.

SEC. 131. [49 U.S.C. 40101 note] NATIONAL AIR
GRANT FELLOWSHIP PROGRAM.

Consolidated Appropriations Act, 2021

(B) DUTIES.—Subject to the supervision of the Administrator, the Director shall administer the National Air Grant Fellowship Program. In addition to any other duty prescribed by law or assigned by the Administrator, the Director shall—

(i) cooperate with institutions of higher education that offer degrees in fields related to aerospace;

(ii) encourage the participation of graduate and post-graduate students in the National Air Grant Fellowship Program; and

(iii) cooperate and coordinate with other Federal activities in fields related to aerospace.

(b) FELLOWSHIPS.—

(1) IN GENERAL.—The Administrator shall support a program of fellowships for qualified individuals at the graduate and post-graduate level. The fellowships shall be in fields related to aerospace and awarded pursuant to guidelines established by the Administrator. The Administrator shall strive to ensure equal access for minority and economically disadvantaged students to the program carried out under this paragraph.

(2) AEROSPACE POLICY FELLOWSHIP.—

(A) IN GENERAL.—The Administrator shall award aerospace policy fellowships to support the placement of individuals at the graduate level of education in fields related to aerospace in positions with—

(i) the executive branch of the United States Government; and

(ii) the legislative branch of the United States Government.

(B) PLACEMENT PRIORITIES FOR LEGISLATIVE FELLOWSHIPS.—

(i) IN GENERAL.—In considering the placement of individuals receiving a fellowship for a legislative branch position under subparagraph (A)(ii), the Administrator shall give priority to placement of such individuals in the following:

(I) Positions in offices of, or with Members on,

SEC. 131. [49 U.S.C. 40101 note] NATIONAL AIR
GRANT FELLOWSHIP PROGRAM.

Consolidated Appropriations Act,

committees of Congress that have jurisdiction over the FAA.

(II) Positions in offices of Members of Congress that have a demonstrated interest in aerospace policy.

(ii) EQUITABLE DISTRIBUTION.—In placing fellows in positions described under clause (i), the Administrator shall ensure that placements are equally distributed among the political parties.

(C) DURATION.—A fellowship awarded under this paragraph shall be for a period of not more than 1 year.

(3) RESTRICTION ON USE OF FUNDS.—Amounts available for fellowships under this subsection, including amounts accepted under subsection (a)(3)(C)(v) or appropriated under subsection (d) to carry out this subsection, shall be used only for award of such fellowships and administrative costs of implementing this subsection.

(c) INTERAGENCY COOPERATION.—Each department, agency, or other instrumentality of the Federal Government that is engaged in or concerned with, or that has authority over, matters relating to aerospace—

(1) may, upon a written request from the Administrator, make available, on a reimbursable basis or otherwise, any personnel (with their consent and without prejudice to their position and rating), service, or facility that the Administrator deems necessary to carry out any provision of this section;

(2) shall, upon a written request from the Administrator, furnish any available data or other information that the Administrator deems necessary to carry out any provision of this section; and

(3) shall cooperate with the FAA and duly authorized officials thereof.

(d) AUTHORIZATION OF APPROPRIATIONS.—There is authorized to be appropriated to the Administrator $15,000,000 for each of fiscal years 2021 through 2028 to carry out this section. Amounts appropriated under the preceding sentence shall remain available until expended.

(e) DEFINITIONS.—In this section:

SEC. 132. [49 U.S.C. 40101 note] EMERGING
SAFETY TRENDS IN AVIATION.

Consolidated Appropriations Act, 2021

(1) DIRECTOR.—The term "Director" means the Director of the National Air Grant Fellowship Program, appointed pursuant to subsection (a)(4).

(2) FIELDS RELATED TO AEROSPACE.—The term "fields related to aerospace" means any discipline or field that is concerned with, or likely to improve, the development, assessment, operation, safety, or repair of aircraft and other airborne objects and systems, including the following:

(A) Aerospace engineering.

(B) Aerospace physiology.

(C) Aeronautical engineering.

(D) Airworthiness engineering.

(E) Electrical engineering.

(F) Human factors.

(G) Software engineering.

(H) Systems engineering.

SEC. 132. [49 U.S.C. 40101 note] EMERGING SAFETY TRENDS IN AVIATION.

(a) GENERAL.—Not later than 180 days after the date of enactment of this title, the Administrator shall enter into an agreement with the Transportation Research Board for the purposes of developing an annual report identifying, categorizing, and analyzing emerging safety trends in air transportation.

(b) FACTORS.—The emerging safety trends report should be based on the following data:

(1) The National Transportation Safety Board's investigation of accidents under section 1132 of title 49, United States Code.

(2) The Administrator's investigations of accidents and incidents under section 40113 of title 49, United States Code.

(3) Information provided by air operators pursuant to safety management systems.

(4) International investigations of accidents and incidents, including reports, data, and information from foreign authorities and ICAO.

(5) Other sources deemed appropriate for establishing

SEC. 133. [49 U.S.C. 40101 note] EMERGING
SAFETY TRENDS IN AVIATION.

Consolidated Appropriations Act,

emerging safety trends in the aviation sector, including the FAA's annual safety culture assessment required under subsection (c).

(c) SAFETY CULTURE ASSESSMENT.—The Administrator shall conduct an annual safety culture assessment through fiscal year 2031, which shall include surveying all employees in the FAA's Aviation Safety organization (AVS) to determine the employees' collective opinion regarding, and to assess the health of, AVS' safety culture and implementation of any voluntary safety reporting program.

(d) EXISTING REPORTING SYSTEMS.—The Executive Director of the Transportation Research Board, in consultation with the Secretary of Transportation and Administrator, may take into account and, as necessary, harmonize data and sources from existing reporting systems within the Department of Transportation and FAA.

(e) BIENNIAL REPORT TO CONGRESS.—One year after the Administrator enters into the agreement with the Transportation Research Board as set forth in subsection (a), and biennially thereafter through fiscal year 2031, the Executive Director, in consultation with the Secretary and Administrator, shall submit to the congressional committees of jurisdiction a report identifying the emerging safety trends in air transportation.

SEC. 133. FAA ACCOUNTABILITY ENHANCEMENT.

(a) ENHANCEMENT OF THE AVIATION SAFETY WHISTLEBLOWER INVESTIGATION OFFICE IN THE FEDERAL AVIATION ADMINISTRATION.—

(1) RENAMING OF THE OFFICE.—

(A) IN GENERAL.—Section 106(t)(1) of title 49, United States Code, is amended by striking "an Aviation Safety Whistleblower Investigation Office" and inserting "the Office of Whistleblower Protection and Aviation Safety Investigations".

(B) CONFORMING AMENDMENT.—The heading of subsection (t) of section 106 of title 49, United States Code, is amended by striking "Aviation Safety Whistleblower Investigation Office" and inserting "Office of Whistleblower Protection and Aviation Safety Investigations".

SEC. 133. [49 U.S.C. 40101 note] EMERGING
SAFETY TRENDS IN AVIATION.

Consolidated Appropriations Act, 2021

(2) DUTIES.—

(A) IN GENERAL.—Section 106(t)(3)(A) of title 49, United States Code, is amended—

(i) in clause (i), by striking "(if the certificate holder does not have a similar in-house whistleblower or safety and regulatory noncompliance reporting process)" and inserting "(if the certificate holder does not have a similar in-house whistleblower or safety and regulatory noncompliance reporting process established under or pursuant to a safety management system)";

(ii) in clause (ii), by striking "and" at the end;

(iii) in clause (iii), by striking the period at the end and inserting a semicolon; and

(iv) by adding at the end the following:

"(iv) receive allegations of whistleblower retaliation by employees of the Agency;

"(v) coordinate with and provide all necessary assistance to the Office of Investigations and Professional Responsibility, the inspector general of the Department of Transportation, and the Office of Special Counsel on investigations relating to whistleblower retaliation by employees of the Agency; and

"(vi) investigate allegations of whistleblower retaliation by employees of the Agency that have been delegated to the Office by the Office of Investigations and Professional Responsibility, the inspector general of the Department of Transportation, or the Office of Special Counsel.".

(B) LIMITATION.—Section 106(t)(2) of title 49, United States Code, is amended by adding at the end the following:

"(E) LIMITATION OF DUTIES.—The Director may only perform duties of the Director described in paragraph (3)(A).".

(C) CONFORMING AMENDMENTS.—Section 106(t)(7) of title 49, United States Code, is amended—

SEC. 133. [49 U.S.C. 40101 note] EMERGING
SAFETY TRENDS IN AVIATION.

Consolidated Appropriations Act,

(i) in the matter preceding subparagraph (A), by striking "October 1" and inserting "November 15"; and

(ii) in subparagraph (A), by striking "paragraph (3)(A)(i) in the preceding 12-month period" and inserting "paragraph (3)(A)(i) in the preceding fiscal year".

(3) REPORT.—Section 106(t)(7) of title 49, United States Code, as amended by paragraph (2)(C), is further amended—

(A) in subparagraph (C)—

(i) by inserting "the resolution of those submissions, including any" before "further"; and

(ii) by striking "and" after the semicolon;

(B) in subparagraph (D) by striking "recommendations." and inserting "recommendations; and"; and

(C) by adding at the end the following:

"(E) A summary of the activities of the Whistleblower Ombudsman, including—

"(i) the number of employee consultations conducted by the Whistleblower Ombudsman in the preceding 12-month period and a summary of such consultations and their resolution (in a de-identified or anonymized form); and

"(ii) the number of reported incidents of retaliation during such period and, if applicable, a description of the disposition of such incidents during such period.".

(b) WHISTLEBLOWER OMBUDSMAN.—Section 106(t) of title 49, United States Code, is further amended by adding at the end the following:

"(8) WHISTLEBLOWER OMBUDSMAN.—

"(A) IN GENERAL.—Within the Office, there shall be established the position of Whistleblower Ombudsman.

"(B) OMBUDSMAN QUALIFICATIONS.—The individual selected as Ombudsman shall have knowledge of Federal labor law and demonstrated government experience in human resource management, and conflict resolution.

"(C) DUTIES.—The Ombudsman shall carry out the following duties:

"(i) Educate Administration employees about prohibitions against materially adverse acts of retaliation and any specific rights or remedies with respect to those retaliatory actions.

"(ii) Serve as an independent confidential resource for Administration employees to discuss any specific retaliation allegation and available rights or remedies based on the circumstances, as appropriate.

"(iii) Coordinate with Human Resource Management, the Office of Accountability and Whistleblower Protection, the Office of Professional Responsibility, and the Office of the Chief Counsel, as necessary.

"(iv) Coordinate with the Office of the Inspector General of the Department of Transportation's Whistleblower Protection Coordinator and the Office of the Special Counsel, as necessary.

"(v) Conduct outreach and assist in the development of training within the Agency to mitigate the potential for retaliation and promote timely and appropriate processing of any protected disclosure or allegation of materially adverse acts of retaliation.".

(c) [49 U.S.C. 40122 note] OFFICE OF INVESTIGATIONS AND PROFESSIONAL RESPONSIBILITY.—The Administrator shall take such action as may be necessary to redesignate the Office of Investigations of the Administration as the Office of Investigations and Professional Responsibility.

(d) MISCONDUCT INVESTIGATIONS.—

(1) IN GENERAL.—The Administrator shall review and revise the Administration's existing investigative policies that govern the investigation of misconduct by a manager of the Administration conducted by the FAA (in this subsection referred to as the "Agency").

(2) PRESERVATION OF COLLECTIVE BARGAINING AGREEMENTS.—The investigative policy established under paragraph (1) shall not apply to, or in the future, be extended by the Administrator to apply to, any employee who is not a

manager or is covered by or eligible to be covered by a collective bargaining agreement entered into by the Agency.

(3) REQUIREMENTS.—In revising the investigative policies, the Administrator shall ensure such policies require—

(A) the utilization of investigative best practices to ensure independent and objective investigation and accurate recording and reporting of such investigation;

(B) the management of case files to ensure the integrity of the information contained in such case files;

(C) interviews be conducted in a manner that ensures, to the greatest extent possible, truthful answers and accurate records of such interviews;

(D) coordination with the Office of the Inspector General of the Department of Transportation, the Office of the Special Counsel, and the Attorney General, as appropriate; and

(E) the completion of investigations in a timely manner.

(4) DEFINITION.—For purposes of this subsection, the term "manager" means an employee of the Agency who is a supervisor or management official, as defined in section 7103(a) of title 5, United States Code.

SEC. 134. AUTHORIZATION OF APPROPRIATIONS FOR THE ADVANCED MATERIALS CENTER OF EXCELLENCE.

Section 44518 of title 49, United States Code, is amended by adding at the end the following:

"(c) AUTHORIZATION OF APPROPRIATIONS.—Out of amounts appropriated under section 48102(a), the Administrator may expend not more than $10,000,000 for each of fiscal years 2021 through 2023 to carry out this section. Amounts appropriated under the preceding sentence for each fiscal year shall remain available until expended.".

SEC. 135. [49 U.S.C. 44515 note] PROMOTING AVIATION REGULATIONS FOR TECHNICAL TRAINING.

(a) NEW REGULATIONS REQUIRED.—

(1) INTERIM FINAL REGULATIONS.—Not later than 90 days after the date of enactment of this section, the Administrator

shall issue interim final regulations to establish requirements for issuing aviation maintenance technician school certificates and associated ratings and the general operating rules for the holders of those certificates and ratings in accordance with the requirements of this section.

(2) REPEAL OF CURRENT REGULATIONS.—Upon the effective date of the interim final regulations required under paragraph (1), part 147 of title 14, Code of Federal Regulations (as in effect on the date of enactment of this title) and any regulations issued under section 624 of the FAA Reauthorization Act of 2018 (Public Law 115-254) shall have no force or effect on or after the effective date of such interim final regulations.

(b) AVIATION MAINTENANCE TECHNICIAN SCHOOL CERTIFICATION REQUIRED.—No person may operate an aviation maintenance technician school without, or in violation of, an aviation maintenance technician school certificate and the operations specifications issued under the interim final regulations required under subsection (a)(1), the requirements of this section, or in a manner that is inconsistent with information in the school's operations specifications under subsection (c)(5).

(c) CERTIFICATE AND OPERATIONS SPECIFICATIONS REQUIREMENTS.—

(1) APPLICATION REQUIREMENTS.—

(A) IN GENERAL.—An application for a certificate or rating to operate an aviation maintenance technician school shall include the following:

(i) A description of the facilities, including the physical address of the certificate holder's primary location for operation of the school, any additional fixed locations where training will be provided, and the equipment and materials to be used at each location.

(ii) A description of the manner in which the school's curriculum will ensure the student has the knowledge and skills necessary for attaining a mechanic certificate and associated ratings under subpart D of part 65 of title 14, Code of Federal Regulations (or any successor regulation).

(iii) A description of the manner in which the school will ensure it provides the necessary qualified

instructors to meet the requirements of subsection
(d)(4).

(B) DOCUMENTED IN THE SCHOOL'S OPERATIONS
SPECIFICATIONS.—Upon issuance of the school's certificate
or rating, the information required under subparagraph
(A) shall be documented in the school's operations
specifications.

(2) CHANGE APPLICATIONS.—

(A) IN GENERAL.—An application for an additional
rating or amended certificate shall include only the
information necessary to substantiate the reason for the
requested additional rating or change.

(B) APPROVED CHANGES.—Any approved changes shall
be documented in the school's operations specifications.

(3) DURATION.—An aviation maintenance technician school
certificate or rating issued under the interim final regulations
required under subsection (a)(1) shall be effective from the
date of issue until the certificate or rating is surrendered,
suspended, or revoked.

(4) CERTIFICATE RATINGS.—An aviation maintenance
technician school certificate issued under the interim final
regulations required under subsection (a)(1) shall specify which
of the following ratings are held by the aviation maintenance
technician school:

(A) Airframe.

(B) Powerplant.

(C) Airframe and Powerplant.

(5) OPERATIONS SPECIFICATIONS.—A certificated aviation
maintenance technician school shall operate in accordance with
operations specifications that include the following:

(A) The certificate holder's name.

(B) The certificate holder's air agency certificate
number.

(C) The name and contact information of the certificate
holder's primary point of contact.

(D) The physical address of the certificate holder's
primary location, as provided under paragraph (1)(A).

(E) The physical address of any additional location of the certificate holder, as provided under subsection (d)(2).

(F) The ratings held, as provided under paragraph (4).

(G) Any regulatory exemption granted to the school by the Administrator.

(d) OPERATIONS REQUIREMENTS.—

(1) FACILITIES, EQUIPMENT, AND MATERIAL REQUIREMENTS.—Each certificated aviation maintenance technician school shall provide and maintain the facilities, equipment, and materials that are appropriate to the 1 or more ratings held by the school and the number of students taught.

(2) TRAINING PROVIDED AT ANOTHER LOCATION.—A certificated aviation maintenance technician school may provide training at any additional location that meets the requirements of the interim final regulations required under subsection (a)(1) and is listed in the certificate holder's operations specifications.

(3) TRAINING REQUIREMENTS.—Each certificated aviation maintenance technician school shall—

(A) establish, maintain, and utilize a curriculum designed to continually align with mechanic airman certification standards as appropriate for the ratings held;

(B) provide training of a quality that meets the requirements of subsection (f)(1); and

(C) ensure students have the knowledge and skills necessary to be eligible to test for a mechanic certificate and associated ratings under subpart D of part 65 of title 14, Code of Federal Regulations (or any successor regulation).

(4) INSTRUCTOR REQUIREMENTS.—Each certificated aviation maintenance technician school shall—

(A) provide qualified instructors to teach in a manner that ensures positive educational outcomes are achieved;

(B) ensure instructors hold a mechanic certificate with 1 or more appropriate ratings (or, with respect to instructors who are not certified mechanics, ensure instructors are otherwise specifically qualified to teach their assigned content); and

(C) ensure the student-to-instructor ratio does not exceed 25:1 for any shop class.

(5) CERTIFICATE OF COMPLETION.—Each certificated aviation maintenance technician school shall provide authenticated documentation to each graduating student, indicating the student's date of graduation and curriculum completed, as described in paragraph (3)(A).

(e) QUALITY CONTROL SYSTEM.—

(1) ACCREDITATION.—Each aviation maintenance technician school shall—

(A) be accredited as meeting the definition of an institution of higher education provided for in section 101 of the Higher Education Act of 1965 (20 U.S.C. 1001); or

(B) establish and maintain a quality control system that meets the requirements specified in paragraph (2) and is approved by the Administrator.

(2) FAA-APPROVED SYSTEM REQUIREMENTS.—In the case of an aviation maintenance technician school that is not accredited as set forth in paragraph (1), the Administrator shall approve a quality control system that provides procedures for recordkeeping, assessment, issuing credit, issuing of final course grades, attendance, ensuring sufficient number of instructors, granting of graduation documentation, and corrective action for addressing deficiencies.

(f) ADDITIONAL REQUIREMENTS.—

(1) MINIMUM PASSAGE RATE.—A certificated aviation maintenance technician school shall maintain a pass rate of at least 70 percent of students who took a written, oral, or practical (or any combination thereof) FAA mechanic tests within 60 days of graduation for the most recent 3-year period .

(2) FAA INSPECTION.—A certificated aviation maintenance technician school shall allow the Administrator such access as the Administrator determines necessary to inspect the 1 or more locations of the school for purposes of determining the school's compliance with the interim final regulations required under subsection (a)(1), the procedures and information outlined in the school's operations specifications according to subsection (c)(5), and the aviation maintenance technician school certificate issued for the school.

(3) DISPLAY OF CERTIFICATE.—A certificated aviation maintenance technician school shall display its aviation maintenance technician school certificate at a location in the school that is visible by and normally accessible to the public.

(4) EARLY TESTING.—A certificated aviation maintenance technician school may issue authenticated documentation demonstrating a student's satisfactory progress, completion of corresponding portions of the curriculum, and preparedness to take the aviation mechanic written general knowledge test, even if the student has not met the experience requirements of section 65.77 of title 14, Code of Federal Regulations (or any successor regulation). Any such documentation shall specify the curriculum the student completed and the completion date.

SEC. 136. INDEPENDENT STUDY ON TYPE CERTIFICATION REFORM.

(a) REPORT AND DEADLINES.—Not later than 30 days after the date of enactment of this title, the Administrator shall enter into an agreement with an appropriate Federally-funded research and development center to review, develop, and submit a report to the Administrator in accordance with the requirements and elements set forth in this section.

(b) ELEMENTS.—The review and report under subsection (a) shall set forth analyses, assessments, and recommendations addressing the following elements for transport category airplanes:

(1) Whether or not aviation safety would improve as the result of institution of a fixed time beyond which a type certificate may not be amended.

(2) Requiring the Administrator, when issuing an amended or supplemental type certificate for a design that does not comply with the latest amendments to the applicable airworthiness standards, to document any exception from the latest amendment to an applicable regulation, issue an exemption in accordance with section 44701 of title 14, United States Code, or make a finding of an equivalent level of safety in accordance with section 21.21(a)(1) of title 14, Code of Federal Regulations.

(3) Safety benefits and costs for certification of transport category airplanes resulting from the implementation of paragraphs (1) and (2).

(4) Effects on the development and introduction of advancements in new safety enhancing design and technologies, and continued operation and operational safety support of products in service in the United States and worldwide, resulting from the implementation of paragraphs (1) and (2).

(c) INVESTIGATIONS AND REPORTS.—The review and report under subsection (a) shall take into consideration investigations, reports, and assessments regarding the Boeing 737 MAX, including but not limited to investigations, reports, and assessments by the Joint Authorities Technical Review, the National Transportation Safety Board, the Department of Transportation Office of the Inspector General, the Department of Transportation Special Committee, the congressional committees of jurisdiction and other congressional committees, and foreign authorities. The review and report under subsection (a) also shall consider the impact of changes made by this title and the amendments made by this title.

(d) REPORT TO CONGRESS.—Not later than 270 days after the report developed under subsection (a) is submitted to the Administrator, the Administrator shall submit a report to the congressional committees of jurisdiction regarding the FAA's response to the findings and recommendations of the report, what actions the FAA will take as a result of such findings and recommendations, and the FAA rationale for not taking action on any specific recommendation

SEC. 137. [49 U.S.C. 40101 note] DEFINITIONS.
In this title:

(1) ADMINISTRATION; FAA.—The terms "Administration" and "FAA" mean the Federal Aviation Administration.

(2) ADMINISTRATOR.—The term "Administrator" means the Administrator of the FAA.

(3) CONGRESSIONAL COMMITTEES OF JURISDICTION.—The term "congressional committees of jurisdiction" means the Committee on Transportation and Infrastructure of the House of Representatives and the Committee on Commerce, Science, and Transportation of the Senate.

(4) ICAO.—The term "ICAO" means the International Civil Aviation Organization.

(5) ORGANIZATION DESIGNATION AUTHORIZATION.—The term "organization designation authorization" has the same meaning given such term in section 44736(c) of title 49, United States Code.

(6) TRANSPORT AIRPLANE.—The term "transport airplane" means a transport category airplane designed for operation by an air carrier or foreign air carrier type-certificated with a passenger seating capacity of 30 or more or an all-cargo or combi derivative of such an airplane.

(7) TYPE CERTIFICATE.—The term "type certificate"—

(A) means a type certificate issued pursuant to section 44704(a) of title 49, United States Code, or an amendment to such certificate; and

(B) does not include a supplemental type certificate issued under section 44704(b) of such section.

AMERICAN SECURITY DRONE ACT

PUBLIC LAW 116-260

National Defense Authorization Act for Fiscal Year 2024

[(Public Law 118–31)]

[As Amended Through P.L. 118–78, Enacted July 30, 2024]

AN ACT To authorize appropriations for fiscal year 2024 for military activities of the Department of Defense and for military construction, and for defense activities of the Department of Energy, to prescribe military personnel strengths for such fiscal year, and for other purposes.

Be it enacted by the Senate and House of Representatives of the United States of America in Congress assembled,

SECTION 1. SHORT TITLE.

This Act may be cited as the "National Defense Authorization Act for Fiscal Year 2024".

SEC. 2. ORGANIZATION OF ACT INTO DIVISIONS; TABLE OF CONTENTS.

* * * * * * *

(b) TABLE OF CONTENTS.—The table of contents for this Act is as follows:

* * * * * * *

DIVISION A—DEPARTMENT OF DEFENSE AUTHORIZATIONS

* * * * * * *

TITLE XVIII—OTHER DEFENSE MATTERS

* * * * * * *

Subtitle B—Drone Security

* * * * * * *

Subtitle B—Drone Security

SEC. 1821. SHORT TITLE.

This subtitle may be cited as the "American Security Drone Act of 2023".

SEC. 1822. DEFINITIONS.

In this subtitle:

(1) COVERED FOREIGN ENTITY.—The term ""covered foreign entity"" means an entity included on a list developed and maintained by the Federal Acquisition Security Council and published in the System for Award Management (SAM). This list will include entities in the following categories:

(A) An entity included on the Consolidated Screening List.

(B) Any entity that is subject to extrajudicial direction from a foreign government, as determined by the Secretary of Homeland Security.

(C) Any entity the Secretary of Homeland Security, in coordination with the Attorney General, Director of National Intelligence, and the Secretary of Defense, determines poses a national security risk.

(D) Any entity domiciled in the People's Republic of China or subject to influence or control by the Government of the People's Republic of China or the Communist Party of the People's Republic of China, as determined by the Secretary of Homeland Security.

(E) Any subsidiary or affiliate of an entity described in subparagraphs (A) through (D).

(2) COVERED UNMANNED AIRCRAFT SYSTEM.—The term ""covered unmanned aircraft system"" has the meaning given the term ""unmanned aircraft system"" in section 44801 of title 49, United States Code.

(3) INTELLIGENCE; INTELLIGENCE COMMUNITY.—The terms "intelligence" and "intelligence community" have the meanings given those terms in section 3 of the National Security Act of 1947 (50 U.S.C. 3003).

SEC. 1823. PROHIBITION ON PROCUREMENT OF COVERED UNMANNED AIRCRAFT SYSTEMS FROM COVERED FOREIGN ENTITIES.

(a) IN GENERAL.—Except as provided under subsections (b) through (f), the head of an executive agency may not procure any covered unmanned aircraft system that is manufactured or assembled by a covered foreign entity, which includes associated elements related to the collection and transmission of sensitive information (consisting of communication links and the components that control the unmanned aircraft) that enable the operator to operate the aircraft in the National Airspace System. The Federal Acquisition Security Council, in coordination with the Secretary of Transportation, shall develop and update a list of associated elements.

(b) EXEMPTION.—The Secretary of Homeland Security, the Secretary of Defense, the Secretary of State, and the Attorney General are exempt from the restriction under subsection (a) if the procurement is required in the national interest of the United States and—

(1) is for the sole purposes of research, evaluation, training, testing, or analysis for electronic warfare, information warfare operations, cybersecurity, or development of unmanned aircraft system or counter-unmanned aircraft system technology;

(2) is for the sole purposes of conducting counterterrorism or counterintelligence activities, protective missions, or Federal criminal or national security investigations, including forensic examinations, or for electronic warfare, information warfare operations, cybersecurity, or development of an unmanned aircraft system or counter-unmanned aircraft system technology; or

(3) is an unmanned aircraft system that, as procured or as modified after procurement but before operational use, can

no longer transfer to, or download data from, a covered foreign entity and otherwise poses no national security cybersecurity risks as determined by the exempting official.

(c) DEPARTMENT OF TRANSPORTATION AND FEDERAL AVIATION ADMINISTRATION EXEMPTION.—The Secretary of Transportation is exempt from the restriction under subsection (a) if the operation or procurement is deemed to support the safe, secure, or efficient operation of the National Airspace System or maintenance of public safety, including activities carried out under the Federal Aviation Administration's Alliance for System Safety of UAS through Research Excellence (ASSURE) Center of Excellence (COE) and any other activity deemed to support the safe, secure, or efficient operation of the National Airspace System or maintenance of public safety, as determined by the Secretary or the Secretary's designee.

(d) NATIONAL TRANSPORTATION SAFETY BOARD EXEMPTION.—The National Transportation Safety Board, in consultation with the Secretary of Homeland Security, is exempt from the restriction under subsection (a) if the operation or procurement is necessary for the sole purpose of conducting safety investigations.

(e) NATIONAL OCEANIC AND ATMOSPHERIC ADMINISTRATION EXEMPTION.—The Administrator of the National Oceanic and Atmospheric Administration (NOAA), in consultation with the Secretary of Homeland Security, is exempt from the restriction under subsection (a) if the procurement is necessary for the purpose of meeting NOAA's science or management objectives or operational mission.

(f) WAIVER.—The head of an executive agency may waive the prohibition under subsection (a) on a case-by-case basis—

(1) with the approval of the Director of the Office of Management and Budget, after consultation with the Federal Acquisition Security Council; and

(2) upon notification to—

(A) the Committee on Homeland Security and Governmental Affairs of the Senate;

(B) the Committee on Oversight and Accountability in the House of Representatives; and

(C) other appropriate congressional committees of jurisdiction.

SEC. 1824. PROHIBITION ON OPERATION OF COVERED UNMANNED AIRCRAFT SYSTEMS FROM COVERED FOREIGN ENTITIES.

(a) PROHIBITION.—

(1) IN GENERAL.—Beginning on the date that is two years after the date of the enactment of this Act, no Federal department or agency may operate a covered unmanned aircraft system manufactured or assembled by a covered foreign entity.

(2) APPLICABILITY TO CONTRACTED SERVICES.—The prohibition under paragraph (1) applies to any covered unmanned aircraft systems that are being used by any executive agency through the method of contracting for the services of covered unmanned aircraft systems.

(b) EXEMPTION.—The Secretary of Homeland Security, the Secretary of Defense, the Secretary of State, and the Attorney General are exempt from the restriction under subsection (a) if the operation is required in the national interest of the United States and—

(1) is for the sole purposes of research, evaluation, training, testing, or analysis for electronic warfare, information warfare operations, cybersecurity, or development of unmanned aircraft system or counter-unmanned aircraft system technology;

(2) is for the sole purposes of conducting counterterrorism or counterintelligence activities, protective missions, or Federal criminal or national security investigations, including forensic examinations, or for electronic warfare, information warfare operations, cybersecurity, or development of an unmanned aircraft system or counter-unmanned aircraft system technology; or

(3) is an unmanned aircraft system that, as procured or as modified after procurement but before operational use, can no longer transfer to, or download data from, a covered foreign entity and otherwise poses no national security cybersecurity risks as determined by the exempting official.

(c) DEPARTMENT OF TRANSPORTATION AND FEDERAL AVIATION ADMINISTRATION EXEMPTION. The Secretary of Transportation is exempt from the restriction under subsection (a) if the operation is deemed to support the safe, secure, or efficient operation of the National Airspace System or maintenance of public safety, including activities carried out under the Federal Aviation Administration's Alliance for System Safety of UAS through Research Excellence (ASSURE) Center of Excellence (COE) and any other activity deemed to support the safe, secure, or efficient operation of the National Airspace System or maintenance of public safety, as determined by the Secretary or the Secretary's designee.

(d) NATIONAL TRANSPORTATION SAFETY BOARD EXEMPTION.—The National Transportation Safety Board, in consultation with the Secretary of Homeland Security, is exempt from the restriction under subsection (a) if the operation is necessary for the sole purpose of conducting safety investigations.

(e) NATIONAL OCEANIC AND ATMOSPHERIC ADMINISTRATION EXEMPTION.—The Administrator of the National Oceanic and Atmospheric Administration (NOAA), in consultation with the Secretary of Homeland Security, is exempt from the restriction under subsection (a) if the procurement is necessary for the purpose of meeting NOAA's science or management objectives or operational mission.

(f) WAIVER.—The head of an executive agency may waive the prohibition under subsection (a) on a case-by-case basis—

(1) with the approval of the Director of the Office of Management and Budget, after consultation with the Federal Acquisition Security Council; and

(2) upon notification to—

(A) the Committee on Homeland Security and Governmental Affairs of the Senate;

(B) the Committee on Oversight and Accountability in the House of Representatives; and

(C) other appropriate congressional committees of jurisdiction.

(g) REGULATIONS AND GUIDANCE.—Not later than 180 days after the date of the enactment of this Act, the Secretary of Homeland Security, in consultation with the Attorney General and the Secretary of Transportation, shall prescribe regulations or guidance to implement this section.

SEC. 1825. PROHIBITION ON USE OF FEDERAL FUNDS FOR PROCUREMENT AND OPERATION OF COVERED UNMANNED AIRCRAFT SYSTEMS FROM COVERED FOREIGN ENTITIES.

(a) IN GENERAL.—Beginning on the date that is two years after the date of the enactment of this Act, except as provided in subsection (b), no Federal funds awarded through a contract, grant, or cooperative agreement, or otherwise made available may be used—

(1) to procure a covered unmanned aircraft system that is manufactured or assembled by a covered foreign entity; or

(2) in connection with the operation of such a drone or unmanned aircraft system.

(b) EXEMPTION.—The Secretary of Homeland Security, the Secretary of Defense, the Secretary of State, and the Attorney General are exempt from the restriction under subsection (a) if the procurement or operation is required in the national interest of the United States and—

(1) is for the sole purposes of research, evaluation, training, testing, or analysis for electronic warfare, information warfare operations, cybersecurity, or development of unmanned aircraft system or counter-unmanned aircraft system technology;

(2) is for the sole purposes of conducting counterterrorism or counterintelligence activities, protective missions, or Federal criminal or national security investigations, including forensic examinations, or for electronic warfare, information warfare operations, cybersecurity, or development of an unmanned aircraft system or counter-unmanned aircraft system technology; or

(3) is an unmanned aircraft system that, as procured or as modified after procurement but before operational use, can no longer transfer to, or download data from, a covered foreign entity and otherwise poses no national security cybersecurity risks as determined by the exempting official.

(c) DEPARTMENT OF TRANSPORTATION AND FEDERAL AVIATION ADMINISTRATION EXEMPTION. The Secretary of Transportation is exempt from the restriction under subsection (a) if the operation or procurement is deemed to support the safe, secure, or efficient operation of the National Airspace System or maintenance of public safety, including activities carried out under the Federal Aviation Administration's Alliance for System Safety of UAS through Research Excellence (ASSURE) Center of Excellence (COE) and any other activity deemed to support the safe, secure, or efficient operation of the National Airspace System or maintenance of public safety, as determined by the Secretary or the Secretary's designee.

(d) NATIONAL OCEANIC AND ATMOSPHERIC ADMINISTRATION EXEMPTION.—The Administrator of the National Oceanic and Atmospheric Administration (NOAA), in consultation with the Secretary of Homeland Security, is exempt from the restriction under subsection (a) if the operation or procurement is necessary for the purpose of meeting NOAA's science or management objectives or operational mission.

(e) WAIVER.—The head of an executive agency may waive the prohibition under subsection (a) on a case-by-case basis—

(1) with the approval of the Director of the Office of Management and Budget, after consultation with the Federal Acquisition Security Council; and

(2) upon notification to—

(A) the Committee on Homeland Security and Governmental Affairs of the Senate;

(B) the Committee on Oversight and Accountability in the House of Representatives; and

(C) other appropriate congressional committees of jurisdiction.

(f) REGULATIONS.—Not later than 180 days after the date of the enactment of this Act, the Federal Acquisition Regulatory Council shall prescribe regulations or guidance, as necessary, to implement the requirements of this section pertaining to Federal contracts.

SEC. 1826. PROHIBITION ON USE OF GOVERNMENT-ISSUED PURCHASE CARDS TO PURCHASE COVERED UNMANNED AIRCRAFT SYSTEMS FROM COVERED FOREIGN ENTITIES.

Effective immediately, Government-issued Purchase Cards may not be used to procure any covered unmanned aircraft system from a covered foreign entity.

SEC. 1827. MANAGEMENT OF EXISTING INVENTORIES OF COVERED UNMANNED AIRCRAFT SYSTEMS FROM COVERED FOREIGN ENTITIES.

(a) IN GENERAL.—All executive agencies must account for existing inventories of covered unmanned aircraft systems manufactured or assembled by a covered foreign entity in their personal property accounting systems, within one year of the date of enactment of this Act, regardless of the original procurement cost, or the purpose of procurement due to the special monitoring and accounting measures necessary to track the items' capabilities.

(b) CLASSIFIED TRACKING.—Due to the sensitive nature of missions and operations conducted by the United States Government, inventory data related to covered unmanned aircraft systems manufactured or assembled by a covered foreign entity may be tracked at a classified level, as determined by the Secretary of Homeland Security or the Secretary's designee.

(c) EXCEPTIONS.—The Department of Defense, the Department of Homeland Security, the Department of Justice, the Department of Transportation, and the National Oceanic and Atmospheric Administration may exclude from the full inventory process, covered unmanned aircraft systems that are deemed expendable due to mission risk such as recovery issues, or that are one-time-use covered unmanned aircraft due to requirements and low cost.

(d) INTELLIGENCE COMMUNITY EXCEPTION.—Nothing in this section shall apply to any element of the intelligence community.

SEC. 1828. COMPTROLLER GENERAL REPORT.

Not later than 275 days after the date of the enactment of this Act, the Comptroller General of the United States shall submit to Congress a report on the amount of commercial off-the-shelf drones and covered unmanned aircraft systems procured by Federal departments and agencies from covered foreign entities, except that nothing in this section shall apply to any element of the intelligence community.

SEC. 1829. GOVERNMENT-WIDE POLICY FOR PROCUREMENT OF UNMANNED AIRCRAFT SYSTEMS.

(a) IN GENERAL.—Not later than 180 days after the date of the enactment of this Act, the Director of the Office of Management and Budget, in coordination with the Department of Homeland Security, Department of Transportation, the Department of Justice, and other Departments as determined by the Director of the Office of Management and Budget, and in consultation with the National Institute of Standards and Technology, shall establish a government-wide policy for the procurement of an unmanned aircraft system—

(1) for non-Department of Defense and non-intelligence community operations; and

(2) through grants and cooperative agreements entered into with non-Federal entities.

(b) INFORMATION SECURITY.—The policy developed under subsection (a) shall include the following specifications, which to the extent practicable, shall be based on industry standards and technical guidance from the National Institute of Standards and Technology, to address the risks associated with processing, storing, and transmitting Federal information in an unmanned aircraft system:

(1) Protections to ensure controlled access to an unmanned aircraft system.

(2) Protecting software, firmware, and hardware by ensuring changes to an unmanned aircraft system are properly managed, including by ensuring an unmanned aircraft system can be updated using a secure, controlled, and configurable mechanism.

(3) Cryptographically securing sensitive collected, stored, and transmitted data, including proper handling of privacy data and other controlled unclassified information.

(4) Appropriate safeguards necessary to protect sensitive information, including during and after use of an unmanned aircraft system.

(5) Appropriate data security to ensure that data is not transmitted to or stored in non-approved locations.

(6) The ability to opt out of the uploading, downloading, or transmitting of data that is not required by law or regulation and an ability to choose with whom and where information is shared when it is required.

(c) REQUIREMENT.—The policy developed under subsection (a) shall reflect an appropriate risk-based approach to information security related to use of an unmanned aircraft system.

(d) REVISION OF ACQUISITION REGULATIONS.—Not later than 180 days after the date on which the policy required under subsection (a) is issued—

(1) the Federal Acquisition Regulatory Council shall revise the Federal Acquisition Regulation, as necessary, to implement

the policy; and

(2) any Federal department or agency or other Federal entity not subject to, or not subject solely to, the Federal Acquisition Regulation shall revise applicable policy, guidance, or regulations, as necessary, to implement the policy.

(e) EXEMPTION.—In developing the policy required under subsection (a), the Director of the Office of Management and Budget shall—

(1) incorporate policies to implement the exemptions contained in this subtitle; and

(2) incorporate an exemption to the policy in the case of a head of the procuring department or agency determining, in writing, that no product that complies with the information security requirements described in subsection (b) is capable of fulfilling mission critical performance requirements, and such determination—

(A) may not be delegated below the level of the Deputy Secretary, or Administrator, of the procuring department or agency;

(B) shall specify—

(i) the quantity of end items to which the waiver applies and the procurement value of those items; and

(ii) the time period over which the waiver applies, which shall not exceed three years;

(C) shall be reported to the Office of Management and Budget following issuance of such a determination; and

(D) not later than 30 days after the date on which the determination is made, shall be provided to the Committee on Homeland Security and Governmental Affairs of the Senate and the Committee on Oversight and Accountability of the House of Representatives.

SEC. 1830. STATE, LOCAL, AND TERRITORIAL LAW ENFORCEMENT AND EMERGENCY SERVICE EXEMPTION.

(a) RULE OF CONSTRUCTION.—Nothing in this subtitle shall prevent a State, local, or territorial law enforcement or emergency service agency from procuring or operating a covered unmanned aircraft system purchased with non-Federal dollars.

(b) CONTINUITY OF ARRANGEMENTS.—The Federal Government may continue entering into contracts, grants, and cooperative agreements or other Federal funding instruments with State, local, or territorial law enforcement or emergency service agencies under which a covered unmanned aircraft system will be purchased or operated if the agency has received approval or waiver to purchase or operate a covered unmanned aircraft system pursuant to section 1825.

SEC. 1831. STUDY.

(a) STUDY ON THE SUPPLY CHAIN FOR UNMANNED AIRCRAFT SYSTEMS AND COMPONENTS.—

(1) REPORT REQUIRED.—Not later than one year after the date of the enactment of this Act, the Under Secretary of Defense for Acquisition and Sustainment shall provide to the appropriate congressional committees a report on the supply chain for covered unmanned aircraft systems, including a discussion of current and projected future demand for covered unmanned aircraft systems.

(2) ELEMENTS.—The report under paragraph (1) shall include the following:

(A) A description of the current and future global and domestic market for covered unmanned aircraft systems that are not widely commercially available except from a covered foreign entity.

(B) A description of the sustainability, availability, cost, and quality of secure sources of covered unmanned aircraft systems domestically and from sources in allied and partner countries.

(C) The plan of the Secretary of Defense to address any gaps or deficiencies identified in subparagraph (B), including through the use of funds available under the Defense Production Act of 1950 (50 U.S.C. 4501 et seq.) and partnerships with the National Aeronautics and Space Administration and other interested persons.

(D) Such other information as the Under Secretary of Defense for Acquisition and Sustainment determines to be appropriate.

(3)   APPROPRIATE   CONGRESSIONAL   COMMITTEES

DEFINED.—In this section, the term "appropriate congressional committees" means the following:

(A) The Committees on Armed Services of the Senate and the House of Representatives.

(B) The Committee on Homeland Security and Governmental Affairs of the Senate and the Committee on Oversight and Accountability of the House of Representatives.

(C) The Committee on Commerce, Science, and Transportation of the Senate and the Committee on Science, Space, and Technology of the House of Representatives.

(D) The Select Committee on Intelligence of the Senate and the Permanent Select Committee on Intelligence of the House of Representatives.

(E) The Committee on Transportation and Infrastructure of the House of Representatives.

(F) The Committee on Homeland Security of the House of Representatives.

(G) The Committee on Foreign Relations of the Senate and the Committee on Foreign Affairs of the House of Representatives.

SEC. 1832. EXCEPTIONS.

(a) EXCEPTION FOR WILDFIRE MANAGEMENT OPERATIONS AND SEARCH AND RESCUE OPERATIONS.—The appropriate Federal agencies, in consultation with the Secretary of Homeland Security, are exempt from the procurement and operation restrictions under sections 1823, 1824, and 1825 to the extent the procurement or operation is necessary for the purpose of supporting the full range of wildfire management operations or search and rescue operations.

(b) EXCEPTION FOR INTELLIGENCE ACTIVITIES.—Sections 1823, 1824, and 1825 shall not apply to any activity subject to the reporting requirements under title V of the National Security Act of 1947 (50 U.S.C. 3091 et seq.), any authorized intelligence activities of the United States, or any activity or procurement that supports an authorized intelligence activity.

(c) EXCEPTION FOR TRIBAL LAW ENFORCEMENT OR EMERGENCY SERVICE AGENCY.—Tribal law enforcement or Tribal emergency

service agencies, in consultation with the Secretary of Homeland
Security, are exempt from the procurement, operation, and
purchase restrictions under sections 1823, 1824, and 1825 to the
extent the procurement or operation is necessary for the purpose of
supporting the full range of law enforcement operations or search
and rescue operations on Indian lands.

SEC. 1833. SUNSET.

Sections 1823, 1824, and 1825 shall cease to have effect on the
date that is five years after the date of the enactment of this Act.

* * * * * * *

PILOTS BILL OF RIGHTS

PUBLIC LAW 112-153

Pilot's Bill of Rights

[(Public Law 112–153)]

[As Amended Through P.L. 118–63, Enacted May 16, 2024]

AN ACT To amend title 49, United States Code, to provide rights for pilots, and for other purposes.

Be it enacted by the Senate and House of Representatives of the United States of America in Congress assembled,

SECTION 1. [49 U.S.C. 40101 note] SHORT TITLE.
This Act may be cited as the "Pilot's Bill of Rights".

SEC. 2. [49 U.S.C. 44703 note] FEDERAL AVIATION ADMINISTRATION ENFORCEMENT PROCEEDINGS AND ELIMINATION OF DEFERENCE.

(a) IN GENERAL.—Any proceeding conducted under subpart C, D, or F of part 821 of title 49, Code of Federal Regulations, relating to denial, amendment, modification, suspension, or revocation of an airman certificate, shall be conducted, to the extent practicable, in accordance with the Federal Rules of Civil Procedure and the Federal Rules of Evidence.

(b) ACCESS TO INFORMATION.—

(1) IN GENERAL.—Except as provided under paragraph (3), the Administrator of the Federal Aviation Administration (referred to in this section as the "Administrator") shall provide timely, written notification to an individual who is the subject of an investigation relating to the approval, denial, suspension, modification, or revocation of an airman certificate under chapter 447 of title 49, United States Code.

(2) INFORMATION REQUIRED.—The notification required under paragraph (1) shall inform the individual—

(A) of the nature of the investigation and the specific activity on which the investigation is based;

(B) that an oral or written response to a Letter of Investigation from the Administrator is not required;

(C) that no action or adverse inference can be taken against the individual for declining to respond to a Letter of Investigation from the Administrator;

(D) that any response to a Letter of Investigation from the Administrator or to an inquiry made by a representative of the Administrator by the individual may be used as evidence against the individual;

(E) that the releasable portions of the Administrator's investigative report will be available to the individual; and

(F) that the individual is entitled to access or otherwise obtain air traffic data described in paragraph (4).

(3) EXCEPTION.—The Administrator may delay notification under paragraph (1) if the Administrator determines that such notification may threaten the integrity of the investigation.

(4) ACCESS TO AIR TRAFFIC DATA.—

(A) FAA AIR TRAFFIC DATA.—The Administrator shall provide an individual described in paragraph (1) with timely access to any air traffic data in the possession of the Federal Aviation Administration that would facilitate the individual's ability to productively participate in a proceeding relating to an investigation described in such paragraph.

(B) AIR TRAFFIC DATA DEFINED.—As used in subparagraph (A), the term "air traffic data" includes—

(i) relevant air traffic communication tapes;

(ii) radar information;

(iii) air traffic controller statements;

(iv) flight data;

(v) investigative reports; and

(vi) any other air traffic or flight data in the Federal Aviation Administration's possession that would facilitate the individual's ability to productively participate in the proceeding.

(C) GOVERNMENT CONTRACTOR AIR TRAFFIC DATA.—

(i) IN GENERAL.—Any individual described in paragraph (1) is entitled to obtain any air traffic data that would facilitate the individual's ability to productively participate in a proceeding relating to an investigation described in such paragraph from a government contractor that provides operational services to the Federal Aviation Administration, including control towers and flight service stations.

(ii) REQUIRED INFORMATION FROM INDIVIDUAL.—The individual may obtain the information described in clause (i) by submitting a request to the Administrator that—

(I) describes the facility at which such information is located; and

(II) identifies the date on which such information was generated.

(iii) PROVISION OF INFORMATION TO INDIVIDUAL.—If the Administrator receives a request under this subparagraph, the Administrator shall—

(I) request the contractor to provide the requested information; and

(II) upon receiving such information, transmitting the information to the requesting individual in a timely manner.

(5) TIMING.—Except when the Administrator determines that an emergency exists under section 44709(e)(2) or 46105(c), the Administrator may not proceed against an individual that is the subject of an investigation described in paragraph (1) during the 30-day period beginning on the date on which the air traffic data required under paragraph (4) is made available to the individual.

(6) RESPONSE TO LETTER OF INVESTIGATION.—

(A) IN GENERAL.—If an individual decides to respond to a Letter of Investigation described in paragraph (2)(B), such individual may respond not later than 30 days after receipt of such Letter, including providing written comments on the incident to the investigating office.

(B) CONSTRUCTION.—Nothing in this paragraph shall be construed to diminish the authority of the Administrator (as of the day before the date of enactment of the FAA Reauthorization Act of 2024) to take emergency action relating to an airman certificate.

(c) [49 U.S.C. 44703] AMENDMENTS TO TITLE 49.—

(1) AIRMAN CERTIFICATES.—Section 44703(d)(2) of title 49, United States Code, is amended by striking "but is bound by all validly adopted interpretations of laws and regulations the Administrator carries out unless the Board finds an interpretation is arbitrary, capricious, or otherwise not according to law".

(2) [49 U.S.C. 44709] AMENDMENTS, MODIFICATIONS, SUSPENSIONS, AND REVOCATIONS OF CERTIFICATES.—Section 44709(d)(3) of such title is amended by striking "but is bound by all validly adopted interpretations of laws and regulations the Administrator carries out and of written agency policy guidance available to the public related to sanctions to be imposed under this section unless the Board finds an interpretation is arbitrary, capricious, or otherwise not according to law".

(3) [49 U.S.C. 44710] REVOCATION OF AIRMAN CERTIFICATES FOR CONTROLLED SUBSTANCE VIOLATIONS.—Section 44710(d)(1) of such title is amended by striking "but shall be bound by all validly adopted interpretations of laws and regulations the Administrator carries out and of written agency policy guidance available to the public related to sanctions to be imposed under this section unless the Board finds an interpretation is arbitrary, capricious, or otherwise not according to law".

(d) APPEAL FROM CERTIFICATE ACTIONS.—

(1) IN GENERAL.—Upon a decision by the National Transportation Safety Board upholding an order or a final decision by the Administrator denying an airman certificate under section 44703(d) of title 49, United States Code, or imposing a punitive civil action or an emergency order of revocation under subsections (d) and (e) of section 44709 of such title, an individual substantially affected by an order of the Board may, at the individual's election, file an appeal in the United States district court in which the individual resides or in which the action in question occurred, or in the United States District Court for the District of Columbia. If the individual

substantially affected by an order of the Board elects not to file an appeal in a United States district court, the individual may file an appeal in an appropriate United States court of appeals.

(2) EMERGENCY ORDER PENDING JUDICIAL REVIEW.—Subsequent to a decision by the Board to uphold an Administrator's emergency order under section 44709(e)(2) of title 49, United States Code, and absent a stay of the enforcement of that order by the Board, the emergency order of amendment, modification, suspension, or revocation of a certificate shall remain in effect, pending the exhaustion of an appeal to a Federal district court as provided in this Act.

(e) STANDARD OF REVIEW.—

(1) IN GENERAL.—In an appeal filed under subsection (d) in a United States district court, the district court shall give full independent review of a denial, suspension, or revocation ordered by the Administrator, including substantive independent and expedited review of any decision by the Administrator to make such order effective immediately.

(2) EVIDENCE.—A United States district court's review under paragraph (1) shall include in evidence any record of the proceeding before the Administrator and any record of the proceeding before the National Transportation Safety Board, including hearing testimony, transcripts, exhibits, decisions, and briefs submitted by the parties.

(f) RELEASE OF INVESTIGATIVE REPORTS.—

(1) IN GENERAL.—

(A) EMERGENCY ORDERS.—In any proceeding conducted under part 821 of title 49, Code of Federal Regulations, relating to the amendment, modification, suspension, or revocation of an airman certificate, in which the Administrator issues an emergency order under subsections (d) and (e) of section 44709, section 44710, or section 46105(c) of title 49, United States Code, or another order that takes effect immediately, the Administrator shall provide, upon request, to the individual holding the airman certificate the releasable portion of the investigative report at the time the Administrator issues the order. If the complete Report of Investigation is not available at the time of the request, the Administrator shall issue all portions of the report that are available at the time and shall provide the full report not later than 5 days after its completion.

(B) OTHER ORDERS.—In any nonemergency proceeding conducted under part 821 of title 49, Code of Federal Regulations, relating to the amendment, modification, suspension, or revocation of an airman certificate, in which the Administrator notifies the certificate holder of a proposed certificate action under subsections (b) and (c) of section 44709 or section 44710 of title 49, United States Code, the Administrator shall, upon the written request of the covered certificate holder and at any time after that notification, provide to the covered certificate holder the releasable portion of the investigative report.

(2) MOTION FOR DISMISSAL.—If the Administrator does not provide the releasable portions of the investigative report to the individual holding the airman certificate subject to the proceeding referred to in paragraph (1) by the time required by that paragraph, the individual may move to dismiss the complaint of the Administrator or for other relief and, unless the Administrator establishes good cause for the failure to provide the investigative report or for a lack of timeliness, the administrative law judge shall order such relief as the judge considers appropriate.

(3) RELEASABLE PORTION OF INVESTIGATIVE REPORT.—For purposes of paragraph (1), the releasable portion of an investigative report is all information in the report, except for the following:

(A) Information that is privileged.

(B) Information that constitutes work product or reflects internal deliberative process.

(C) Information that would disclose the identity of a confidential source.

(D) Information the disclosure of which is prohibited by any other provision of law.

(E) Information that is not relevant to the subject matter of the proceeding.

(F) Information the Administrator can demonstrate is withheld for good cause.

(G) Sensitive security information, as defined in section 15.5 of title 49, Code of Federal Regulations (or any corresponding similar ruling or regulation).

(4) RULE OF CONSTRUCTION.—Nothing in this subsection shall be construed to prevent the Administrator from releasing to an individual subject to an investigation described in subsection (b)(1)—

(A) information in addition to the information included in the releasable portion of the investigative report; or

(B) a copy of the investigative report before the Administrator issues a complaint.

SEC. 3. [49 U.S.C. 44701 note] NOTICES TO AIRMEN.

(a) IN GENERAL.—

(1) DEFINITION.—In this section, the term "NOTAM" means Notices to Airmen.

(2) IMPROVEMENTS.—Not later than 180 days after the date of the enactment of the Fairness for Pilots Act, the Administrator of the Federal Aviation Administration shall complete the implementation of a Notice to Airmen Improvement Program (in this section referred to as the "NOTAM Improvement Program")—

(A) to improve the system of providing airmen with pertinent and timely information regarding the national airspace system;

(B) to continue developing and modernizing the NOTAM repository, in a public central location, to maintain and archive all NOTAMs, including the original content and form of the notices, the original date of publication, and any amendments to such notices with the date of each amendment, in a manner that is Internet-accessible, machine-readable, and searchable;

(C) to apply filters so that pilots can prioritize critical flight safety information from other airspace system information; and

(D) to specify the times during which temporary flight restrictions are in effect and the duration of a designation of special use airspace in a specific area.

(b) GOALS OF PROGRAM.—The goals of the NOTAM Improvement Program are—

(1) to decrease the overwhelming volume of NOTAMs an airman receives when retrieving airman information prior to a flight in the national airspace system;

(2) make the NOTAMs more specific and relevant to the airman's route and in a format that is more useable to the airman;

(3) to provide a full set of NOTAM results in addition to specific information requested by airmen;

(4) to provide a document that is easily searchable; and

(5) to provide a filtering mechanism similar to that provided by the Department of Defense Notices to Airmen.

(c) ADVICE FROM PRIVATE SECTOR GROUPS.—The Administrator shall establish a NOTAM Improvement Panel, which shall be comprised of representatives of relevant nonprofit and not-for-profit general aviation pilot groups, to advise the Administrator in carrying out the goals of the NOTAM Improvement Program under this section.

(d) DESIGNATION OF REPOSITORY AS SOLE SOURCE FOR NOTAMS.—

(1) IN GENERAL.—The Administrator—

(A) shall consider the repository for NOTAMs under subsection (a)(2)(B) to be the sole location for airmen to check for NOTAMs; and

(B) may not consider a NOTAM to be announced or published until the NOTAM is included in the repository for NOTAMs under subsection (a)(2)(B).

(2) PROHIBITION ON TAKING ACTION FOR VIOLATIONS OF NOTAMS NOT IN REPOSITORY.—

(A) IN GENERAL.—Except as provided in subparagraph (B), beginning on the date that the repository under subsection (a)(2)(B) is final and published, the Administrator may not take any enforcement action against an airman for a violation of a NOTAM during a flight if—

(i) that NOTAM is not available through the repository before the commencement of the flight; and

(ii) that NOTAM is not reasonably accessible and identifiable to the airman.

(B) EXCEPTION FOR NATIONAL SECURITY.—Subparagraph (A) shall not apply in the case of an enforcement action for a violation of a NOTAM that directly relates to national security.

SEC. 4. [49 U.S.C. 44703 note] MEDICAL CERTIFICATION.

(a) ASSESSMENT.—

(1) IN GENERAL.—Not later than 180 days after the date of the enactment of this Act, the Comptroller General of the United States shall initiate an assessment of the Federal Aviation Administration's medical certification process and the associated medical standards and forms.

(2) REPORT.—The Comptroller General shall submit a report to Congress based on the assessment required under paragraph (1) that examines—

(A) revisions to the medical application form that would provide greater clarity and guidance to applicants;

(B) the alignment of medical qualification policies with present-day qualified medical judgment and practices, as applied to an individual's medically relevant circumstances; and

(C) steps that could be taken to promote the public's understanding of the medical requirements that determine an airman's medical certificate eligibility.

(b) GOALS OF THE FEDERAL AVIATION ADMINISTRATION'S MEDICAL CERTIFICATION PROCESS.—The goals of the Federal Aviation Administration's medical certification process are—

(1) to provide questions in the medical application form that—

(A) are appropriate without being overly broad;

(B) are subject to a minimum amount of misinterpretation and mistaken responses;

(C) allow for consistent treatment and responses during the medical application process; and

(D) avoid unnecessary allegations that an individual has intentionally falsified answers on the form;

(2) to provide questions that elicit information that is relevant to making a determination of an individual's medical qualifications within the standards identified in the Administrator's regulations;

(3) to give medical standards greater meaning by ensuring the information requested aligns with present-day medical judgment and practices; and

(4) to ensure that—

(A) the application of such medical standards provides an appropriate and fair evaluation of an individual's qualifications; and

(B) the individual understands the basis for determining medical qualifications.

(c) ADVICE FROM PRIVATE SECTOR GROUPS.—The Administrator shall establish a panel, which shall be comprised of representatives of relevant nonprofit and not-for-profit general aviation pilot groups, aviation medical examiners, and other qualified medical experts, to advise the Administrator in carrying out the goals of the assessment required under this section.

(d) FEDERAL AVIATION ADMINISTRATION RESPONSE.—Not later than 1 year after the issuance of the report by the Comptroller General pursuant to subsection (a)(2), the Administrator shall take appropriate actions to respond to such report.

SEC. 5. [49 U.S.C. 44703 note] REEXAMINATION OF AN AIRMAN CERTIFICATE.

(a) IN GENERAL.—The Administrator shall provide timely, written notification to an individual subject to a reexamination of an airman certificate issued under chapter 447 of title 49, United States Code.

(b) INFORMATION REQUIRED.—In providing notification under subsection (a), the Administrator shall inform the individual—

(1) of the nature of the reexamination and the specific activity on which the reexamination is necessitated;

(2) that the reexamination shall occur within 1 year from the date of the notice provided by the Administrator, however, if the reexamination is not conducted within 30 days, the Administrator may restrict passenger carrying operations;

(3) that if such reexamination is not conducted after 1 year from date of notice, the airman certificate of the individual may be suspended or revoked; and

(4) when, as determined by the Administrator, an oral or written response to the notification from the Administrator is not required.

(c)   EXCEPTION.—Nothing   in   this   section   prohibits   the Administrator   from   reexamining   a   certificate   holder   if   the Administrator has reasonable grounds—

(1) to establish that an airman may not be qualified to exercise the privileges of a certificate or rating based upon an act or omission committed by the airman while exercising such privileges or performing ancillary duties associated with the exercise of such privileges; or

(2) to demonstrate that the airman obtained such a certificate or rating through fraudulent means or through an examination that was inadequate to establish the qualifications of an airman.

(d)   STANDARD   OF   REVIEW.—An   order   issued   by   the Administrator to amend, modify, suspend, or revoke an airman certificate after reexamination of the airman is subject to the standard of review provided for under section 2 of this Act.

FAA REAUTHORIZATION ACT OF 2024

PUBLIC LAW 118-63

FAA Reauthorization Act of 2024

[(Public Law 118–63)]

[This law has not been amended]

AN ACT To amend title 49, United States Code, to reauthorize and improve the Federal Aviation Administration and other civil aviation programs, and for other purposes.

Be it enacted by the Senate and House of Representatives of the United States of America in Congress assembled,

SECTION 1. SHORT TITLE; TABLE OF CONTENTS.

(a) [40 U.S.C. 40101 note] SHORT TITLE.—This Act may be cited as the "FAA Reauthorization Act of 2024".

(b) TABLE OF CONTENTS.—The table of contents for this Act is as follows:

250

TITLE IX—NEW ENTRANTS AND AEROSPACE INNOVATION

Subtitle A—Unmanned Aircraft Systems

Subtitle B—Advanced Air Mobility

* * * * * * *

SEC. 2. [49 U.S.C. 40101 note] DEFINITIONS.

In this Act:

(1) ADMINISTRATOR.—Unless otherwise specified, the term ""Administrator"" means the Administrator of the Federal Aviation Administration.

(2) APPROPRIATE COMMITTEES OF CONGRESS.—The term ""appropriate committees of Congress"" means the Committee on Commerce, Science, and Transportation of the Senate and the Committee on Transportation and Infrastructure of the House of Representatives.

(3) COMPTROLLER GENERAL.—The term ""Comptroller General"" means the Comptroller General of the United States.

(4) FAA.—The term ""FAA"" means the Federal Aviation Administration.

(5) NEXTGEN.—The term ""NextGen"" means the Next Generation Air Transportation System.

(6) SECRETARY.—Unless otherwise specified, the term ""Secretary"" means the Secretary of Transportation.

TITLE I—AUTHORIZATIONS

SEC. 101. AIRPORT PLANNING AND DEVELOPMENT AND NOISE COMPATIBILITY PLANNING AND PROGRAMS.

(a) AUTHORIZATION.—Section 48103(a) of title 49, United States Code, is amended—

(1) in paragraph (6) by striking "and" at the end;

(2) by striking paragraph (7) and inserting the following:

"(7) $3,350,000,000 for fiscal year 2024;

"(8) $4,000,000,000 for fiscal year 2025;

"(9) $4,000,000,000 for fiscal year 2026;

"(10) $4,000,000,000 for fiscal year 2027; and

"(11) $4,000,000,000 for fiscal year 2028."

(b) OBLIGATION AUTHORITY.—Section 47104(c) of title 49, United States Code, is amended in the matter preceding paragraph (1) by striking "May 10, 2024" and inserting "September 30, 2028".

SEC. 102. FACILITIES AND EQUIPMENT.

Section 48101(a) of title 49, United States Code, is amended by striking paragraphs (1) through (7) and inserting the following:

"(1) $3,191,250,000 for fiscal year 2024.

"(2) $3,575,000,000 for fiscal year 2025.

"(3) $3,625,000,000 for fiscal year 2026.

"(4) $3,675,000,000 for fiscal year 2027.

"(5) $3,725,000,000 for fiscal year 2028."

SEC. 103. OPERATIONS.

(a) IN GENERAL.—Section 106(k)(1) of title 49, United States Code, is amended by striking subparagraphs (A) through (G) and inserting the following:

"(A) $12,729,627,000 for fiscal year 2024;

"(B) $13,055,000,000 for fiscal year 2025;

"(C) $13,354,000,000 for fiscal year 2026;

"(D) $13,650,000,000 for fiscal year 2027; and

"(E) $13,954,000,000 for fiscal year 2028."

(b) AUTHORIZED EXPENDITURES.—Section 106(k)(2)(D) of title 49, United States Code, is amended—

(1) by striking clauses (i) through (v);

(2) by redesignating clause (vi) as clause (i); and

(3) by adding at the end the following:

"(ii) $42,018,000 for fiscal year 2024.

"(iii) $52,985,000 for fiscal year 2025.

"(iv) $59,044,000 for fiscal year 2026.

"(v) $65,225,000 for fiscal year 2027.

"(vi) $71,529,000 for fiscal year 2028."

(c) AUTHORITY TO TRANSFER FUNDS.—Section 106(k)(3) of title 49, United States Code, is amended—

(1) by striking "Notwithstanding" and inserting the following:

"(A) IN GENERAL.—Notwithstanding"

;

(2) by striking "in each of fiscal years 2018 through 2023 and for the period beginning on October 1, 2023, and ending on May 10, 2024" and inserting "in each of fiscal years 2024

through 2028"; and

(3) by adding at the end the following:

"(B) PRIORITIZATION.—In reducing non-safety-related activities of the Administration under subparagraph (A), the Secretary shall prioritize such reductions from amounts other than amounts authorized under this subsection, section 48101, or section 48103.

"(C) SUNSET.—This paragraph shall cease to be effective on October 1, 2028."

SEC. 104. EXTENSION OF MISCELLANEOUS EXPIRING AUTHORITIES.

(a) AUTHORITY TO PROVIDE INSURANCE.—Section 44310(b) of title 49, United States Code, is amended by striking "May 10, 2024" and inserting "September 30, 2028".

(b) MARSHALL ISLANDS, MICRONESIA, AND PALAU.—Section 47115(i) of title 49, United States Code, is amended by striking "fiscal years 2018 through 2023, and for the period beginning on October 1, 2023, and ending on May 10, 2024," and inserting "fiscal years 2024 through 2028,".

(c) WEATHER REPORTING PROGRAMS.—Section 48105 of title 49, United States Code, is amended by striking paragraph (5) and adding at the end the following:

"(5) $60,000,000 for each of fiscal years 2024 through 2028."

(d) MIDWAY ISLAND AIRPORT.—Section 186(d) of the Vision 100—Century of Aviation Reauthorization Act (Public Law 108-176) is amended by striking "fiscal years 2018 through 2023 and for the period beginning on October 1, 2023, and ending on May 10, 2024," and inserting "for fiscal years 2024 through 2028,".

(e) [49 U.S.C. 44701 note] EXTENSION OF THE SAFETY OVERSIGHT AND CERTIFICATION ADVISORY COMMITTEE.—Section 202(h) of the FAA Reauthorization Act of 2018 (Public Law 115-254) is amended by striking "shall terminate" and all that follows through the period at the end and inserting "shall terminate on October 1, 2028.".

TITLE II—FAA OVERSIGHT AND ORGANIZATIONAL REFORM

* * * * * * *

SEC. 206. FUTURE OF NEXTGEN.

(a) [49 U.S.C. 40101 note] KEY PROGRAMS.—Not later than December 31, 2025, the Administrator shall operationalize all of the key programs under the NextGen program as described in the deployment plan of the FAA.

(b) OFFICE TERMINATION.—The NextGen Office of the FAA shall terminate on December 31, 2025.

(c) TRANSFER OF RESIDUAL NEXTGEN IMPLEMENTATION FUNCTIONS.—If the Administrator does not complete the air traffic modernization project known as the NextGen program by the deadline specified in subsection (a), the Administrator shall transfer the residual functions for completing the NextGen program to the Airspace Modernization Office of the FAA established under section 207.

(d) TRANSFER OF NEXTGEN ADVISORY COMMITTEE.—Not later than December 31, 2025, management of the NextGen Advisory Committee shall transfer to the Chief Operating Officer of the air traffic control system.

(e) TRANSFER OF ADVANCED AIR MOBILITY FUNCTIONS.—Not later than 90 days after the date of enactment of this Act, any advanced air mobility relevant functions, duties, and responsibilities of the NAS Systems Engineering and Integration Office or other offices within the Office of NextGen of the FAA shall be incorporated into the Office of Aviation Safety of the FAA.

(f) REMAINING ACTIVITIES.—In carrying out subsection (a), and after implementing subsections (c) through (e), the Administrator shall transfer any remaining duties, authorities, activities, personnel, and assets managed by the Office of NextGen of the FAA to other offices of the FAA, as appropriate.

* * * * * * *

SEC. 207. [49 U.S.C. 106 note] AIRSPACE MODERNIZATION OFFICE.

(a) ESTABLISHMENT.—

SEC. 207. [49 U.S.C. 106 note] AIRSPACE
MODERNIZATION OFFICE.

FAA Reauthorization Act of 2

(1) IN GENERAL.— On January 1, 2026, the Administrator shall establish within the FAA an Airspace Modernization Office (in this section referred to as the "Office").

(2) PLACEMENT.— The Administrator may task an existing office of the FAA with the functions of the Office.

(3) DUTIES.— The Office shall be responsible for—

(A) the research and development, systems engineering, enterprise architecture, and portfolio management for the continuous modernization of the national airspace system;

(B) the development of an information-centric national airspace system, including digitization of the processes and technology that supports such system;

(C) improving the interoperability of FAA systems and third-party systems that support safe operations in the national airspace system; and

(D) developing and periodically updating an integrated plan for the future state of the national airspace system in coordination with other offices of the FAA.

(b) INTEGRATED PLAN REQUIREMENTS.— The integrated plan developed by the Office shall be designed to ensure that the national airspace system meets future safety, security, mobility, efficiency, and capacity needs of a diverse and growing set of airspace users. The integrated plan shall include the following:

(1) A description of the demand for services that will be required of the future air transportation system, and an explanation of how the demand projections were derived, including—

(A) the most likely range of average annual resources required over the duration of the plan to cost effectively maintain the safety, sustainability, and other characteristics of national airspace operation and the mission of the FAA; and

(B) an estimate of FAA resource requirements by user group, including expectations concerning the growth of new entrants and potential new users.

(2) A roadmap for creating and implementing the integrated plan, including—

SEC. 207. [49 U.S.C. 106 note] AIRSPACE
MODERNIZATION OFFICE.

FAA Reauthorization Act of 2024

(A) the most significant technical, operational, and personnel obstacles and the activities necessary to overcome such obstacles, including the role of other Federal agencies, corporations, institutions of higher learning, and nonprofit organizations in carrying out such activities;

(B) the annual anticipated cost of carrying out such activities;

(C) the technical milestones that will be used to evaluate the activities; and

(D) identifying technology gaps that the Administrator or industry may need to address to fully implement the integrated plan.

(3) A description of the operational concepts to meet the system performance requirements for all system users and a timeline and anticipated expenditures needed to develop and deploy the system.

(4) A description of the management of the enterprise architecture framework for the introduction of any operational improvements and to inform FAA financial decision-making.

(5) A justification for the operational improvements that the Office determines will need to be developed and deployed by 2040 to meet the needs of national airspace users, including the benefits, costs, and risks of the preferred and alternative options.

(c) CONSIDERATIONS.—In developing an initial integrated plan required under subsection (b) and carrying out such plan, the Office shall consider—

(1) the results and recommendations of the independent report on implementation of the NextGen program under section 603;

(2) the status of the transition to, and deployment of, trajectory-based operations within the national airspace system; and

(3) the findings of the audit required by section 622, and the resulting plan to replace or enhance the identified legacy systems within a reasonable timeframe.

(d) CONSULTATION.—In developing and carrying out the integrated plan, the Office shall consult with the NextGen Advisory

SEC. 209. [49 U.S.C. 106 note] AIRSPACE
MODERNIZATION OFFICE.

FAA Reauthorization Act of

Committee of the FAA.

(e) PLAN DEADLINE; BRIEFINGS.—

(1) PLAN DEADLINE.—Not later than 3 years after the date
of enactment of this Act, the Administrator shall submit to
the Committee on Commerce, Science, and Transportation of
the Senate, the Committee on Appropriations of the Senate,
the Committee on Transportation and Infrastructure of the
House of Representatives, the Committee on Science, Space,
and Technology of the House of Representatives, and the
Committee on Appropriations of the House of Representatives
an initial integrated plan required under subsection (a)(3)(D).

(2) ANNUAL BRIEFINGS.—The Administrator shall provide
the committees of Congress specified in paragraph (1) with
an annual briefing describing the progress in carrying out the
integrated plan required under subsection (a)(3)(D), including
any changes to the plan, through 2028.

(f) DOT INSPECTOR GENERAL REVIEW.—Not later than 180 days
after submission of the initial integrated plan under subsection
(e)(1), the inspector general of the Department of Transportation
shall begin a review of the integrated plan and submit to the
committees of Congress specified in subsection (e)(1) a report that—

(1) assesses the justification for the integrated plan;

(2) provides any recommendations for improving the
integrated plan; and

(3) includes any other information that the inspector
general determines appropriate.

* * * * * * *

SEC. 209. SENSE OF CONGRESS ON FAA ENGAGEMENT DURING
RULEMAKING ACTIVITIES.

It is the sense of Congress that—

(1) the Administrator should—

(A) engage with aviation stakeholder groups and the
public during pre-drafting stages of rulemaking activities
and use, to the greatest extent practicable, properly
docketed ex parte discussions during rulemaking activities
in order to—

(i) inform the work of the Administrator;

(ii) assist the Administrator in developing the scope of a rule; and

(iii) reduce the timeline for issuance of proposed and final rules;

(B) rely on documented data and safety trends when determining whether or not to proceed with a rulemaking activity; and

(C) not consider a rulemaking activity required in statute, for the purposes of ex parte communications, as having been established on the date of enactment of the related public law, but rather upon obtainment of a regulation identifier number; and

(2) when it would reduce the time required for the Administrator to adjudicate public comments, the Administrator should publicly provide information describing the rationale behind a regulatory decision included in proposed regulations in order to better allow for the public to provide clear and informed comments on such regulations.

* * * * * * *

SEC. 217. [49 U.S.C. 40131 note] CYBERSECURITY LEAD.

(a) IN GENERAL.—The Administrator shall designate an executive of the FAA to serve as the lead for the cybersecurity of FAA systems and hardware (in this section referred to as the "Cybersecurity Lead").

(b) DUTIES.—The Cybersecurity Lead shall carry out duties and powers prescribed by the Administrator, including the management of activities required under subtitle B of title III.

(c) BRIEFING.—Not later than 1 and 3 years after the date of enactment of this Act, the Cybersecurity Lead shall brief the appropriate committees of Congress on the implementation of subtitle B of title III.

* * * * * * *

SEC. 221. [49 U.S.C. 106 note] FAA TELEWORK.

(a) IN GENERAL.—The Administrator—

(1) may establish telework policies for employees of the

FAA that allow for the Administrator to reduce the office footprint and associated expenses of the FAA, if appropriate, increase workforce retention, and provide flexibilities that the Administrator demonstrates increases efficiency and effectiveness of the Administration, while requiring that any such policy—

(A) does not adversely impact the mission of the FAA;

(B) does not reduce the safety or efficiency of the national airspace system;

(C) for any employee that is designated as an officer or executive in the FAA Executive System or a political appointee (as such term is defined in section 106 of title 49, United States Code)—

(i) maximizes time at a duty station for such employee, excluding official travel; and

(ii) may include telework provisions as determined appropriate by the Administrator, commensurate with official duties for such employee;

(D) provides for on-the-job training opportunities for FAA personnel that are not less than such opportunities available in 2019;

(E) reflects the appropriate work status of employees based on the job functions of such employee;

(F) optimizes the work status of inspectors, investigators, and other personnel performing safety-related functions to ensure timely completion of safety oversight activities;

(G) provides for personnel, including such personnel performing work related to aircraft certification and flight standards, who are responsible for actively working with regulated entities, external stakeholders, or other members of the public to be—

(i) routinely available on a predictable basis for in-person and virtual communications with external persons; and

(ii) not hindered from meeting with, visiting, auditing, or inspecting facilities or projects of regulated persons due to any telework policy; and

(H) provides opportunities for in-person dialogue, collaboration, and ideation for all employees;

(2) ensures that locality pay for an employee of the FAA accurately reflects the telework status and duty station of such employee;

(3) may not establish a telework policy for an employee of the FAA unless such employee will be provided with secure network capacity, communications tools, necessary and secure access to appropriate agency data assets and Federal records, and equipment sufficient to enable such employee to be fully productive; and

(4) not later than 2 years after the date of enactment of this Act, shall evaluate and address any telework policies in effect on the day before such date of enactment to ensure that such policies meet the requirements of paragraph (1).

(b) CONGRESSIONAL UPDATE.—Not later than 1 year after the date of enactment of this Act, and 1 year thereafter, the Administrator shall brief the appropriate committees of Congress on any telework policies currently in place, the implementation of such policies, and the benefits of such policies.

(c) CONSULTATION.—If the Administrator determines that telework agreements need to be updated to implement the requirements of subsection (a), the Administrator shall, prior to updating such agreements, consult with—

(1) exclusive bargaining representatives of air traffic controllers certified under section 7111 of title 5, United States Code; and

(2) labor organizations certified under such section as the exclusive bargaining representative of airway transportation systems specialists and aviation safety inspectors and engineers of the FAA.

* * * * * * *

SEC. 224. [49 U.S.C. 106 note] FAA PARTICIPATION IN INDUSTRY STANDARDS ORGANIZATIONS.

(a) IN GENERAL.—The Administrator shall encourage the participation of employees of the FAA, as appropriate, in the activities of recognized industry standards organizations to advance the adoption, reference, and acceptance rate of standards and means of compliance developed by such organizations by the Administrator.

(b) PARTICIPATION.—An employee of the FAA directed by the Administrator to participate in a working group, task group, committee, or similar body of a recognized industry standards organization shall—

(1) actively participate in the discussions and work of such organization;

(2) accurately represent the position of the Administrator on the subject matter of such discussions and work;

(3) contribute to the development of work products of such organization, unless determined to be inappropriate by such organization;

(4) make reasonable efforts to identify and make any concerns of the Administrator relating to such work products known to such organization, including through providing formal comments, as may be allowed for under the procedures of such organization;

(5) provide regular updates to other FAA employees and management on the progress of such work products; and

(6) seek advice and input from other FAA employees and management, as needed.

(c) RECOGNIZED INDUSTRY STANDARDS ORGANIZATION DEFINED.—In this section, the term "recognized industry standards organization" means a domestic or international organization that—

(1) uses agreed upon procedures to develop aviation-related industry standards or means of compliance, including standards or means of compliance that satisfy FAA requirements or guidance;

(2) is comprised of members of the public, including subject matter experts, industry representatives, academics and researchers, and government employees; and

(3) has had at least 1 standard or means of compliance accepted by the Administrator or referenced in guidance material or a regulation issued by the FAA after the date of enactment of the Vision 100—Century of Aviation

Reauthorization Act (Public Law 108-176).

SEC. 225. SENSE OF CONGRESS ON USE OF VOLUNTARY CONSENSUS STANDARDS.

It is the sense of Congress that the Administrator should make every effort to abide by the policies set forth in the circular of the Office of Management and Budget, titled "Federal Participation in the Development and Use of Voluntary Consensus Standards and Conformity Assessment Activities" (A-119).

* * * * * * *

SEC. 229. [49 U.S.C. 44501 note] ADVANCED AVIATION TECHNOLOGY AND INNOVATION STEERING COMMITTEE.

(a) ESTABLISHMENT.— Not later than 180 days after the date of enactment of this Act, the Administrator shall establish an Advanced Aviation Technology and Innovation Steering Committee (in this section referred to as the "Steering Committee") to assist the FAA in planning for and integrating advanced aviation technologies.

(b) PURPOSE.— The Steering Committee shall—

(1) create and regularly update a comprehensive strategy and action plan for integrating advanced aviation technologies into the national airspace system and aviation ecosystem; and

(2) provide direction and resolution for complex issues related to advanced aviation technologies that span multiple offices or lines of business of the FAA, as needed.

(c) CHAIR.— The Deputy Administrator of the FAA shall serve as the Chair of the Steering Committee.

(d) COMPOSITION.— In addition to the Chair, the Steering Committee shall consist of the Assistant or Associate Administrator, or the designee of such Administrator, of each of the following FAA offices:

(1) Office of Aviation Safety.

(2) Air Traffic Organization.

(3) Office of Airports.

(4) Office of Commercial Space Transportation.

(5) Office of Finance and Management.

(6) Office of the Chief Counsel.

SEC. 308. [49 U.S.C. 44701 note] SCALABILITY OF SAFETY MANAGEMENT SYSTEMS.

FAA Reauthorization Act of

(7) Office of Rulemaking and Regulatory Improvement.

(8) Office of Policy, International Affairs, and Environment.

(9) Office of Security and Hazardous Materials Safety.

(10) Any other Office the Administrator determines necessary.

* * * * * * *

TITLE III—AVIATION SAFETY IMPROVEMENTS

Subtitle A—General Provisions

* * * * * * *

SEC. 308. [49 U.S.C. 44701 note] SCALABILITY OF SAFETY MANAGEMENT SYSTEMS.

In conducting any rulemaking to require, or implementing a regulation requiring, a safety management system, the Administrator shall consider the scalability of such safety management system requirements, to the full range of entities in terms of size or complexity that may be affected by such rulemaking or regulation, including—

(1) how an entity can demonstrate compliance using various documentation, tools, and methods, including, as appropriate, systems with multiple small operators collectively monitoring for and addressing risks;

(2) a review of traditional safety management techniques and the suitability of such techniques for small entities;

(3) the applicability of existing safety management system programs implemented by an entity;

(4) the suitability of existing requirements under part 5 of title 14, Code of Federal Regulations, for small entities; and

(5) other unique challenges relating to small entities the Administrator determines appropriate to consider.

* * * * * * *

SEC. 314. [49 U.S.C. 44709 note] RISK MODEL
FOR PRODUCTION FACILITY INSPECTIONS.

FAA Reauthorization Act of 2024

SEC. 314. [49 U.S.C. 44709 note] RISK MODEL FOR PRODUCTION FACILITY INSPECTIONS.

(a) IN GENERAL.— Not later than 12 months after the date of enactment of this Act, and periodically thereafter, the Administrator shall—

(1) conduct a review of the risk-based model used by certification management offices of the FAA to inform the frequency of aircraft manufacturing or production facility inspections; and

(2) update the model to ensure such model adequately accounts for risk at facilities during periods of increased production.

(b) BRIEFINGS.— Not later than 60 days after the date on which the review is completed under subsection (a), the Administrator shall brief the appropriate committees of Congress on—

(1) the results of the review;

(2) any changes made to the risk-based model described in subsection (a); and

(3) how such changes would help improve the in-plant inspection process.

SEC. 315. [49 U.S.C. 40101 note] REVIEW OF FAA USE OF AVIATION SAFETY DATA.

(a) IN GENERAL.— Not later than 2 years after the date of enactment of this Act, the Administrator shall seek to enter into an appropriate arrangement with a qualified third-party organization or consortium to evaluate the collection, collation, analysis, and use of aviation data across the FAA.

(b) CONSULTATION.— In completing the evaluation under subsection (a), the qualified third-party organization or consortium shall—

(1) seek the input of experts in data analytics, including at least 1 expert in the commercial data services or analytics solutions sector;

(2) consult with the National Transportation Safety Board and the Transportation Research Board; and

(3) consult with appropriate federally funded research and development centers, to the extent that such centers are not

SEC. 315. [49 U.S.C. 40101 note] REVIEW OF
FAA USE OF AVIATION SAFETY DATA.

FAA Reauthorization Act of

already involved in the evaluation.

(c) SUBSTANCE OF EVALUATION.— In completing the evaluation under subsection (a), the qualified third-party organization or consortium shall—

(1) compile a list of internal and external sources, databases, and streams of information the FAA receives or has access to that provide the FAA with operational or safety information and data about the national airspace system, its users, and other regulated entities of the FAA;

(2) review data sets to determine completeness and accuracy of relevant information;

(3) identify gaps in information that the FAA could fill through sharing agreements, partnerships, or other means that would add value during safety trend analysis;

(4) assess the capabilities of the FAA, including analysis systems and workforce skillsets, to analyze relevant data and information to make informed decisions;

(5) review data and information for proper storage, identification controls, and data privacy—

(A) as required by law; and

(B) consistent with best practices for data collection, storage, and use;

(6) review the format of such data and identify methods to improve the usefulness of such data;

(7) assess internal and external access to data for—

(A) appropriateness based on data type and level of detail;

(B) proper data access protocols and precautions; and

(C) maximizing availability of safety-related data that could support the improvement of safety management systems of and trend identification by regulated entities and the FAA;

(8) examine the collation and dissemination of data within offices and between offices of the FAA;

(9) review and recommend improvements to the data analysis techniques of the FAA; and

(10) recommend investments the Administrator should

SEC. 315. [49 U.S.C. 40101 note] REVIEW OF
FAA USE OF AVIATION SAFETY DATA.

FAA Reauthorization Act of 2024

consider to better collect, manage, and analyze data sets, including within and between offices of the FAA.

(d) ACCESS TO INFORMATION.— The Administrator shall provide the qualified third-party organization or consortium and the experts described in subsection (b) with adequate access to safety and operational data collected by and held by the agency across all offices of the FAA, except if specific access is otherwise prohibited by law.

(e) NONDISCLOSURE.— Prior to participating in the review, the Administrator shall ensure that each person participating in the evaluation under this section enters into an agreement with the Administrator in which the person shall be prohibited from disclosing at any time, except as required by law, to any person, foreign or domestic, any non-public information made accessible to the federally funded research and development center under this section.

(f) REPORT.— The qualified third-party organization or consortium carrying out the evaluation under this section shall provide a report of the findings of the center to the Administrator and include recommendations to improve the FAA's collection, collation, analysis, and use of aviation data, including recommendations to—

(1) improve data access across offices within the FAA, as necessary, to support efficient execution of safety analysis and programs across such offices;

(2) improve data storage best practices;

(3) develop or refine methods for collating data from multiple FAA and industry sources; and

(4) procure or use available analytics tools to draw conclusions and identify previously unrecognized trends or miscategorized risks in the aviation system, particularly when identification of such information requires the analysis of multiple sets of data from multiple sources.

(g) IMPLEMENTATION OF RECOMMENDATIONS.— Not later than 6 months after the receipt of the report under subsection (f), the Administrator shall review, develop an implementation plan, and, if appropriate, begin the implementation of the recommendations received in such report.

(h) REVIEW OF IMPLEMENTATION.— The qualified third-party

organization or consortium that conducted the initial evaluation, and any experts who contributed to such evaluation pursuant to subsection (b)(1), shall provide regular feedback and advice to the Administrator on the implementation plan developed under subsection (g) and any implementation activities for at least 2 years beginning on the date of the receipt of the report under subsection (f).

(i) REPORT TO CONGRESS.— The Administrator shall submit to the appropriate committees of Congress the report described in subsection (f) and the implementation plan described in subsection (g).

(j) EXISTING REPORTING SYSTEMS.— Consistent with section 132 of the Aircraft Certification, Safety, and Accountability Act (Public Law 116-260), the Executive Director of the Transportation Research Board, in consultation with the Secretary and the Administrator, may further harmonize data and sources following the implementation of recommendations under subsection (g).

(k) RULE OF CONSTRUCTION.— Nothing in this section shall be construed to permit the public disclosure of information submitted under a voluntary safety reporting program or that is otherwise protected under section 44735 of title 49, United States Code.

* * * * * * *

SEC. 320. [49 U.S.C. 44737 note] CRASH-RESISTANT FUEL SYSTEMS IN ROTORCRAFT.

(a) IN GENERAL.—The Administrator shall task the Aviation Rulemaking Advisory Committee to—

(1) review the data analysis conducted and the recommendations developed by the Aviation Rulemaking Advisory Committee Rotorcraft Occupant Protection Working Group of the Administration;

(2) update the 2018 report of such working group on rotorcraft occupant protection by—

(A) reviewing National Transportation Safety Board data from 2016 through 2023 on post-crash fires in helicopter accidents; and

(B) determining whether and to what extent crash-resistant fuel systems could have prevented fatalities in the accidents covered by the data reviewed under subparagraph (A); and

(3) develop recommendations for either the Administrator or the helicopter industry to encourage helicopter owners and operators to expedite the installation of crash-resistant fuel systems in the aircraft of such owners and operators regardless of original certification and manufacture date.

(b) SCHEDULE.—

(1) DEADLINE.—Not later than 18 months after the Administrator tasks the Aviation Rulemaking Advisory Committee under subsection (a), the Committee shall submit the recommendations developed under subsection (a)(2) to the Administrator.

(2) IMPLEMENTATION.—If applicable, and not later than 180 days after receiving the recommendations under paragraph (1), the Administrator shall—

(A) begin implementing, as appropriate, any safety recommendations the Administrator receives from the Aviation Rulemaking Advisory Committee, and brief the appropriate committees of Congress on any recommendations the Administrator does not implement; and

(B) partner with the United States Helicopter Safety Team, as appropriate, to facilitate implementation of any recommendations for the helicopter industry pursuant to subsection (a)(2).

SEC. 321. [49 U.S.C. 44505 note] REDUCING TURBULENCE-RELATED INJURIES ON PART 121 AIRCRAFT OPERATIONS.

(a) IN GENERAL.—Not later than 2 years after the date of enactment of this Act, the Administrator shall review the recommendations made by the Chair of the National Transportation Safety Board to the Administrator contained in the safety research report titled "Preventing Turbulence-Related Injuries in Air Carrier Operations Conducted Under Title 14 Code of Federal Regulations Part 121", issued on August 10, 2021 (NTSB/SS-21/01) and provide a briefing to the appropriate committees of Congress with any planned actions in response to the recommendations of the report.

(b) IMPLEMENTATION.—Not later than 3 years after the date

of enactment of this Act, the Administrator shall implement, as appropriate, the recommendations in the safety research report described in subsection (a).

(c) REPORT.—

(1) IN GENERAL.—Not later than 2 years after completing the review under subsection (a), and every 2 years thereafter, the Administrator shall submit to the appropriate committees of Congress a report on the implementation status of the recommendations in the safety research report described in subsection (a) until the earlier of—

(A) the date on which such recommendations have been adopted or adjudicated as described in paragraph (2); or

(B) the date that is 10 years after the date of enactment of this Act.

(2) CONTENTS.—If the Administrator decides not to implement a recommendation in the safety research report described in subsection (a), the Administrator shall provide, as a part of the report required under paragraph (1), a description of why the Administrator did not implement such recommendation.

* * * * * * *

SEC. 324. LITHIUM-ION POWERED WHEELCHAIRS.

(a) IN GENERAL.—Not later than 2 years after the date of enactment of this Act, the Secretary shall task the Air Carrier Access Act Advisory Committee (in this section referred to as the "Committee") to conduct a review of regulations related to lithium-ion battery powered wheelchairs and mobility aids on commercial aircraft and provide recommendations to the Secretary to ensure safe transport of such wheelchairs and mobility aids in air transportation.

(b) CONSIDERATIONS.—In conducting the review required under subsection (a), the Committee shall consider the following:

(1) Any existing or necessary standards for lithium-ion batteries, including casings or other similar components, in such wheelchairs and mobility aids.

(2) The availability of necessary containment or storage

devices, including fire containment covers or fire-resistant storage containers, for such wheelchairs and mobility aids.

(3) The policies of each air carrier (as such term is defined in part 121 of title 14, Code of Federal Regulations) pertaining to lithium-ion battery powered wheelchairs and mobility aids (as in effect on the date of enactment of this Act).

(4) Any other considerations the Secretary determines appropriate.

(c) CONSULTATION REQUIREMENT.—In conducting the review required under subsection (a), the Committee shall consult with the Administrator of the Pipeline and Hazardous Materials Safety Administration.

(d) NOTIFICATION.—

(1) IN GENERAL.—Upon completion of the review conducted under subsection (a), the Committee shall notify the Secretary if an air carrier does not have a policy pertaining to lithium-ion battery powered wheelchairs and mobility aids in effect.

(2) NOTIFICATION.—The Secretary shall notify an air carrier described in paragraph (1) of the status of such air carrier.

(e) REPORT TO CONGRESS.—Not later than 90 days after submission of the recommendations to the Secretary, the Secretary shall submit to the appropriate committees of Congress any recommendations under subsection (a), in the form of a report.

(f) PUBLICATION.—The Secretary shall publish the report required under subsection (e) on the public website of the Department of Transportation.

SEC. 325. [49 U.S.C. 44701 note] NATIONAL SIMULATOR PROGRAM POLICIES AND GUIDANCE.

(a) REVIEW.—Not later than 2 years after the date of enactment of this Act, the Administrator shall review relevant policies and guidance, including all advisory circulars, information bulletins, and directives, pertaining to part 60 of title 14, Code of Federal Regulations.

(b) UPDATES.—Upon completion of the review required under subsection (a), the Administrator shall, at a minimum, update relevant policies and guidance, including all advisory circulars, information bulletins, and directives, pertaining to part 60 of title

14, Code of Federal Regulations.

(c) CONSULTATION.—In carrying out the review required under subsection (a), the Administrator shall convene and consult with entities required to comply with part 60 of title 14, Code of Federal Regulations, including representatives of—

(1) air carriers;

(2) flight schools certificated under part 141 of title 14, Code of Federal Regulations;

(3) training centers certificated under part 142 of title 14, Code of Federal Regulations; and

(4) manufacturers and suppliers of flight simulation training devices (as defined in part 1 of title 14, Code of Federal Regulations, and Appendix F to part 60 of such title).

(d) GAO STUDY ON FAA NATIONAL SIMULATOR PROGRAM.—

(1) IN GENERAL.—Not later than 18 months after the date of enactment of this Act, the Comptroller General shall conduct a study on the National Simulator Program of the FAA that is part of the Training and Simulation Group of the Air Transportation Division.

(2) CONSIDERATIONS.—In conducting the study required under paragraph (1), the Comptroller General shall, at a minimum, assess—

(A) how the program described in paragraph (1) is maintained to reflect and account for advancement in technologies pertaining to flight simulation training devices (as defined in part 1 of title 14, Code of Federal Regulations, and appendix F to part 60 of such title);

(B) the staffing levels, critical competencies, and skills gaps of FAA personnel responsible for carrying out and supporting the program described in paragraph (1); and

(C) how the program described in paragraph (1) engages air carriers and relevant industry stakeholders, including flight schools, to ensure efficient compliance with part 60 of title 14, Code of Federal Regulations.

(3) REPORT.—Not later than 18 months after the date of enactment of this Act, the Comptroller General shall submit to the appropriate committees of Congress a report on the findings of the study conducted under paragraph (1).

* * * * * * *

SEC. 328. [49 U.S.C. 40101 note] RESTRICTED CATEGORY AIRCRAFT MAINTENANCE AND OPERATIONS.

Notwithstanding any other provision of law, the Administrator shall have sole regulatory and oversight jurisdiction over the maintenance and operations of aircraft owned by civilian operators and type-certificated in the restricted category under section 21.25 of title 14, Code of Federal Regulations.

* * * * * * *

SEC. 330. TASK FORCE ON HUMAN FACTORS IN AVIATION SAFETY.

(a) IN GENERAL.—Not later than 6 months after the date of enactment of this Act, and notwithstanding section 127 of the Aircraft Certification Safety and Accountability Act (49 U.S.C. 44513 note), the Administrator shall convene a task force on human factors in aviation safety (in this section referred to as the "Task Force").

(b) COMPOSITION.—

(1) MEMBERS.—The Administrator shall appoint members of the Task Force—

(A) that have expertise in an operational or academic discipline that is relevant to the analysis of human errors in aviation, which may include air carrier operations, line pilot expertise, air traffic control, technical operations, aeronautical information, aircraft maintenance and mechanics psychology, linguistics, human-machine integration, general aviation operations, and organizational behavior and culture;

(B) that sufficiently represent all relevant operational or academic disciplines described in subparagraph (A);

(C) with expertise on human factors but whose experience and training are not in aviation and who have not previously been engaged in work related to the FAA or the aviation industry;

(D) that are representatives of pilot labor organizations and certificated mechanic labor organizations;

(E) that are employees of the FAA that have expertise in safety; and

(F) that are employees of other Federal agencies with expertise on human factors.

(2) NUMBER OF MEMBERS.—In appointing members under paragraph (1), the Administrator shall ensure that—

(A) at least half of the members appointed have expertise in aviation;

(B) at least one member appointed represents an exclusive bargaining representative of air traffic controllers certified under section 7111 of title 5, United States Code; and

(C) 3 members are employees of the FAA and 1 member is an employee of the National Transportation Safety Board.

(3) VOTING.—The members described in paragraph (2)(C) shall be non-voting members of the Task Force.

(c) DURATION.—

(1) IN GENERAL.—Members of the Task Force shall be appointed for the duration of the Task Force.

(2) LENGTH OF EXISTENCE.—

(A) IN GENERAL.—The Task Force shall have an initial duration of 2 years.

(B) OPTION.—The Administrator may extend the duration of the Task Force for an additional period of up to 2 years.

(d) DUTIES.—In coordination with the Research, Engineering, and Development Advisory Committee, the Task Force shall—

(1) not later than the date on which the duration of the Task Force expires under subsection (c), produce a written report in which the Task Force—

(A) to the greatest extent possible, identifies the most significant human factors and the relative contribution of such factors to aviation safety risk;

(B) identifies new research priorities for research in human factors in aviation safety;

(C) reviews existing products by other working groups

related to human factors in aviation safety including the work of the Commercial Aviation Safety Team pertaining to flight crew responses to abnormal events;

(D) provides recommendations on potential revisions to any FAA regulations and guidance pertaining to the certification of aircraft under part 25 of title 14, Code of Federal Regulations, including sections related to presumed pilot response times and assumptions about the reliability of pilot performance during unexpected, stressful events;

(E) reviews rules, regulations, or standards regarding flight crew and maintenance personnel rest and fatigue that are used by a sample of international air carriers, including rules, regulations, or standards determined to be more stringent and less stringent than the current standards pertaining to air carriers (as such term is defined in section 40102 of title 49, United States Code), and identifies risks to the national airspace system from any variation in such rules, regulations, or standards across countries;

(F) reviews pilot training requirements and recommends any revisions necessary to ensure adequate understanding of automated systems on aircraft;

(G) reviews approach and landing misalignment and makes any recommendations for reducing misalignment events;

(H) identifies ways to enhance instrument landing system maintenance schedules;

(I) determines how a real-time smart system should be developed to inform the air traffic control system, air carriers, and airports about any changes in the state of runway and taxiway lights and identifies how such real-time smart system could be connected to the maintenance system of the FAA;

(J) analyzes, with respect to human errors related to aviation safety of air carriers operating under part 121 of title 14, Code of Federal Regulations—

(i) fatigue and distraction during critical phases of work among pilots or other aviation personnel;

(ii) tasks and workload;

(iii) organizational culture;

(iv) communication among personnel;

(v) adherence to safety procedures;

(vi) mental state of personnel; and

(vii) any other relevant factors that are the cause or potential cause of human error related to aviation safety;

(K) includes a tabulation of the number of accidents, incidents, or aviation safety database entries received in which an item identified under subparagraph (J) was a cause or potential cause of human error related to aviation safety; and

(L) includes a list of causes or potential causes of human error related to aviation safety about which the Administrator believes additional information is needed; and

(2) if the Administrator extends the duration of the Task Force pursuant to subsection (c)(2)(B), not later than the date that is 2 years after the date on which the Task Force is established, produce an interim report containing the information described in paragraph (1).

(e) METHODOLOGY.—In carrying out the duties under subparagraphs (J) through (L) of subsection (d)(1), the Task Force shall consult with the National Transportation Safety Board and use all available data compiled and analysis conducted on safety incidents and irregularities collected during the relevant fiscal year from the following:

(1) Flight Operations Quality Assurance.

(2) Aviation Safety Action Program.

(3) Aviation Safety Information Analysis and Sharing.

(4) The Aviation Safety Reporting System.

(5) Aviation safety recommendations and investigation findings of the National Transportation Safety Board.

(6) Other relevant programs or sources.

(f) CONSISTENCY.—Nothing in this section shall be construed to require changes to, or duplication of, work as required by section

127 of the Aircraft Certification Safety and Accountability Act (49 U.S.C. 44513 note).

* * * * * * *

SEC. 335. SERVICE DIFFICULTY REPORTS.

(a) CONGRESSIONAL BRIEFING.—Not later than 18 months after the date of enactment of this Act, and annually thereafter through 2027, the Administrator shall brief the appropriate committees of Congress on compliance with requirements relating to service difficulty reports during the preceding year.

(b) SCOPE.—The Administrator shall include in the briefing required under subsection (a) information relating to—

(1) operators required to comply with section 121.703 of title 14, Code of Federal Regulations;

(2) approval or certificate holders required to comply with section 183.63 of title 14, Code of Federal Regulations; and

(3) FAA offices that investigate service difficulty reports, as documented in the following FAA Orders (and any subsequent revisions of such orders):

(A) FAA Order 8900.1A, titled "Flight Standards Information Management System" and issued on October 27, 2022.

(B) FAA Order 8120.23A, titled "Certificate Management of Production Approval Holders" and issued on March 6, 2017.

(C) FAA Order 8110.107B, titled "Monitor Safety/ Analyze Data" and issued on October 13, 2023.

(c) REQUIREMENTS.—The Administrator shall include in the briefing required under subsection (a) the following information with respect to the year preceding the year in which the briefing is provided:

(1) An identification of categories of service difficulties reported.

(2) An identification of service difficulties for which repeated reports are made.

(3) A general description of the causes of all service difficulty reports, as determined by the Administrator.

(4) A description of actions taken by, or required by, the Administrator to address identified causes of service difficulties.

(5) A description of violations of title 14, Code of Federal Regulations, related to service difficulty reports and any actions taken by the Administrator in response to such violations.

SEC. 336. CONSISTENT AND TIMELY PILOT CHECKS FOR AIR CARRIERS.

(a) ESTABLISHMENT OF WORKING GROUP.—Not later than 180 days after the date of enactment of this Act, unless the requirements of this section are assigned to working groups under subsection (b)(2), the Administrator shall establish a working group for purposes of reviewing and evaluating all regulations and policies related to check airmen and authorized check airmen for air carrier operations conducted under part 135 of title 14, Code of Federal Regulations.

(b) MEMBERSHIP.—

(1) IN GENERAL.—The working group established under this section shall include, at a minimum—

(A) employees of the FAA who serve as check airmen;

(B) representatives of air carriers operating under part 135 of title 14, Code of Federal Regulations; and

(C) industry associations representing such air carriers.

(2) EXISTING WORKING GROUP.—The Administrator may assign the duties described in subsection (c) to an existing FAA working group if—

(A) such working group includes representatives from the list of required members under paragraph (1); or

(B) the membership of such existing working group can be modified to include representatives from the list of required members under paragraph (1).

(c) DUTIES.—A working group shall review, evaluate, and make recommendations on the following:

(1) Methods by which authorized check airmen for air carriers operating under part 135 of title 14, Code of Federal Regulations, are selected, trained, and approved by the

SEC. 338. [49 U.S.C. 44701 note] TARMAC
OPERATIONS MONITORING STUDY.

FAA Reauthorization Act of 2024

Administrator.

(2) Staffing and utilization rates of authorized check airmen by such air carriers.

(3) Differences in qualification standards applied to—

(A) employees of the FAA who serve as check airmen; and

(B) authorized check airmen of such air carriers.

(4) Methods to harmonize the qualification standards between authorized check airmen and employees of the FAA who serve as check airmen.

(5) Methods to improve the training and qualification of authorized check airmen.

(6) Prior recommendations made by FAA advisory committees or working groups regarding check airmen functions.

(7) Petitions for rulemaking submitted to the FAA regarding check airmen functions.

(d) BRIEFING TO CONGRESS.—Not later than 1 year after the date on which the Administrator tasks a working group with the duties described in subsection (c), the Administrator shall brief the appropriate committees of Congress on the progress and recommendations of the working group and the efforts of the Administrator to implement such recommendations.

(e) AUTHORIZED CHECK AIRMAN DEFINED.—In this section, the term "authorized check airman" means an individual employed by an air carrier that meets the qualifications and training requirements of sections 135.337 and 135.339 of title 14, Code of Federal Regulations, and is approved to evaluate and certify the knowledge and skills of pilots employed by such air carrier.

* * * * * * *

SEC. 338. [49 U.S.C. 44701 note] TARMAC OPERATIONS MONITORING STUDY.

(a) IN GENERAL.—The Director of the Bureau of Transportation Statistics, in consultation with relevant offices within the Office of the Secretary and the FAA (as determined by the Secretary), shall conduct a study to explore the capture, storage, analysis, and feasibility of monitoring ground source data at airports.

(b) OBJECTIVES.—The objectives of the study conducted under subsection (a) shall include the following:

(1) Determining the current state of ground source data coverage at airports.

(2) Understanding the technology requirements for monitoring ground movements at airports through sensors, receivers, or other technologies.

(3) Conducting data collection through a pilot program established under subsection (c) and collecting ground-based tarmac delay statistics.

(4) Performing an evaluation and feasibility analysis of potential system-level tarmac operations monitoring solutions.

(c) PILOT PROGRAM.—

(1) IN GENERAL.—Not later than 180 days after the date of enactment of this Act, the Director shall establish a pilot program to collect data and develop ground-based tarmac delay statistics or other relevant statistics with respect to airports.

(2) REQUIREMENTS.—The pilot program established under paragraph (1) shall—

(A) include up to 6 airports that the Director determines reflect a diversity of factors, including geography, size, and air traffic;

(B) terminate not more than 3 years after the date of enactment of this Act; and

(C) be subject to any guidelines issued by the Director.

(d) REPORT.—Not later than 4 years after the date of enactment of this Act, the Director shall publish the results of the study conducted under subsection (a) and the pilot program established under subsection (c) on a publicly available website.

* * * * * * *

SEC. 342. DON YOUNG ALASKA AVIATION SAFETY INITIATIVE.

* * * * * * *

(d) [49 U.S.C. 47101 note] RUNWAY LENGTH.—The Administrator—

(1) may not restrict funding made available under chapter

SEC. 344. [49 U.S.C. 44704 note] CHANGED
PRODUCT RULE REFORM.

FAA Reauthorization Act of 2024

471 of title 49, United States Code, from being used at an airport in Alaska to rehabilitate, resurface, or reconstruct the full length and width of an existing runway within Alaska based solely on reduced current or forecasted aeronautical activity levels or critical design type standards;

(2) may not reject requests for runway projects at airports in Alaska if such projects address critical community needs, including projects—

(A) that support economic development by expanding a runway to meet new demands; or

(B) that preserve the length of runways used by aircraft to deliver necessary cargo, including heating fuel and gasoline, for the community served by the airport; and

(3) shall, not later than 60 days after receiving a request for a runway rehabilitation or reconstruction project at an airport in Alaska, review each such request on a case-by-case basis.

(e) IMPLEMENTATION OF NTSB RECOMMENDATIONS.—

(1) IN GENERAL.—Not later than 3 years after the date of enactment of this Act, the Administrator shall take such actions as may be necessary to implement National Transportation Safety Board recommendations A-22-25 and A-22-26 (as contained in Aviation Investigation Report AIR-22-09, adopted November 16, 2022).

(2) COORDINATION.—In taking actions under paragraph (1), the Administrator shall coordinate with the State of Alaska, airports in Alaska, air carriers operating in Alaska, private pilots (including tour operators) based in Alaska, and such other members of the Alaska aviation community or other stakeholders as the Administrator determines appropriate.

* * * * * * *

* * * * * * *

SEC. 344. [49 U.S.C. 44704 note] CHANGED PRODUCT RULE REFORM.

(a) IN GENERAL.—Not later than 18 months after the date of enactment of this Act, the Administrator shall issue a notice of proposed rulemaking to revise section 21.101 of title 14, Code of Federal Regulations, to achieve the following objectives:

SEC. 346. [49 U.S.C. 44704 note] CHANGED
PRODUCT RULE REFORM.

FAA Reauthorization Act of

(1) For any significant design change, as determined by the Administrator, to require that the exception related to impracticality under subsection (b)(3) of such section from the requirement to comply with the latest amendments of the applicable airworthiness standards in effect on the date of application for the change be approved only after providing public notice and opportunity to comment on such exception.

(2) To ensure appropriate documentation of any exception or exemption from airworthiness requirements in title 14, Code of Federal Regulations, as in effect on the date of application for the change.

(b) CONGRESSIONAL BRIEFING.—Not later than 1 year after the date of enactment of this Act, the Administrator shall provide to the appropriate committees of Congress a briefing on the implementation by the FAA of the recommendations of the Changed Product Rule International Authorities Working Group, established for purposes of carrying out the requirements of section 117 of the Aircraft Certification, Safety, and Accountability Act (49 U.S.C. 44704 note), including recommendations on harmonized changes and reforms regarding the impractical exception.

(c) FINAL RULE.—Not later than 3 years after the date of enactment of this Act, the Administrator shall issue a final rule based on the notice of proposed rulemaking issued under subsection (a).

(d) ANNUAL REPORT.—Beginning in 2025 and annually thereafter through 2028, the Administrator shall submit to the appropriate committees of Congress an annual report detailing the number of all significant design change exceptions approved and denied under paragraphs (1) through (3) of section 21.101(b) of title 14, Code of Federal Regulations.

* * * * * * *

SEC. 346. STUDY ON AIRWORTHINESS STANDARDS COMPLIANCE.

(a) STUDY.— The Administrator shall seek to enter into an agreement with a federally funded research and development center to conduct a study, in consultation with appropriate aviation safety engineers of the FAA, on the occurrences and potential consequences of a transport airplane design found to not comply with applicable airworthiness standards.

SEC. 346. [49 U.S.C. 44704 note] CHANGED PRODUCT RULE REFORM.

FAA Reauthorization Act of 2024

(b) SCOPE.— In conducting the study pursuant to subsection (a), the federally funded research and development center shall identify each final airworthiness directive issued by the FAA or another civil aviation authority—

(1) applicable to transport airplanes during the 10-year period prior to the date of enactment of this Act; and

(2) to address an unsafe condition resulting from an approved design that was noncompliant with an applicable airworthiness standard.

(c) REQUIREMENTS.— For each such airworthiness directive identified under subsection (b), the federally funded research and development center shall examine—

(1) the airworthiness standard with which the transport airplane failed to comply;

(2) the resulting unsafe condition and whether such condition resulted in an accident;

(3) the methods by which the noncompliance was discovered and brought to the attention of the FAA or another civil aviation authority, to the extent such methods can be identified;

(4) an analysis of the method used by the applicant to show compliance during the certification process and whether other compliance methods may have reasonably identified the noncompliance during the certification process;

(5) the date of approval of the relevant type design and the date of issuance of the airworthiness directive;

(6) any corrective action mandated to address the identified unsafe condition;

(7) the period of time specified for the incorporation of the corrective action, during which the affected transport airplanes were allowed to operate before the unsafe condition was corrected; and

(8) the total cost of compliance estimated in the final rule adopting the airworthiness directive.

(d) COORDINATION.—In conducting the study under subsection (a), the federally funded research and development center shall coordinate with, and solicit comments from—

(1) transport category aircraft manufacturers; and

(2) employees of the Administration, including the official bargaining representative of aircraft certification services engineers and of aviation safety engineers under section 7111 of title 5, United States Code, involved in developing airworthiness directives, as necessary.

(e) REPORT TO CONGRESS.—Not later than 2 years after the date of enactment of this Act, the Administrator shall submit to the appropriate committees of Congress a report that includes—

(1) the results of the study conducted under subsection (a);

(2) actions the Administrator determines necessary to improve safety as a result of the findings under subsection (a) and any root causes of an unsafe condition that were identified;

(3) the comments solicited under subsection (d); and

(4) any other recommendations for legislative or administrative action determined appropriate by the Administrator.

(f) DEFINITIONS.—In this section:

(1) AIR CARRIER; FOREIGN AIR CARRIER.—The terms "air carrier" and "foreign air carrier" have the meanings given such terms in section 40102 of title 49, United States Code.

(2) TRANSPORT AIRPLANE.—The term "transport airplane" means a transport category airplane designed for operation by an air carrier or foreign air carrier type-certificated with a passenger seating capacity of 30 or more or an all-cargo or combi derivative.

SEC. 347. ZERO TOLERANCE FOR NEAR MISSES, RUNWAY INCURSIONS, AND SURFACE SAFETY RISKS.

* * * * * * *

(b) [49 U.S.C. 47101 note] RUNWAY SAFETY COUNCIL.—

(1) IN GENERAL.—Not later than 6 months after the date of enactment of this Act, the Administrator shall establish a council, to be known as the "Runway Safety Council" (in this section referred to as the "Council"), to develop a systematic management strategy to address airport surface safety risks.

(2) DUTIES.—The duties of the Council shall include, at a minimum, advancing the development of risk-based, data driven, integrated systems solutions and strategies to enhance

airport surface safety risk mitigation.

    (3) MEMBERSHIP.—

        (A) IN GENERAL.—In establishing the Council, the Administrator shall appoint at least 1 member from each of the following:

            (i) Airport operators.

            (ii) Air carriers.

            (iii) Aircraft operators.

            (iv) Avionics manufacturers.

            (v) Flight schools.

            (vi) The exclusive collective bargaining representative of aviation safety professionals for the FAA certified under section 7111 of title 5, United States Code.

            (vii) The exclusive bargaining representative of the air traffic controllers certified under section 7111 of title 5, United States Code.

            (viii) Other safety experts the Administrator determines appropriate.

        (B) ADDITIONAL MEMBERS.—The Administrator may appoint members representing any other stakeholder organization that the Administrator determines appropriate to the Runway Safety Council.

    (c) [49 U.S.C. 47101 note] AIRPORT SURFACE SAFETY TECHNOLOGIES.—

        (1) IDENTIFICATION.—Not later than 6 months after the date of enactment of this Act, the Administrator shall, in coordination with the Council, consult with relevant stakeholders to identify technologies, equipment, systems, and process changes, that—

        (A) may provide airport surface surveillance capabilities at airports lacking such capabilities;

        (B) may augment existing airport surface detection and surveillance system; or

        (C) may improve onboard situational awareness for flight crewmembers, including technologies for use in an aircraft that—

(i) reduce the risk of collision on the runway with other aircraft or vehicles;

(ii) calculate safe landing distances; and

(iii) prompt actions to bring the aircraft to a safe stop.

(2) CRITERIA.—Not later than 1 year after the date of enactment of this Act, the Administrator shall—

(A) based on the information obtained pursuant to paragraph (1)(A) and (1)(B), identify airport surface detection and surveillance systems that meet the standards of the FAA and may be able to—

(i) provide airport surface surveillance capabilities at airports lacking such capabilities; or

(ii) augment existing airport surface detection and surveillance systems, such as Airport Surface Detection System—Model X or the Airport Surface Surveillance Capability;

(B) establish a timeline and action plan for replacing, maintaining, or enhancing the operational capability provided by existing airport surface detection and surveillance systems, and implementing runway safety technologies at airports without airport surface detection and surveillance systems, as needed, to improve runway safety;

(C) based on the information obtained pursuant to paragraph (1)(C), identify safety technologies and systems in transport airplanes that meet the standards of the FAA that will—

(i) enhance runway safety for transport airplanes that lack the capabilities of such technologies and systems, as appropriate; or

(ii) augment existing onboard situational awareness runway traffic alerting and runway landing safety technologies installed on transport airplanes; and

(D) establish clear and quantifiable criteria relating to operational factors, including ground traffic and air traffic activity and the rate of runway and terminal airspace safety events (including runway incursions), that determine when the installation and deployment of an airport surface detection or surveillance system, or other runway safety system (including runway status lights), at an airport is required.—

(3) DEPLOYMENT.—Not later than 5 years after the date of enactment of this Act, the Administrator shall ensure that airport surface detection and surveillance systems are deployed and operational at—

(A) all airports described in paragraph (2)(A); and

(B) all medium and large hub airports.

(4) BRIEFING.—Not later than 3 years after the date of enactment of this Act, the Administrator shall brief the appropriate committees of Congress on the progress of the deployment described in paragraph (3).

(d) [49 U.S.C. 47101 note] FOREIGN OBJECT DEBRIS DETECTION.—

(1) IN GENERAL.—Not later than 3 years after the date of enactment of this Act, the Administrator shall assess, in coordination with the Council, automated foreign object debris monitoring and detection systems at not less than 3 airports that are using such systems.

(2) CONSIDERATIONS.—In conducting the assessment under paragraph (1), the Administrator shall consider the following:

(A) The categorization of an airport.

(B) The potential frequency of foreign object debris incidents on airport runways or adjacent ramp areas.

(C) The availability of funding for the installation and maintenance of foreign object debris monitoring and detection systems.

(D) The impact of such systems on the airfield operations of an airport.

(E) The effectiveness of available foreign object debris monitoring and detection systems.

(F) Any other factors relevant to assessing the return on investment of foreign object debris monitoring and detection systems.

(3) CONSULTATION.—In carrying out this subsection, the

Administrator and the Council shall consult with manufacturers and suppliers of foreign object debris detection technology and any other relevant stakeholders.

(e) [49 U.S.C. 47101 note] RUNWAY SAFETY STUDY.—

(1) IN GENERAL.—Not later than 2 years after the date of enactment of this Act, the Administrator shall seek to enter into appropriate arrangements with a federally funded research and development center to conduct a study of runway incursions, airport surface incidents, operational errors, or losses of standard separation of aircraft in the approach or departure phase of flight to determine how advanced technologies and future airport development projects may be able to reduce the frequency of such events and enhance aviation safety.

(2) CONSIDERATIONS.—In conducting the study under paragraph (1), the federally funded research and development center shall—

(A) examine data relating to recurring runway incursions, surface incidents, operational errors, or losses of standard separation of aircraft in the approach or departure phase of flight at airports to identify the underlying factors that caused such events;

(B) assess metrics used to identify when such events are increasing at an airport;

(C) assess available and developmental technologies, including and beyond such technologies considered in subsection (c), that may augment existing air traffic management capabilities of surface surveillance and terminal airspace equipment;

(D) consider growth trends in airport size, staffing and communication complexities to identify—

(i) future gaps in information exchange between aerospace stakeholders; and

(ii) methods for meeting future near real-time information sharing needs; and

(E) examine airfield safety training programs used by airport tenants and other stakeholders operating on airfields of airports, including airfield familiarization training programs for employees, to assess scalability to handle future growth in airfield capacity and traffic.

(3) RECOMMENDATIONS.—In conducting the study required by paragraph (1), the federally funded research and development center shall develop recommendations for the strategic planning efforts of the Administration to appropriately maintain surface safety considering future increases in air traffic and based on the considerations described in paragraph (2).

(4) REPORT TO CONGRESS.—Not later than 90 days after the completion of the study required by paragraph (1), the Administrator shall submit to the appropriate committees of Congress a report on the findings of such study and any recommendations developed under paragraph (3).

(f) [49 U.S.C. 47101 note] DEFINITIONS.—In this section:

(1) AIR CARRIER; FOREIGN AIR CARRIER.—The terms "air carrier" and "foreign air carrier" have the meanings given such terms in section 40102 of title 49, United States Code.

(2) AIRPORT SURFACE DETECTION AND SURVEILLANCE SYSTEM.—The term "airport surface detection and surveillance system" means an airport surveillance system that is—

(A) designed to track surface movement of aircraft and vehicles; or

(B) capable of alerting air traffic controllers or flight crewmembers of a possible runway incursion, misaligned approach, or other safety event.

(3) TRANSPORT AIRPLANE.—The term "transport airplane" means a transport category airplane designed for operation by an air carrier or foreign air carrier jet type-certificated with a passenger seating capacity of at least 10 seats or a maximum takeoff weight above 12,500 pounds or an all-cargo or combi derivative of such an airplane.

SEC. 348. [49 U.S.C. 44701 note] IMPROVEMENTS TO AVIATION SAFETY INFORMATION ANALYSIS AND SHARING PROGRAM.

(a) IN GENERAL.—Not later than 3 years after the date of enactment of this Act, the Administrator shall implement improvements to the Aviation Safety Information Analysis and Sharing Program with respect to safety data sharing and risk mitigation.

(b) REQUIREMENTS.—In carrying out subsection (a), the

Administrator shall—

(1) identify methods to increase the rate at which data is collected, processed, and analyzed to expeditiously share safety intelligence;

(2) develop predictive capabilities to anticipate emerging safety risks;

(3) identify methods to improve shared data environments with external stakeholders;

(4) establish a robust process for prioritizing requests for safety information;

(5) establish guidance to encourage regular safety inspector review of non-confidential aviation safety and performance data;

(6) identify industry segments not yet included and conduct outreach to such industry segments to increase the rate of participation, including—

(A) general aviation;

(B) air transportation and commercial aviation;

(C) rotorcraft operations;

(D) air ambulance operations; and

(E) aviation maintenance;

(7) establish processes for obtaining and analyzing comprehensive and aggregate data for new and future industry segments; and

(8) integrate safety data from unmanned aircraft system operators, as appropriate.

(c) IMPLEMENTATION.—In carrying out subsection (a), the Administrator shall—

(1) prioritize production-ready configurable solutions over custom development, as appropriate, to support FAA critical aviation safety programs; and

(2) ensure that adequate market research is completed in accordance with FAA acquisition management system requirements, including appropriate demonstrations of proposed solutions, as part of the evaluation criteria.

(d) RULE OF CONSTRUCTION.—Nothing in this section shall be construed—

(1) to require the Administrator to share confidential or proprietary information and data to safety inspectors for purposes of enforcement; or

(2) to limit the applicability of section 44735 of title 49, United States Code, to the Aviation Safety Information Analysis and Sharing Program.

(e) BRIEFING.—Not later than 180 days after the date of enactment of this Act, and every 6 months thereafter until the improvements under subsection (a) are made, the Administrator shall brief the appropriate committees of Congress on the progress of implementation of the Aviation Safety Information Analysis and Sharing Program, including—

(1) an assessment of the progress of the FAA toward achieving milestones for such program identified by the inspector general of the Department of Transportation and the Special Committee to Review FAA Aircraft Certification Reports;

(2) a description of the plan to use appropriate deployable commercial solutions to assist the FAA in meeting such milestones;

(3) steps taken to make improvements under subsection (b); and

(4) a summary of the efforts of the FAA to address gaps in safety data provided from any of the industry segments described in subsection (b)(6).

SEC. 349. [49 U.S.C. 44704 note] INSTRUCTIONS FOR CONTINUED AIRWORTHINESS AVIATION RULEMAKING COMMITTEE.

(a) IN GENERAL.—The Administrator shall convene an aviation rulemaking committee to review, and develop findings and recommendations regarding, instructions for continued airworthiness (as described in section 21.50 of title 14, Code of Federal Regulations), and provide to the Administrator a report on such findings and recommendations and for other related purposes as determined by the Administrator.

(b) COMPOSITION.—The aviation rulemaking committee established pursuant to subsection (a) shall consist of members appointed by the Administrator, including representatives of—

(1) holders of type certificates (as described in subpart B of

part 21, title 14, Code of Federal Regulations);

(2) holders of production certificates (as described in subpart G of part 21, title 14, Code of Federal Regulations);

(3) holders of parts manufacturer approvals (as described in subpart K of part 21, title 14, Code of Federal Regulations);

(4) holders of technical standard order authorizations (as described in subpart O of part 21, title 14, Code of Federal Regulations);

(5) operators under parts 121, 125, or 135 of title 14, Code of Federal Regulations;

(6) holders of repair station certificates (as described in section 145 of title 14, Code of Federal Regulations) that are not also type certificate holders as included under paragraph (1), production certificate holders as included under paragraph (2), or aircraft operators as included under paragraph (5) (or associated with any such entities);

(7) the certified bargaining representative of aviation safety inspectors and engineers for the Administration;

(8) general aviation operators;

(9) mechanics certificated under part 65 of title 14, Code of Federal Regulations;

(10) holders of supplemental type certificates (as described in subpart E of part 21 of title 14, Code of Federal Regulations);

(11) designated engineering representatives employed by repair stations described in paragraph (6); and

(12) aviation safety experts with specific knowledge of instructions for continued airworthiness policies and regulations.

(c) CONSIDERATIONS.—The aviation rulemaking committee established pursuant to subsection (a) shall consider—

(1) existing standards, regulations, certifications, assessments, and guidance related to instructions for continued airworthiness and the clarity of such standards, regulations, certifications, assessments, and guidance to all parties;

(2) the sufficiency of safety data used in preparing instructions for continued airworthiness;

(3) the sufficiency of maintenance data used in preparing

SEC. 350. [49 U.S.C. 44903 note] SECONDARY
COCKPIT BARRIERS.

FAA Reauthorization Act of 2024

instructions for continued airworthiness;

(4) the protection of proprietary information and intellectual property in instructions for continued airworthiness;

(5) the availability of instructions for continued airworthiness, as needed, for maintenance activities;

(6) the need to harmonize or deconflict proposed and existing regulations with other Federal regulations, guidance, and policies;

(7) international collaboration, where appropriate and consistent with the interests of safety in air commerce and national security, with other civil aviation authorities, international aviation and standards organizations, and any other appropriate entities; and

(8) any other matter the Administrator determines appropriate.

(d) DUTIES.—The Administrator shall—

(1) not later than 1 year after the date of enactment of this Act, submit to the appropriate committees of Congress a copy of the aviation rulemaking committee report under subsection (a); and

(2) not later than 180 days after the date of submission of the report under paragraph (1), initiate a rulemaking activity or make such policy and guidance updates necessary to address any consensus recommendations reached by the aviation rulemaking committee established pursuant to subsection (a), as determined appropriate by the Administrator.

SEC. 350. [49 U.S.C. 44903 note] SECONDARY COCKPIT BARRIERS.

(a) IN GENERAL.—Not later than 6 months after the date of enactment of this Act, the Administrator shall convene an aviation rulemaking committee to review and develop findings and recommendations to require installation of a secondary cockpit barrier on commercial passenger aircraft operated under the provisions of part 121 of title 14, Code of Federal Regulations, that are not captured under another regulation or proposed regulation.

(b) MEMBERSHIP.—The Administrator shall appoint a chair and members of the rulemaking committee convened under subsection (a), which shall be comprised of at least 1 representative from the

SEC. 350. [49 U.S.C. 44903 note] SECONDARY
COCKPIT BARRIERS.

FAA Reauthorization Act of

constituencies of—

(1) mainline air carriers;

(2) regional air carriers;

(3) aircraft manufacturers;

(4) passenger aircraft pilots represented by a labor group;

(5) flight attendants represented by a labor group;

(6) airline passengers; and

(7) other stakeholders the Administrator determines appropriate.

(c) CONSIDERATIONS.—The aviation rulemaking committee convened under subsection (a) shall consider—

(1) minimum dimension requirements for secondary barriers on all aircraft types operated under part 121 of title 14, Code of Federal Regulations;

(2) secondary barrier performance standards manufacturers and air carriers must meet for such aircraft types;

(3) the availability of certified secondary barriers suitable for use on such aircraft types;

(4) the development, certification, testing, manufacturing, installation, and training for secondary barriers for such aircraft types;

(5) flight duration and stage length;

(6) the location of lavatories on such aircraft as related to operational complexities;

(7) operational complexities;

(8) any risks to safely evacuate passengers of such aircraft; and

(9) other considerations the Administrator determines appropriate.

(d) REPORT TO CONGRESS.—Not later than 12 months after the convening of the aviation rulemaking committee described in subsection (a), the Administrator shall submit to the appropriate committees of Congress a report based on the findings and recommendations of the aviation rulemaking committee convened under subsection (a), including—

(1) if applicable, any dissenting positions on the findings and the rationale for each position; and

(2) any disagreements with the recommendations, including the rationale for each disagreement and the reasons for the disagreement.

(e) INSTALLATION OF SECONDARY COCKPIT BARRIERS OF EXISTING AIRCRAFT.—Not later than 36 months after the date of the submission of the report under subsection (d), the Administrator shall, taking into consideration the final reported findings and recommendations of the aviation rulemaking committee, issue a final rule requiring installation of a secondary cockpit barrier on each commercial passenger aircraft operated under the provisions of part 121 of title 14, Code of Federal Regulations.

SEC. 351. [49 U.S.C. 44701 note] PART 135 DUTY AND REST.

(a) PART 91 TAIL-END FERRY RULEMAKING.—Not later than 3 years after the date of enactment of this Act, the Administrator shall require that any operation conducted by a flight crewmember during an assigned duty period under the operational control of an operator holding a certificate under part 135 of title 14, Code of Federal Regulations, before, during, or after the duty period (including any operations under part 91 of title 14, Code of Federal Regulations), without an intervening rest period, shall count towards the flight time and duty period limitations of such flight crewmember under part 135 of title 14, Code of Federal Regulations.

(b) RECORD KEEPING.—Not later than 1 year after the date of enactment of this Act, the Administrator shall update any Administration policy and guidance regarding complete and accurate record keeping practices for operators holding a certificate under part 135 of title 14, Code of Federal Regulations, in order to properly document, at a minimum—

(1) flight crew assignments;

(2) flight crew prospective rest notifications;

(3) compliance with flight and duty times limitations and post-duty rest requirements; and

(4) duty period start and end times.

(c) SAFETY MANAGEMENT SYSTEM OVERSIGHT.—The Administrator, in performing oversight of the safety management

SEC. 353. [49 U.S.C. 44701 note] RAMP
WORKER SAFETY CALL TO ACTION.

FAA Reauthorization Act of

system of an operator holding a certificate under part 135 of title 14, Code of Federal Regulations, following the implementation of the final rule issued based on the final rule titled "Safety Management Systems", and published on April 26, 2024 (89 Fed. Reg. 33068), shall ensure such operator is evaluating and appropriately mitigating aviation safety risks, including, at minimum, risks associated with—

(1) inadequate flight crewmember duty and rest periods; and

(2) incomplete records pertaining to flight crew rest, duty, and flight times.

(d) ORGAN TRANSPORTATION FLIGHTS.—In updating guidance and policy pursuant to subsection (b), the Administrator shall consider and allow for appropriate accommodations, including accommodations related to subsections (b)(2) and (b)(4) for operators—

(1) performing organ transportation operations; and

(2) who have in place a means by which to identify and mitigate risks associated with flight crew duty and rest.

* * * * * * *

SEC. 353. [49 U.S.C. 44701 note] RAMP WORKER SAFETY CALL TO ACTION.

(a) CALL TO ACTION RAMP WORKER SAFETY REVIEW.—Not later than 180 days after the date of enactment of this Act, the Administrator shall initiate a Call to Action safety review of airport ramp worker safety and ways to minimize or eliminate ingestion zone and jet blast zone accidents.

(b) CONTENTS.—The Call to Action safety review required pursuant to subsection (a) shall include—

(1) a description of Administration regulations, guidance, and directives related to airport ramp worker safety procedures and oversight of such processes;

(2) a description of reportable accidents and incidents involving airport ramp workers in 5-year period preceding the date of enactment of this Act, including any identified contributing factors to the reportable accident or incident;

(3) training and related educational materials for airport

ramp workers, including supervisory and contract employees;

(4) any recommended devices and methods for communication on the airport ramp, including considerations of requirements for operable radios and headsets;

(5) a review of markings on the airport ramp that define restriction, staging, safety, or hazard zones, including markings to clearly define and graphically indicate the engine ingestion zones and envelope of safety for the variety of aircraft that may park at the same gate of the airport;

(6) a review of aircraft jet blast and engine intake safety markings, including incorporation of markings on aircraft to indicate engine inlet danger zones; and

(7) a process for stakeholders, including airlines, aircraft manufacturers, airports, labor, and aviation safety experts, to provide feedback and share best practices.

(c) REPORT AND ACTIONS.—Not later than 180 days after the conclusion of the Call to Action safety review pursuant to subsection (a), the Administrator shall—

(1) submit to the appropriate committees of Congress a report on the results of the review and any recommendations for actions or best practices to improve airport ramp worker safety, including the identification of risks and possible ways to mitigate such risks to be considered in any applicable safety management system of air carriers and airports; and

(2) initiate such actions as are necessary to act upon the findings of the review.

(d) TRAINING MATERIALS.—Not later than 6 months after the completion of the safety review required under subsection (a), the Administrator shall develop and publish training and related educational materials about aircraft engine ingestion and jet blast hazards for ground crews, including supervisory and contract employees, that includes information on—

(1) the specific dangers and consequences of entering engine ingestion or jet blast zones;

(2) proper protocols to avoid entering an engine ingestion or jet blast zone; and

(3) on-the-job, instructor-led training to physically demonstrate the engine ingestion zone boundaries and jet blast

zones for each kind of aircraft the ground crew may encounter.

(e) CONSULTATION.—In carrying out this section, the Administrator shall consult with aviation safety experts, air carriers, aircraft manufacturers, relevant labor organizations, and airport operators.

(f) TRAINING REQUIREMENTS.—Not later than 6 months after the publication of the training and related educational materials required under subsection (d), the Administrator may require any ramp worker, as appropriate, to receive the relevant engine ingestion and jet blast zone hazard training before such ramp worker may perform work on any airport ramp.

* * * * * * *

SEC. 355. [49 U.S.C. 44718 note] TOWER MARKING NOTICE OF PROPOSED RULEMAKING.

(a) IN GENERAL.—Not later than 1 year after the date of enactment of this Act, the Administrator shall issue a notice of proposed rulemaking to implement section 2110 of the FAA Extension, Safety, and Security Act of 2016 (49 U.S.C. 44718 note).

(b) REPORT.—If the Administrator fails to issue the notice of proposed rulemaking pursuant to subsection (a), the Administrator shall submit to the appropriate committees of Congress an annual report on the status of such rulemaking, including—

(1) the reasons that the Administrator has failed to issue the rulemaking; and

(2) a list of fatal aircraft accidents associated with unmarked towers that have occurred during the 5-year period preceding the date of submission of the report.

* * * * * * *

SEC. 358. GLOBAL AVIATION SAFETY.

* * * * * * *

(c) BILATERAL AVIATION SAFETY AGREEMENTS; TECHNICAL ASSISTANCE.—

* * * * * * *

(3) [49 U.S.C. 40104 note] VALIDATION OF POWERED-LIFT

AIRCRAFT.—In carrying out section 40104(d) of title 49, United States Code (as amended by this Act), the Administrator shall ensure coordination with international civil aviation authorities regarding the establishment of mutual processes for efficient validation, acceptance, and working arrangements of certificates and approvals for powered-lift aircraft, products, and articles.

(4) REPORT ON INTERNATIONAL VALIDATION PROGRAM PERFORMANCE.—

(A) IN GENERAL.—Not later than 2 years after the date of enactment of this Act, the Secretary shall initiate a review to evaluate the performance of the type certificate validation program of the FAA under bilateral or multilateral aviation safety agreements, with a focus on agreed to implementation procedures.

(B) CONTENTS.—In conducting the review under subparagraph (A), the Secretary shall consider, at minimum, the following:

(i) Actions taken for the purposes of carrying out section 243(a) of the FAA Reauthorization Act of 2018 (49 U.S.C. 44701 note).

(ii) Metrics from validation programs carried out prior to the initiation of such review, including the number and types of projects, timeline milestones, and trends relating to the repeated use of non-basic criteria.

(iii) Training on the minimum standards of established validation work plans, including any guidance on the level of involvement of the validating authority, established justifications for involvement, and procedures for compliance document requests.

(iv) The perspectives of—

(I) FAA employees responsible for type validation projects;

(II) bilateral civil aviation regulatory partners; and

(III) industry applicants seeking validation.

(v) Adequacy of the funding and staffing levels of

the International Validation Branch of the Compliance and Airworthiness Division of the Aircraft Certification Service of the FAA.

(vi) Effectiveness of FAA training for FAA employees.

(vii) Effectiveness of outreach conducted to improve and enforce validation processes.

(viii) Efforts undertaken to strengthen relationships with international certification authorities.

(ix) Number of approvals issued by other certifying authorities in compliance with applicable bilateral agreements and implementation procedures.

(C) REPORT.—Not later than 60 days after the completion of the review initiated under this subsection, the Administrator shall submit to the appropriate committees of Congress a report regarding such review.

(D) DEFINITIONS.—In this paragraph, the terms "ODA holder" and "ODA unit" have the meanings given such terms in section 44736(c) of title 49, United States Code.

* * * * * * *

(e) [49 U.S.C. 40104 note] POWERED-LIFT AIRCRAFT.—In developing the methodology required under section 40104(d)(7)(H) of title 49, United States Code (as added by subsection (d)), the Administrator shall—

(1) perform an assessment of existing bilateral aviation safety agreements, implementation procedures, and other associated bilateral arrangements to determine how current and future powered-lift products and articles can utilize the most appropriate validation mechanisms and procedures;

(2) facilitate global acceptance of the approach of the FAA to certification of powered-lift aircraft, products, and articles; and

(3) consider any other information determined appropriated by the Administrator.

* * * * * * *

SEC. 360. [49 U.S.C. 44704 note] WILDFIRE SUPPRESSION.

(a) IN GENERAL.—Not later than 18 months after the date of enactment of this Act, to ensure that sufficient firefighting resources are available to suppress wildfires and protect public safety and property, and notwithstanding any other provision of law or agency regulation, the Administrator shall issue a rule under which—

(1) an operation described in section 21.25(b)(7) of title 14, Code of Federal Regulations, shall allow for the transport of firefighters to and from the site of a wildfire to perform ground wildfire suppression and designate the firefighters conducting such an operation as essential crewmembers on board a covered aircraft operated on a mission to suppress wildfire;

(2) the aircraft maintenance, inspections, and pilot training requirements under part 135 of such title 14 may apply to such an operation, if determined by the Administrator to be necessary to maintain the safety of firefighters carrying out wildfire suppression missions; and

(3) the noise standards described in part 36 of such title 14 shall not apply to such an operation.

(b) SURPLUS MILITARY AIRCRAFT.—In issuing a rule under subsection (a), the Administrator may not enable any aircraft of a type that has been—

(1) manufactured in accordance with the requirements of, and accepted for use by, the armed forces (as defined in section 101 of title 10, United States Code); and

(2) later modified to be used for wildfire suppression operations.

(c) CONFORMING AMENDMENTS TO FAA DOCUMENTS.—In issuing a rule under subsection (a), the Administrator shall revise the order of the FAA titled "Restricted Category Type Certification", issued on February 27, 2006 (FAA Order 8110.56), as well as any corresponding policy or guidance material, to reflect the requirements of this section.

(d) SAVINGS PROVISION.—Nothing in this section shall be construed to limit the authority of the Administrator to take action otherwise authorized by law to protect aviation safety or passenger safety.

(e) DEFINITIONS.—In this section:

(1) COVERED AIRCRAFT.—The term "covered aircraft" means an aircraft type-certificated in the restricted category under section 21.25 of title 14, Code of Federal Regulations, used for transporting firefighters to and from the site of a wildfire in order to perform ground wildfire suppression for the purpose of extinguishing a wildfire on behalf of, or pursuant to a contract with, a Federal, State, or local government agency.

(2) FIREFIGHTERS.—The term "firefighters" means a trained fire suppression professional the transport of whom is necessary to accomplish a wildfire suppression operation.

SEC. 361. CONTINUOUS AIRCRAFT TRACKING AND TRANSMISSION FOR HIGH ALTITUDE BALLOONS.

(a) STUDY ON EFFECTS OF HIGH ALTITUDE BALLOONS ON AVIATION SAFETY.—

(1) IN GENERAL.—Not later than 180 days after the date of enactment of this Act, the Administrator, in coordination with the heads of other relevant Federal agencies, shall brief the appropriate committees of Congress on the effects of high altitude balloon operations that do not emit electronic or radio signals for identification purposes and are launched within the United States and the territories of the United States on aviation safety.

(2) CONSIDERATIONS.—In carrying out this subsection, the Administrator shall consider—

(A) current technology available and employed to track high altitude balloon operations described under paragraph (1);

(B) how the flights of such operations have affected, or could affect, aviation safety;

(C) how such operations have contributed, or could contribute, to misidentified threats to civil or military aviation operations or infrastructure; and

(D) how such operations have impacted, or could impact, national security and air traffic control operations.

(b) HIGH ALTITUDE BALLOON TRACKING AVIATION RULEMAKING COMMITTEE.—

(1) ESTABLISHMENT.—Not later than 180 days after the date of enactment of this Act, the Administrator shall establish

an Aviation Rulemaking Committee (in this section referred to as the "Committee") to review and develop findings and recommendations to inform a standard for any high altitude balloon to be equipped with a system for continuous aircraft tracking that transmits, at a minimum, the altitude, location, and identity of the high altitude balloon in a manner that is accessible to air traffic controllers and ensures the safe integration of high altitude balloons into the national airspace system.

(2) COMPOSITION.—The Committee shall consist of members appointed by the Administrator, including the following:

(A) Representatives of industry.

(B) Aviation safety experts, including experts with specific knowledge—

(i) of high altitude balloon operations; or

(ii) FAA tracking and surveillance systems.

(C) Non-governmental researchers and educators.

(D) Representatives of the Department of Defense.

(E) Representatives of Federal agencies that conduct high altitude balloon operations.

(3) REPORT.—Not later than 18 months after the date of enactment of this Act, the Committee shall submit to the Administrator a report detailing the findings and recommendations developed under paragraph (1), including recommendations regarding the following:

(A) How to update sections 91.215, 91.225, and 99.13 of title 14, Code of Federal Regulations, to require all high altitude balloons to have a continuous aircraft tracking and transmission system.

(B) Any necessary updates to the requirements for high altitude balloons under subpart D of part 101 of title 14, Code of Federal Regulations.

(C) Any necessary updates to other FAA regulations or requirements deemed appropriate and necessary by the Administrator to—

(i) ensure any high altitude balloon has a continuous aircraft tracking and transmission system;

(ii) ensure all data relating to the altitude, location, and identity of any high altitude balloon is made available to air traffic controllers;

(iii) determine criteria and provide approval guidance for new equipment that provides continuous aircraft tracking and transmission for high altitude balloons and meets the performance requirements described under section 91.225 of title 14, Code of Federal Regulations, including portable, battery-powered Automatic Dependent Surveillance-Broadcast Out equipage; and

(iv) maintain airspace safety.

(4) USE OF PRIOR WORK.—In developing the report under paragraph (3), the Committee may make full use of any research, comments, data, findings, or recommendations made by any prior aviation rulemaking committee.

(5) NEW TECHNOLOGIES AND SOLUTIONS.—Nothing in this subsection shall require the Committee to develop recommendations requiring equipage of high altitude balloons with an Automatic Dependent Surveillance-Broadcast Out system or an air traffic control transponder transmission system, or preclude the Committee from making recommendations for the adoption of new systems or solutions that may require that a high altitude balloon be equipped with a system that can transmit, at a minimum, the altitude, location, and identity of the high altitude balloon.

(6) BRIEFING.—Not later than 6 months after receiving the report required under paragraph (3), the Administrator shall brief the appropriate committees of Congress on the contents of such report and the status of any recommendation received pursuant to such report.

(c) DEFINITIONS.—In this section, the term "high altitude balloon" means a manned or unmanned free balloon operating not less than 18,000 feet above mean sea level.

SEC. 362. [49 U.S.C. 40101 note] CABIN AIR SAFETY.

(a) DEADLINE FOR 2018 STUDY ON BLEED AIR.—Not later than 6 months after the date of enactment of this Act, the Administrator shall complete the requirements of section 326 of the FAA

Reauthorization Act of 2018 (49 U.S.C. 40101 note) and submit to the appropriate Congressional committees the following:

(1) The completed study required under subsection (c) of such section.

(2) The report on the feasibility, efficacy, and cost-effectiveness of certification and installation of systems to evaluate bleed air quality required under subsection (d) of such section.

(b) REPORTING SYSTEM FOR SMOKE OR FUME EVENTS ONBOARD COMMERCIAL AIRCRAFT.—

(1) IN GENERAL.—Not later than 180 days after the date of the enactment of this Act, the Administrator shall develop a standardized submission system for air carrier employees to voluntarily report fume or smoke events onboard passenger-carrying aircraft operating under part 121 of title 14, Code of Federal Regulations.

(2) COLLECTED INFORMATION.—In developing the system under paragraph (1), the Administrator shall ensure that the system includes a method for submitting information about a smoke or fume event that allows for the collection of the following information, if applicable:

(A) Identification of the flight number, type, and registration of the aircraft.

(B) The date of the reported fume or smoke event onboard the aircraft.

(C) Description of fumes or smoke in the aircraft, including the nature, intensity, and visual consistency or smell (if any).

(D) The location of the fumes or smoke in the aircraft.

(E) The source (if discernible) of the fumes or smoke in the aircraft.

(F) The phase of flight during which fumes or smoke first became present.

(G) The duration of the fume or smoke event.

(H) Any required onboard medical attention for passengers or crew members.

(I) Any additional factors as determined appropriate by the Administrator or crew member submitting a report.

(3) GUIDELINES FOR SUBMISSION.—The Administrator shall issue guidelines on how to submit the information described in paragraph (2).

(4) CONFIRMATION OF SUBMISSION.—Upon submitting the information described in paragraph (2), the submitting party shall receive a duplicate record of the submission and confirmation of receipt.

(5) USE OF INFORMATION.—The Administrator—

(A) may not publicly publish any—

(i) information specific to a fume or smoke event that is submitted pursuant to this section; and

(ii) any information that may be used to identify the party submitting such information;

(B) may only publicly publish information submitted pursuant to this section that has been aggregated if—

(i) such information has been validated; and

(ii) the availability of such information would improve aviation safety;

(C) shall maintain a database of such information;

(D) at the request of an air carrier, shall provide to such air carrier any information submitted pursuant to this section that is relevant to such air carrier, except any information that may be used to identify the party submitting such information;

(E) may not, without validation, assume that information submitted pursuant to this section is accurate for the purposes of initiating rulemaking or taking an enforcement action;

(F) may use information submitted pursuant to this section to inform the oversight of the safety management system of an air carrier; and

(G) may use information submitted pursuant to this section for the purpose of performing a study or supporting a study sponsored by the Administrator.

(c) NATIONAL ACADEMIES STUDY ON OVERALL CABIN AIR QUALITY.—

(1) IN GENERAL.—Not later than 3 years after the date of

enactment of this Act, the Administrator shall seek to enter into the appropriate arrangements with the National Academies to conduct a study and issue recommendations to be made publicly available pertaining to cabin air quality and any risk of, and potential for, persistent and accidental fume or smoke events onboard a passenger-carrying aircraft operating under part 121 of title 14, Code of Federal Regulations.

(2) SCOPE.—In carrying out a study pursuant to paragraph (1), the National Academies shall examine—

(A) the report issued pursuant to section 326 of the FAA Reauthorization Act of 2018 (49 U.S.C. 40101 note) and any identified assumptions or gaps described in such report;

(B) the information collected through the system established pursuant to subsection (b);

(C) any health risks or impacts of fume or smoke events on flight crews, including flight attendants and pilots, and passengers onboard aircraft operating under part 121 of title 14, Code of Federal Regulations;

(D) instances of persistent or regularly occurring (as determined by the National Academies) fume or smoke events in such aircraft;

(E) instances of accidental, unexpected, or irregularly occurring (as determined by the National Academies) fume or smoke events on such aircraft, including whether such accidental events are more frequent during various phases of operations, including ground operations, taxiing, take off, cruise, and landing;

(F) the air contaminants present during the instances described in subparagraphs (D) and (E) and the probable originating materials of such air contaminants;

(G) the frequencies, durations, and likely causes of the instances described in subparagraphs (D) and (E); and

(H) any additional data on fume or smoke events, as determined appropriate by the National Academies.

(3) RECOMMENDATIONS.—As a part of the study conducted under paragraph (1), the National Academies shall provide recommendations—

(A) that, at minimum, address how to—

(i) improve overall cabin air quality of passenger-carrying aircraft;

(ii) improve the detection, accuracy, and reporting of fume or smoke events; and

(iii) reduce the frequency and impact of fume or smoke events; and

(B) to establish or update standards, guidelines, or regulations that could help achieve the recommendations described in subparagraph (A).

(4) REPORT TO CONGRESS.—Not later than 1 month after the completion of the study conducted under paragraph (1), the Administrator shall submit to the appropriate committees of Congress a copy of such study and recommendations submitted with such study.

(d) RULEMAKING.—Not later than 1 year after the completion of the study conducted under subsection (c), the Administrator may, as appropriate to address the safety risks identified as a result of the actions taken pursuant to this section, issue a notice of proposed rulemaking to establish requirements for scheduled passenger air carrier operations under part 121 of title 14, Code of Federal Regulations that may include the following:

(1) Training for flight attendants, pilots, aircraft maintenance technicians, airport first responders, and emergency responders on how to respond to incidents on aircraft involving fume or smoke events.

(2) Required actions and procedures for air carriers to take after receiving a report of an incident involving a fume or smoke event in which at least 1 passenger or crew member required medical attention as a result of such incident.

(3) Installation onboard aircraft of detectors and other air quality monitoring equipment.

(e) FUME OR SMOKE EVENT DEFINED.—In this section, the term "fume or smoke event" means an event in which there is an atypical noticeable or persistent presence of fumes or air contaminants in the cabin, including, at a minimum, a smoke event.

SEC. 363. [49 U.S.C. 44705 note] COMMERCIAL AIR TOUR AND SPORT PARACHUTING SAFETY.

(a) SAFETY REQUIREMENTS FOR COMMERCIAL AIR TOUR OPERATORS.—

(1) SAFETY REFORMS.—

(A) AUTHORITY TO CONDUCT NONSTOP COMMERCIAL AIR TOURS.—

(i) IN GENERAL. —Subject to clause (ii), beginning on the date that is 2 years after the date a final rule is published pursuant to paragraph (3), no person may conduct commercial air tours unless such person either—

(I) holds a certificate identifying the person as an air carrier or commercial operator under part 119 of title 14, Code of Federal Regulations and conducts all commercial air tours under the applicable provisions of part 121 or part 135 of title 14, Code of Federal Regulations; or

(II) conducts all commercial air tours pursuant to the requirements established by the Administrator under the final rule published pursuant to paragraph (3).

(ii) SMALL BUSINESS EXCEPTION.—The provisions of clause (i) shall not apply to a person who conducts 100 or fewer commercial air tours in a calendar year.

(B) ADDITIONAL SAFETY REQUIREMENTS.—

(i) IN GENERAL.—Not later than 3 years after the date of enactment of this Act, the Administrator shall issue new or revised regulations to require a commercial air tour operator seeking to conduct an operation with a removed or modified door and a person conducting aerial photography operations seeking to conduct an operation with a removed or modified door to receive approval from the Administrator prior to conducting such operation.

(ii) CONDITIONS AND RESTRICTIONS.—In issuing new or revised regulations under clause (i), the Administrator may impose such conditions and restrictions as determined necessary for safety.

(iii) CONSIDERATIONS.—In issuing new or revised regulations under clause (i), the Administrator shall require a commercial air tour operator to demonstrate to any representative of the FAA, upon request, that a pilot authorized to operate such an air tour has received avoidance training for controlled flight into terrain and in-flight loss of control. Such training shall address reducing the risk of accidents involving unintentional flight into instrument meteorological conditions to address day, night, and low-visibility environments with special attention paid to research available as of the date of enactment of this Act on human factors issues involved in such accidents, including, at a minimum—

(I) specific terrain, weather, and infrastructure challenges relevant in the local operating environment that increase the risk of such accidents;

(II) pilot decision-making relevant to the avoidance of instrument meteorological conditions while operating under visual flight rules;

(III) use of terrain awareness displays;

(IV) spatial disorientation risk factors and countermeasures; and

(V) strategies for maintaining control, including the use of automated systems.

(2) AVIATION RULEMAKING COMMITTEE.—

(A) IN GENERAL. —The Administrator shall convene an aviation rulemaking committee to review and develop findings and recommendations to increase the safety of commercial air tours.

(B) CONSIDERATIONS.—The aviation rulemaking committee convened under subparagraph (A) shall consider, at a minimum—

(i) potential changes to operations regulations or requirements for commercial air tours, including requiring—

(I) the adoption of pilot training standards that are comparable, as applicable, to the standards under subpart H of part 135 of title 14, Code of Federal Regulations; and

(II) the adoption of maintenance standards that are comparable, as applicable, to the standards under subpart J of part 135 of title 14, Code of Federal Regulations;

(ii) establishing a performance-based standard for flight data monitoring for all commercial air tour operators that reviews all available data sources to identify deviations from established areas of operation and potential safety issues;

(iii) requiring all commercial air tour operators to install flight data recording devices capable of supporting collection and dissemination of the data incorporated in the Flight Operational Quality Assurance Program under section 13.401 of title 14, Code of Federal Regulations (or, if an aircraft cannot be retrofitted with such equipment, requiring the commercial air tour operator for such aircraft to collect and maintain flight data through alternative methods);

(iv) requiring all commercial air tour operators to implement a flight data monitoring program, such as a Flight Operational Quality Assurance Program;

(v) establishing methods to provide effective terrain awareness and warning; and

(vi) establishing methods to provide effective traffic avoidance in identified high-traffic tour areas, such as requiring commercial air tour operators that operate within such areas be equipped with an automatic dependent surveillance-broadcast out- and in-supported traffic advisory system that—

(I) includes both visual and aural alerts;

(II) is driven by an algorithm designed to eliminate nuisance alerts; and

(III) is operational during all flight operations.

(vii) codifying and uniformly applying Living History Flight Experience exemption conditions and limitations.

(C) MEMBERSHIP.—The aviation rulemaking committee convened under subparagraph (A) shall consist of members appointed by the Administrator, including—

(i) representatives of industry, including manufacturers of aircraft and aircraft technologies;

(ii) air tour operators or organizations that represent such operators; and

(iii) aviation safety experts with specific knowledge of safety management systems and flight data monitoring programs under part 135 of title 14, Code of Federal Regulations.

(D) DUTIES.—

(i) IN GENERAL. —The Administrator shall direct the aviation rulemaking committee to make findings and submit recommendations regarding each of the matters specified in clauses (i) through (vi) of subparagraph (B).

(ii) CONSIDERATIONS.—In carrying out the duties of the aviation rulemaking committee under clause (i), the Administrator shall direct the aviation rulemaking committee to consider—

(I) recommendations of the National Transportation Safety Board;

(II) recommendations of previous aviation rulemaking committees that reviewed flight data monitoring program requirements for commercial operators under part 135 of title 14, Code of Federal Regulations;

(III) recommendations from industry safety organizations, including the Vertical Aviation Safety Team, the General Aviation Joint Safety Committee, and the United States Helicopter Safety Team;

(IV) scientific data derived from a broad range of flight data recording technologies capable of continuously transmitting and that support a measurable and viable means of assessing data to identify and correct hazardous trends;

(V) appropriate use of data for modifying behavior to prevent accidents;

(VI) the need to accommodate technological advancements in flight data recording technology;

(VII) data gathered from aviation safety reporting programs;

(VIII) appropriate methods to provide effective terrain awareness and warning system protections while mitigating nuisance alerts for aircraft;

(IX) the need to accommodate the diversity of airworthiness standards under part 27 and part 29 of title 14, Code of Federal Regulations;

(X) the need to accommodate diversity of operations and mission sets;

(XI) benefits of third-party data analysis for large and small operations;

(XII) accommodations necessary for small businesses; and

(XIII) other issues, as necessary.

(E) REPORTS AND REGULATIONS.—Not later than 20 months after the date of enactment of this Act, the Administrator shall submit to the appropriate committees of Congress a report based on the findings of the aviation rulemaking committee.

(3) RULEMAKING REQUIRED.—

(A) NOTICE OF PROPOSED RULEMAKING.—Not later than 1 year after the date the Administrator submits a report under paragraph (2)(E), the Administrator shall issue a notice of proposed rulemaking establishing increasing safety regulations for commercial air tour operators based on the recommendations of the rulemaking committee established under paragraph (2).

(B) CONTENTS.—The notice of proposed rulemaking under subparagraph (A) shall require, at a minimum—

(i) the adoption of pilot training standards that are comparable, as applicable, to the standards under subpart H of part 135 of title 14, Code of Federal Regulations for commercial tour operators;

(ii) the adoption of maintenance standards that

are comparable, as applicable, to the standards under subpart J of part 135 of title 14, Code of Federal Regulations for commercial tour operators; and

(iii) that beginning on a date determined appropriate by the Administrator, a helicopter operated by a commercial air tour operator be equipped with an approved flight data monitoring system capable of recording flight performance data.

(C) FINAL RULE. —Not later than 2 years after the issuance of a notice of proposed rulemaking under subparagraph (A), the Administrator shall finalize the rule.

(b) SAFETY REQUIREMENTS FOR SPORT PARACHUTE OPERATIONS.—

(1) AVIATION RULEMAKING COMMITTEE. —The Administrator shall convene an aviation rulemaking committee to review and develop findings and recommendations to increase the safety of sport parachute operations.

(2) CONTENTS.—This aviation rulemaking committee convened under paragraph (1) shall consider, at a minimum—

(A) potential regulatory action governing parachute operations that are conducted in the United States and are subject to the requirements of part 105 of title 14, Code of Federal Regulations, to address—

(i) whether FAA-approved aircraft maintenance and inspection programs that consider, at a minimum, minimum equipment standards informed by recommended maintenance instructions of engine manufacturers, such as service bulletins and service information letters for time between overhauls and component life limits, should be implemented; and

(ii) initial and annual recurrent pilot training and proficiency checks for pilots conducting parachute operations that address, at a minimum, operation- and aircraft-specific weight and balance calculations, preflight inspections, emergency and recovery procedures, and parachutist egress procedures for each type of aircraft flown; and

(B) the revision of guidance material contained in the advisory circular of the FAA titled "Sport Parachuting"

(AC 105-2E) to include guidance for parachute operations in implementing the FAA-approved aircraft maintenance and inspection program and the pilot training and pilot proficiency checking programs required under any new or revised regulations; and

(C) the revision of guidance materials issued in the order of the FAA titled "Flight Standards Information Management System" (FAA Order 8900.1), to include guidance for FAA inspectors who oversee an operation conducted under—

(i) part 91 of title 14, Code of Federal Regulations; and

(ii) an exception specified in section 119.1(e) of title 14, Code of Federal Regulations.

(3) MEMBERSHIP. —The aviation rulemaking committee under paragraph (1) shall consist of members appointed by the Administrator, including—

(A) representatives of industry, including manufacturers of aircraft and aircraft technologies;

(B) parachute operators, or organizations that represent such operators; and

(C) aviation safety experts with specific knowledge of safety management systems and flight data monitoring programs under part 135 and part 105 of title 14, Code of Federal Regulations.

(4) DUTIES.—

(A) IN GENERAL. —The Administrator shall direct the aviation rulemaking committee to make findings and submit recommendations regarding each of the matters specified in subparagraphs (A) through (C) of paragraph (2).

(B) CONSIDERATIONS.—In carrying out its duties under subparagraph (A), the Administrator shall direct the aviation rulemaking committee to consider—

(i) findings and recommendations of the National Transportation Safety Board, as relevant, and specifically such findings and recommendations related to parachute operations, including the June 21,

2019, incident in Mokuleia, Hawaii;

(ii) recommendations of previous aviation rulemaking committees that considered similar issues;

(iii) recommendations from industry safety organizations, including, at a minimum, the United States Parachute Association;

(iv) appropriate use of data for modifying behavior to prevent accidents;

(v) data gathered from aviation safety reporting programs;

(vi) the need to accommodate diversity of operations and mission sets;

(vii) accommodations necessary for small businesses; and

(viii) other issues as necessary.

(5) REPORTS AND REGULATIONS.—

(A) IN GENERAL.—Not later than 36 months after the date of enactment of this Act, the Administrator shall submit to the appropriate committees of Congress a report based on the findings of the aviation rulemaking committee.

(B) CONTENTS. —The report under subparagraph (A) shall include—

(i) any recommendations submitted by the aviation rulemaking committee; and

(ii) any actions the Administrator intends to initiate, if necessary, as a result of such recommendations.

(c) DEFINITIONS.—In this section:

(1) AIR CARRIER.—The term "air carrier" has the meaning given such term in section 40102 of title 49, United States Code.

(2) COMMERCIAL AIR TOUR.—The term "commercial air tour" has the meaning given such term in section 136.1 of title 14, Code of Federal Regulations.

(3) COMMERCIAL AIR TOUR OPERATOR.—The term "commercial air tour operator" has the meaning given such term in section 136.1 of title 14, Code of Federal Regulations.

SEC. 364. [49 U.S.C. 44715 note] HAWAII AIR
NOISE AND SAFETY TASK FORCE.

FAA Reauthorization Act of 2024

(4) PARACHUTE OPERATION.—The term "parachute operation" has the meaning given such term in section 105.3 of title 14, Code of Federal Regulations (or any successor regulation).

SEC. 364. [49 U.S.C. 44715 note] HAWAII AIR NOISE AND SAFETY TASK FORCE.

(a) PARTICIPATION.—To the extent acceptable to the State of Hawaii, the Administrator shall participate as a technical advisor in the air noise and safety task force established by State legislation in the State of Hawaii.

(b) RULEMAKING. —Not later than 18 months after the date on which the task force described in subsection (a) delivers findings and consensus recommendations to the FAA, the Administrator shall, consistent with maintaining the safety and efficiency of the national airspace system—

(1) issue an intent to proceed with a proposed rulemaking;

(2) take other action sufficient to carry out feasible, consensus recommendations; or

(3) issue a statement determining that no such rule or other action is warranted, including a detailed explanation of the rationale for such determination.

(c) CONSIDERATIONS.—In determining whether to proceed with a proposed rulemaking, guidance, or other action under subsection (b) and, if applicable, in developing the proposed rule, guidance, or carrying out the other action, the Administrator shall consider the findings and consensus recommendations of the task force described in subsection (a).

(d) AUTHORITIES.—In issuing the rule, guidance, or carrying out the other action described in subsection (b), the Administrator may take actions in the State of Hawaii to—

(1) provide commercial air tour operators with preferred routes, times, and minimum altitudes for the purpose of noise reduction, so long as such recommendations do not negatively impact safety conditions;

(2) provide commercial air tour operators with information regarding quiet aircraft technology; and

(3) establish a method for residents of the State of Hawaii to publicly report noise disruptions due to commercial air tours

and for commercial air tour operators to respond to complaints.

(e) RULE OF CONSTRUCTION.—Nothing in this section shall be construed as providing the Administrator with authority to ban commercial air tour flights in the State of Hawaii for the purposes of noise reduction.

(f) DEFINITIONS.—In this section:

(1) COMMERCIAL AIR TOUR.—The term "commercial air tour" has the meaning given such term in section 136.1 of title 14, Code of Federal Regulations.

(2) COMMERCIAL AIR TOUR OPERATOR.—The term "commercial air tour operator" has the meaning given such term in section 136.1 of title 14, Code of Federal Regulations.

SEC. 365. [49 U.S.C. 44701 note] MODERNIZATION AND IMPROVEMENTS TO AIRCRAFT EVACUATION.

(a) STUDY.—

(1) IN GENERAL. —Not later than 1 year after the date of enactment of this Act, the Administrator shall conduct a study on improvements to the safety and efficiency of evacuation standards for manufacturers and carriers of transport category airplanes, as described in parts 25 and 121 of title 14, Code of Federal Regulations.

(2) CONTENTS.—

(A) REQUIREMENTS.—The study required under paragraph (1) shall include—

(i) a prospective risk analysis, as well as an evaluation of relevant past incidents with respect to evacuation safety and evacuation standards;

(ii) an assessment of the evacuation testing procedures described in section 25.803 of such title 14, as well as recommendations for how to revise such testing procedures to ensure that the testing procedures assess, in a safe manner, the ability of passengers with disabilities, including passengers who use wheelchairs or other mobility assistive devices, to safely and efficiently evacuate an aircraft;

(iii) an assessment of the evacuation demonstration procedures described in such part 121, as well as recommendations for how to improve such demonstration procedures to ensure that the demonstration procedures assess, in a safe manner, the ability of passengers with disabilities, including passengers who use wheelchairs or other mobility assistive devices, to safely and efficiently evacuate an aircraft;

(iv) the research proposed in National Transportation Safety Board Safety Recommendation A-18-009; and

(v) any other analysis determined appropriate by the Administrator.

(B) CONSIDERATIONS.—In conducting the study under paragraph (1), the Administrator shall assess the following:

(i) The ability of passengers of different ages (including infants, children, and senior citizens) to safely and efficiently evacuate a transport category airplane.

(ii) The ability of passengers of different heights and weights to safely and efficiently evacuate a transport category airplane.

(iii) The ability of passengers with disabilities to safely and efficiently evacuate a transport category airplane.

(iv) The ability of passengers who cannot speak, have difficulty speaking, use synthetic speech, or are non-vocal or non-verbal to safely and efficiently evacuate a transport category airplane.

(v) The ability of passengers who do not speak English to safely and efficiently evacuate a transport category airplane.

(vi) The impact of the presence of carry-on luggage and personal items (such as a purse, briefcase, laptop, or backpack) on the ability of passengers to safely and efficiently evacuate a transport category airplane.

(vii) The impact of seat size and passenger seating space and pitch on the ability of passengers to safely and efficiently evacuate a transport category airplane.

(viii) The impact of seats and other obstacles in the pathway to the exit opening from the nearest aisle on the ability of passengers to safely and efficiently evacuate a transport category airplane.

(ix) With respect to aircraft with parallel longitudinal aisles, the impact of seat pods or other seating configurations that block access between such aisles within a cabin on the ability of passengers to safely and efficiently evacuate a transport category airplane.

(x) The impact of passenger load on the ability of passengers to safely and efficiently evacuate a transport category airplane.

(xi) The impact of animals approved to accompany a passenger, including service animals, on the ability of passengers to safely and efficiently evacuate a transport category airplane.

(xii) Whether an applicant for a type certificate (as defined in section 44704(e)(7) of title 49, United States Code) should be required to demonstrate compliance with FAA emergency evacuation regulations (as described in section 25.803 and Appendix J of part 25 of title 14, Code of Federal Regulations) through live testing in any case in which the Administrator determines that the new aircraft design is significant.

(xiii) Any other factor determined appropriate by the Administrator.

(C) DEFINITIONS.—In this paragraph:

(i) PASSENGER LOAD.—The term "passenger load" means the number of passengers relative to the number of seats onboard the aircraft.

(ii) PASSENGERS WITH DISABILITIES.—The term "passengers with disabilities" means any qualified individual with a disability, as defined in section 382.3 of title 14, Code of Federal Regulations.

(b) AVIATION RULEMAKING COMMITTEE FOR EVACUATION STANDARDS.—

(1) IN GENERAL. —Not later than 180 days after the completion of the study conducted under subsection (a), the

Administrator shall establish an aviation rulemaking committee (in this section referred to as the "Committee") to—

(A) review the findings of the study; and

(B) develop and submit to the Administrator recommendations regarding improvements to the evacuation standards described in parts 25 and 121 of title 14, Code of Federal Regulations.

(2) COMPOSITION.—The Committee shall consist of members appointed by the Administrator, including the following:

(A) Representatives of industry.

(B) Representatives of aviation labor organizations.

(C) Aviation safety experts with specific knowledge of the evacuation standards and requirements under such parts 25 and 121.

(D) Representatives of individuals with disabilities with specific knowledge of accessibility standards regarding evacuations in emergency circumstances.

(E) Representatives of the senior citizen community.

(F) Representatives of pediatricians.

(3) CONSIDERATIONS.—In reviewing the findings of the study conducted under subsection (a) and developing recommendations regarding the improvement of the evacuation standards under subsection (b)(1)(B), the Committee shall consider the following:

(A) The recommendations made by any prior aviation rulemaking committee regarding the evacuation standards described in such parts 25 and 121.

(B) Scientific data derived from the study conducted under subsection (a).

(C) Any data gathered from aviation safety reporting programs.

(D) The cost-benefit analysis and risk analysis of any recommended standards.

(E) Any other item determined appropriate by the Committee.

(c) REPORT TO CONGRESS.—Not later than 180 days after the

SEC. 366. [49 U.S.C. 44701 note] 25-HOUR
COCKPIT VOICE RECORDER.

FAA Reauthorization Act of 2

date on which the Committee submits to the Administrator the
recommendations under subsection (b)(1)(B), the Administrator
shall submit to the appropriate committees of Congress a report
on—

(1) the findings of the study conducted under subsection (a);

(2) the recommendations of the Committee under
subsection (b)(1)(B); and

(3) the Administrator's plan, if any, to implement such
recommendations.

(d) RULEMAKING. —Not later than 90 days after submitting to
Congress the report under subsection (c), the Administrator shall
issue a notice of proposed rulemaking to implement the
recommendations of the Committee that the Administrator
considers appropriate.

SEC. 366. [49 U.S.C. 44701 note] 25-HOUR COCKPIT VOICE
RECORDER.

(a) IN GENERAL.—

(1) COCKPIT VOICE RECORDER FOR NEWLY MANUFACTURED
AIRCRAFT.—A covered operator may not operate a covered
aircraft manufactured later than the date that is 1 year after
the date of enactment of this Act unless such aircraft has a
cockpit voice recorder installed that retains the last 25 hours of
recorded information using a recorder that meets the standards
of Technical Standard Order TSO-C123c, or any later revision.

(2) COCKPIT VOICE RECORDER FOR COVERED AIRCRAFT.—Not
later than 6 years after the date of enactment of this Act, a
covered operator may not operate a covered aircraft unless such
aircraft has a cockpit voice recorder installed that retains the
last 25 hours of recorded information using a recorder that
meets the standards of Technical Standard Order TSO-C123c,
or any later revision.

(b) PROHIBITED USE.—The Administrator or any covered
operator may not use a cockpit voice recorder recording for a
certificate action, civil penalty, or disciplinary proceedings against
a flight crewmember.

(c) RULEMAKING.—Not later than 3 years after the date of
enactment of this Act, the Administrator shall—

(1) issue a final rule to update applicable regulations, as

necessary, to conform to the requirements of subsection (a)(2); and

(2) issue a rule to update applicable regulations, as necessary, to ensure, to the greatest extent practicable, that any data from a cockpit voice recorder—

(A) is protected from unlawful or unauthorized disclosure to the public;

(B) is used exclusively by a Federal agency or a foreign accident investigative agency for a criminal investigation, aircraft accident, or aircraft incident investigation; and

(C) is not deliberately erased or tampered with following a National Transportation Safety Board reportable event under part 830 of title 49, Code of Federal Regulations, for which civil and criminal penalties may be assessed in accordance with section 1155 of title 49, United States Code, and section 32 of title 18, United States Code.

(d) SAVINGS CLAUSE.—Nothing in this section shall be construed as rescoping, constraining, or otherwise mandating delays to FAA actions in the notice of proposed rulemaking titled "25-Hour Cockpit Voice Recorder (CVR) Requirements, New Aircraft Production", issued on December 4, 2023 (88 Fed. Reg. 84090).

(e) RULE OF CONSTRUCTION.—Nothing in this section shall be construed to affect—

(1) the confidentiality of recording and transcripts under section 1114(c) of title 49, United States Code;

(2) the ban on recording for civil penalty or certificate under section 121.359(h) of title 14, Code of Federal Regulations; or

(3) the prohibition against use of data from flight operational quality assurance programs for enforcement purposes under section 13.401 of title 14, Code of Federal Regulations.

(f) DEFINITIONS.—In this section:

(1) COVERED AIRCRAFT.—The term "covered aircraft" means—

(A) an aircraft operated by an air carrier under part 121 of title 14, Code of Federal Regulations; or

(B) a transport category aircraft designed for operations by an air carrier or foreign air carrier type-certificated with a passenger seating capacity of 30 or more or an all-cargo or combi derivative of such an aircraft.

(2) COVERED OPERATOR.—The term "covered operator" means the operator of a covered aircraft.

SEC. 367. SENSE OF CONGRESS REGARDING MANDATED CONTENTS OF ONBOARD EMERGENCY MEDICAL KITS.

It is the sense of Congress that—

(1) a regularly scheduled panel of experts should reexamine and provide an updated list of mandated contents of onboard emergency medical kits that is thorough and practical, keeping passenger safety and well-being paramount; and

(2) such panel should consider including on the list of mandated contents of such medical kits, at a minimum, opioid overdose reversal medication.

SEC. 368. [49 U.S.C. 44701 note] PASSENGER AIRCRAFT FIRST AID AND EMERGENCY MEDICAL KIT EQUIPMENT AND TRAINING.

(a) IN GENERAL.—Not later than 2 years after the date of enactment of this Act, the Administrator shall issue a notice of proposed rulemaking regarding first aid and emergency medical kit equipment and training required for flight crewmembers, as provided in part 121 of title 14, Code of Federal Regulations, applicable to all certificate holders operating passenger aircraft under such part.

(b) CONSIDERATIONS.—In carrying out subsection (a), the Administrator shall consider—

(1) the benefits and costs (including the costs of flight diversions and emergency landings) of requiring any new medications or equipment necessary to be included in approved emergency medical kits;

(2) whether the contents of the emergency medical kits include, at a minimum, appropriate medications and equipment that can practicably be administered to address—

(A) the emergency medical needs of children and pregnant women;

(B) opioid overdose reversal;

(C) anaphylaxis; and

(D) cardiac arrest;

(3) what contents of the emergency medical kits should be readily available, to the extent practicable, for use by flight crews without prior approval by a medical professional.

(c) REGULAR REVIEW.—Not later than 5 years after the issuance of the final rule under subsection (a), and every 5 years thereafter, the Administrator shall evaluate and revise, if appropriate—

(1) the first aid and emergency medical kit equipment and training required for flight crewmembers; and

(2) any required training for flight crewmembers regarding the content, location, and function of such kit.

* * * * * * *

SEC. 372. [49 U.S.C. 44703 note] ENHANCED QUALIFICATION PROGRAM FOR RESTRICTED AIRLINE TRANSPORT PILOT CERTIFICATE.

(a) PROGRAM.—

(1) IN GENERAL.—Not later than 6 months after the date of enactment of this Act, the Administrator shall establish the requirements for a program to be known as the Enhanced Qualification Program (in this section referred to as the "Program") under which—

(A) qualified air carriers are certified by the Administrator to provide enhanced training for eligible pilots seeking to obtain restricted airline transport certificates, either directly by the air carrier or by a certified training institution under part 141 or part 142 of title 14, Code of Federal Regulations, that is under contract with the qualified air carrier; and

(B) qualified instructors and evaluators provide enhanced training to eligible pilots pursuant to the curriculum requirements under paragraph (4).

(2) QUALIFIED INSTRUCTORS AND EVALUATORS.—Under the Program—

(A) all testing and training shall be performed by qualified instructors; and

331

(B) all evaluations shall be performed by qualified evaluators.

(3) PILOT ASSESSMENT.—Under the Program, the Administrator shall establish guidelines for an assessment that prospective pilots are required to pass in order to participate in the training under the Program. Such assessment shall include an evaluation of the pilot's aptitude, ability, and readiness for operation of transport category aircraft.

(4) PROGRAM CURRICULUM.—Under the Program, the Administrator shall establish requirements for the curriculum to be provided under the Program. Such curriculum shall include—

(A) a nationally standardized, non-air carrier or aircraft-specific training curriculum which shall—

(i) ensure prospective pilots have appropriate knowledge at the commercial pilot certificate, multi-engine rating, and instrument rating level;

(ii) introduce the pilots to concepts associated with air carrier operations;

(iii) meet all requirements for an ATP Certification Training Program under part 61.156 or part 142 of title 14, Code of Federal Regulations; and

(iv) include a course of instruction designed to prepare the prospective pilot to take the ATP Multiengine Airplane Knowledge Test;

(B) an aircraft-specific training curriculum, developed by the air carrier using objectives and learning standards developed by the Administrator, which shall—

(i) only be administered to prospective pilots who have completed the requirements under subparagraph (A);

(ii) resemble a type rating training curriculum that includes aircraft ground and flight training that culminates in—

(I) the completion of a maneuvers evaluation that incorporates elements of a type rating practical test; or

(II) at the discretion of the air carrier, an

actual type rating practical test resulting in the issuance of a type rating for the specific aircraft; and

(iii) ensure the prospective pilot has an adequate understanding and working knowledge of transport category aircraft automation and autoflight systems; and

(C) air carrier-specific procedures using objectives and learning standards developed by the Administrator to further expand on the concepts described in subparagraphs (A) and (B), which shall—

(i) only be administered to prospective pilots who have completed requirements under subparagraphs (A) and (B) and an ATP Multiengine Airplane Knowledge Test;

(ii) include instructions on air carrier checklist usage and standard operating procedures; and

(iii) integrate aircraft-specific training in appropriate flight simulation training devices representing the specific aircraft type, including complete crew resource management and scenario-based training.

(5) APPLICATION AND CERTIFICATION.—Under the Program, the Administrator shall establish a process for air carriers to apply for training program certification. Such process shall include a review to ensure that the training provided by the air carrier will meet the requirements of this section, including—

(A) the assessment requirements under paragraph (3);

(B) the curriculum requirements under paragraph (4);

(C) the requirements for qualified instructors under subsection (d)(5); and

(D) the requirements for eligible pilots under subsection (d)(2).

(6) DATA.—Under the Program, the Administrator shall require that each qualified air carrier participating in the Program collect and submit to the Administrator such data from the Program that the Administrator determines is appropriate for the Administrator to provide for oversight of the

Program.

(7) REGULAR INSPECTION.—Under the Program, the Administrator shall provide for the regular inspection of qualified air carriers certified under paragraph (5) to ensure that the air carrier continues to meet the requirements under the Program.

(b) REGULATIONS.—The Administrator may issue regulations or guidance as determined necessary to carry out the Program.

(c) CLARIFICATION REGARDING REQUIRED FLIGHT HOURS.—The provisions of this section shall have no effect on the total flight hours required under part 61.159 of title 14, Code of Federal Regulations, to receive an airline transport pilot certificate, or the Administrator's authority under section 217(d) of the Airline Safety and Federal Aviation Administration Extension Act of 2010 (49 U.S.C. 44701 note) (as in effect on the date of enactment of this section).

(d) DEFINITIONS.—In this section:

(1) AIR CARRIER.—The term "air carrier" has the meaning given that term in section 40102 of title 49, United States Code.

(2) ELIGIBLE PILOT.—The term "eligible pilot" means a pilot that—

(A) has—

(i) graduated from a United States Armed Forces undergraduate pilot training school;

(ii) obtained a degree with an aviation major from an institution of higher education (as defined in part 61.1 of title 14, Code of Federal Regulations) that has been issued a letter of authorization by the Administrator under part 61.169 of such title 14; or

(iii) completed flight and ground training for a commercial pilot certificate in the airplane category and an airplane instrument rating at a certified training institution under part 141 of such title 14;

(B) has a current commercial pilot certificate under part 61.123 of such title 14, with airplane category multi-engine and instrument ratings under part 61.129 of such title 14; and

(C) meets the pilot assessment requirements under

subsection (a)(3).

(3) QUALIFIED AIR CARRIER.—The term "qualified air carrier" means an air carrier that has been issued a part 119 operating certificate for conducting operations under part 121 of title 14, Code of Federal Regulations.

(4) QUALIFIED EVALUATOR.—The term "qualified evaluator" means an individual that meets the requirements for a training center evaluator under part 142.55 of title 14, Code of Federal Regulations, or for check airmen under part 121.411 of such title.

(5) QUALIFIED INSTRUCTOR.—The term "qualified instructor" means an individual that—

(A) is qualified in accordance with the minimum training requirements for an ATP Certification Training Program under paragraphs (1) through (3) of part 121.410(b) of title 14, Code of Federal Regulations;

(B) if the instructor is a flight instructor, is qualified in accordance with part 121.410(b)(4) of such title;

(C) if the instructor is administering type rating practical tests, is qualified as an appropriate examiner for such rating;

(D) received training in threat and error management, facilitation, and risk mitigation determined appropriate by the Administrator; and

(E) meets any other requirement determined appropriate by the Administrator.

Subtitle B—Aviation Cybersecurity

SEC. 391. FINDINGS.

Congress finds the following:

(1) Congress has tasked the FAA with responsibility for securing the national airspace system, including the air traffic control system and other air navigation services, civil aircraft, and aeronautical products and articles through safety regulation and oversight. These mandates have included protecting against cyber threats affecting aviation safety or the Administration's provision of safe, secure, and efficient air

navigation services and airspace management.

(2) In 2016, Congress passed the FAA Extension, Safety, and Security Act of 2016, pursuant to which the FAA enhanced the cybersecurity of the national airspace system by—

(A) developing a cybersecurity strategic plan;

(B) coordinating with other Federal agencies to identify cyber vulnerabilities;

(C) developing a cyber threat model; and

(D) completing a comprehensive, strategic policy framework to identify and mitigate cybersecurity risks to the air traffic control system.

(3) In 2018, Congress passed the FAA Reauthorization Act of 2018 which—

(A) authorized funding for the construction of FAA facilities dedicated to improving the cybersecurity of the national airspace system;

(B) required the FAA to review and update its comprehensive, strategic policy framework for cybersecurity to assess the degree to which the framework identifies and addresses known cybersecurity risks associated with the aviation system, and evaluate existing short- and long-term objectives for addressing cybersecurity risks to the national airspace system;

(C) created a Chief Technology Officer position within the FAA to be responsible for, among other things, coordinating the implementation, operation, maintenance, and cybersecurity of technology programs relating to the air traffic control system with the aviation industry and other Federal agencies; and

(D) directed the National Academy of Sciences to study the cybersecurity workforce of the FAA in order to develop recommendations to increase the size, quality, and diversity of such workforce.

(4) Congress has declared that the FAA is the primary Federal agency to assess and address the threats posed from cyber incidents relating to FAA-provided air traffic control and air navigation services and the threats posed from cyber incidents relating to civil aircraft, aeronautical products and

articles, aviation networks, aviation systems, services, and operations, and the aerospace industry affecting aviation safety or the provision of safe, secure, and efficient air navigation services and airspace management by the Administration.

* * * * * * *

SEC. 395. [49 U.S.C. 40131 note] CIVIL AVIATION CYBERSECURITY RULEMAKING COMMITTEE.

(a) IN GENERAL.—Not later than 1 year after the date of enactment of this Act, the Administrator shall convene an aviation rulemaking committee on civil aircraft cybersecurity to conduct reviews (as segmented under subsection (c)) and develop findings and recommendations on cybersecurity standards for civil aircraft, aircraft ground support information systems, airports, air traffic control mission systems, and aeronautical products and articles.

(b) DUTIES.—The Administrator shall—

(1) for each segmented review conducted by the committee convened under subsection (a), submit to the appropriate committees of Congress a report based on the findings of such review; and

(2) not later than 180 days after the date of submission of a report under paragraph (1) and, in consultation with other agencies as the Administrator determines necessary, for consensus recommendations reached by such aviation rulemaking committee—

(A) undertake a rulemaking, if appropriate, based on such recommendations; and

(B) submit to the appropriate committees of Congress a supplemental report with explanations for each consensus recommendation not addressed, if applicable, by a rulemaking under subparagraph (A).

(c) SEGMENTATION.—In tasking the aviation rulemaking committee with developing findings and recommendations relating to aviation cybersecurity, the Administrator shall direct such committee to segment and sequence work by the topic or subject matter of regulation, including by directing the committee to establish subgroups to consider different topics and subject matters.

(d) COMPOSITION.—The aviation rulemaking committee

convened under subsection (a) shall consist of members appointed by the Administrator, including representatives of—

(1) aircraft manufacturers, to include at least 1 manufacturer of transport category aircraft;

(2) air carriers;

(3) unmanned aircraft system stakeholders, including operators, service suppliers, and manufacturers of hardware components and software applications;

(4) manufacturers of powered-lift aircraft;

(5) airports;

(6) original equipment manufacturers of ground and space-based aviation infrastructure;

(7) aviation safety experts with specific knowledge of aircraft cybersecurity; and

(8) a nonprofit which operates 1 or more federally funded research and development centers with specific knowledge of aviation and cybersecurity.

(e) MEMBER ELIGIBILITY.—Prior to a member's appointment under subsection (c), the Administrator shall establish appropriate requirements related to nondisclosure, background investigations, security clearances, or other screening mechanisms for applicable members of the aviation rulemaking committee who require access to sensitive security information or other protected information relevant to the member's duties on the rulemaking committee. Members shall protect the sensitive security information in accordance with part 1520 of title 49, Code of Federal Regulations.

(f) PROHIBITION ON COMPENSATION.—The members of the aviation rulemaking committee convened under subsection (a) shall not receive pay, allowances, or benefits from the Government by reason of their service on such committee.

(g) CONSIDERATIONS.—The Administrator may direct such committee to consider—

(1) existing aviation cybersecurity standards, regulations, policies, and guidance, including those from other Federal agencies, and the need to harmonize or deconflict proposed and existing standards, regulations, policies, and guidance;

(2) threat- and risk-based security approaches used by the aviation industry, including the assessment of the potential

costs and benefits of cybersecurity actions;

(3) data gathered from cybersecurity or safety reporting;

(4) the diversity of operations and systems on aircraft and amongst air carriers;

(5) design approval holder aircraft network security guidance for operators;

(6) FAA services, aviation industry services, and aircraft use of positioning, navigation, and timing data in the context of Executive Order No. 13905, as in effect on the date of enactment of this Act;

(7) updates needed to airworthiness regulations and systems safety assessment methods used to show compliance with airworthiness requirements for design, function, installation, and certification of civil aircraft, aeronautical products and articles, and aircraft networks;

(8) updates needed to air carrier operating and maintenance regulations to ensure continued adherence with processes and procedures established in airworthiness regulations to provide cybersecurity protections for aircraft systems, including for continued airworthiness;

(9) policies and procedures to coordinate with other Federal agencies, including intelligence agencies, and the aviation industry in sharing information and analyses related to cyber threats to civil aircraft information, data, networks, systems, services, operations, and technology and aeronautical products and articles;

(10) the response of the Administrator and aviation industry to, and recovery from, cyber incidents, including by coordinating with other Federal agencies, including intelligence agencies;

(11) processes for members of the aviation industry to voluntarily report to the FAA cyber incidents that may affect aviation safety in a manner that protects trade secrets and confidential business information;

(12) appropriate cybersecurity controls for aircraft networks, aircraft systems, and aeronautical products and articles to protect aviation safety, including airworthiness;

(13) appropriate cybersecurity controls for airports relative

to the size and nature of airside operations of such airports to ensure aviation safety;

(14) minimum standards for protecting civil aircraft, aeronautical products and articles, aviation networks, aviation systems, services, and operations from cyber threats and cyber incidents;

(15) international collaboration, where appropriate and consistent with the interests of aviation safety in air commerce and national security, with other civil aviation authorities, international aviation and standards organizations, and any other appropriate entities to protect civil aviation from cyber incidents and cyber threats;

(16) activities of the Administrator under section 506 of the FAA Reauthorization Act of 2018 (49 U.S.C. 44704 note) (as amended by section 394); and

(17) any other matter the Administrator determines appropriate.

(h) DEFINITIONS.—The definitions set forth in section 40131 of title 49, United States Code (as added by this subtitle), shall apply to this section.

* * * * * * *

TITLE IV—AEROSPACE WORKFORCE

* * * * * * *

SEC. 402. [49 U.S.C. 44703 note] CIVIL AIRMEN STATISTICS.

(a) PUBLICATION FREQUENCY.—The Administrator shall publish the study commonly referred to as the "U.S. Civil Airmen Statistics" on a monthly basis.

(b) PRESENTATION OF DATA.—The Administrator shall make the data from the study under subsection (a) publicly available on the website of the Administration in a user-friendly, downloadable format.

(c) EXPANDED DATA CRITERIA.—Not later than 1 year after the date of enactment of this Act, the Administrator shall ensure that data sets and tables published as part of the study described in subsection (a) display information relating to the sex of certificate holders in more instances.

(d) HISTORICAL DATA.—Not later than 1 year after the date of
enactment of this Act, the Administrator shall make all previously
published annual data from the study described in subsection (a)
available on the website of the Administration.

SEC. 403. BESSIE COLEMAN WOMEN IN AVIATION ADVISORY
COMMITTEE.

(a) ESTABLISHMENT.—Not later than 6 months after the date
of enactment of this Act, the Secretary shall establish the Bessie
Coleman Women in Aviation Advisory Committee (in this section
referred to as the "Committee").

(b) PURPOSE.—The Committee shall advise the Secretary and
the Administrator on matters and policies related to promoting
the recruitment, retention, employment, education, training, career
advancement, and well-being of women in the aviation industry and
aviation-focused Federal civil service positions.

(c) FORM OF DIRECTIVES.—All activities carried out by the
Committee, including special committees, shall be in response to
written terms of work from the Secretary or taskings approved
by a majority of the voting members of the Committee and may
not duplicate the objectives of the Air Carrier Training Aviation
Rulemaking Committee.

(d) FUNCTIONS.—In carrying out the directives described in
subsection (c), the functions of the Committee are as follows:

(1) Foster industry collaboration in an open and
transparent manner by engaging, as prescribed by this section,
with representatives of the private sector associated with an
entity described in subsection (e)(1)(B).

(2) Make recommendations for strategic objectives,
priorities, and policies that would improve the recruitment,
retention, training, and career advancement of women in
aviation professions.

(3) Evaluate opportunities for the Administration to
improve the recruitment and retention of women in the
Administration.

(4) Periodically review and update the recommendations
directed to the FAA and non-FAA entities produced by the
Advisory Board created pursuant to section 612 of the FAA

Reauthorization Act of 2018 (49 U.S.C. 40101 note) to improve the implementation of such recommendations.

(5) Coordinate with the Office of Civil Rights of the Department of Transportation and the Federal Women's Program of the FAA to ensure directives described in subsection (c) do not duplicate objectives of such office or program.

(e) MEMBERSHIP.—

(1) VOTING MEMBERS.—The Committee shall be composed of the following members:

(A) The Administrator, or the designee of the Administrator.

(B) At least 25 individuals, appointed by the Secretary, representing the following:

(i) Aircraft manufacturers and aerospace companies.

(ii) Public and private aviation labor organizations, including collective bargaining representatives of—

(I) aviation safety inspectors and safety engineers of the FAA;

(II) air traffic controllers;

(III) certified aircraft maintenance technicians; and

(IV) commercial airline crewmembers.

(iii) General aviation operators.

(iv) Air carriers.

(v) Business aviation operators, including powered-lift operators.

(vi) Unmanned aircraft systems operators.

(vii) Aviation safety management experts.

(viii) Aviation maintenance, repair, and overhaul entities.

(ix) Airport owners, operators, and employees.

(x) Institutions of higher education (as defined in section 101 of the Higher Education Act of 1965 (20 U.S.C. 1001)), a postsecondary vocational institution (as defined in section 102(c) of the Higher Education Act of 1965 (20 U.S.C. 1002)), or a high school or secondary school (as such terms are defined in section 8101 of the Elementary and Secondary Education Act of 1965 (20 U.S.C. 7801)).

(xi) A flight school that provides flight training, as defined in part 61 of title 14, Code of Federal Regulations, or that holds a pilot school certificate under part 141 of title 14, Code of Federal Regulations.

(xii) Aviation maintenance technician schools governed under part 147 of title 14, Code of Federal Regulations.

(xiii) Engineering business associations.

(xiv) Civil Air Patrol.

(xv) Nonprofit organizations within the aviation industry.

(2) NONVOTING MEMBERS.—

(A) IN GENERAL.—In addition to the members appointed under paragraph (1), the Committee shall be composed of not more than 5 nonvoting members appointed by the Secretary from among officers or employees of the FAA, at least 1 of which shall be an employee of the Office of Civil Rights of the FAA.

(B) ADDITIONAL NONVOTING MEMBERS.—The Secretary may invite representatives from the Department of Education and Department of Labor to serve as nonvoting members on the Committee.

(C) DUTIES.—The nonvoting members may—

(i) take part in deliberations of the Committee; and

(ii) provide subject matter expertise with respect to reports and recommendations of the Committee.

(D) LIMITATION.—The nonvoting members may not represent any stakeholder interest other than that of the respective Federal agency of the member.

(3) TERMS.—Each voting member and nonvoting member of the Committee appointed by the Secretary shall be appointed for a term that expires not later than the date on which the

authorization of the Committee expires under subsection (k).

(4) COMMITTEE CHARACTERISTICS.—The Committee shall have the following characteristics:

(A) The ability to obtain necessary information from additional experts in the aviation and aerospace communities.

(B) A membership that enables the Committee to have substantive discussions and reach consensus on issues in a timely manner.

(C) Appropriate expertise, including expertise in human resources, human capital management, policy, labor relations, employment training, workforce development, and youth outreach.

(5) DATE.—Not later than 9 months after the date of enactment of this Act, the Secretary shall make the appointments described in this subsection.

(f) CHAIRPERSON.—

(1) IN GENERAL.—The Committee shall select a chairperson from among the voting members of the Committee.

(2) TERM.—The Chairperson shall serve a 2-year term.

(g) MEETINGS.—

(1) FREQUENCY.—The Committee shall meet at least twice each year at the call of the Chairperson or the Secretary.

(2) PUBLIC ATTENDANCE.—The meetings of the Committee shall be open and accessible to the public.

(3) ADMINISTRATIVE SUPPORT.—The Secretary shall furnish the Committee with logistical and administrative support to enable the Committee to perform the duties of the Committee.

(h) SPECIAL COMMITTEES.—

(1) ESTABLISHMENT.—The Committee may establish special committees composed of industry representatives, members of the public, labor representatives, and other relevant parties in complying with the consultation and participation requirements under subsection (d).

(2) APPLICABLE LAW.—Chapter 10 of title 5, United States Code, shall not apply to a special committee established by the Committee.

(i) PERSONNEL MATTERS.—

(1) NO COMPENSATION OF MEMBERS.—

(A) NON-FEDERAL EMPLOYEES.—A member of the Committee who is not an officer or employee of the Government shall serve without compensation.

(B) FEDERAL EMPLOYEES.—A member of the Committee who is an officer or employee of the Federal Government shall serve without compensation in addition to the compensation received for the services of the member as an officer or employee of the Federal Government.

(2) DEATH OR RESIGNATION.—If a member of the Committee dies or resigns during the term of service of such member, the Secretary shall designate a successor for the unexpired term of such member.

(j) REPORTS.—

(1) TASK REPORTS.—The Committee shall submit to the Secretary and the appropriate committees of Congress annual reports detailing the completion of each directive summarizing the—

(A) findings and associated recommendations of the Committee for any legislative and administrative actions the Committee considers appropriate to improve the advancement of women in aviation; and

(B) planned activities of the Committee, as directed by the Secretary or approved by a majority of voting members of the Committee, and proposed terms of work to fulfill each activity.

(2) ADDITIONAL REPORTS.—The Committee may submit to the appropriate committees of Congress, the Secretary, and the Administrator additional reports and recommendations related to education, training, recruitment, retention, and advancement of women in the aviation industry as the Committee determines appropriate.

(k) SUNSET.—The authorization of the Committee shall expire on October 1, 2028.

SEC. 404. [49 U.S.C. 106 note] FAA ENGAGEMENT AND COLLABORATION WITH HBCUS AND MSIS.

(a) IN GENERAL.—The Administrator—

(1) shall continue—

(A) to partner with and conduct outreach to Historically Black Colleges and Universities and minority serving institutions to promote awareness of educational and career opportunities, including the Educational Partnership Initiative of the FAA, and develop curriculum related to aerospace, aviation, and air traffic control; and

(B) operation of the Minority Serving Institutions Internship Program; and

(2) may—

(A) make internship placements under the Minority Serving Institutions Internship Program available during academic sessions throughout the year; and

(B) extend an internship placement under the Minority Serving Institutions Internship Program for a student beyond a single academic session.

(b) PROGRAM DATA.—In carrying out the Minority Serving Institutions Internship Program, the Administrator shall track data, including annual metrics measuring the following with respect to such Program:

(1) The total number of applicants.

(2) The total number of applicants offered an internship and the total number of applicants who accept an internship.

(3) The line of business in which each intern is placed.

(4) The conversion rate of interns in the Program who are hired as full-time FAA employees.

(c) MINORITY SERVING INSTITUTION DEFINED.—In this section, the term "minority serving institution" means an institution described in paragraphs (1) through (7) of section 371(a) of the Higher Education Act of 1965 (20 U.S.C. 1067q(a)).

* * * * * * *

SEC. 406. AIRMAN CERTIFICATION STANDARDS.

(a) IN GENERAL.—The Administrator shall use the Aviation Rulemaking Advisory Committee Airman Certification System Working Group (in this section referred to as the "Working Group")

SEC. 407. [49 U.S.C. 44703 note] AIRMAN'S
MEDICAL BILL OF RIGHTS.

FAA Reauthorization Act of 2024

to review airman certification standards and ensure that airman proficiency and knowledge correlates and corresponds to regulations, procedures, equipment, aviation infrastructure, and safety trends at the time of such review.

(b) DUTIES.—In carrying out subsection (a), the Working Group shall—

(1) obtain industry recommendations on maintaining and updating airman certification standards, including guidance documents and airman tests;

(2) ensure tasks carried out by the Working Group are addressed and completed in a timely and efficient manner; and

(3) recommend to the Administrator a means by which the FAA may communicate to industry the process for establishing, updating, and maintaining airman certification standards, including relevant guidance documents, handbooks, and airman test materials.

SEC. 407. [49 U.S.C. 44703 note] AIRMAN'S MEDICAL BILL OF RIGHTS.

(a) IN GENERAL.—

(1) DEVELOPMENT.—Not later than 1 year after the date of enactment of this Act, the Administrator shall develop a document (in this section referred to as the "Airman's Medical Bill of Rights") detailing the rights of an individual before, during, and after a medical examination conducted by an Aviation Medical Examiner.

(2) CONTENTS.—The Airman's Medical Bill of Rights required under paragraph (1) shall, at a minimum, contain information about the right of an individual to—

(A) bring a trusted companion or request to have a chaperone present for a medical examination;

(B) terminate an exam in accordance with guidelines from the Administrator for appropriately terminating such exam;

(C) receive medical examination with respect and recognition of the dignity of the individual;

(D) be assured of privacy and confidentiality;

(E) select an Aviation Medical Examiner of the choice

SEC. 407. [49 U.S.C. 44703 note] AIRMAN'S
MEDICAL BILL OF RIGHTS.

FAA Reauthorization Act of 2

of the individual, as long as the Aviation Medical Examiner has the required designations;

(F) privacy when changing, undressing, and using the restroom;

(G) ask questions about FAA medical standards and the applicability to the current health status of the individual;

(H) report an incident of misconduct by an Aviation Medical Examiner to the appropriate authorities, including to the State licensing board of the Aviation Medical Examiner or the FAA;

(I) report to the Administrator an allegation regarding alleged Aviation Medical Examiner misconduct without fear of retaliation or negative action relating to an airman certificate of the individual; and

(J) be advised of any known conflicts of interest an Aviation Medical Examiner may have with respect to the medical examination of the individual.

(3) PUBLIC AVAILABILITY.—The Airman's Medical Bill of Rights required under paragraph (1) shall be—

(A) made available to, and acknowledged by, an individual in the MedXpress system (or any successor system);

(B) made available in a hard-copy format by an Aviation Medical Examiner at the time of exam upon request by an individual; and

(C) displayed in a common space in the office of the Aviation Medical Examiner.

(b) EXPECTATIONS FOR MEDICAL EXAMINATIONS.—

(1) IN GENERAL.—Not later than 1 year after the date of enactment of this Act, the Administrator shall develop a simplified document explaining the standard procedures performed during a medical examination conducted by an Aviation Medical Examiner.

(2) PUBLIC AVAILABILITY.—The document required under paragraph (1) shall be—

(A) made available to, and acknowledged by, an individual in the MedXpress system (or any successor system);

(B) made available in a hard-copy format by an
Aviation Medical Examiner at the time of exam upon
request by an individual; and

(C) displayed in a common space in the office of the
Aviation Medical Examiner.

SEC. 408. [49 U.S.C. 44703 note] IMPROVED DESIGNEE
MISCONDUCT REPORTING PROCESS.

(a) IMPROVED DESIGNEE MISCONDUCT REPORTING PROCESS.—

(1) IN GENERAL.—Not later than 1 year after the date of
enactment of this Act, the Administrator shall establish a
streamlined process for individuals involved in incidents of
alleged misconduct by a designee to report such incidents in
a manner that protects the privacy and confidentiality of such
individuals.

(2) PUBLIC ACCESS TO REPORTING PROCESS.—The process
for reporting alleged misconduct by a designee shall be made
available to the public on the website of the Administration,
including—

(A) the designee locator search webpage; and

(B) the webpage of the Office of Audit and Evaluation
of the FAA.

(3) OBLIGATION TO REPORT CRIMINAL CHARGES.—Not later
than 90 days after the date of enactment of this Act, the
Administrator shall revise the orders and policies governing
the Designee Management System to clarify that designees are
obligated to report any arrest, indictment, or conviction for
violation of a local, State, or Federal law within a period of time
specified by the Administrator.

(4) AUDIT OF REPORTING PROCESS BY INSPECTOR GENERAL.—

(A) IN GENERAL.—Not later than 3 years after the date
on which the Administrator finalizes the update of the
reporting process under paragraph (1), the inspector
general of the Department of Transportation shall conduct
an audit of such reporting process.

(B) CONTENTS.—In conducting the audit of the
reporting process described in subparagraph (A), the

SEC. 410. [49 U.S.C. 44516 note] HUMAN
FACTORS PROFESSIONALS.

FAA Reauthorization Act of

inspector general shall, at a minimum—

(i) review the efforts of the Administration to improve the reporting process and solutions developed to respond to and investigate allegations of misconduct;

(ii) analyze reports of misconduct brought to the Administrator prior to any changes made to the reporting process as a result of the enactment of this Act, including the ultimate outcomes of those reports and whether any reports resulted in the Administrator taking action against the accused designee;

(iii) determine whether the reporting process results in appropriate action, including reviewing, investigating, and closing out reports; and

(iv) if applicable, make recommendations to improve the reporting process.

(C) REPORT.—Not later than 1 year after the date of initiation of the audit described in subparagraph (A), the inspector general shall submit to the appropriate committees of Congress a report on the results of such audit, including findings and recommendations.

(b) DESIGNEE DEFINED.—In this section, the term "designee" means an individual who has been designated to act as a representative of the Administrator as—

(1) an Aviation Medical Examiner (as described in section 183.21 of title 14, Code of Federal Regulations);

(2) a pilot examiner (as described in section 183.23 of such title); or

(3) a technical personnel examiner (as described in section 183.25 of such title).

* * * * * * *

SEC. 410. [49 U.S.C. 44516 note] HUMAN FACTORS PROFESSIONALS.
The Administrator shall take such actions as may be necessary to establish a new work code for human factors professionals who—

(1) perform work involving the design and testing of technologies, processes, and systems which require effective and safe human performance;

(2) generate and apply theories, principles, practical concepts, systems, and processes related to the design and testing of technologies, systems, and training programs to support and evaluate human performance in work contexts; and

(3) meet education or experience requirements as determined by the Administrator.

SEC. 411. [49 U.S.C. 44703 note] AEROMEDICAL INNOVATION AND MODERNIZATION WORKING GROUP.

(a) ESTABLISHMENT.—Not later than 180 days after the date of enactment of this Act, the Administrator shall establish a working group (in this section referred to as the "working group") to review the medical processes, policies, and procedures of the Administration and to make recommendations to the Administrator on modernizing such processes, policies, and procedures to ensure timely and efficient certification of airmen.

(b) MEMBERSHIP.—

(1) IN GENERAL.—The working group shall consist of—

(A) 2 co-chairs described in paragraph (2); and

(B) not less than 15 individuals appointed by the Administrator, each of whom shall have knowledge or a background in aerospace medicine, psychiatry, neurology, cardiology, or internal medicine.

(2) CO-CHAIRS.—The working group shall be co-chaired by—

(A) the Federal Air Surgeon of the FAA; and

(B) a member described under paragraph (1)(A) to be selected by members of the working group.

(3) PREFERENCE.—The Administrator, in appointing members pursuant to paragraph (1)(B), shall give preference to—

(A) Aviation Medical Examiners (as described in section 183.21 of title 14, Code of Federal Regulations);

(B) licensed medical physicians;

(C) practitioners holding a pilot certificate; and

(D) individuals having demonstrated research and expertise in aeromedical research or sciences.

(c) ACTIVITIES.—In reviewing the aeromedical decision-making processes, policies, and procedures of the Administration in accordance with subsection (a), the working group, at a minimum, shall—

(1) assess the medical conditions an Aviation Medical Examiner may issue a medical certificate directly to an individual;

(2) determine the appropriateness of the list of such medical conditions as of the date of enactment of this Act;

(3) assess the special issuance process;

(4) determine the appropriateness of whether a renewal of a special issuance can be based on a medical evaluation and treatment plan by the treating medical specialist of the individual pursuant to approval from an Aviation Medical Examiner;

(5) evaluate advancements in technologies to address forms of red-green color blindness and determine whether such technologies may be approved for use by airmen;

(6) review policies and guidance relating to Attention-Deficit Hyperactivity Disorder and Attention Deficit Disorder;

(7) evaluate whether medications used to treat such disorders may be safely prescribed to airmen;

(8) review protocols pertaining to the Human Intervention Motivation Study of the FAA;

(9) review protocols and policies relating to—

(A) neurological disorders; and

(B) cardiovascular conditions to ensure alignment with medical best practices, latest research;

(10) review mental health protocols and medications approved for treating such mental health conditions, including such actions taken resulting from recommendations by the Mental Health and Aviation Medical Clearances Rulemaking Committee;

(11) assess processes and protocols pertaining to recertification of airmen receiving disability insurance post-recovery from the medical condition, injury, or disability that precludes airmen from exercising the privileges of an airman certificate;

(12) assess processes and protocols pertaining to the certification of veterans reporting a disability rating from the Department of Veterans Affairs; and

(13) assess and evaluate the user interface and information-sharing capabilities of any online medical portal administered by the FAA.

(d) AVIATION WORKFORCE MENTAL HEALTH TASK GROUP.—

(1) ESTABLISHMENT.—Not later than 120 days after the working group pursuant to subsection (a) is established, the co-chairs of such working group shall establish an aviation workforce mental health task group (referred to in this subsection as the "task group") to oversee, monitor, and evaluate efforts of the Administrator related to supporting the mental health of the aviation workforce.

(2) COMPOSITION.—The co-chairs of such working group shall appoint—

(A) a Chair of the task group; and

(B) members of the task group from among the members of the working group appointed by the Administrator under subsection (b)(1).

(3) DUTIES.—The duties of the task group shall include—

(A) carrying out the activities described in subsection (c)(10);

(B) soliciting feedback from aviation industry professionals or other licensed professionals representing air carrier operations under part 121 and part 135 of title 14, Code of Federal Regulations, and general aviation operations under part 91 of title 14, Code of Federal Regulations;

(C) reviewing and evaluating guidance issued by the International Civil Aviation Organization on aviation workforce mental health;

(D) providing advice, as appropriate, on the implementation of the final recommendations issued by the inspector general of the Department of Transportation in the report titled, "FAA Conduct Comprehensive Evaluations of Pilots With Mental Health Challenges, but Opportunities Exist to Further Mitigate Safety Risks", published on July 12, 2023 (AV2023038);

(E) monitoring and evaluating the implementation of recommendations by the Mental Health and Aviation Medical Clearances Rulemaking Committee;

(F) expanding and improving mental health outreach, education, and assistance programs for the aviation workforce; and

(G) reducing the stigma associated with mental healthcare in the aviation workforce.

(4) REPORT.—Not later than 2 years after the date of the establishment of the task group, the task group shall submit to the Secretary and the appropriate committees of Congress a report detailing—

(A) the results of the review under paragraph (3)(A); and

(B) progress on the implementation of recommendations pursuant to subparagraphs (D) and (E) of paragraph (3); and

(C) the activities carried out pursuant to fulfilling the duties described in subparagraphs (F) and (G) of paragraph (3).

(e) SUPPORT.—The Administrator shall seek to enter into 1 or more agreements with the National Academies to support the activities of the working group described in subsection (c).

(f) FINDINGS AND RECOMMENDATIONS.—Not later than 1 year after the date of enactment of this Act, and annually thereafter, the working group shall submit to the Administrator and the appropriate committees of Congress a report on the findings and recommendations resulting from the activities carried out under subsection (c).

(g) IMPLEMENTATION.—Not later than 1 year after receiving recommendations outlined in the report under subsection (f), the Administrator may take such action, as appropriate, to implement such recommendations.

(h) SUNSET.—The working group shall terminate on October 1, 2028.

* * * * * * *

SEC. 413. [49 U.S.C. 44703 note] MEDICAL PORTAL MODERNIZATION TASK GROUP.

(a) ESTABLISHMENT.— Not later than 120 days after the working group pursuant to section 411 is established, the co-chairs of such working group shall establish a medical portal modernization task group (in this section referred to as the "task group") to evaluate the user interface and information sharing capabilities of an online medical portal administered by the FAA.

(b) COMPOSITION.— The co-chairs of the working group provided for in section 411 shall appoint—

(1) a Chair of the task group; and

(2) members of the task group from among the members of the working group appointed by the Administrator under section 411(b).

(c) ASSESSMENT; RECOMMENDATIONS.— The task group shall, at a minimum, assess and evaluate the capabilities of any such medical portal and provide recommendations to improve the following:

(1) The cybersecurity protections and protocols of any such medical portal, including the secure exchange of health information and records between Aviation Medical Examiners and pilots, or their designee, including the ability for airmen to submit additional information requested by the Administrator.

(2) The status of an airman's medical application and the disclosure of how long an airman can expect to wait for a final determination to be issued by the Administrator.

(3) The disclosure of the name and contact information of the Administrator's representative managing an airman's case so that an Aviation Medical Examiner has a point of contact within the Administration who is familiar with an airman's application.

(d) CONSULTATION.— In carrying out the duties described in subsection (c), the task group may consult with cybersecurity experts and individuals with a knowledge of securing electronic health care transactions.

(e) REPORT.— Not later than 1 year after the date of the establishment of the task group, the task group shall submit to the Administrator and the appropriate committees of Congress a report detailing activities and recommendations of the task group.

(f) IMPLEMENTATION.—Not later than 1 year after receiving the report described in subsection (e), the Administrator may take such action as may be necessary to implement recommendations of the task group to improve any such medical portal.

* * * * * * *

SEC. 415. [49 U.S.C. 44506 note] IMPROVED ACCESS TO AIR TRAFFIC CONTROL SIMULATION TRAINING.

(a) IN GENERAL.—The Administrator shall continue making tower simulator systems (in this section referred to as "TSS") more accessible to all air traffic controller specialists assigned to an air traffic control tower of the FAA (in this section referred to as an "ATCT"), regardless of facility assignment.

(b) CLOUD-BASED VISUAL DATABASE AND SOFTWARE SYSTEM.—Not later than 30 months after the date of enactment of this Act, the Administrator shall develop and implement a cloud-based visual database and software system that is compatible with existing and future TSS that, at a minimum, includes—

(1) the unique runway layout, approach paths, and lines of sight of every ATCT; and

(2) specifications that meet all applicable data security requirements.

(c) TSS UPGRADES.—Not later than 2 years after the date of enactment of this Act, the Administrator shall upgrade existing, permanent TSS so that the TSS is, at a minimum, capable of—

(1) securely and quickly downloading data from the cloud-based visual database and software system described in subsection (b); and

(2) running scenarios for each ATCT involving differing levels of air traffic volume and varying complexities, including, aircraft emergencies, rapidly changing weather, issuance of safety alerts, special air traffic procedures for events of national or international significance, and recovering from unforeseen events or losses of separation.

(d) MOBILE TSS.—Not later than 4 years after the date of enactment of this Act, the Administrator shall acquire and implement mobile TSS at each ATCT that is without an existing, permanent TSS so that the mobile TSS is capable of, at a minimum, the capabilities described in paragraphs (1) and (2) of subsection (c).

(e) COLLABORATION.—In carrying out this section, the Administrator may collaborate with the exclusive bargaining representative of air traffic controllers certified under section 7111 of title 5, United States Code.

* * * * * * *

SEC. 418. [49 U.S.C. 40132 note] PILOT PROGRAM TO PROVIDE VETERANS WITH PILOT TRAINING SERVICES.

(a) IN GENERAL.—The Secretary, in consultation with the Secretary of Education and the Secretary of Veterans Affairs, shall establish a pilot program to provide grants to eligible entities to provide pilot training activities and related education to support a pathway for veterans to become commercial aviators.

(b) ELIGIBLE ENTITY.—In this section, the term "eligible entity" means a pilot school or provisional pilot school that—

(1) holds an Air Agency Certificate under part 141 of title 14, Code of Federal Regulations; and

(2) has an established employment pathway with at least 1 air carrier operating under part 121 or 135 of title 14, Code of Federal Regulations.

(c) PRIORITY APPLICATION.—In selecting eligible entities under this section, the Secretary shall prioritize eligible entities that meet the following criteria:

(1) An eligible entity accredited (as defined in section 61.1 of title 14, Code of Federal Regulations) by an accrediting agency recognized by the Secretary of Education.

(2) An eligible entity that holds a letter of authorization issued in accordance with section 61.169 of title 14, Code of Federal Regulations.

(d) USE OF FUNDS.—Amounts from a grant received by an eligible entity under the pilot program established under subsection (a) shall be used for the following:

(1) Administrative costs related to implementation of the program described in subsection (a) not to exceed 5 percent of the amount awarded.

(2) To provide guidance and pilot training services, including tuition and flight training fees for veterans enrolled

with an eligible entity, to support such veterans in obtaining any of the following pilot certificates and ratings:

(A) Private pilot certificate with airplane single-engine or multi-engine ratings.

(B) Instrument rating.

(C) Commercial pilot certificate with airplane single-engine or multi-engine ratings.

(D) Multi-engine rating.

(E) Certificated flight instructor single-engine certificate, if applicable to the degree sought.

(F) Certificated flight instructor multi-engine certificate, if applicable to the degree sought.

(G) Certificated flight instructor instrument certificate, if applicable to the degree sought.

(3) To provide educational materials, training materials, and equipment to support pilot training activities and related education for veterans enrolled with the eligible entity.

(4) To provide periodic reports to the Secretary on use of the grant funds, including documentation of training completion of the certificates and ratings described in subparagraphs (A) through (G) of paragraph (2).

(e) AWARD AMOUNT LIMIT.—An award granted to an eligible entity shall not exceed more than $750,000 in any given fiscal year.

(f) APPROPRIATIONS.—To carry out this section, there is authorized to be appropriated $5,000,000 for each of fiscal years 2025 through 2028.

SEC. 419. [49 U.S.C. 44720 note] PROVIDING NON-FEDERAL WEATHER OBSERVER TRAINING TO AIRPORT PERSONNEL.

The Administrator may take such actions as are necessary to provide training that is easily accessible and streamlined for airport personnel to become certified as non-Federal weather observers so that such personnel can manually provide weather observations in any case in which automated surface observing systems and automated weather observing systems experience outages and errors to ensure operational safety at airports.

* * * * * * *

SEC. 424. SENSE OF CONGRESS ON IMPROVING UNMANNED AIRCRAFT SYSTEM STAFFING AT FAA.

It is the sense of Congress that the Administrator should leverage the Unmanned Aircraft System Collegiate Training Initiative to address any staffing challenges and skills gaps within the FAA to support efforts to facilitate the safe integration of unmanned aircraft systems and other new airspace entrants into the national airspace system.

SEC. 425. JOINT AVIATION EMPLOYMENT TRAINING WORKING GROUP.

(a) ESTABLISHMENT.—Not later than 120 days after the date of enactment of this Act, the Secretary shall establish an interagency working group (in this section referred to as the "working group") to advise the Secretary and the Secretary of Defense on matters and policies related to increasing awareness of the eligibility, training, and experience requirements needed to become an FAA-certified or a military-covered aviation professional in order to improve career transitions between the military and civilian workforces.

(b) MEMBERSHIP.—

(1) IN GENERAL.—The working group shall consist of—

(A) 2 co-chairs described in paragraph (2);

(B) not less than 6 representatives of the FAA, to be appointed by the co-chair described in paragraph (2)(A); and

(C) not less than 1 representative of each component of the armed forces (as such term is defined in section 101 of title 10, United States Code), to be appointed by the co-chair described in paragraph (2)(B).

(2) CO-CHAIRS.—The working group shall be co-chaired by—

(A) a representative of the Department of Transportation, to be appointed by the Secretary; and

(B) a representative of the Department of Defense, to be appointed by the Secretary of Defense.

(c) ACTIVITIES.—The working group shall—

(1) evaluate and compare all eligibility, training, and experience requirements for individuals interested in becoming

FAA-certified, or serving in the armed forces, as covered aviation professionals, including agency policies, guidance, and orders affecting covered aviation professionals;

(2) identify challenges that inhibit recruitment, training, and retention within the respective workforces of such professionals;

(3) assess methods to improve outreach, engagement, and awareness of eligibility, training, and experience requirements needed to enter careers of covered aviation professionals;

(4) consult with representatives from nonprofit organizations supporting veterans and representatives from aviation industry organizations representing covered aviation professionals in the development of recommendations required pursuant to subsection (d)(2)(B); and

(5) identify opportunities for increased interagency information sharing across workforces on matters related to certification pathways, including knowledge testing, affecting covered aviation professionals.

(d) INITIAL REPORT TO CONGRESS.—

(1) IN GENERAL.—Not later than 1 year after the date on which the Secretary establishes the working group, the working group shall submit to the covered committees of Congress an initial report on the activities of the working group.

(2) CONTENTS.—The report required under paragraph (1) shall include—

(A) a detailed description of the findings of the working group pursuant to the activities required under subsection (c), including feedback offered by representatives described in subsection (c)(4); and

(B) recommendations for regulatory, policy, or legislative action to improve awareness of the eligibility, training, and experience requirements needed to become FAA-certified or military-covered aviation professionals across the civilian and military workforces.

(e) ANNUAL REPORTING.—Not later than 1 year after the date on which the working group submits the initial report under subsection (d), and annually thereafter, the working group shall submit to the covered committees of Congress a report—

(1) describing the continued activities of the working group;

(2) describing any progress made by the Secretary or Secretary of Defense in implementing the recommendations described in subsection (d)(2)(B); and

(3) containing any other recommendations the working group may have with respect to efforts to improve the employment and training of covered aviation professionals in the civilian and military workforces.

(f) SUNSET.—The working group shall terminate on the date that is 4 years after the date on which the working group submits the initial report to Congress pursuant to subsection (d).

(g) DEFINITIONS.—In this section:

(1) COVERED COMMITTEES OF CONGRESS.—The term "covered committees of Congress" means—

(A) the Committee on Armed Services of the House of Representatives;

(B) the Committee on Armed Services of the Senate;

(C) the Committee on Transportation and Infrastructure of the House of Representatives; and

(D) the Committee on Commerce, Science, and Transportation of the Senate.

(2) COVERED AVIATION PROFESSIONAL.—The term "covered aviation professional" means—

(A) an airman;

(B) an aircraft maintenance and repair technician;

(C) an air traffic controller; and

(D) any other aviation-related professional that has comparable tasks and duties across the civilian and military workforces, as determined jointly by the co-chairs of the working group.

SEC. 426. [49 U.S.C. 44703 note] MILITARY AVIATION MAINTENANCE TECHNICIANS RULE.

(a) STREAMLINED CERTIFICATION FOR ELIGIBLE MILITARY MAINTENANCE TECHNICIANS.—

(1) RULEMAKING.—Not later than 18 months after the date of enactment of this Act, the Administrator shall issue a notice

of proposed rulemaking to revise part 65 of title 14, Code of Federal Regulations, to—

(A) create a military mechanic written competency test that addresses gaps between military and civilian experience; and

(B) develop, as necessary, a relevant Airman Certification Standard to qualify eligible military maintenance technicians for a civilian mechanic certificate with airframe or powerplant ratings.

(2) CONSIDERATION.—In carrying out paragraph (1), the Administrator shall evaluate and consider—

(A) whether to allow a certificate of eligibility from the Joint Services Aviation Maintenance Technician Certification Council (in this section referred to as the "JSAMTCC") evidencing completion of a training curriculum for any rating sought to serve as a substitute to fulfill the requirement under such part 65 for oral and practical tests administered by a designated mechanic examiner for eligible military maintenance technicians;

(B) aeronautical knowledge subject areas contained in the Aviation Mechanic General, Airframe, and Powerplant Airman Certification Standards as described in section 65.75 of title 14, Code of Federal Regulations, as appropriate, to the rating sought; and

(C) any applicable recommendations by the Aviation Rulemaking Advisory Committee Airman Certification System Working Group.

(b) EXPANSION OF TESTING LOCATIONS.—Not later than 1 year after the date of enactment of this Act, the Administrator, in consultation with the Secretary of Defense and the Secretary of Homeland Security, shall determine—

(1) whether an expansion of the number of active testing locations operated within military installation testing centers would increase access to testing; and

(2) how to implement such expansion, if appropriate.

(c) OUTREACH AND AWARENESS.—Not later than 1 year after the date of enactment of this Act, the Administrator, in coordination with the Secretary of Defense, the Secretary of Veterans Affairs, and the Secretary of Homeland Security, shall develop a plan to increase outreach and awareness regarding services made available by the JSAMTCC and how such services can assist in facilitating the transition between military and civilian aviation maintenance careers.

(d) BRIEFINGS.—

(1) INITIAL BRIEFING.—Not later than 180 days after the date on which the Administrator develops the outreach and awareness plan pursuant to subsection (c), the Administrator shall provide to the Committee on Commerce, Science, and Transportation and the Committee on Veterans' Affairs of the Senate and the Committee on Transportation and Infrastructure and the Committee on Veterans' Affairs of the House of Representatives a briefing on the activities planned to implement the outreach and awareness plan.

(2) PERIODIC BRIEFING.—Not later than 2 years after the date of enactment of this Act, and 2 years thereafter, the Administrator shall provide to the Committee on Commerce, Science, and Transportation and the Committee on Veterans' Affairs of the Senate and the Committee on Transportation and Infrastructure and the Committee on Veterans' Affairs of the House of Representatives a briefing on any rulemaking activities carried out pursuant to subsection (a), including a timeline for the issuance of a final rule.

(e) ELIGIBLE MILITARY MAINTENANCE TECHNICIAN DEFINED.—For purposes of this section, the term "eligible military maintenance technician" means an individual who—

(1) has been a maintenance technician during service in the armed forces who was honorably discharged or has retired from the armed forces (as defined in section 101 of title 10, United States Code);

(2) presents an official record of service in the armed forces confirming that the individual has been a military aviation maintenance technician, holding an appropriate Military Occupational Specialty Code, as determined by the Administrator, in coordination with the Secretary of Defense; and

(3) presents documentary evidence of experience in accordance with the requirements under section 65.77 of title 14, Code of Federal Regulations.

SEC. 428. [49 U.S.C. 44502 note] DIRECT-HIRE
AUTHORITY UTILIZATION.

FAA Reauthorization Act of 2

* * * * * * *

SEC. 428. [49 U.S.C. 44502 note] DIRECT-HIRE AUTHORITY
UTILIZATION.

(a) IN GENERAL.—The Administrator shall utilize direct hire
authorities (as such authorities existed on the day before the date of
enactment of this Act) to hire individuals on a non-competitive basis
for positions related to aircraft certification and aviation safety.
In utilizing such authorities, the Administrator shall take into
consideration any staffing gaps in the safety workforce of the FAA,
including in positions supporting the safe integration of unmanned
aircraft systems and other new airspace entrants.

(b) CONGRESSIONAL BRIEFING.—Not later than 180 days after
the date of enactment of this Act, and annually thereafter through
2028, the Administrator shall brief the appropriate committees of
Congress on the—

(1) utilization of the Administrator's direct-hire authorities
described in subsection (a);

(2) utilization of the Administrator's direct-hire authorities
with respect to the Unmanned Aircraft System Collegiate
Training Initiative of the FAA; and

(3) number of employees hired as a result of the utilization
of such authorities by the Administrator, the relevant lines of
business or offices in which such employees were hired, and the
occupational series of the positions filled.

* * * * * * *

SEC. 430. [49 U.S.C. 44701 note] STAFFING MODEL FOR AVIATION
SAFETY INSPECTORS.

(a) IN GENERAL.—Not later than 2 years after the date of
enactment of this Act, the Administrator shall review and, as
necessary, revise the staffing model for aviation safety inspectors.

(b) REQUIREMENTS.—

(1) CONSIDERATION OF PRIOR STUDIES AND REPORTS.—In
reviewing and revising the model, the Administrator shall take
into consideration the contents and recommendations
contained in the following:

(A) The 2006 report released by the National Research

Council titled "Staffing Standards for Aviation Safety Inspectors".

(B) The 2007 study released by the National Academy of Sciences titled "Staffing Standards for Aviation Safety Inspectors".

(C) The 2013 report released by Grant Thornton LLP, titled "ASTARS Gap Analysis Study: Comparison of the AVS Staffing Model for Aviation Safety Inspectors to the National Academy of Sciences' Recommendations Final Report".

(D) The 2021 report released by the inspector general of the Department of Transportation titled "FAA Can Increase Its Inspector Staffing Model's Effectiveness by Implementing System Improvements and Maximizing Its Capabilities".

(E) The FAA Fiscal Year 2023 Aviation Safety Workforce Plan conducted to satisfy the requirements of section 104 of the Aircraft Certification, Safety, and Accountability Act, as enacted in the Consolidated Appropriations Act, 2021 (49 U.S.C. 44701 note).

(2) ASSESSMENTS.—In carrying out this section, the Administrator shall assess the following:

(A) Projected staffing needs at the service and office level.

(B) Forecasted attrition of the aviation safety inspector workforce.

(C) Forecasted workload of aviation safety inspectors, including responsibilities associated with overseeing aviation manufacturers and new airspace entrants.

(D) Means by which field managers use the model to assess aviation safety inspector staffing and provide feedback on resources needed at the office level.

(E) Work performed by aviation safety inspectors in comparison to designees acting on behalf of the Administrator.

(F) Any associated performance metrics to inform periodic comparisons to actual aviation safety inspector staffing level results.

(3) CONSULTATION.—In carrying out this section, the Administrator shall consult with interested persons, including the exclusive collective bargaining representative for aviation safety inspectors certified under section 7111 of title 5, United States Code.

SEC. 431. [49 U.S.C. 44701 note] SAFETY-CRITICAL STAFFING.

(a) IMPLEMENTATION OF STAFFING STANDARDS FOR SAFETY INSPECTORS.—Upon completion of the revised staffing model for aviation safety inspectors under section 430, and validation of the model by the Administrator, the Administrator shall take all appropriate actions in response to the number of aviation safety inspectors, aviation safety technicians, and operation support positions that are identified in such model to meet the responsibilities of the Flight Standards Service and Aircraft Certification Service, including potentially increasing the number of safety critical positions in the Flight Standards Service and Aircraft Certification Service each fiscal year, as appropriate, so long as such staffing increases are measured relative to the number of individuals serving in safety-critical positions as of September 30, 2023.

(b) AVAILABILITY OF APPROPRIATIONS.—Any increase in safety critical staffing pursuant to this subsection shall be subject to the availability of appropriations.

(c) SAFETY-CRITICAL POSITIONS DEFINED.—In this section, the term "safety-critical positions" means—

(1) aviation safety inspectors, aviation safety specialists (1801 job series), aviation safety technicians, and operations support positions in the Flight Standards Service; and

(2) manufacturing safety inspectors, pilots, engineers, Chief Scientist Technical Advisors, aviation safety specialists (1801 job series), safety technical specialists, and operational support positions in the Aircraft Certification Service.

SEC. 432. [49 U.S.C. 44701 note] DETERRING CREWMEMBER INTERFERENCE.

(a) TASK FORCE.—

(1) IN GENERAL.—Not later than 120 days after the date of enactment of this Act, the Administrator shall convene a task force to develop voluntary standards and best practices relating

SEC. 434. [49 U.S.C. 44701 note] DETERRING CREWMEMBER INTERFERENCE.

FAA Reauthorization Act of 2024

to suspected violations of sections 46318, 46503, and 46504 of title 49, United States Code, including—

(A) proper and consistent incident documentation and reporting techniques;

(B) best practices for flight crew and cabin crew response, including de-escalation;

(C) improved coordination between stakeholders, including flight crew and cabin crew, airport staff, other Federal agencies as appropriate, and law enforcement; and

(D) appropriate enforcement actions.

(2) MEMBERSHIP.—The task force convened under paragraph (1) shall be comprised of representatives of—

(A) air carriers;

(B) airport sponsors and airport law enforcement agencies;

(C) other Federal agencies determined necessary by the Administrator;

(D) labor organizations representing air carrier pilots;

(E) labor organizations representing flight attendants; and

(F) labor organizations representing ticketing, check-in, or other customer service representatives employed by air carriers.

(b) ANNOUNCEMENTS.—Not later than 90 days after the date of enactment of this Act, the Administrator shall initiate such actions as may be necessary to include in the briefing of passengers before takeoff required under section 121.571 of title 14, Code of Federal Regulations, a statement informing passengers that it is against Federal law to assault or threaten to assault any individual on an aircraft or interfere with the duties of a crewmember.

(c) DEFINITIONS.—For purposes of this section, the definitions in section 40102(a) of title 49, United States Code, shall apply to terms in this section.

* * * * * * *

SEC. 434. EMPLOYEE ASSAULT PREVENTION AND RESPONSE PLAN STANDARDS AND BEST PRACTICES.

(a) SENSE OF CONGRESS.—It is the sense of Congress that—

(1) each air carrier operating under part 121 of title 14, Code of Federal Regulations, shall submit to the Administrator an Employee Assault Prevention and Response Plan pursuant to section 551 of the FAA Reauthorization Act of 2018 (49 U.S.C. 44903 note);

(2) each such air carrier should have in place and deploy an Employee Assault Prevention and Response Plan to facilitate appropriate protocols, standards, and training to equip employees with best practices and the experience necessary to respond effectively to hostile situations and disruptive behavior and maintain a safe traveling experience; and

(3) any air carrier formed after the date of enactment of this Act should develop and implement an Employee Assault Prevention and Response Plan.

* * * * * * *

SEC. 435. [49 U.S.C. 44903 note] FORMAL POLICY ON SEXUAL ASSAULT AND HARASSMENT ON AIR CARRIERS.

(a) IN GENERAL.—Not later than 180 days after the date of enactment of this Act, passenger air carriers operating under part 121 of title 14, Code of Federal Regulations, shall issue, in consultation with labor unions representing personnel, a formal policy with respect to sexual assault or harassment incidents.

(b) CONTENTS.—Each policy required under subsection (a) shall include—

(1) a statement indicating that no sexual assault or harassment incident is acceptable under any circumstance;

(2) procedures that facilitate the reporting of a sexual assault or harassment incident, including—

(A) appropriate public outreach activities; and

(B) confidential phone and internet-based opportunities for reporting;

(3) procedures that personnel should follow upon the reporting of a sexual assault or harassment incident, including actions to protect affected individuals from continued sexual assault or harassment and to notify law enforcement, including the Federal Bureau of Investigation, when appropriate;

(4) procedures that may limit or prohibit, to the extent practicable, future travel with the air carrier by any passenger who commits a sexual assault or harassment incident; and

(5) training that is required for all appropriate personnel with respect to each such policy, including specific training for personnel who may receive reports of sexual assault or harassment incidents.

(c) PASSENGER INFORMATION.—An air carrier described in subsection (a) shall display, on the website of the air carrier and through the use of appropriate signage, a written statement that informs passengers and personnel of the procedure for reporting a sexual assault or harassment incident.

(d) STANDARD OF CARE.—Compliance with the requirements of this section, and any policy issued thereunder, shall not determine whether the air carrier described in subsection (a) has acted with any requisite standard of care.

(e) RULES OF CONSTRUCTION.—

(1) EFFECT ON AUTHORITIES.—Nothing in this section shall be construed as granting the Secretary any additional authorities beyond ensuring that a passenger air carrier operating under part 121 of title 14, Code of Federal Regulations issues a formal policy and displays required information in compliance with this section.

(2) EFFECT ON OTHER LAWS.—Nothing in this section shall be construed to alter existing authorities of the Equal Employment Opportunity Commission, the Department of Labor, or the Department of Justice to enforce applicable employment and sexual assault and sexual harassment laws.

(f) DEFINITIONS.—In this section:

(1) PERSONNEL.—The term "personnel" means an employee or contractor of passenger air carrier operating under part 121 of title 14, Code of Federal Regulations.

(2) SEXUAL ASSAULT.—The term "sexual assault" means the occurrence of an act that constitutes any nonconsensual sexual act proscribed by Federal, tribal, or State law, including when the victim lacks capacity to consent.

(3) SEXUAL ASSAULT OR HARASSMENT INCIDENT.—The term "sexual assault or harassment incident" means the occurrence, or reasonably suspected occurrence, of an act that—

SEC. 437. [49 U.S.C. 44506 note] AIR TRAFFIC
CONTROL WORKFORCE STAFFING.

FAA Reauthorization Act of 2

(A) constitutes sexual assault or sexual harassment; and

(B) is committed—

(i) by a passenger or personnel against another passenger or personnel; and

(ii) within an aircraft or in an area in which passengers are entering or exiting an aircraft.

* * * * * * *

SEC. 437. [49 U.S.C. 44506 note] AIR TRAFFIC CONTROL WORKFORCE STAFFING.

(a) MAXIMUM HIRING.—Subject to the availability of appropriations, for each of fiscal years 2024 through 2028, the Administrator shall set as the minimum hiring target for new air traffic controllers (excluding individuals described in section 44506(f)(1)(A) of title 49, United States Code) the maximum number of individuals able to be trained at the Federal Aviation Administration Academy.

(b) TRANSPORTATION RESEARCH BOARD ASSESSMENT.—

(1) REVIEW.—Not later than 30 days after the date of enactment of this Act, the Administrator shall submit an attestation to the appropriate committees of Congress demonstrating an agreement entered into with the with the National Academies Transportation Research Board to—

(A) compare the Certified Professional Controller (in this section referred to as "CPC") operational staffing models and methodologies in determining the FAA Controller Staffing Standard included in the 2023 Air Traffic Controller Workforce Plan of the FAA, with such models and methodologies developed by the Collaborative Resource Workgroup of the FAA (in this subsection referred to as "CRWG") to determine CPC operational staffing targets necessary to meet facility operational, statutory, contractual and safety requirements, including—

(i) the availability factor multiplier and other formula components;

(ii) the independent facility staffing targets of

SEC. 437. [49 U.S.C. 44506 note] AIR TRAFFIC
CONTROL WORKFORCE STAFFING.

FAA Reauthorization Act of 2024

CPCs able to control traffic;

(iii) air traffic controller position utilization;

(iv) attrition rates at each air traffic control facility operated by the Administration; and

(v) the time needed to meet facility operational, statutory, and contractual requirements, including relevant resources to develop, evaluate, and implement processes and initiatives affecting the national airspace system;

(B) examine the current and estimated budgets of the FAA to implement the FAA Controller Staffing Standard included in the 2023 Controller Workforce Plan in comparison to the funding needed to implement the CRWG CPC operational staffing targets;

(C) assess future needs of the air traffic control system and potential impacts on staffing standards, including projected air traffic in the airspace of each air traffic control facility operated by the Administration; and

(D) determine which staffing models and methodologies evaluated pursuant to this subsection best accounts for the operational staffing needs of the air traffic control system and provide a justification for such determination.

(2) REPORT.—Not later than 180 days after the agreement entered into pursuant to paragraph (b)(1), the Transportation Research Board of the National Academies shall submit a report to the Administrator and appropriate committees of Congress on the findings and recommendations under this subsection, including the determination pursuant to subparagraph (D).

(3) CONSULTATION.—In conducting the assessment under this subsection, the Transportation Research Board shall consult with—

(A) the exclusive bargaining representatives of air traffic control specialists of the Administration certified under section 7111 of title 5, United States Code;

(B) front line managers of the air traffic control system;

(C) managers and employees responsible for training

SEC. 437. [49 U.S.C. 44506 note] AIR TRAFFIC CONTROL WORKFORCE STAFFING.

FAA Reauthorization Act of 2

air traffic controllers;

(D) the MITRE Corporation;

(E) the Chief Operating Officer of the Air Traffic Organization of the FAA, and other Federal Government representatives;

(F) users and operators in the air traffic control system;

(G) relevant industry representatives; and

(H) other parties determined appropriate by the Transportation Research Board of the National Academies.

(c) REQUIRED IMPLEMENTATION OF IDENTIFIED STAFFING MODEL.—

(1) USE OF STAFFING MODEL.—The Administrator shall, as appropriate, take such action that may be necessary to implement and use the staffing model identified by the Transportation Research Board pursuant to subsection (b)(1)(D), including any recommendations for improving such model, not later than one year after enactment of this Act.

(2) BRIEFING.—Not later than 90 days after taking such actions to implement and use the staffing model identified by the Transportation Research Board pursuant to subsection (b)(1)(D), the Administrator shall brief the appropriate committees of Congress regarding the reasons for why any recommendation by the Transportation Research Board study was not incorporated into the implemented staffing model.

(d) REVISED STAFFING STANDARDS.—The Administration shall revise the FAA CPC operational staffing standards of the Administration implemented under subsection (c) to—

(1) provide that the controller and management workforce is sufficiently staffed to safely and efficiently manage and oversee the air traffic control system;

(2) account for the target number of CPCs able to control traffic at each independent facility; and

(3) avoid any required or requested reduction of national airspace system capacity or aircraft operations as a result of inadequate air traffic control system staffing.

(e) INTERIM ADOPTION OF COLLABORATIVE RESOURCE WORKGROUP MODELS.—

SEC. 439. [49 U.S.C. 44506 note] AIR TRAFFIC
CONTROL WORKFORCE STAFFING.

FAA Reauthorization Act of 2024

(1) IN GENERAL.—In submitting a Controller Workforce Plan of the FAA to Congress published after the date of enactment of this Act, the Administrator shall adopt and use the staffing models and methodologies developed by the Collaborative Resource Workgroup that were recommended in the 2023 Controller Workforce Plan.

* * * * * * *

(3) EFFECTIVE DATE.—The requirements of paragraph (1) shall cease to be effective upon the adoption and implementation of a revised staffing model by the Administrator as required under subsection (c).

(f) CONTROLLER TRAINING.—In any Controller Workforce Plan of the FAA published after the date of enactment of this Act, the Administrator shall—

(1) identify all limiting factors on the ability of the Administrator to hire and train controllers in line with the staffing standards target set out in such Plan; and

(2) describe what actions the Administrator intends to take to rectify any impediments to meeting staffing standards targets and identify contributing factors that are outside the control of the Administrator.

* * * * * * *

SEC. 439. FEDERAL AVIATION ADMINISTRATION ACADEMY AND FACILITY EXPANSION PLAN.

(a) PLAN.—

(1) IN GENERAL.—No later than 90 days after the date of enactment of this Act, the Administrator shall initiate the development of a plan to expand overall FAA capacity relating to facilities, instruction, equipment, and training resources to grow the number of developmental air traffic controllers enrolled per fiscal year and support increases in FAA air controller staffing to advance the safety of the national airspace system.

(2) CONSIDERATIONS.—In developing the plan under paragraph (1), the Administrator shall consider—

(A) the resources needed to support an increase in the total number of developmental air traffic controllers

SEC. 439. [49 U.S.C. 44506 note] AIR TRAFFIC
CONTROL WORKFORCE STAFFING.

FAA Reauthorization Act of

enrolled at the FAA Academy;

(B) the resources needed to lessen FAA Academy attrition per fiscal year;

(C) how to modernize the education and training of developmental air traffic controllers, including through the use of new techniques and technologies to support instruction;

(D) the equipment needed to support expanded instruction, including air traffic control simulation systems, virtual reality, and other virtual training platforms;

(E) projected staffing needs associated with FAA Academy expansion and the operation of education platforms, including the number of on-the-job instructors needed to educate and train additional developmental air traffic controllers;

(F) the costs of expanding FAA capacity at the existing air traffic control academy (as described in paragraph (1)(A));

(G) soliciting input from, and coordinating with, relevant stakeholders as appropriate, including the exclusive bargaining representative of air traffic control specialists of the FAA certified under section 7111 of title 5, United States Code; and

(H) other logistical and financial considerations as determined appropriate by the Administrator.

(b) REPORT.—Not later than 1 year after the date of enactment of this Act, the Administrator shall submit to the appropriate committees of Congress the plan developed under subsection (a).

(c) BRIEFING.—Not later than 180 days after the submission of the plan under subsection (b), the Administrator shall brief the appropriate committees of Congress on the plan, including the implementation of the plan.

* * * * * * *

TITLE V—PASSENGER EXPERIENCE IMPROVEMENTS

SEC. 511. [49 U.S.C. 6302 note] BUREAU OF TRANSPORTATION STATISTICS.

FAA Reauthorization Act of 2024

Subtitle A—Consumer Enhancements

* * * * * * *

SEC. 511. [49 U.S.C. 6302 note] BUREAU OF TRANSPORTATION STATISTICS.

(a) RULEMAKING.—Not later than 60 days after the date of enactment of this Act, the Director of the Bureau of Transportation Statistics shall initiate a rulemaking to revise section 234.4 of title 14, Code of Federal Regulations, to create a new "cause of delay" category (or categories) that identifies and tracks information on delays and cancellations of air carriers (as defined in section 40102 of title 49, United States Code) that are due to instructions from the FAA Air Traffic Control System and to make any other changes necessary to carry out this section.

(b) AIR CARRIER CODE.—The following causes shall not be included within the Air Carrier code specified in section 234.4 of title 14, Code of Federal Regulations, for cancelled and delayed flights:

(1) Aircraft cleaning necessitated by the death of a passenger.

(2) Aircraft damage caused by extreme weather, foreign object debris, or sabotage.

(3) A baggage or cargo loading delay caused by an outage of a bag system not controlled by a carrier or its contractor.

(4) Cybersecurity attacks (provided that the air carrier is in compliance with applicable cybersecurity regulations).

(5) A shutdown or system failure of government systems that directly affects the ability of an air carrier to safely conduct flights and is unexpected.

(6) Overheated brakes due to a safety incident resulting in the use of emergency procedures.

(7) Unscheduled maintenance, including in response to an airworthiness directive, manifesting outside a scheduled maintenance program that cannot be deferred or must be addressed before flight.

(8) An emergency that required medical attention through no fault of the carrier.

SEC. 512. [49 U.S.C. 6302 note] BUREAU OF
TRANSPORTATION STATISTICS.

FAA Reauthorization Act of 2

(9) The removal of an unruly passenger.

(10) An airport closure due to the presence of volcanic ash, wind, or wind shear.

(c) FAMILY SEATING COMPLAINTS.—

(1) IN GENERAL.—The Director of the Bureau of Transportation Statistics shall update the reporting framework of the Bureau to create a new category to identify and track information on complaints related to family seating.

(2) SUNSET.—The requirements in paragraph (1) shall cease to be effective on the date on which the rulemaking required by section 513 is effective.

(d) AIR TRAVEL CONSUMER REPORT.—

(1) ATCSCC DELAYS.—The Secretary shall include information on delays and cancellations that are due to instructions from the FAA Air Traffic Control System Command Center in the Air Travel Consumer Report issued by the Office of Aviation Consumer Protection of the Department of Transportation.

(2) FAMILY SEATING COMPLAINTS.—The Secretary shall include information on complaints related to family seating—

(A) in the Air Travel Consumer Report issued by the Office of Aviation Consumer Protection of the Department of Transportation; and

(B) on the family seating dashboard required by subsection (a)(2).

(3) SUNSET.—The requirements in paragraph (2) shall cease to be effective on the date on which the rulemaking required by section 513 is effective.

SEC. 512. REIMBURSEMENT FOR INCURRED COSTS.

(a) IN GENERAL.—Not later than 1 year after the date of enactment of this Act, the Secretary shall direct all air carriers providing scheduled passenger interstate or intrastate air transportation to establish policies regarding reimbursement for lodging, transportation between such lodging and the airport, and meal costs incurred due to a flight cancellation or significant delay directly attributable to the air carrier.

(b) DEFINITION OF SIGNIFICANTLY DELAYED.—In this section,

SEC. 517. [49 U.S.C. 6302 note] BUREAU OF
TRANSPORTATION STATISTICS.

FAA Reauthorization Act of 2024

the term "significantly delayed" means, with respect to air transportation, the departure or arrival at the originally ticketed destination associated with such transportation has changed—

(1) in the case of a domestic flight, 3 or more hours after the original scheduled arrival time; and

(2) in the case of an international flight, 6 or more hours after the original scheduled arrival time.

(c) RULE OF CONSTRUCTION.—Nothing in this section shall be construed as providing the Secretary with any additional authorities beyond the authority to require air carriers establish the policies referred to in subsection (a).

* * * * * * *

SEC. 517. PASSENGER EXPERIENCE ADVISORY COMMITTEE.

(a) IN GENERAL.—The Secretary shall establish an advisory committee to advise the Secretary and the Administrator in carrying out activities relating to the improvement of the passenger experience in air transportation customer service. The advisory committee shall not duplicate the work of any other advisory committee.

(b) MEMBERSHIP.—The Secretary shall appoint the members of the advisory committee, which shall be comprised of at least 1 representative of each of—

(1) mainline air carriers;

(2) air carriers with a low-cost or ultra-low-cost business model;

(3) regional air carriers;

(4) large hub airport sponsors and operators;

(5) medium hub airport sponsors and operators;

(6) small hub airport sponsors and operators;

(7) nonhub airport sponsors and operators;

(8) ticket agents;

(9) representatives of intermodal transportation companies that operate at airports;

(10) airport concessionaires;

(11) nonprofit public interest groups with expertise in

SEC. 517. [49 U.S.C. 6302 note] BUREAU OF
TRANSPORTATION STATISTICS.

FAA Reauthorization Act of 2

consumer protection matters;

(12) senior managers of the FAA Air Traffic Organization;

(13) aircraft manufacturers;

(14) entities representing individuals with disabilities;

(15) certified labor organizations representing aviation workers, including—

(A) FAA employees;

(B) airline pilots working for air carriers operating under part 121 of title 14, Code of Federal Regulations;

(C) flight attendants working for air carriers operating under part 121 of title 14, Code of Federal Regulations; and

(D) other customer-facing airline and airport workers;

(16) other organizations or industry segments as determined by the Secretary; and

(17) other Federal agencies that directly interface with passengers at airports.

(c) VACANCIES.—A vacancy in the advisory committee under this section shall be filled in a manner consistent with subsection (b).

(d) TRAVEL EXPENSES.—Members of the advisory committee under this section shall serve without pay but shall receive travel expenses, including per diem in lieu of subsistence, in accordance with subchapter I of chapter 57 of title 5, United States Code.

(e) CHAIR.—The Secretary shall designate an individual among the individuals appointed under subsection (b) to serve as Chair of the advisory committee.

(f) DUTIES.—The duties of the advisory committee shall include—

(1) evaluating ways to improve the comprehensive passenger experience, including—

(A) transportation between airport terminals and facilities;

(B) baggage handling;

(C) wayfinding;

(D) the security screening process; and

(E) the communication of flight delays and

cancellations;

(2) evaluating ways to improve efficiency in the national airspace system affecting passengers;

(3) evaluating ways to improve the cooperation and coordination between the Department of Transportation and other Federal agencies that directly interface with aviation passengers at airports;

(4) responding to other taskings determined by the Secretary; and

(5) providing recommendations to the Secretary and the Administrator, if determined necessary during the evaluations considered in paragraphs (1) through (4).

(g) REPORT TO CONGRESS.—Not later than 1 year after the date of enactment of this Act, and every 2 years thereafter, the Secretary shall submit to Congress a report containing—

(1) consensus recommendations made by the advisory committee since such date of enactment or the previous report, as appropriate; and

(2) an explanation of how the Secretary has implemented such recommendations and, for such recommendations not implemented, the Secretary's reason for not implementing such recommendation.

(h) DEFINITION.—The definitions in section 40102 of title 49, United States Code, shall apply to this section.

(i) SUNSET.—This section shall cease to be effective on October 1, 2028.

(j) TERMINATION OF DOT ACCESS ADVISORY COMMITTEE.—The ACCESS Advisory Committee of the Department of Transportation shall terminate on the date of enactment of this Act.

SEC. 518. [49 U.S.C. 44701 note] UPDATING PASSENGER INFORMATION REQUIREMENT REGULATIONS.

(a) ARAC TASKING.—Not later than 3 years after the date of enactment of this Act, the Administrator shall task the Aviation Rulemaking Advisory Committee with—

(1) reviewing passenger information requirement regulations under section 121.317 of title 14, Code of Federal Regulation, and such other related regulations as the

Administrator determines appropriate; and

(2) making recommendations to update and improve such regulations.

(b) FINAL REGULATION.—Not later than 6 years after the date of enactment of this Act, the Administrator shall issue a final regulation revising section 121.317 of title 14, Code of Federal Regulations, and such other related regulations as the Administrator determines appropriate, to—

(1) update such section and regulations to incorporate exemptions commonly issued by the Administrator;

(2) reflect civil penalty inflation adjustments; and

(3) incorporate such updates and improvements recommended by the Aviation Rulemaking Advisory Committee that the Administrator determines appropriate.

* * * * * * *

Subtitle B—Accessibility

* * * * * * *

SEC. 542. [49 U.S.C. 41728 note] IMPROVED TRAINING STANDARDS FOR ASSISTING PASSENGERS WHO USE WHEELCHAIRS.

(a) RULEMAKING.—Not later than 6 months after the date of enactment of this Act, the Secretary shall issue a notice of proposed rulemaking to develop requirements for minimum training standards for airline personnel or contractors who assist wheelchair users who board or deplane using an aisle chair or other boarding device.

(b) REQUIREMENTS.—The training standards developed under subsection (a) shall require, at a minimum, that airline personnel or contractors who assist passengers who use wheelchairs who board or deplane using an aisle chair or other boarding device—

(1) before being allowed to assist a passenger using an aisle chair or other boarding device to board or deplane, be able to successfully demonstrate skills (during hands-on training sessions) on—

(A) how to safely use the aisle chair, or other boarding device, including the use of all straps, brakes, and other safety features;

(B) how to assist in the transfer of passengers to and
from their wheelchair, the aisle chair, and the aircraft's
passenger seat, either by physically lifting the passenger or
deploying a mechanical device for the lift or transfer; and

(C) how to effectively communicate with, and take
instruction from, the passenger;

(2) are trained regarding the availability of accessible
lavatories and on-board wheelchairs and the right of a qualified
individual with a disability to request an on-board wheelchair;
and

(3) complete refresher training within 18 months of an
initial training and be recertified on the job every 18 months
thereafter by a relevant superior in order to remain qualified
for providing aisle chair assistance.

(c) CONSIDERATIONS.—In conducting the rulemaking under
subsection (a), the Secretary shall consider, at a minimum—

(1) whether to require air carriers and foreign air carriers
to partner with national disability organizations and disabled
veterans organizations representing individuals with
disabilities who use wheelchairs and scooters in developing,
administering, and auditing training;

(2) whether to require air carriers and foreign air carriers
to use a lift device, instead of an aisle chair, to board and
deplane passengers with mobility disabilities; and

(3) whether individuals able to provide boarding and
deplaning assistance for passengers with limited or no mobility
should receive training incorporating procedures from medical
professionals on how to properly lift these passengers.

(d) FINAL RULE.—Not later than 12 months after the date of
enactment of this Act, the Secretary shall issue a final rule
pursuant to the rulemaking conducted under this section.

(e) PENALTIES.—The Secretary may assess a civil penalty in
accordance with section 46301 of title 49, United States Code, to any
air carrier or foreign air carrier who fails to meet the requirements
established under the final rule under subsection (d).

SEC. 543. [49 U.S.C. 41728 note] TRAINING STANDARDS FOR
STOWAGE OF WHEELCHAIRS AND SCOOTERS.

(a) RULEMAKING.—Not later than 6 months after the date of enactment of this Act, the Secretary shall issue a notice of proposed rulemaking to develop minimum training standards related to stowage of wheelchairs and scooters used by passengers with disabilities on aircraft.

(b) REQUIREMENTS.—The training standards developed under subsection (a) shall require, at a minimum, that personnel and contractors of air carriers and foreign air carriers who stow wheelchairs and scooters on aircraft—

(1) before being allowed to handle or stow a wheelchair or scooter, be able to successfully demonstrate skills (during hands-on training sessions) on—

(A) how to properly handle and configure, at a minimum, the most commonly used power and manual wheelchairs and scooters for stowage on each aircraft type operated by the air carrier or foreign air carrier;

(B) how to properly review any wheelchair or scooter information provided by the passenger or the wheelchair or scooter manufacturer; and

(C) how to properly load, secure, and unload wheelchairs and scooters, including how to use any specialized equipment for loading or unloading, on each aircraft type operated by the air carrier or foreign air carrier; and

(2) complete refresher training within 18 months of an initial training and be recertified on the job every 18 months thereafter by a relevant superior in order to remain qualified for handling and stowing wheelchairs and scooters.

(c) CONSIDERATIONS.—In conducting the rulemaking under subsection (a), the Secretary shall consider, at a minimum, whether to require air carriers and foreign air carriers to partner with wheelchair or scooter manufacturers, national disability and disabled veterans organizations representing individuals who use wheelchairs and scooters, and aircraft manufacturers, in developing, administering, and auditing training.

(d) FINAL RULE.—Not later than 12 months after the date of enactment of this Act, the Secretary shall issue a final rule pursuant to the rulemaking conducted under this section.

(e) PENALTIES.—The Secretary may assess a civil penalty in

accordance with section 46301 of title 49, United States Code, to any air carrier or foreign air carrier who fails to meet the requirements established under the final rule under subsection (d).

SEC. 544. [49 U.S.C. 41728 note] MOBILITY AIDS ON BOARD IMPROVE LIVES AND EMPOWER ALL.

(a) PUBLICATION OF CARGO HOLD DIMENSIONS.—

(1) IN GENERAL.—Not later than 2 years after the date of enactment of this Act, the Secretary shall require air carriers to publish in a prominent and easily accessible place on the public website of the air carrier, information describing the relevant dimensions and other characteristics of the cargo holds of all aircraft types operated by the air carrier, including the dimensions of the cargo hold entry, that would limit the size, weight, and allowable type of cargo.

(2) PROPRIETARY INFORMATION.—The Secretary shall allow an air carrier to protect the confidentiality of any trade secret or proprietary information submitted in accordance with paragraph (1), as appropriate.

(b) REFUND REQUIRED FOR INDIVIDUAL TRAVELING WITH WHEELCHAIR.—In the case of a qualified individual with a disability traveling with a wheelchair who has purchased a ticket for a flight from an air carrier, but who cannot travel on the aircraft for such flight because the wheelchair of such qualified individual cannot be physically accommodated in the cargo hold of the aircraft, the Secretary shall require such air carrier to offer a refund to such qualified individual of any previously paid fares, fees, and taxes applicable to such flight.

(c) EVALUATION OF DATA REGARDING DAMAGED WHEELCHAIRS.—Not later than 12 months after the date of enactment of this Act, and annually thereafter, the Secretary shall—

(1) evaluate data regarding the type and frequency of incidents of the mishandling of wheelchairs on aircraft and delineate such data by—

(A) types of wheelchairs involved in such incidents; and

(B) the ways in which wheelchairs are mishandled, including the type of damage to wheelchairs (such as broken drive wheels or casters, bent or broken frames, damage to electrical connectors or wires, control input devices, joysticks, upholstery or other components, loss, or delay of return);

(2) determine whether there are trends with respect to the data evaluated under paragraph (1); and

(3) make available on the public website of the Department of Transportation, in an accessible manner, a report containing the results of the evaluation of data and determination made under paragraphs (1) and (2) and a description of how the Secretary plans to address such results.

(d) REPORT TO CONGRESS ON MISHANDLED WHEELCHAIRS.—Upon completion of each annual report required under subsection (c), the Secretary shall transmit to the appropriate committees of Congress such report.

(e) FEASIBILITY OF IN-CABIN WHEELCHAIR RESTRAINT SYSTEMS.—

(1) ROADMAP.—Not later than 1 year after the date of enactment of this Act, the Secretary shall submit to the appropriate committees of Congress a publicly available strategic roadmap that describes how the Department of Transportation and the United States Access Board, respectively, shall, in accordance with the recommendations from the National Academies of Science, Engineering, and Mathematics Transportation Research Board Special Report 341—

(A) establish a program of research, in collaboration with the Rehabilitation Engineering and Assistive Technology Society of North America, the assistive technology industry, air carriers, original equipment manufacturers, national disability and disabled veterans organizations, and any other relevant stakeholders, to test and evaluate an appropriate selection of WC19-compliant wheelchairs and accessories in accordance with applicable FAA crashworthiness and safety performance criteria, including the issues and considerations set forth in such Special Report 341; and

(B) sponsor studies that assess issues and considerations, including those set forth in such Special

Report 341, such as—

(i) the likely demand for air travel by individuals who are nonambulatory if such individuals could remain seated in their personal wheelchairs in flight; and

(ii) the feasibility of implementing seating arrangements that would accommodate passengers in wheelchairs in the main cabin in flight.

(2) STUDY.—If determined to be technically feasible by the Secretary, not later than 2 years after making such determination, the Secretary shall commence a study to assess the economic and financial feasibility of air carriers and foreign air carriers implementing seating arrangements that accommodate passengers with wheelchairs in the main cabin during flight. Such study shall include an assessment of—

(A) the cost of such seating arrangements, equipment, and installation;

(B) the demand for such seating arrangements;

(C) the impact of such seating arrangements on passenger seating and safety on aircraft;

(D) the impact of such seating arrangements on the cost of operations and airfare; and

(E) any other information determined appropriate by the Secretary.

(3) REPORT.—Not later than 1 year after the date on which the study under paragraph (2) is completed, the Secretary shall submit to the appropriate committees of Congress a publicly available report describing the results of the study conducted under paragraph (2) and any recommendations the Secretary determines appropriate.

(f) DEFINITIONS.—In this section:

(1) AIR CARRIER.—The term "air carrier" has the meaning given such term in section 40102 of title 49, United States Code.

(2) DISABILITY; QUALIFIED INDIVIDUAL WITH A DISABILITY.—The terms "disability" and "qualified individual with a disability" have the meanings given such terms in section 382.3 of title 14, Code of Federal Regulations (as in effect on date of enactment of this Act).

(3) WHEELCHAIR.—The term "wheelchair" has the meaning given such term in section 37.3 of title 49, Code of Federal Regulations (as in effect on date of enactment of this Act), and includes power wheelchairs, manual wheelchairs, and scooters.

SEC. 545. [49 U.S.C. 41728 note] PRIORITIZING ACCOUNTABILITY AND ACCESSIBILITY FOR AVIATION CONSUMERS.

(a) ANNUAL REPORT.—Not later than 1 year after the date of enactment of this Act, and annually thereafter, the Secretary shall submit to the appropriate committees of Congress, and make publicly available, a report on aviation consumer complaints related to passengers with a disability filed with the Department of Transportation.

(b) CONTENTS.—Each annual report submitted under subsection (a) shall, at a minimum, include the following:

(1) The number of aviation consumer complaints reported to the Secretary related to passengers with a disability filed with the Department of Transportation during the calendar year preceding the year in which such report is submitted.

(2) The nature of such complaints, including reported issues with—

(A) an air carrier, including an air carrier's staff training or lack thereof;

(B) mishandling of passengers with a disability or their accessibility equipment, including mobility aids and wheelchairs;

(C) the condition, availability, or lack of accessibility of equipment operated by an air carrier or a contractor of an air carrier;

(D) the accessibility of in-flight services, including accessing and using on-board lavatories, for passengers with a disability;

(E) difficulties experienced by passengers with a disability in communicating with air carrier personnel;

(F) difficulties experienced by passengers with a disability in being moved, handled, or otherwise assisted;

(G) an air carrier changing the flight itinerary of a passenger with a disability without the consent of such passenger;

(H) issues experienced by passengers with a disability traveling with a service animal; and

(I) such other issues as the Secretary determines appropriate.

(3) An overview of the review process for such complaints received during such calendar year.

(4) The median length of time for how quickly review of such complaints was initiated by the Secretary.

(5) The median length of time for how quickly such complaints were resolved or otherwise addressed.

(6) Of the complaints that were found to violate section 41705 of title 49, United States Code—

(A) the number of such complaints for which a formal enforcement order was issued; and

(B) the number of such complaints for which a formal enforcement order was not issued.

(7) How many aviation consumer complaints related to passengers with a disability were referred to the Department of Justice for an enforcement action under—

(A) section 504 of the Rehabilitation Act of 1973 (29 U.S.C. 794);

(B) the Americans with Disabilities Act of 1990 (42 U.S.C. 12101 et seq.); or

(C) any other provision of law.

(8) How many aviation consumer complaints related to passengers with a disability filed with the Department of Transportation that involved airport staff (or other matters under the jurisdiction of the FAA) were referred to the FAA.

(9) The number of disability-related aviation consumer complaints filed with the Department of Transportation involving Transportation Security Administration staff that were referred to the Transportation Security Administration or the Department of Homeland Security.

(c) DEFINITIONS.—

(1) IN GENERAL.—Except as provided in paragraph (2), the definitions set forth in section 40102 of title 49, United States

Code, and section 382.3 of title 14, Code of Federal Regulations, apply to this section.

(2) AIR CARRIER.—The term "air carrier" means an air carrier conducting passenger operations under part 121 of title 14, Code of Federal Regulations.

(3) PASSENGERS WITH A DISABILITY.—In this section, the term "passengers with a disability" has the meaning given the term "qualified individual with a disability" in section 382.3 of title 14, Code of Federal Regulations.

SEC. 546. [49 U.S.C. 41728 note] ACCOMMODATIONS FOR QUALIFIED INDIVIDUALS WITH DISABILITIES.

(a) IN GENERAL.—

(1) ADVANCED NOTICE OF PROPOSED RULEMAKING.—Not later than 180 days after the date of enactment of this Act, the Secretary shall issue an advanced notice of proposed rulemaking regarding seating accommodations for any qualified individual with a disability.

(2) NOTICE OF PROPOSED RULEMAKING.—Not later than 18 months after the date on which the advanced notice of proposed rulemaking under paragraph (1) is completed, the Secretary shall issue a notice of proposed rulemaking regarding seating accommodations for any qualified individual with a disability.

(3) FINAL RULE.—Not later than 30 months after the date on which the notice of proposed rulemaking under subparagraph (B) is completed, the Secretary shall issue a final rule pursuant to the rulemaking conducted under this subsection.

(b) CONSIDERATIONS.—In carrying out the advanced notice of proposed rulemaking required in subsection (a)(1), the Secretary shall consider the following:

(1) The scope and anticipated number of qualified individuals with a disability who—

(A) may need to be seated with a companion to receive assistance during a flight; or

(B) should be afforded bulkhead seats or other seating considerations.

(2) The types of disabilities that may need seating

accommodations.

(3) Whether such qualified individuals with a disability are unable to obtain, or have difficulty obtaining, appropriate seating accommodations.

(4) The scope and anticipated number of individuals assisting a qualified individual with a disability who should be afforded an adjoining seat pursuant to section 382.81 of title 14, Code of Federal Regulations.

(5) Any notification given to qualified individuals with a disability regarding available seating accommodations.

(6) Any method that is adequate to identify fraudulent claims for seating accommodations.

(7) Any other information determined appropriate by the Secretary.

(c) KNOWN SERVICE ANIMAL TRAVEL PILOT PROGRAM.—

(1) IN GENERAL.—The Secretary shall establish a pilot program to allow approved program participants as known service animals for purposes of exemption from the documentation requirements under part 382 of title 14, Code of Federal Regulations, with respect to air travel with a service animal.

(2) REQUIREMENTS.—The pilot program established under paragraph (1) shall—

(A) be optional for a service animal accompanying a qualified individual with a disability;

(B) provide for assistance for applicants, including over-the-phone assistance, throughout the application process for the program; and

(C) with respect to any web-based components of the pilot program, meet or exceed the standards described in section 508 of the Rehabilitation Act of 1973 (29 U.S.C. 794d) and the regulations implementing that Act as set forth in part 1194 of title 36, Code of Federal Regulations (or any successor regulations).

(3) CONSULTATION.—In establishing the pilot program under paragraph (1), the Secretary shall consult with—

(A) disability organizations, including advocacy and nonprofit organizations that represent or provide services to individuals with disabilities;

    (B) air carriers and foreign air carriers;

    (C) accredited service animal training programs and authorized registrars, such as the International Guide Dog Federation, Assistance Dogs International, and other similar organizations and foreign and domestic governmental registrars of service animals;

    (D) other relevant departments or agencies of the Federal Government; and

    (E) other entities determined to be appropriate by the Secretary.

(4) ELIGIBILITY.—To be eligible to participate in the pilot program under this subsection, an individual shall—

    (A) be a qualified individual with a disability;

    (B) require the assistance of a service animal because of a disability; and

    (C) submit an application to the Secretary at such time, in such manner, and containing such information as the Secretary may require.

(5) CLARIFICATION.—The Secretary may award a grant or enter into a contract or cooperative agreement in order to carry out this subsection.

(6) NOMINAL FEE.—The Secretary may require an applicant to pay a nominal fee, not to exceed $25, to participate in the pilot program.

(7) REPORTS TO CONGRESS.—Not later than 1 year after the establishment of the pilot program under this subsection, and annually thereafter until the date described in paragraph (8), the Secretary shall submit to the appropriate committees of Congress and make publicly available report on the progress of the pilot program.

(8) SUNSET.—The pilot program shall terminate on the date that is 5 years after the date of enactment of this Act.

(d) ACCREDITED SERVICE ANIMAL TRAINING PROGRAMS AND AUTHORIZED REGISTRARS.—Not later than 6 months after the date of enactment of this Act, the Secretary shall publish and maintain, on the website of the Department of Transportation, a list of—

    (1) accredited programs that train service animals; and

(2) authorized registrars that evaluate service animals.

(e) REPORT TO CONGRESS ON SERVICE ANIMAL REQUESTS.—Not later than 1 year after the date of enactment of this Act, and annually thereafter, the Secretary shall submit to the appropriate committees of Congress a report on requests for air travel with service animals, including—

(1) during the reporting period, how many requests to board an aircraft with a service animal were made in total, and how many requests were made by qualified individuals with disabilities; and

(2) the number and percentage of such requests, categorized by type of request, that were reported by air carriers or foreign air carriers as—

(A) granted;

(B) denied but not fraudulent; or

(C) denied as fraudulent.

(f) TRAINING.—

(1) IN GENERAL.—Not later than 180 days after the date of enactment of this section, the Secretary shall, in consultation with the Air Carrier Access Act Advisory Committee, issue guidance regarding improvements to training for airline personnel (including contractors) in recognizing when a qualified individual with a disability is traveling with a service animal.

(2) REQUIREMENTS.—The guidance issued under paragraph (1) shall—

(A) take into account respectful engagement with and assistance for individuals with a wide range of visible and nonvisible disabilities;

(B) provide information on—

(i) service animal behavior and whether the service animal is appropriately harnessed, leashed, or otherwise tethered; and

(ii) the various types of service animals, such as guide dogs, hearing or signal dogs, psychiatric service dogs, sensory or social signal dogs, and seizure response dogs; and

(C) outline the rights and responsibilities of the

SEC. 547. [49 U.S.C. 41728 note] EQUAL
ACCESSIBILITY TO PASSENGER PORTALS.

FAA Reauthorization Act of

handler of the service animal.

(g) DEFINITIONS.—In this section:

(1) AIR CARRIER.—The term "air carrier" has the meaning given that term in section 40102 of title 49, United States Code.

(2) FOREIGN AIR CARRIER.—The term "foreign air carrier" has the meaning given that term in section 40102 of title 49, United States Code.

(3) QUALIFIED INDIVIDUAL WITH A DISABILITY.—The term "qualified individual with a disability" has the meaning given that term in section 382.3 of title 14, Code of Federal Regulations.

(4) SERVICE ANIMAL.—The term "service animal" has the meaning given that term in section 382.3 of title 14, Code of Federal Regulations.

SEC. 547. [49 U.S.C. 41728 note] EQUAL ACCESSIBILITY TO PASSENGER PORTALS.

(a) APPLICATIONS AND INFORMATION COMMUNICATION TECHNOLOGIES.—Not later than 2 years after the date of enactment of this Act, the Secretary shall, in consultation with the United States Architectural and Transportation Barriers Compliance Board, issue regulations setting forth minimum standards to ensure that individuals with disabilities are able to access customer-focused kiosks, software applications, and websites of air carriers, foreign air carriers, and airports, in a manner that is equally as effective, and has a substantially equivalent ease of use, as for individuals without disabilities.

(b) CONSISTENCY WITH GUIDELINES.—The standards set forth under subsection (a) shall be consistent with the standards contained in the Web Content Accessibility Guidelines 2.1 Level AA of the Web Accessibility Initiative of the World Wide Web Consortium or any subsequent version of such Guidelines.

(c) REVIEW.—

(1) AIR CARRIER ACCESS ACT ADVISORY COMMITTEE REVIEW.—The Air Carrier Access Act Advisory Committee shall periodically review, and make appropriate recommendations regarding, the accessibility of websites, kiosks, and information communication technology of air carriers, foreign air carriers, and airports, and make such recommendations publicly

available.

(2) DOT REVIEW.—Not later than 5 years after issuing regulations under subsection (a), and every 5 years thereafter, the Secretary shall—

(A) review the recommendations of the Air Carrier Access Act Advisory Committee regarding the regulations issued under this subsection; and

(B) update such regulations as necessary.

SEC. 548. [49 U.S.C. 41728 note] AIRCRAFT ACCESS STANDARDS.

(a) AIRCRAFT ACCESS STANDARDS.—

(1) STANDARDS.—

(A) ADVANCE NOTICE OF PROPOSED RULEMAKING.—Not later than 1 year after the date of enactment of this Act, the Secretary shall issue an advanced notice of proposed rulemaking regarding standards to ensure that the aircraft boarding and deplaning process is accessible, in terms of design for, transportation of, and communication with, individuals with disabilities, including individuals who use wheelchairs.

(B) NOTICE OF PROPOSED RULEMAKING.—Not later than 1 year after the date on which the advanced notice of proposed rulemaking under subparagraph (A) is completed, the Secretary shall issue a notice of proposed rulemaking regarding standards addressed in subparagraph (A).

(C) FINAL RULE.—Not later than 1 year after the date on which the notice of proposed rulemaking under subparagraph (B) is completed, the Secretary shall issue a final rule.

(2) COVERED AIRPORT, EQUIPMENT, AND FEATURES.—The standards prescribed under paragraph (1)(A) shall address, at a minimum—

(A) boarding and deplaning equipment;

(B) improved procedures to ensure the priority cabin stowage for manual assistive devices pursuant to section 382.67 of title 14, Code of Federal Regulations; and

(C) improved cargo hold storage to prevent damage to

assistive devices.

(3) CONSULTATION.—For purposes of the rulemaking under this subsection, the Secretary shall consult with the Access Board and any other relevant department or agency to determine appropriate accessibility standards.

(b) IN-FLIGHT ENTERTAINMENT RULEMAKING.—Not later than 1 year after the date of the enactment of this Act, the Secretary shall issue a notice of proposed rulemaking in accordance with the November 22, 2016, resolution of the Department of Transportation ACCESS Committee and the consensus recommendation set forth in the Term Sheet Reflecting Agreement of the Access Committee Regarding In-Flight Entertainment.

(c) NEGOTIATED RULEMAKING ON IN-CABIN WHEELCHAIR RESTRAINT SYSTEMS AND ENPLANING AND DEPLANING STANDARDS.—

(1) TIMING.—

(A) IN GENERAL.—Not later than 1 year after completion of the report required by section 544(e)(2), and if such report finds economic and financial feasibility of air carriers and foreign air carriers implementing seating arrangements that accommodate individuals with disabilities using wheelchairs (including power wheelchairs, manual wheelchairs, and scooters) in the main cabin during flight, the Secretary shall conduct a negotiated rulemaking on new type certificated aircraft standards for seating arrangements that accommodate such individuals in the main cabin during flight or an accessible route to a minimum of 2 aircraft passenger seats for passengers to access from personal assistive devices of such individuals.

(B) REQUIREMENT.—The negotiated rulemaking under subparagraph (A) shall include participation of representatives of—

(i) air carriers;

(ii) aircraft manufacturers;

(iii) national disability organizations;

(iv) aviation safety experts; and

(v) mobility aid manufacturers.

(2) NOTICE OF PROPOSED RULEMAKING.—Not later than 1 year after the completion of the negotiated rulemaking required under paragraph (1), the Secretary shall issue a notice of proposed rulemaking regarding the standards described in paragraph (1).

(3) FINAL RULE.—Not later than 1 year after the date on which the notice of proposed rulemaking under paragraph (2) is completed, the Secretary shall issue a final rule regarding the standards described in paragraph (1).

(4) CONSIDERATIONS.—In the negotiated rulemaking and rulemaking required under this subsection, the Secretary shall consider—

(A) a reasonable period for the design, certification, and construction of aircraft that meet the requirements;

(B) the safety of all persons on-board the aircraft, including necessary wheelchair standards and wheelchair compliance with FAA crashworthiness and safety performance criteria; and

(C) the costs of design, installation, equipage, and aircraft capacity impacts, including partial fleet equipage and fare impacts.

(d) VISUAL AND TACTILELY ACCESSIBLE ANNOUNCEMENTS.—The Advisory Committee established under section 439 of the FAA Reauthorization Act of 2018 (49 U.S.C. 41705 note) shall examine technical solutions and the feasibility of visually and tactilely accessible announcements on-board aircraft.

(e) AIRPORT FACILITIES.—Not later than 2 years after the date of enactment of this Act, the Secretary shall, in direct consultation with the Access Board, prescribe regulations setting forth minimum standards under section 41705 of title 49, United States Code, that ensure all gates (including counters), ticketing areas, and customer service desks covered under such section at airports are accessible to and usable by all individuals with disabilities, including through the provision of visually and tactilely accessible announcements and full and equal access to aural communications.

(f) DEFINITIONS.—In this section:

(1) ACCESS BOARD.—The term "Access Board" means the Architectural and Transportation Barriers Compliance Board.

(2) AIR CARRIER.—The term "air carrier" has the meaning

SEC. 551. [49 U.S.C. 41728 note] ON-BOARD
WHEELCHAIRS IN AIRCRAFT CABIN.

FAA Reauthorization Act of 2

given such term in section 40102 of title 49, United States Code.

(3) INDIVIDUAL WITH A DISABILITY.—The term "individual with a disability" has the meaning given such term in section 382.3 of title 14, Code of Federal Regulations.

(4) FOREIGN AIR CARRIER.—The term "foreign air carrier" has the meaning given such term in section 40102 of title 49, United States Code.

* * * * * * *

SEC. 551. [49 U.S.C. 41728 note] ON-BOARD WHEELCHAIRS IN AIRCRAFT CABIN.

(a) IN GENERAL.—If an individual informs an air carrier or foreign air carrier at the time of booking a ticket for air transportation on a covered aircraft that the individual requires the use of any wheelchair, the air carrier or foreign air carrier shall provide information regarding the provision and use of on-board wheelchairs, including the rights and responsibilities of the air carrier and passenger as such rights and responsibilities relate to the provision and use of on-board wheelchairs.

(b) AVAILABILITY OF INFORMATION.—An air carrier or foreign air carrier that operates a covered aircraft shall provide on a publicly available website of the carrier information regarding the rights and responsibilities of both passengers on such aircraft and the air carrier or foreign air carrier relating to on-board wheelchairs, including—

(1) that an air carrier or foreign air carrier is required to equip aircraft that have more than 60 passenger seats and that have an accessible lavatory (whether or not having such a lavatory is required by section 382.63 of title 14, Code of Federal Regulations) with an on-board wheelchair, unless an exception described in such section 382.65 applies;

(2) that a qualified individual with a disability (as defined in section 382.3 of title 14, Code of Federal Regulations (as in effect on date of enactment of this Act)) may request an on-board wheelchair on aircraft with more than 60 passenger seats even if the lavatory is not accessible and that the basis of such request must be that the individual can use an inaccessible lavatory but cannot reach it from a seat without using an on-board wheelchair;

(3) that the air carrier or foreign air carrier may require the qualified individual with a disability to provide the advance notice specified in section 382.27 of title 14, Code of Federal Regulations, in order for the individual to be provided with the on-board wheelchair; and

(4) if the air carrier or foreign air carrier requires the advance notice described in paragraph (3), information on how such a qualified individual with a disability can make such a request.

(c) DEFINITIONS.—In this section:

(1) APPLICABILITY OF TERMS.—The definitions contained in section 40102 of title 49, United States Code, apply to this section.

(2) COVERED AIRCRAFT.—The term "covered aircraft" means an aircraft that is required to be equipped with on-board wheelchairs in accordance with section 382.65 of title 14, Code of Federal Regulations.

* * * * * * *

Subtitle C—Air Service Development

* * * * * * *

SEC. 564. ESSENTIAL AIR SERVICE IN PARTS OF ALASKA.

Not later than September 1, 2024, the Secretary, in consultation with the appropriate State authority of Alaska, shall review all domestic points in the State of Alaska that were deleted from carrier certificates between July 1, 1968, and October 24, 1978, and that were not subsequently determined to be an eligible place prior to January 1, 1982, as a result of being unpopulated at that time due to destruction during the 1964 earthquake and its resultant tidal wave, to determine whether such points have been resettled or relocated and should be designated as an eligible place entitled to receive a determination of the level of essential air service supported, if necessary, with Federal funds.

* * * * * * *

SEC. 568. [49 U.S.C. 41731 note] RESPONSE TIME FOR

APPLICATIONS TO PROVIDE ESSENTIAL AIR SERVICE.

The Secretary shall take such actions as are necessary to respond with an approval or denial of any application filed by an applicant to provide essential air service under subchapter II of chapter 417 of title 49, United States Code, to the greatest extent practicable not later than 6 months after receiving such application. The Assistant General Counsel for International and Aviation Economic Law shall ensure the timely review of all orders proposed by the Essential Air Service Office, and such timeliness shall be analyzed annually by the General Counsel of the Department of Transportation.

* * * * * * *

TITLE VI—MODERNIZING THE NATIONAL AIRSPACE SYSTEM

SEC. 601. INSTRUMENT LANDING SYSTEM INSTALLATION.

(a) IN GENERAL.—Not later than January 1, 2025, the Administrator shall expedite the installation of at least 15 instrument landing systems (in this section referred to as "ILS") in the national airspace system by utilizing the existing ILS contract vehicle and the employees of the FAA.

(b) REQUIREMENTS.—In carrying out subsection (a), the Administrator shall—

(1) incorporate lessons learned from installations under section 44502(a)(4) of title 49, United States Code;

(2) record metrics of cost and time savings of expedited installations;

(3) consider opportunities to further develop ILS technical expertise among the employees of the FAA; and

(4) consider the cost-benefit analysis of utilizing the existing ILS contract vehicle, the employees of the FAA, or both, to accelerate the installation and deployment of procured equipment.

(c) BRIEFING TO CONGRESS.—Not later than June 30, 2025, the Administrator shall brief the appropriate committees of Congress—

(1) on the installation of ILS under this section;

(2) describing any planned near-term ILS installations; and

(3) outlining the approach of the FAA to accelerate future procurement and installation of ILS throughout the national airspace system in a manner consistent with the requirements of title VIII of division J of the Infrastructure Investment and Jobs Act (Public Law 117-58).

* * * * * * *

SEC. 603. NEXTGEN ACCOUNTABILITY REVIEW.

(a) IN GENERAL.—Not later than December 31, 2026, the Administrator shall seek to enter into an agreement with the National Academy of Public Administration to initiate a review to assess the performance of the FAA in delivering and implementing quantifiable operational benefits to the national airspace system within the NextGen program.

(b) REVIEW REQUIREMENTS.—In conducting the review required under subsection (a), the National Academy of Public Administration shall—

(1) leverage metrics used by the FAA to quantify the benefits of NextGen technology and investments;

(2) validate metrics and identify additional metrics the FAA can use to track national airspace system throughput and savings as a result of NextGen investments—

(A) by calculating a per flight average, weighted by distance, of the—

(i) reduction and cumulative savings of track miles and time savings;

(ii) reduction and cumulative savings of emissions and fuel burn; and

(iii) reduction of aircraft operation time; and

(B) by using any other metrics that the National Academy determines may provide insights into the quantifiable benefits for operators in the national airspace system; and

(3) validate current metrics and identify additional metrics the FAA can use to track and assess fleet equipage across operators in the national airspace system, including

identifying—

(A) the percentage of aircraft equipped with NextGen avionics equipment as recommended in the report of the NextGen Advisory Committee titled "Minimum Capabilities List (MCL) Ad Hoc Team NAC Task 19-1 Report", issued on November 17, 2020;

(B) quantified costs and benefits for an operator to properly equip an aircraft with baseline NextGen avionics equipment over the lifecycle of such aircraft; and

(C) cumulative unrealized NextGen benefits associated with rates of mixed equipage across operators.

(c) INDUSTRY CONSULTATION.—In conducting the review required under subsection (a), the National Academy of Public Administration may consult with aviation industry stakeholders.

(d) REPORT.—Not later than 270 days after the initiation of the review under subsection (a), the National Academy shall submit to the Administrator and the appropriate committees of Congress a report containing any findings and recommendations under such review.

(e) PUBLICATION.—Not later than 180 days after receiving the report required under subsection (d), the Administrator shall establish a website of the FAA that can be used to monitor and update—

(1) the metrics identified by the review conducted under subsection (a) on a quarterly and annual basis through 2030, as appropriate; and

(2) the total amount invested in NextGen technologies and resulting quantifiable benefits on a quarterly basis until the Administrator announces the completion of NextGen implementation.

SEC. 604. [49 U.S.C. 40103 note] AIRSPACE ACCESS.

(a) COALESCING AIRSPACE.—

(1) REVIEW OF NATIONAL AIRSPACE SYSTEM.—Not later than 3 years after the date of enactment of this Act, the Administrator, in coordination with the Secretary of Defense, shall conduct a comprehensive review of the airspace of the national airspace system, including special use airspace.

(2) STREAMLINING AND EXPEDITING ACCESS.—In carrying out paragraph (1), the Administrator shall identify methods to streamline, expedite, and provide greater flexibility of access to certain categories of airspace for users of the national airspace system who may not regularly have such access.

(b) BRIEFING.—

(1) IN GENERAL.—Not later than 3 months after the completion of review the under subsection (a), the Administrator shall brief the appropriate committees of Congress on the findings of such review and a proposed action plan to improve access to airspace for users of the national airspace system.

(2) CONTENTS.—In the briefing under paragraph (1), the Administrator shall include, at a minimum, the following:

(A) An identification of current challenges and barriers faced by airspace users in accessing certain categories of airspace, including special use airspace.

(B) An evaluation of existing procedures, regulations, and requirements that may impede or delay access to certain categories of airspace for certain users of the national airspace system.

(C) Actions for streamlining and expediting the airspace access process, including potential regulatory changes, technological advancements, and enhanced coordination among relevant stakeholders and Federal agencies.

(D) If determined appropriate, an implementation plan for a framework that allows for temporary access to certain categories of airspace, including special use airspace, by users of the national airspace system who do not have regular access to such airspace.

(E) An assessment of the impact of airspace access improvements described in paragraph (1) on the safety of, efficiency of, and economic opportunities for airspace users, including—

(i) military operators;

(ii) commercial operators; and

(iii) general aviation operators.

SEC. 606. [49 U.S.C. 47124 note] AIR TRAFFIC
CONTROL TOWER SAFETY.

FAA Reauthorization Act of 2

(3) IMPLEMENTATION AND FOLLOW-UP.—

(A) ACTION PLAN.—The Administrator shall take such actions as are necessary to implement the action plan developed pursuant to this section.

(B) COORDINATION.—In implementing the action plan under subparagraph (A), the Administrator shall coordinate with relevant stakeholders, including airspace users and the Secretary of Defense, to ensure effective implementation of such action plan, and ongoing collaboration in addressing airspace access challenges.

(C) PROGRESS REPORTS.—The Administrator shall provide to the appropriate committees of Congress periodic briefings on the implementation of the action plan developed under this subparagraph (A), including updates on—

(i) the adoption of streamlined procedures;

(ii) technological enhancements; and

(iii) any regulatory changes necessary to improve airspace access and flexibility.

* * * * * * *

SEC. 606. [49 U.S.C. 47124 note] AIR TRAFFIC CONTROL TOWER SAFETY.

In designing, adopting a design, or constructing an air traffic control tower based on a previously adopted design, the Administrator shall prioritize the safety of the national airspace system, the safety of employees of the Administration, the operational reliability of such air traffic control tower, and the costs of such tower.

* * * * * * *

SEC. 608. CONSIDERATION OF SMALL HUB CONTROL TOWERS.

In selecting projects for the replacement of federally owned air traffic control towers from funds made available under the heading "Federal Aviation Administration—Facilities and Equipment" in title VIII of division J of the Infrastructure Investment and Jobs Act (Public Law 117-58), the Administrator shall consider selecting projects at small hub commercial service airports with control

SEC. 609. [49 U.S.C. 44505 note] FLIGHT
PROFILE OPTIMIZATION.

FAA Reauthorization Act of 2024

towers that are at least 50 years old.

SEC. 609. [49 U.S.C. 44505 note] FLIGHT PROFILE OPTIMIZATION.

(a) PILOT PROGRAM.—

(1) ESTABLISHMENT.—The Administrator shall establish a pilot program to award grants to air traffic flow management technology providers to develop prototype capabilities to incorporate flight profile optimization (in this section referred to as "FPO") into the trajectory based-operations air traffic flow management system of the FAA.

(2) CONSIDERATIONS.—In establishing the pilot program under paragraph (1), the Administrator shall consider the following:

(A) The extent to which developed FPO capabilities may reduce strain on the national airspace system infrastructure while facilitating safe and efficient flow of future air traffic volumes and diverse range of aircraft and advanced aviation aircraft.

(B) The extent to which developed FPO capabilities may achieve environmental benefits and time savings.

(C) The perspectives of FAA employees responsible for air traffic flow management development projects, bilateral civil aviation regulatory partners, and industry applicants on the performance of the FAA in carrying out air traffic flow management system development projects.

(D) Any other information the Administrator determines appropriate.

(3) APPLICATION.—To be eligible to receive a grant under the program, an air traffic flow management technology provider shall submit an application to the Administrator at such time, in such manner, and containing such information as the Administrator may require.

(4) MAXIMUM AMOUNT.—A grant awarded under the program may not exceed $2,000,000 to a single air traffic flow management technology provider.

(b) BRIEFING TO CONGRESS.—Not later than 1 year after the date of enactment of this Act, and annually thereafter until the termination of the pilot program under subsection (d) established under this section, the Administrator shall brief the appropriate committees of Congress on the progress of such pilot program, including any implementation challenges of the program, detailed metrics of the program, and any recommendations to achieve the adoption of FPO.

(c) TRAJECTORY-BASED OPERATIONS DEFINED.—In this section, the term "trajectory-based operations" means an air traffic flow management method for strategically planning, managing, and optimizing flights that uses time-based management, performance-based navigation, and other capabilities and processes to achieve air traffic flow management operational objectives and improvements.

(d) SUNSET.—The pilot program under this section shall terminate on October 1, 2028.

* * * * * * *

SEC. 611. [49 U.S.C. 47124 note] FEDERAL CONTACT TOWER WAGE DETERMINATIONS AND POSITIONS.

(a) IN GENERAL.—The Secretary shall request that the Secretary of Labor—

(1) review and update, as necessary, including to account for cost-of-living adjustments, the basis for the wage determination for air traffic controllers who are employed at air traffic control towers operated under the Contract Tower Program established under section 47124 of title 49, United States Code;

(2) reassess the basis for air traffic controller occupation codes;

(3) create a new wage determination category or occupation code for managers of air traffic controllers who are employed at air traffic control towers operated under the Contract Tower Program; and

(4) consult with the Administrator in carrying out the requirements of paragraphs (1) through (3).

(b) REPORT.—Not later than 2 years after the date of enactment of this Act, the Secretary, in consultation with the Secretary of Labor, shall submit to the appropriate committees of Congress a report that includes—

(1) a description of the findings and conclusions of the review and reassessment made under subsection (a);

(2) an explanation of and justification for the basis for the wage determination; and

(3) a description of the actions taken by the Department of Transportation and the Department of Labor to ensure that contract tower air traffic controller wages are adjusted for inflation and are assigned the appropriate occupation codes.

* * * * * * *

SEC. 613. [49 U.S.C. 44505 note] AERONAUTICAL MOBILE COMMUNICATIONS SERVICES.

(a) SATELLITE VOICE COMMUNICATIONS SERVICES.—The Administrator shall evaluate the addition of satellite voice communication services (in this section referred to as "SatVoice") to the Aeronautical Mobile Communications program (in this section referred to as the "AMCS program") that provides for the delivery of air traffic control messages in oceanic and remote continental airspace.

(b) ANALYSIS AND IMPLEMENTATION PROCEDURES.—Not later than 1 year after the date of enactment of this Act, the Administrator shall begin to develop the safety case analysis and implementation procedures for SatVoice instructions over the controlled oceanic and remote continental airspace regions of the FAA.

(c) REQUIREMENTS.—The analysis and implementation procedures required under subsection (b) shall include, at a minimum, the following:

(1) Network and protocol testing and integration with satellite service providers.

(2) Operational testing with aircraft to identify and resolve performance issues.

(3) A definition of Satcom Standards and Recommended Practices established through a collaboration with the International Civil Aviation Organization, which shall include an RCP-130 performance standard as well as SatVoice standards.

(4) Training for radio operators on new operation procedures and protocols.

(5) A phased implementation plan for incorporating

SatVoice services into the AMCS program.

(6) The estimated cost of the implementation procedures for relevant stakeholders.

(d) HF/VHF MINIMUM EQUIPAGE.—

(1) RULE OF CONSTRUCTION.—Nothing in this section shall be construed to affect the HF/VHF equipage requirement for communications in oceanic and remote continental airspace as of the date of enactment of this Act.

(2) MAINTENANCE OF HF/VHF SERVICES.—The Administrator shall maintain HF/VHF services existing as of the date of enactment of this Act as minimum equipage under the AMCS program to provide for auxiliary communication and maintain safety in the event of a satellite outage.

SEC. 614. [49 U.S.C. 44505 note] DELIVERY OF CLEARANCE TO PILOTS VIA INTERNET PROTOCOL.

(a) IN GENERAL.—Not later than 18 months after the date of enactment of this Act, the Administrator shall establish a pilot program to conduct testing and an evaluation to determine the feasibility of the use, in air traffic control towers, of technology for mobile clearance delivery for general aviation and on-demand air carriers operating under part 135 of title 14, Code of Federal Regulations, at suitable airports that do not have tower data link services.

(b) AIRPORT SELECTION.—

(1) IN GENERAL.—The Administrator shall designate 5 suitable airports for participation in the program established under subsection (a) after consultation with the exclusive representatives of air traffic controllers certified under section 7111 of title 5, United States Code, airport sponsors, aircraft and avionics manufacturers, MITRE, and aircraft operators

(2) AIRPORT SIZE AND COMPLEXITY.—In designating airports under paragraph (1), the Administrator shall designate airports of different size and complexity.

(c) PROGRAM OBJECTIVE.—The program established under subsection (a) shall address and include safety, security, and operational requirements for mobile clearance delivery at airports and heliports across the United States.

(d) REPORT.—Not later than 1 year after the date on which

the program under subsection (a) is established, the Administrator shall submit to the appropriate committees of Congress a report on the safety, security, and operational performance of mobile clearance delivery at airports pursuant to this section and recommendations on how best to improve the program.

(e) DEFINITIONS.—In this section:

(1) MOBILE CLEARANCE DELIVERY.—The term "mobile clearance delivery" means the delivery of access to departure clearance and clearance cancellation via internet protocol via applications to pilots while aircraft are on the ground where traditional data link installations are not feasible or possible.

(2) TOWER DATA LINK SERVICES.—The term "tower data link services" means communications between controllers and pilots using controller-pilot data link communications.

(3) SUITABLE AIRPORT.—The term "suitable airport" means towered airports, non-towered airports, and heliports.

* * * * * * *

SEC. 619. [49 U.S.C. 40101 note] NEXTGEN PROGRAMS.

(a) IN GENERAL.—Not later than 180 days after the date of enactment of this Act, and periodically thereafter as the Administrator determines appropriate, the Administrator shall convene FAA officials to evaluate and expedite the implementation of NextGen programs and capabilities.

(b) NEXTGEN PROGRAM PRIORITIZATION.—In allocating amounts appropriated pursuant to section 48101(a) of title 49, United States Code, the Secretary shall give priority to the following activities:

(1) Performance-based navigation.

(2) Data communications.

(3) Terminal flight data manager.

(4) Aeronautical information management.

(5) Other activities as recommended by the NextGen Advisory Committee and determined by the Administrator to be appropriate.

(c) PERFORMANCE-BASED NAVIGATION.—

(1) IN GENERAL.—Not later than 3 years after the date of enactment of this Act, the Administrator shall fully implement

performance-based navigation procedures for all terminal and enroute routes, including approach and departure procedures for covered airports.

(2) SPECIFIC PROCEDURES.—Pursuant to paragraph (1), the Administrator shall prioritize the following performance-based navigation procedures:

(A) Trajectory-based operations.

(B) Optimized profile descents.

(C) Multiple airport route separation.

(D) Established on required navigation performance.

(E) Converging runway display aids.

(3) PERFORMANCE-BASED NAVIGATION BASELINE EQUIPAGE REQUIREMENTS. —In carrying out paragraph (1), the Administrator shall issue such regulations as may be required, and publish applicable advisory circulars, to establish the equipage baseline appropriate for aircraft to safely use performance-based navigation procedures.

(4) UTILIZATION ACTION PLAN.—Not later than 180 days after enactment of this Act, the Administrator shall, in consultation with certified labor representatives of air traffic controllers and the NextGen Advisory Committee, develop an action plan to utilize performance-based navigation procedures as a primary means of navigation to further reduce the dependency on legacy systems within the national airspace system.

(d) DATA COMMUNICATIONS.—

(1) IN GENERAL.—Not later than 2 years after the date of enactment of this Act, the Administrator shall fully implement the use of data communications.

(2) SPECIFIC CAPABILITIES.—In carrying out subsection (a) and this subsection, the Administrator shall prioritize the following data communications capabilities:

(A) Ground-to-ground message exchange for surface aircraft operations and runway safety at airports.

(B) Automated message generation and receipt.

(C) Message routing and transmission.

(D) Direct communications with aircraft avionics.

(E) Implementation of data communications at all Air Route Traffic Control Centers.

(F) The Future Air Navigation System.

(e) TERMINAL FLIGHT DATA MANAGER AND OTHER SYSTEMS.—

(1) TERMINAL FLIGHT DATA MANAGER. —Not later than 4 years after the date of enactment of this Act, the Administrator shall install the Terminal Flight Data Manager system at not less than 89 airports in the United States based on the highest number of annual aircraft operations or a determination of operational need and the impact of installation and deployment on the national airspace system.

(2) ELECTRONIC FLIGHT STRIPS.—At a minimum, the Administrator shall implement electronic flight strips at the air traffic control towers of airports described in paragraph (1).

(3) FLOW MANAGEMENT DATA AND SERVICES.—Not later than 4 years after the date of enactment of this Act, if the Administrator finds that Terminal Flight Data Manager systems would be beneficial to safety or efficiency, the Administrator shall install Flow Management Data and Services at airports described under paragraph (1).

(4) APPROPRIATIONS.—The activities under paragraphs (1), (2), and (3) of this subsection shall be contingent on the appropriation of funds to carry out this subsection.

(f) AERONAUTICAL INFORMATION MANAGEMENT SYSTEMS.—

(1) IN GENERAL.—Not later than 3 years after the date of enactment of this Act, the Administrator shall fully modernize the aeronautical information management systems of the FAA to improve the functionality, useability, durability, and reliability of such systems used in the national airspace system.

(2) REQUIREMENTS.—In carrying out paragraph (1), the Administrator shall—

(A) improve the distribution of critical safety information to pilots, air traffic control, and other relevant aviation stakeholders;

(B) fully develop and implement the Enterprise Information Display System; and

(C) notwithstanding a centralized aeronautical information management system, restructure the back-up systems of aeronautical information management systems to be independent and self-sufficient from one another.

(g) NEXTGEN EQUIPAGE PLAN.—

(1) IN GENERAL.—Not later than 14 months after the date of enactment of this Act, the Administrator shall develop a 2-year implementation plan to further incentivize the acceleration of the equipage rates of certain NextGen avionics within the fleets of air carriers (as such term is defined in section 40102(a) of title 49, United States Code.

(2) CONTENTS.—In developing the plan required under paragraph (1), the Administrator shall, at a minimum—

(A) provide for further implementation and deployment of NextGen operational improvements to incentivize universal equipage of commercial and regional aircraft with certain NextGen avionics;

(B) identify any remaining barriers for operators of commercial and regional aircraft to properly equip such aircraft with certain NextGen avionics, including any methods to address such barriers;

(C) provide for the use of the best methods to highlight and enhance to operators of commercial and regional aircraft the benefits of equipping such aircraft with certain NextGen avionics; and

(D) include in such plan any equipage guidelines and regulations the Administrator determines necessary and appropriate.

(3) CONSULTATION.—In developing the plan under paragraph (1), the Administrator shall consult with representatives from—

(A) trade associations representing air carriers;

(B) trade associations representing avionics manufacturers;

(C) certified labor organizations representing air traffic controllers; and

(D) any other representatives the Administrator determines appropriate.

(4) SUBMISSION OF PLAN.—Not later than 15 months after the date of enactment of this Act, the Administrator shall

submit to the appropriate committees of Congress the plan required under this subsection.

(5) IMPLEMENTATION.—Not later than 18 months after the date of enactment of this Act, the Administrator shall initiate such actions necessary to implement the plan developed under paragraph (1), including initiating any required rulemaking.

(6) DEFINITION.—In this subsection, the term "certain NextGen avionics" means those avionics and baseline capabilities as recommended in the report of the NextGen Advisory Committee titled "Minimum Capabilities List (MCL) Ad Hoc Team NAC Task 19-1 Report", issued on November 17, 2020.

(h) EFFECT OF FAILURE TO MEET DEADLINE.—

(1) NOTIFICATION OF CONGRESS.—For each deadline established under subsections (a) through (g), if the Administrator determines that the Administrator has not met or will not meet each such deadline, the Administrator shall, not later than 30 days after such determination, notify the appropriate committees of Congress about the failure to meet each deadline.

(2) CONTENTS OF NOTIFICATION.—Each notification under paragraph (1) shall be accompanied by the following:

(A) An explanation as to why the Administrator will not or did not meet the deadline described in such paragraph.

(B) A description of the actions the Administrator plans to take to meet the deadline described in such paragraph.

(C) Actions Congress can take to assist the Administrator in meeting the deadline described in such paragraph.

(3) BRIEFING.—If the Administrator is required to provide notice under paragraph (1), the Administrator shall provide the appropriate committees of Congress quarterly briefings as to the progress made by the Administrator regarding implementation under the respective subsection for which the deadline will not be or was not met until such time as the Administrator has completed the required work under such subsection.

(i) NEXTGEN ADVISORY COMMITTEE CONSULTATION.—

(1) IN GENERAL.—The Administrator shall consult and task the NextGen Advisory Committee with providing recommendations on ways to expedite, prioritize, and fully implement the NextGen program to realize the operational benefits of such programs.

(2) CONSIDERATIONS.—In providing recommendations under paragraph (1), the NextGen Advisory Committee shall consider—

(A) air traffic throughput of the national airspace system;

(B) daily operational performance, including delays and cancellations; and

(C) the potential need for performance-based operational metrics related to the NextGen program and subsequent air traffic modernization programs and efforts.

* * * * * * *

SEC. 622. [49 U.S.C. 44505 note] AUDIT OF LEGACY SYSTEMS.

(a) IN GENERAL.—Not later than 120 days after the date of enactment of this Act, the Administrator shall initiate an audit of all legacy systems of the national airspace system to determine the level of operational risk, functionality, and security of such systems and the compatibility of such systems with current and future technology.

(b) SCOPE OF AUDIT.—The audit required under subsection (a)—

(1) shall be conducted by an independent third-party contractor or a federally funded research and development center selected by the Administrator;

(2) shall include an assessment of whether a legacy system is an outdated, insufficient, unsafe, or unstable legacy system;

(3) with respect to any legacy systems identified in the audit as an outdated, insufficient, unsafe, or unstable legacy system, shall include—

(A) an analysis of the operational risks associated with using such legacy systems;

(B) recommendations for replacement or enhancement of such legacy systems; and

(C) an analysis of any potential impact on aviation safety and efficiency; and

(4) shall include recommended performance metrics by which the Administrator can assess the circumstances in which safety-critical communication, navigation, and surveillance aviation infrastructure within the national airspace system can remain in operational service, which take into account—

(A) the expected lifespan of such aviation infrastructure;

(B) the number and type of mechanical failures of such aviation infrastructure;

(C) the average annual costs of maintaining such aviation infrastructure over a 5-year period and whether such costs exceed the cost to replace such aviation infrastructure; and

(D) the availability of replacement parts or labor capable of maintaining such aviation infrastructure.

(c) DEADLINE.—Not later than 15 months after the date of enactment of this Act, the audit required under subsection (a) shall be completed.

(d) REPORT.—Not later than 180 days after the audit required under subsection (a) is completed, the Administrator shall provide to the appropriate committees of Congress a report on the findings and recommendations of such audit, including—

(1) an inventory of the legacy systems in use;

(2) an assessment of the operational condition of the legacy systems in use, including the interoperability of such systems;

(3) the average age of such legacy systems and, for each such legacy system, the intended design life of the system, by type; and

(4) the availability of replacement parts, equipment, or technology to maintain such legacy systems.

(e) PLAN TO ACCELERATE DRAWDOWN, REPLACEMENT, OR ENHANCEMENT OF IDENTIFIED LEGACY SYSTEMS.—

(1) IN GENERAL.—Not later than 120 days after the date on which the Administrator provides the report under subsection

(d), the Administrator shall develop and implement a plan, in consultation with industry representatives, to accelerate the drawdown, replacement, or enhancement of any legacy systems that are identified in the audit required under subsection (a) as outdated, insufficient, unsafe, or unstable legacy systems.

(2) PRIORITIES.—In developing the plan under paragraph (1), the Administrator shall prioritize the drawdown, replacement, or enhancement of such legacy systems based on the operational risks such legacy systems pose to aviation safety and the costs associated with the replacement or enhancement of such legacy systems.

(3) COLLABORATION WITH EXTERNAL EXPERTS.—In carrying out this subsection, the Administrator shall—

(A) collaborate with industry representatives and other external experts in information technology to develop the plan under paragraph (1) within a reasonable timeframe;

(B) identify technologies in existence or in development that, with or without adaptation, are expected to be suitable to meet the technical information technology needs of the FAA; and

(C) maintain consistency with the acquisition management system established and updated pursuant to section 40110(d) of title 49, United States Code.

(4) PROGRESS UPDATES.—The Administrator shall provide the appropriate committees of Congress with semiannual updates through September 30, 2028 on the progress made in carrying out the plan under paragraph (1).

(5) INSPECTOR GENERAL REVIEW.—

(A) IN GENERAL.—Not later than 3 years after the Administrator develops the plan required under paragraph (1), the inspector general of the Department of Transportation shall assess such efforts of the Administration to drawdown, replace, or enhance any legacy systems identified under subsection (a).

(B) REPORT.—The inspector general shall submit to the appropriate committees of Congress a report on the results of the review carried out under subparagraph (A).

(f) DEFINITIONS.—In this section:

(1) INDUSTRY.—The term "industry" means aviation industry organizations with expertise in aviation-dedicated network systems, systems engineering platforms, aviation software services, air traffic management, flight operations, and International Civil Aviation Organization standards.

(2) LEGACY SYSTEM.—The term "legacy system" means any communication, navigation, surveillance, or automation or network applications or ground-based aviation infrastructure, or other critical software and hardware systems owned by the FAA, that were deployed prior to the year 2000, including the Notice to Air Missions system.

(3) OUTDATED, INSUFFICIENT, UNSAFE, OR UNSTABLE LEGACY SYSTEM.—The term "outdated, insufficient, unsafe, or unstable legacy system" means a legacy system for which the likelihood of failure of such system creates a risk to air safety or security due to the age, ability to be maintained in a cost-effective manner, vulnerability to degradation, errors, or malicious attacks of such system, or any other factors that may compromise the performance or security of such system, including a legacy system—

(A) that is vulnerable or susceptible to mechanical failure; and

(B) with a risk of a single point of failure or that lacks sufficient contingencies in the event of such failure.

* * * * * * *

SEC. 624. AIR TRAFFIC CONTROL TOWER REPLACEMENT PROCESS REPORT.

(a) REPORT REQUIRED.—Not later than 120 days after the date of enactment of this Act, the Administrator shall submit to Congress a report on the process by which air traffic control tower facilities are chosen for replacement.

(b) CONTENTS.—The report required under subsection (a) shall contain—

(1) the process by which air traffic control tower facilities are chosen for replacement, including which divisions of the Administration control or are involved in the replacement decision making process;

(2) the criteria the Administrator uses to determine which air traffic control tower facilities to replace, including—

(A) the relative importance of each such criteria;

(B) why the Administrator uses each such criteria; and

(C) the reasons for the relative importance of each such criteria;

(3) what types of investigation the Administrator carries out to determine if an air traffic control tower facility should be replaced;

(4) a timeline of the replacement process for an individual air traffic control tower facility replacement;

(5) the list of facilities established under subsection (c), including the reason for selecting each such facility; and

(6) any other information the Administrator considers relevant.

(c) [49 U.S.C. 47124 note] LIST OF REPLACED AIR TRAFFIC CONTROL TOWER FACILITIES.—The Administrator shall establish, maintain, and publish on the website of the FAA a list of the following:

(1) All air traffic control tower facilities replaced within the 10-year period preceding the date of enactment of this Act.

(2) Any air traffic control tower facilities for which the Administrator has made a determination requiring replacement, but for which such replacement has not yet been completed.

SEC. 625. CONTRACT TOWER PROGRAM SAFETY ENHANCEMENTS.

(a) [49 U.S.C. 47124 note] PILOT PROGRAM FOR TRANSITIONING TO FAA TOWERS.—

(1) IN GENERAL.—Not later than 18 months after the date of enactment of this Act, the Administrator shall establish a pilot program to convert high-activity air traffic control towers operating under the Contract Tower Program as established under section 47124 of title 49, United States Code, (in this section referred to as the "Contract Tower Program") to a level I (Visual Flight Rules) tower staffed by the FAA.

(2) PRIORITY.—In selecting air traffic control towers to

participate in the pilot program established under paragraph (1), the Administrator shall prioritize air traffic control towers operating under the Contract Tower Program that—

(A) either—

(i) had over 200,000 annual tower operations in calendar year 2022; or

(ii) served a small hub airport with more than 900,000 passenger enplanements in calendar year 2021;

(B) are either currently owned by the FAA or are constructed to FAA standards; and

(C) operate within complex airspace, including airspace that serves air carrier, general aviation, and military aircraft.

(3) TOWER SELECTION.—The number of air traffic control towers selected to participate in the pilot program established under paragraph (1) shall be determined based on the availability of funds for the pilot program and the interest of the airport sponsor related to such facility.

(4) CONTROLLER RETENTION.—With respect to any high-activity air traffic control tower selected to be converted under the pilot program established under paragraph (1), the Administrator shall appoint to the position of air traffic controller any air traffic controller who—

(A) is employed at such air traffic control tower as of the date on which the Administrator selects such tower to be converted;

(B) meets the qualifications contained in section 44506(f)(1)(A) of title 49, United States Code; and

(C) has all other pre-employment qualifications required by law to be a certified controller of the FAA.

(5) SAFETY ANALYSIS.—

(A) IN GENERAL.—The Administrator shall conduct a safety analysis to determine whether the conversion of any air traffic control tower described in paragraph (1) negatively impacts aviation safety at such air traffic control tower and take such actions needed to address any negative impact.

(B) REPORT.—Not later than 3 years after the date of enactment of this Act, the Administrator shall submit to the appropriate committees of Congress a report describing the results of the safety analysis under subparagraph (A), any actions taken to address any negative impacts to safety, and the overall results of the pilot program established under this subsection.

(6) AUTHORIZATION OF APPROPRIATIONS.—Out of amounts made available under section 106(k) of title 49, United States Code, there is authorized to be appropriated to carry out this subsection $30,000,000 to remain available for 5 fiscal years.

(b) AIR TRAFFIC CONTROLLER STAFFING LEVELS AT SMALL AND MEDIUM HUB AIRPORTS.—Section 47124(b)(2) of title 49, United States Code, is amended—

(1) by striking "The Secretary may" and inserting the following:

"(A) IN GENERAL.—The Secretary may"

; and

(2) by adding at the end the following:

"(B) SMALL OR MEDIUM HUB AIRPORTS.—In the case of a contract entered into on or after the date of enactment of this subparagraph to operate an airport traffic control tower at a small or medium hub airport, the contract shall require the Secretary, after coordination with the airport sponsor and the entity, State, or subdivision, and not later than 18 months after the date of enactment of the FAA Reauthorization Act of 2024, to provide funding sufficient for the cost of wages and benefits of at least 2 air traffic controllers for each tower operating shift."

(c) PRIORITIES FOR FACILITY SELECTION.—Section 47124(b)(3)(C) of title 49, United States Code, is amended by adding at the end the following:

"(viii) Air traffic control towers at airports with safety or operational problems related to the lack of an existing tower.

"(ix) Air traffic control towers at airports with projected commercial and military increases in aircraft or flight operations.

"(x) Air traffic control towers at airports with a variety of aircraft operations, including a variety of commercial and military flight operations."

SEC. 626. SENSE OF CONGRESS ON USE OF ADVANCED SURVEILLANCE IN OCEANIC AIRSPACE.

It is the sense of Congress the FAA shall continue to evaluate the potential uses for space-based automatic dependent surveillance broadcast to improve surveillance coverage of domestic airspace including improving surveillance coverage over remote terrain and in oceanic airspace. If determined appropriate by the Administrator, the FAA shall consider whether additional testing would meaningfully contribute to the FAA's processes for developing separation standards and more efficient routes.

SEC. 627. LOW-ALTITUDE ROUTES FOR VERTICAL FLIGHT.

(a) SENSE OF CONGRESS.—It is the sense of Congress that the national airspace system requires additional rotorcraft, powered-lift aircraft, and low-altitude instrument flight rules, routes leveraging advances in performance based navigation in order to provide direct, safe, and reliable routes that ensure sufficient separation from higher altitude fixed wing aircraft traffic.

(b) [49 U.S.C. 40103 note] LOW-ALTITUDE ROTORCRAFT AND POWERED-LIFT AIRCRAFT INSTRUMENT FLIGHT ROUTES.—

(1) IN GENERAL.—Not later than 3 years after the date of enactment of this Act, the Administrator shall initiate a rulemaking process to establish or update, as appropriate, low altitude routes and flight procedures to ensure safe rotorcraft and powered-lift aircraft operations in the national airspace system.

(2) REQUIREMENTS.—In carrying out this subsection, the Administrator shall—

(A) incorporate instrument flight rules rotorcraft operations into the low-altitude performance based navigation procedure infrastructure;

(B) prioritize the development of new helicopter area navigation instrument flight rules routes as part of the United States air traffic service route structure that utilize performance based navigation, such as Global Positioning

System and Global Navigation Satellite System equipment;
and

(C) consider the impact of such low altitude flight
routes on other airspace users and impacted communities
to ensure that such routes are designed to minimize—

(i) the potential for conflict with existing national
airspace system operations;

(ii) the workload of air traffic controllers; and

(iii) negative effects to impacted communities.

(3) CONSULTATION.—In carrying out the rulemaking
process under paragraph (1), the Administrator shall consult
with—

(A) stakeholders in the airport, heliport, rotorcraft
manufacturer and operator, general aviation operator,
powered-lift operator, air carrier, and performance based
navigation technology manufacturer sectors;

(B) the United States Helicopter Safety Team;

(C) exclusive bargaining representatives of air traffic
controllers certified under section 7111 of title 5, United
States Code; and

(D) other stakeholders determined appropriate by the
Administrator.

* * * * * * *

SEC. 630. AIRSPACE INTEGRATION FOR SPACE LAUNCH AND REENTRY.

(a) SENSE OF CONGRESS.—It is the Sense of Congress that—

(1) a safe and efficient national airspace system that
successfully supports existing users and integrates new
entrants is of the utmost importance;

(2) both commercial aviation and space launch and reentry
operations are vital to United States global leadership, national
security, and economic opportunity;

(3) aircraft hazard areas are necessary during space launch
and reentry operations to ensure public safety; and

(4) the Administrator should prioritize the development
and deployment of technologies to improve visibility of space

launch and reentry operations within FAA computer systems and minimize operational workload to air traffic controllers associated with routing traffic during spaceflight launch and reentry operations.

(b) SPACE LAUNCH AND REENTRY AIRSPACE INTEGRATION TECHNOLOGY.—Out of amounts made available under section 48101 of title 49, United States Code, $10,000,000 for each of the fiscal years 2025 through 2028 (or until such time as the Administrator determines that the project meeting the requirements of this section has reached an operational status) is available for the Administrator to carry out a project to expedite the development, acquisition, and deployment of technologies or capabilities to aid in space launch and reentry integration with the objective of operational readiness not later than December 31, 2026, which may include—

(1) technologies recommended by the Airspace Access Priorities aviation rulemaking committee in the final report titled "ARC Recommendations Final Report", issued on August 21, 2019;

(2) systems to enable the integration of launch and reentry data directly onto air traffic controller displays; and

(3) automated systems to enable near real-time planning and dynamic rerouting of commercial aircraft during and following commercial space launch and reentry operations.

* * * * * * *

TITLE VII—MODERNIZING AIRPORT INFRASTRUCTURE

Subtitle A—Airport Improvement Program Modifications

* * * * * * *

SEC. 711. [49 U.S.C. 47101 note] PROHIBITION ON PROVISION OF AIRPORT IMPROVEMENT GRANT FUNDS TO CERTAIN ENTITIES THAT HAVE VIOLATED INTELLECTUAL PROPERTY RIGHTS OF UNITED STATES ENTITIES.

(a) IN GENERAL.—Beginning on the date that is 30 days after the date of enactment of this Act, amounts provided as project grants under subchapter I of chapter 471 of title 49, United States Code, may not be used to enter into a covered contract with any entity on the list required under subsection (b).

(b) LIST REQUIRED.—

(1) IN GENERAL.—Not later than 30 days after the date of enactment of this Act, and thereafter as required under paragraph (2), the United States Trade Representative, the Attorney General, and the Administrator shall make available to the Administrator a publicly-available list of entities manufacturing airport passenger boarding infrastructure or equipment that—

(A) are owned, directed by, or subsidized in whole or in part by the People's Republic of China;

(B) have been determined by a Federal court to have misappropriated intellectual property or trade secrets from an entity organized under the laws of the United States or any jurisdiction within the United States;

(C) own or control, are owned or controlled by, are under common ownership or control with, or are successors to an entity described in subparagraph (A); or

(D) have entered into an agreement with or accepted funding from, whether in the form of minority investment interest or debt, have entered into a partnership with, or have entered into another contractual or other written arrangement with an entity described in subparagraph (A).

(2) UPDATES TO LIST.—The United States Trade Representative shall update the list required under paragraph (1), based on information provided by the Attorney General and the Administrator—

(A) not less frequently than every 90 days during the 180-day period following the initial publication of the list under paragraph (1); and

(B) not less frequently than annually thereafter.

(c) DEFINITIONS.—In this section:

(1) IN GENERAL.—The definitions in section 47102 of title 49, United States Code, shall apply.

(2) COVERED CONTRACT.—The term "covered contract" means a contract or other agreement for the procurement of infrastructure or equipment for a passenger boarding bridge at an airport.

* * * * * * *

SEC. 713. PFC TURNBACK REDUCTION.

* * * * * * *

(b) [49 U.S.C. 47114 note] APPLICABILITY.—For an airport that increased in categorization from a small hub to a medium hub in any fiscal year beginning after the date of enactment of the FAA Reauthorization Act of 2018 (Public Law 115-254) and prior to the date of enactment of this Act, the amendment to section 47114(f)(2) of title 49, United States Code, under subsection (a) shall be applied as though the airport increased in categorization from a small hub to a medium hub in the calendar year prior to the first fiscal year in which such amendment is applicable.

* * * * * * *

SEC. 730. MINORITY AND DISADVANTAGED BUSINESS PARTICIPATION.

(a) FINDINGS.—Congress finds the following:

(1) While significant progress has occurred due to the establishment of the airport disadvantaged business enterprise program and the airport concessions disadvantaged business enterprise program under sections 47113 and 47107(e) of title 49, United States Code, respectively, discrimination and related barriers continue to pose significant obstacles for minority- and women-owned businesses seeking to do business in airport-related markets across the Nation.

(2) Congress has received and reviewed testimony and documentation of race and gender discrimination from numerous sources, including congressional hearings and roundtables, scientific reports, reports issued by public and private agencies, news stories, reports of discrimination by organizations and individuals, and discrimination lawsuits. Such testimony and documentation show that race- and gender-neutral efforts alone are insufficient to address the problem.

SEC. 732. [49 U.S.C. 47103 note] POPULOUS
COUNTIES WITHOUT AIRPORTS.

FAA Reauthorization Act of 2

(3) The testimony and documentation described in paragraph (2) demonstrate that race and gender discrimination pose a barrier to full and fair participation in airport-related businesses of women business owners and minority business owners in the racial groups detailed in parts 23 and 26 of title 49, Code of Federal Regulations, and has impacted firm development and other aspects of airport-related business in the public and private markets.

(4) The testimony and documentation described in paragraph (2) provide a strong basis that there is a compelling need for the continuation of the airport disadvantaged business enterprise program and the airport concessions disadvantaged business enterprise program to address race and gender discrimination in airport-related business.

* * * * * * *

SEC. 732. [49 U.S.C. 47103 note] POPULOUS COUNTIES WITHOUT AIRPORTS.

Notwithstanding any other provision of law, the Secretary may not deny inclusion in the national plan of integrated airport systems maintained under section 47103 of title 49, United States Code, to an airport or proposed airport if the airport or proposed airport—

(1) is located in the most populous county (as such term is defined in section 2 of title 1, United States Code) of a State that does not have an airport listed in the national plan;

(2) has an airport sponsor that was established before January 1, 2017;

(3) is located more than 15 miles away from another airport listed in the national plan;

(4) demonstrates how the airport will meet the operational activity required, through a forecast validated by the Secretary, within the first 10 years of operation;

(5) meets FAA airport design standards;

(6) submits a benefit-cost analysis;

(7) presents a detailed financial plan to accomplish construction and ongoing maintenance; and

(8) has the documented support of the State government for the entry of the airport or proposed airport into the national

plan.

SEC. 733. [49 U.S.C. 47101 note] AIP HANDBOOK UPDATE.

(a) IN GENERAL.—Not later than 3 years after the date of enactment of this Act, the Administrator shall revise the Airport Improvement Program Handbook (FAA Order 5100.38D) (in this section referred to as the "AIP Handbook") to account for legislative changes to the airport improvement program under subchapter I of chapter 471 and chapter 475 of title 49, United States Code, and to make such other changes as the Administrator determines necessary.

(b) REQUIREMENTS RELATING TO ALASKA.—In revising the AIP Handbook under subsection (a) (and in any subsequent revision), the Administrator, in consultation with the Governor of Alaska, shall identify and incorporate reasonable exceptions to the general requirements of the AIP Handbook to meet the unique circumstances, and advance the safety needs, of airports in Alaska, including with respect to the following:

(1) Snow Removal Equipment Building size and configuration.

(2) Expansion of lease areas.

(3) Shared governmental use of airport equipment and facilities in remote locations.

(4) Ensuring the resurfacing or reconstruction of legacy runways to support—

(A) aircraft necessary to support critical health needs of a community;

(B) remote fuel deliveries; and

(C) firefighting response.

(5) The use of runway end identifier lights at airports in Alaska.

(c) ADDITIONAL REQUIREMENT.—In revising the AIP Handbook under subsection (a), the Administrator shall include updates to reflect whether a light emitting diode system is an appropriate replacement for any existing halogen system.

(d) PUBLIC COMMENT.—

(1) IN GENERAL.—Not later than 2 years after the date of enactment of this Act, the Administrator shall publish a draft

revision of the AIP Handbook and make such draft available for public comment for a period of not less than 90 days.

(2) REVIEW.—The Administrator shall—

(A) review all comments submitted during the public comment period described under paragraph (1);

(B) as the Administrator considers appropriate, incorporate changes based on such comments into the final revision of the Handbook; and

(C) provide a response to all significant comments.

(e) INTERIM IMPLEMENTATION OF CHANGES.—

(1) IN GENERAL.—Except as provided in paragraph (2), not later than 1 year after the date of enactment of this Act, the Administrator shall issue program guidance letters to provide for the interim implementation of amendments made by this Act to the Airport Improvement Program.

(2) ALASKA EXCEPTIONS.—Not later than 60 days after the date on which the Administrator identified reasonable exceptions under subsection (b), the Administrator, in consultation with the Regional Administrator of the FAA Alaskan Region, shall issue program guidance letters to provide for the interim application of such exceptions.

* * * * * * *

SEC. 739. SPECIAL RULE FOR RECLASSIFICATION OF CERTAIN UNCLASSIFIED AIRPORTS.

(a) REQUEST FOR RECLASSIFICATION.—

(1) IN GENERAL.—Not later than September 30, 2024, a privately owned reliever airport (as such term is defined in section 47102 of title 49, United States Code) that is identified as unclassified in the National Plan of Integrated Airport Systems of the FAA titled "National Plan of Integrated Airport Systems (NPIAS) 2023-2027", published on September 30, 2022 may submit to the Secretary a request to reclassify the airport according to the criteria used to classify a publicly owned airport.

(2) REQUIRED INFORMATION.—In submitting a request under paragraph (1), a privately owned reliever airport shall include the following information:

(A) A sworn statement and accompanying documentation that demonstrates how the airport would satisfy the requirements of FAA Order 5090.5, titled "Formulation of the NPIAS and ACIP" (or any successor guidance), to be classified as "Local" or "Basic" if the airport was publicly owned.

(B) A report that—

(i) identifies the role of the airport to the aviation system; and

(ii) describes the long-term fiscal viability of the airport based on demonstrated aeronautical activity and associated revenues relative to ongoing operating and maintenance costs.

(b) ELIGIBILITY REVIEW.—

(1) IN GENERAL.—Not later than 60 days after receiving a request from a privately owned reliever airport under subsection (a), the Secretary shall perform an eligibility review with respect to the airport, including an assessment of the safety, security, capacity, access, compliance with Federal grant assurances, and protection of natural resources of the airport and the quality of the environment, as prescribed by the Secretary.

(2) PUBLIC SPONSOR.—In performing the eligibility review under paragraph (1), the Secretary—

(A) may require the airport requesting reclassification to provide information regarding the outlook (whether positive or negative) for obtaining a public sponsor; and

(B) may not require the airport to obtain a public sponsor.

(c) RECLASSIFICATION BY SECRETARY.—

(1) IN GENERAL.—Not later than 60 days after receiving a request from a privately owned reliever airport under subsection (a)(1), the Secretary shall grant such request if the following criteria are met:

(A) The request includes the required information under subsection (a)(2).

(B) The privately owned reliever airport, to the satisfaction of the Secretary—

(i) passes the eligibility review performed under subsection (b); or

(ii) submits a corrective action plan in accordance with paragraph (2).

(2) CORRECTIVE ACTION PLAN.—With respect to a privately owned reliever airport that does not, to the satisfaction of the Secretary, pass the eligibility review performed under subsection (b), the Secretary shall provide notice of disapproval to such airport not later than 60 days after receiving the request under subsection (a)(1), and such airport may resubmit to the Secretary a reclassification request along with a corrective action plan that—

(A) resolves any shortcomings identified in such eligibility review; and

(B) proves that any necessary corrective action has been completed by the airport.

(d) EFFECTIVE DATE.—The reclassification of any privately owned reliever airport under this section shall take effect not later than—

(1) October 1, 2025, for any request granted under subsection (c)(1); and

(2) October 1, 2026, for any request granted after the submission of a corrective action plan under subsection (c)(2).

* * * * * * *

SEC. 741. SECONDARY RUNWAYS.

In approving grants for projects with funds made available pursuant to title VIII of division J of the Infrastructure Investment and Jobs Act (Public Law 117-58) under the heading "Federal Aviation Administration—Airport Infrastructure Grants", the Administrator shall consider permitting a nonhub or small hub airport to use such funds to extend secondary runways, notwithstanding the level of operational activity at such airport.

* * * * * * *

SEC. 744. [49 U.S.C. 44718 note] PROTECTION OF SAFE AND EFFICIENT USE OF AIRSPACE AT AIRPORTS.

(a) AIRSPACE REVIEW PROCESS REQUIREMENTS.—The

Administrator shall consider the following additional factors in the evaluation of cumulative impacts when making a determination of hazard or no hazard, or objection or no objection, as applicable, under part 77 of title 14, Code of Federal Regulations, regarding proposed construction or alteration within 3 miles of the runway ends and runway centerlines (as depicted in the FAA-approved Airport Layout Plan of the airport) on any land not owned by any such airport:

(1) The accumulation and spacing of structures or other obstructions that might constrain radar or communication capabilities, thereby reducing the capacity of an airport, flight procedure minimums or availability, or aircraft takeoff or landing capabilities.

(2) Safety risks of lasers, lights, or light sources, inclusive of lighted billboards and screens, affixed to structures, that may pose hazards to air navigation.

(3) Water features or hazardous wildlife attractants, as defined by the Administrator.

(4) Impacts to visual flight rule traffic patterns for both fixed and rotary wing aircraft, inclusive of special visual flight rule procedures established by Letters of Agreement between air traffic facilities, the airport, and flight operators.

(5) Impacts to FAA-funded airport improvement projects, improvements depicted on or described in FAA-approved Airport Layout Plans and master plans, and preservation of the navigable airspace necessary for achieving the objectives and utilization of the projects and plans.

(b) REQUIRED INFORMATION.—A notice submitted under part 77 of title 14, Code of Federal Regulations, shall include the following:

(1) Actual designs of an entire project and property, without regard to whether a proposed construction or alteration within 3 miles of the end of a runway of an airport and runway centerlines as depicted in the FAA-approved Airport Layout Plan of the airport is limited to a singular location on a property.

(2) If there are any changes to such designs or addition of equipment, such as cranes used to construct a building, after submission of such a notice, all information included with the notice submitted before such change or addition shall be

resubmitted, along with information regarding the change or addition.

(c) EXPIRATION.—

(1) IN GENERAL.—Unless extended, revised, or terminated, each determination of no hazard issued by the Administrator under part 77 of title 14, Code of Federal Regulations, shall expire 18 months after the effective date of the determination, or on the date the proposed construction or alteration is abandoned, whichever is earlier.

(2) AFTER EXPIRATION.—Determinations under paragraph (1) are no longer valid with regard to whether a proposed construction or alteration would be a hazard to air navigation after such determination has expired.

(d) AUTHORITY TO CONSOLIDATE OEI SURFACE CRITERIA.—The Administrator may develop a single set of One Engine Inoperative surface criteria that is specific to an airport. The Administrator shall consult with the airport operator and flight operators that use such airport, on the development of such surface criteria.

(e) DEVELOPMENT OF POLICIES TO PROTECT OEI SURFACES.—Not later than 6 months after the date of enactment of this Act, the Administrator shall brief the appropriate committees of Congress regarding the status of the efforts of the FAA to protect One Engine Inoperative surfaces from encroachment at United States certificated and federally obligated airports, including the current status of efforts to incorporate such protections into FAA Obstruction Evaluation/Airport Airspace Analysis processes.

(f) AUTHORITY TO CONSULT WITH OTHER AGENCIES.—The Administrator may consult with other Federal, State, or local agencies as necessary to carry out the requirements of this section.

(g) APPLICABILITY.—This section shall only apply to an airport in a county adjacent to 2 States with converging intersecting cross runway operations within 12 nautical miles of an Air Force base.

SEC. 745. [49 U.S.C. 44504 note] ELECTRIC AIRCRAFT INFRASTRUCTURE PILOT PROGRAM.

(a) IN GENERAL.—The Secretary may establish a pilot program under which airport sponsors may use funds made available under chapter 471 or section 48103 of title 49, United States Code, for use at up to 10 airports to carry out—

SEC. 747. [49 U.S.C. 47101 note] NOTICE OF
FUNDING OPPORTUNITY.

FAA Reauthorization Act of 2024

(1) activities associated with the acquisition, by purchase or lease, operation, and installation of equipment to support the operations of electric aircraft, including interoperable electric vehicle charging equipment; and

(2) the construction or modification of infrastructure to facilitate the delivery of power or services necessary for the use of electric aircraft, including—

(A) on airport utility upgrades; and

(B) associated design costs.

(b) ELIGIBILITY.—A public-use airport is eligible for participation in the pilot program under this section if the Secretary finds that funds made available under subsection (a) would support—

(1) electric aircraft operators at such airport, or using such airport; or

(2) electric aircraft operators planning to operate at such airport with an associated agreement in place.

(c) SUNSET.—The pilot program established under subsection (a) shall terminate on October 1, 2028.

* * * * * * *

SEC. 747. [49 U.S.C. 47101 note] NOTICE OF FUNDING OPPORTUNITY.

Notwithstanding part 200 of title 2, Code of Federal Regulations, or any other provision of law, funds made available as part of the Airport Improvement Program under subchapter I of chapter 471 or chapter 475 of title 49, United States Code, shall not be subject to any public notice of funding opportunity requirement.

SEC. 748. [49 U.S.C. 47115 note] RUNWAY SAFETY PROJECTS.

In awarding grants under section 47115 of title 49, United States Code, for runway safety projects, the Administrator shall, to the maximum extent practicable—

(1) reduce unnecessary or undesirable project segmentation; and

(2) complete the entire project in an expeditious manner.

SEC. 749. [49 U.S.C. 44502 note] AIRPORT DIAGRAM TERMINOLOGY.

(a) IN GENERAL.—The Administrator shall update Airport Diagram Order JO 7910.4 and any related advisory circulars, policy, and guidance to ensure the clear and consistent use of terms to delineate the types of parking available to general aviation pilots.

(b) COLLABORATION.—In carrying out subsection (a), the Administrator shall collaborate with industry stakeholders, commercial service airports, and general aviation airports in—

(1) facilitating basic standardization of general aviation parking terms;

(2) accounting for the majority of uses of general aviation parking terms; and

(3) providing clarity for chart users.

(c) IAC SPECIFICATIONS.—The Administrator shall encourage the Interagency Air Committee to incorporate the terms developed pursuant to subsection (a) in publications produced by the Committee.

* * * * * * *

SEC. 752. [49 U.S.C. 47106 note] PROHIBITION ON CERTAIN RUNWAY LENGTH REQUIREMENTS.

Notwithstanding any other provision of law, the Secretary may not require an airport to shorten the length or width of the runway, apron, or taxiway of the airport as a condition for the receipt of federal financial assistance if the airport directly supports a base of the United States Air Force or the Air National Guard at the airport, regardless of the stationing of military aircraft.

* * * * * * *

SEC. 755. GAO STUDY ON TRANSIT ACCESS.

(a) IN GENERAL.—Not later than 18 months after the date of enactment of this Act, the Comptroller General shall conduct a study on transit access to airports and submit to the appropriate committees of Congress a report on the results of such study.

(b) CONTENTS.—In carrying out the study under subsection (a), the Comptroller General shall review public transportation access to commercial service airports throughout the United States, including accessibility and other potential barriers for individuals.

SEC. 756. BANNING MUNICIPAL AIRPORT.

(a) IN GENERAL.—The United States, acting through the Administrator, shall release the City of Banning, California, from all restrictions, conditions, and limitations on the use, encumbrance, conveyance, and closure of the Banning Municipal Airport, as described in the most recent airport layout plan approved by the FAA, to the extent such restrictions, conditions, and limitations are enforceable by the Administrator.

(b) CONDITIONS.—The release under subsection (a) shall not be executed before the City of Banning, California, or its designee, transfers to the United States Government the following:

(1) A reimbursement for 1983 grant the City of Banning, California received from the FAA for the purchase of 20 acres of land, at an amount equal to the fair market value for the highest and best use of the Banning Municipal Airport property determined in good faith by 2 independent and qualified real estate appraisers and an independent review appraiser on or after the date of the enactment of this Act.

(2) An amount equal to the unamortized portion of any Federal development grants other than land paid to the City of Banning for use at the Banning Municipal Airport, which may be paid with, and shall be an allowable use of, airport revenue notwithstanding section 47107 or 47133 of title 49, United States Code.

(3) For no consideration, all airport and aviation-related equipment of the Banning Municipal Airport owned by the City of Banning and determined by the FAA or the Department of Transportation of the State of California to be salvageable for use at other airports.

(c) RULE OF CONSTRUCTION.—Nothing in this section shall be construed to limit the applicability of—

(1) the requirements and processes under section 46319 of title 49, United States Code;

(2) the requirements under the National Environmental Policy Act of 1969 (42 U.S.C. 4321 et seq.);

(3) the requirements and processes under part 157 of title 14, Code of Federal Regulations; or

(4) the public notice requirements under section 47107(h)(2) of title 49, United States Code.

SEC. 757. [49 U.S.C. 47101 note] DISPUTED CHANGES OF SPONSORSHIP AT FEDERALLY OBLIGATED, PUBLICLY OWNED AIRPORT.

(a) APPROVAL AUTHORITY.—

(1) IN GENERAL.—Subject to paragraph (2), in the case of a disputed change of airport sponsorship, the Administrator shall have the sole legal authority to approve any change in the sponsorship of, or operational responsibility for, the airport from the airport sponsor of record to another public or private entity.

(2) EXCLUSION.—This section shall not apply to a change of sponsorship or ownership of a privately-owned airport, a transfer under the Airport Investment Partnership Program, a change when the Federal Government exercises a right of reverter, or a change that is not disputed.

(b) CONDITIONS FOR APPROVAL.—

(1) IN GENERAL.—Subject to paragraphs (2) and (3), the Administrator shall not approve any disputed change of airport sponsorship unless the Administrator receives—

(A) written documentation from the airport sponsor of record consenting to the change in sponsorship or operation;

(B) notice of a final, non-reviewable judicial decision requiring such change; or

(C) notice of a legally-binding agreement between the parties involved.

(2) PENDING JUDICIAL REVIEW.—The Administrator may not evaluate or approve a disputed change of airport sponsorship where a legal dispute is pending before a court of competent jurisdiction.

(3) TECHNICAL ASSISTANCE.—

(A) IN GENERAL.—Any State or local legislative body or public agency considering whether to take an action (including by drafting legislation) that would impact the ownership, sponsorship, governance, or operations of a federally obligated, publicly owned airport may request from the Administrator, at any point in the deliberative process—

(i) technical assistance regarding the interrelationship between Federal and State or local requirements applicable to any such action; and

(ii) review and comment on such action.

(B) FAILURE TO SEEK TECHNICAL ASSISTANCE.—The Administrator may deny a change in the ownership, sponsorship, or governance of, or operational responsibility for, a federally obligated, publicly owned airport if a State or local legislative body or public agency does not seek technical assistance under subparagraph (A) with respect to such change.

(c) FINAL DECISION AUTHORITY.—In addition to the conditions outlined in subsection (b), the Administrator shall independently determine whether the proposed sponsor or operator is able to satisfy Federal requirements for airport sponsorship or operation and shall ensure, by requiring whatever terms and conditions the Administrator determines necessary, that any change in the ownership, sponsorship, or governance of, or operational responsibility for, a federally obligated, publicly owned airport is consistent with existing Federal law, regulations, existing grant assurances, and Federal land conveyance obligations.

(d) DEFINITION OF DISPUTED CHANGE OF AIRPORT SPONSORSHIP.—In this section, the term "disputed change of airport sponsorship" means any action that seeks to change the ownership, sponsorship, or governance of, or operational responsibility for, a federally obligated, publicly owned airport, including any such change directed by judicial action or State or local legislative action, where the airport sponsor of record initially does not consent to such change.

SEC. 758. [49 U.S.C. 47101 note] PROCUREMENT REGULATIONS APPLICABLE TO FAA MULTIMODAL PROJECTS.

(a) IN GENERAL.—Any multimodal airport development project that uses grant funding from funds made available to the Administrator to carry out subchapter I of chapter 471 of title 49, United States Code, or airport infrastructure projects under the Infrastructure Investment and Jobs Act (Public Law 117-58) shall abide by the procurement regulations applicable to—

(1) the FAA; and

(2) subject to subsection (b), the component of the project relating to transit, highway, or rail, respectively.

(b) MULTIPLE COMPONENT PROJECTS.—In the case of a multimodal airport development project described in subsection (a) that involves more than 1 component described in paragraph (2) of such subsection, such project shall only be required to apply the procurement regulations applicable to the component where the greatest amount of Federal financial assistance will be expended.

SEC. 759. BUCKEYE 940 RELEASE OF DEED RESTRICTIONS.

(a) PURPOSE.—The purpose of this section is to authorize the Secretary to issue a Deed of Release from all terms, conditions, reservations, restrictions, and obligations contained in the Quitclaim Deed and to permit the State of Arizona to deposit all proceeds of the disposition of Buckeye 940 in the appropriate fund for the benefit of the beneficiaries of the Arizona State Land Trust.

(b) RELEASE OF ANY AND ALL INTEREST IN BUCKEYE 940.—

(1) IN GENERAL.—Notwithstanding any other provision of law, the United States, acting through the Secretary, shall issue to the State of Arizona a Deed of Release to release all terms, conditions, reservations, restrictions, and obligations contained in the Quitclaim Deed, including any and all reversionary interest of the United States in Buckeye 940.

(2) TERMS AND CONDITIONS.—The Deed of Release described in paragraph (1) shall be subject to such additional terms and conditions, consistent with such paragraph, as the Secretary considers appropriate to protect the interests of the United States.

(3) NO RESTRICTION ON USE OF PROCEEDS.—Notwithstanding any other provision of law, the State of Arizona may dispose of Buckeye 940 and any proceeds thereof, including proceeds already collected by the State and held in a suspense account, without regard to any restriction imposed by the Quitclaim Deed or by section 155.7 of title 14, Code of Federal Regulations.

(4) MINERAL RESERVATION.—The Deed of Release described in paragraph (1) shall include the release of all interests of the United States to the mineral rights on Buckeye 940 included in the Quitclaim Deed.

(c) DEFINITIONS.—In this section:

(1) BUCKEYE 940.—The term "Buckeye 940" means all of section 12, T.1 N., R.3 W. and all of adjoining fractional section 7, T.1 N., R.2 W., Gila and Salt River Meridian, Arizona, which property was the subject of the Quitclaim Deed between the United States and the State of Arizona, dated July 11, 1949, and which is currently owned by the State of Arizona and held in trust for the beneficiaries of the Arizona State Land Trust.

(2) QUITCLAIM DEED.—The term "Quitclaim Deed" means the Quitclaim Deed between the United States and the State of Arizona, dated July 11, 1949.

* * * * * * *

SEC. 762. PROGRESS REPORTS ON THE NATIONAL TRANSITION PLAN RELATED TO A FLUORINE-FREE FIREFIGHTING FOAM.

(a) IN GENERAL.—Not later than 180 days after the date of enactment of this Act, and every 180 days thereafter until the progress report termination date described in subsection (c), the Administrator, in consultation with the Administrator of the Environmental Protection Agency and the Secretary of Defense, shall submit to the appropriate committees of Congress a progress report on the development and implementation of a national transition plan related to a fluorine-free firefighting foam that meets the performance standards referenced in chapter 6 of the advisory circular of the FAA titled "Aircraft Fire Extinguishing Agents", issued on July 8, 2004 (Advisory Circular 150/5210-6D) and is acceptable under section 139.319(l) of title 14, Code of Federal Regulations, for use at part 139 airports.

(b) REQUIRED INFORMATION.—Each progress report under subsection (a) shall include the following:

(1) An assessment of the progress made by the FAA with respect to providing part 139 airports with—

(A) guidance from the Environmental Protection Agency on acceptable environmental limits relating to fluorine-free firefighting foam;

(B) guidance from the Department of Defense on the transition of the Department of Defense to a fluorine-free firefighting foam;

SEC. 767. [49 U.S.C. 44706 note] PFAS-
RELATED RESOURCES FOR AIRPORTS.

FAA Reauthorization Act of 2

(C) best practices for the decontamination of existing aircraft rescue and firefighting vehicles, systems, and other equipment used to deploy firefighting foam at part 139 airports; and

(D) timelines for the release of policy and guidance relating to the development of implementation plans for part 139 airports to obtain approved military specification products and firefighting personnel training.

(2) A comprehensive list of the amount of aqueous film-forming firefighting foam at each part 139 airport as of the date of the submission of the progress report, including the amount of such firefighting foam held in firefighting equipment and the number of gallons regularly kept in reserve at each such airport.

(3) An assessment of the progress made by the FAA with respect to providing airports that are not part 139 airports and local authorities with responsibility for inspection and oversight with guidance described in subparagraphs (A) and (B) of paragraph (1) as such guidance relates to the use of fluorine-free firefighting foam at such airports.

(4) Any other information that the Administrator determines is appropriate.

(c) PROGRESS REPORT TERMINATION DATE.—The progress report termination date described in this subsection is the date on which the Administrator notifies the appropriate committees of Congress that development and implementation of the national transition plan described in subsection (a) is complete.

(d) PART 139 AIRPORT DEFINED.—In this section, the term "part 139 airport" means an airport certified under part 139 of title 14, Code of Federal Regulations.

* * * * * * *

SEC. 767. [49 U.S.C. 44706 note] PFAS-RELATED RESOURCES FOR AIRPORTS.

(a) PFAS REPLACEMENT PROGRAM FOR AIRPORTS.—Not later than 90 days after the date of enactment of this Act, the Secretary, in consultation with the Administrator of the Environmental Protection Agency, shall establish a program to reimburse sponsors of eligible airports for the reasonable and appropriate costs incurred

SEC. 767. [49 U.S.C. 44706 note] PFAS-
RELATED RESOURCES FOR AIRPORTS.

FAA Reauthorization Act of 2024

after September 12, 2023, and associated with any of the following:

(1) The one-time initial acquisition by the sponsor of an eligible airport of an approved fluorine-free firefighting agent under Military Specification MIL-PRE-32725, dated January 12, 2023, in a quantity of—

(A) the capacity of all required aircraft rescue and firefighting equipment listed in the most recent FAA-approved Airport Certification Manual, regardless of how the equipment was initially acquired; and

(B) twice the quantity carried onboard each required truck available in the fire station for the eligible airport.

(2) The disposal of perfluoroalkyl or polyfluoroalkyl products, including fluorinated aqueous film-forming agents, to the extent such disposal is necessary to facilitate the transition to such approved fluorine-free firefighting agent, including aqueous film-forming agents currently in firefighting equipment and vehicles and any wastewater generated during the cleaning of firefighting equipment and vehicles.

(3) The cleaning or disposal of existing equipment or components thereof, to the extent such cleaning or disposal is necessary to facilitate the transition to such approved fluorine-free firefighting agent.

(4) The acquisition of any equipment, or components thereof, necessary to facilitate the transition to such approved fluorine-free firefighting agent.

(5) The replacement of any aircraft rescue and firefighting equipment determined necessary to be replaced by the Secretary.

(b) DISTRIBUTION OF FUNDS.—

(1) GRANTS TO REPLACE AIRCRAFT RESCUE AND FIREFIGHTING VEHICLES.—

(A) IN GENERAL.—Of the amounts made available to carry out the PFAS replacement program, the Secretary shall reserve up to $30,000,000 to make grants to each eligible airport that is designated under part 139 as an Index A airport and does not have existing capabilities to produce fluorine-free firefighting foam for the replacement of aircraft rescue and firefighting vehicles.

SEC. 767. [49 U.S.C. 44706 note] PFAS-
RELATED RESOURCES FOR AIRPORTS.

FAA Reauthorization Act of

(B) AMOUNT.—The maximum amount of a grant made under subparagraph (A) may not exceed $2,000,000.

(2) REMAINING AMOUNTS.—

(A) DETERMINATION OF NEED.—With respect to the amount of firefighting foam concentrate required for foam production commensurate with applicable aircraft rescue and firefighting equipment required in accordance with the most recent FAA-approved Airport Certification Manual, the Secretary shall determine—

(i) for each eligible airport, the total amount of such concentrate required for all of the federally required aircraft rescue and firefighting vehicles that meet index requirements under part 139, in gallons; and

(ii) for all eligible airports, the total amount of firefighting foam concentrate, in gallons.

(B) DETERMINATION OF GRANT AMOUNTS.—The Secretary shall make a grant to the sponsor of each eligible airport in an amount equal to the product of—

(i) the amount of funds made available to carry out this section that remain available after the Secretary reserves the amount described in paragraph (1); and

(ii) the ratio of the amount determined under subparagraph (A)(i) for such eligible airport to the amount determined under subparagraph (A)(ii).

(c) PROGRAM REQUIREMENTS.—

(1) IN GENERAL.—The Secretary shall determine the eligibility of costs payable under the PFAS replacement program by taking into account all engineering, technical, and environmental protocols and generally accepted industry standards that are developed or established for approved fluorine-free firefighting foams.

(2) COMPLIANCE WITH APPLICABLE LAW.—To be eligible for reimbursement under the program established under subsection (a), the sponsor of an eligible airport shall carry out all actions related to the acquisition, disposal, and transition to approved fluorine-free firefighting foams, including the cleaning and disposal of equipment, in full compliance with all applicable Federal laws in effect at the time of obligation of a

grant under this section.

(3) FEDERAL SHARE.—The Federal share of allowable costs under the PFAS replacement program shall be 100 percent.

(d) AUTHORIZATION OF APPROPRIATIONS.—

(1) IN GENERAL.—There is authorized to be appropriated not more than $350,000,000 to carry out the PFAS replacement program.

(2) REQUIREMENTS.—Amounts made available to carry out the PFAS replacement program shall—

(A) remain available for expenditure for a period of 5 fiscal years; and

(B) be available in addition to any other funding available for similar purposes under any other Federal, State, local, or Tribal program.

(e) DEFINITIONS.—In this section:

(1) ELIGIBLE AIRPORT.—The term "eligible airport" means an airport holding an Airport Operating Certificate issued under part 139.

(2) PART 139.—The term "part 139" means part 139 of title 14, Code of Federal Regulations.

(3) PFAS REPLACEMENT PROGRAM.—The term "PFAS replacement program" means the program established under subsection (a).

* * * * * * *

SEC. 771. AVIATION FUEL IN ALASKA.

(a) [49 U.S.C. 44714 note] IN GENERAL.—

(1) PROHIBITION ON RESTRICTION OF FUEL USAGE OR AVAILABILITY.—The Administrator of the Federal Aviation Administration and the Administrator of the Environmental Protection Agency shall not restrict the continued use or availability of 100-octane low lead aviation gasoline in the State of Alaska until the earlier of—

(A) December 31, 2032; or

(B) 6 months after the date on which the Administrator of the Federal Aviation Administration finds that an unleaded aviation fuel is widely commercially available at airports throughout the State of Alaska that—

(i) has been authorized for use by the Administrator of the Federal Aviation Administration as a replacement for 100-octane low lead aviation gasoline; and

(ii) meets either an industry consensus standard or other standard that facilitates and ensures the safe use, production, and distribution of such unleaded aviation fuel.

(2) SAVINGS CLAUSE.—Nothing in this section shall limit the authority of the Administrator of the Federal Aviation Administration or the Administrator of the Environmental Protection Agency to address the endangerment to public health and welfare posed by lead emissions—

(A) in the United States outside of the State of Alaska; or

(B) within the State of Alaska after the date specified in paragraph (1).

* * * * * * *

SEC. 773. PROHIBITION ON USE OF AMOUNTS TO PROCESS OR ADMINISTER ANY APPLICATION FOR THE JOINT USE OF HOMESTEAD AIR RESERVE BASE WITH CIVIL AVIATION.

No amounts appropriated or otherwise made available to the Federal Aviation Administration for fiscal years 2024 through 2028 may be used to process or administer any application for the joint use of Homestead Air Reserve Base, Homestead, Florida, by the Air Force and civil aircraft.

* * * * * * *

SEC. 774A. [49 U.S.C. 44738 note] AIRPORT HUMAN TRAFFICKING PREVENTION GRANTS.

(a) IN GENERAL.—The Secretary shall establish a grant program to provide grants to airports described in subsection (b)(1) to address human trafficking awareness, education, and prevention efforts, including by—

(1) coordinating human trafficking prevention efforts across multimodal transportation operations within a

community; and

(2) accomplishing the best practices and recommendations provided by the Department of Transportation Advisory Committee on Human Trafficking.

(b) DISTRIBUTION.—

(1) IN GENERAL.—The Secretary shall distribute amounts made available for grants under this section to—

(A) the 75 airports in the United States with the highest number of passenger enplanements annually, based on the most recent data available; and

(B) as the Secretary determines to be appropriate, an airport not described in subparagraph (A) that serves an area with a high prevalence of human trafficking, on application of the airport.

(2) PRIORITY; CONSIDERATIONS.—In distributing amounts made available for grants under this section, the Secretary shall—

(A) give priority in grant amounts to airports referred to in paragraph (1) that serve regions with a higher prevalence of human trafficking; and

(B) take into consideration the effect the amounts would have on surrounding areas.

(3) CONSULTATION.—In distributing amounts made available for grants under this section, the Secretary shall consult with the Department of Transportation Advisory Committee on Human Trafficking in determining the amounts to be distributed to each grant recipient to ensure the best use of the funds.

(c) AUTHORIZATION OF APPROPRIATIONS.—There is authorized to be appropriated to the Secretary to carry out this section $10,000,000 for each of fiscal years 2025 through 2028.

* * * * * * *

Subtitle C—Noise And Environmental Programs And Streamlining

* * * * * * *

SEC. 787. [49 U.S.C. 47501 note] REDUCING
COMMUNITY AIRCRAFT NOISE EXPOSURE.

FAA Reauthorization Act of 2

SEC. 787. [49 U.S.C. 47501 note] REDUCING COMMUNITY AIRCRAFT
NOISE EXPOSURE.

In implementing or substantially revising a flight procedure,
the Administrator shall consider the following actions (to the extent
that such actions do not negatively affect aviation safety or
efficiency) to reduce undesirable aircraft noise:

(1) Implement flight procedures that can mitigate the
impact of aircraft noise, based on a consensus community
recommendation.

(2) Work with airport sponsors and potentially impacted
neighboring communities in establishing or modifying aircraft
arrival and departure routes.

(3) In collaboration with local governments, discourage
local encroachment of residential or other buildings near
airports that could create future aircraft noise complaints or
impact airport operations or aviation safety.

SEC. 788. [49 U.S.C. 47171 note] CATEGORICAL EXCLUSIONS.

(a) CATEGORICAL EXCLUSION FOR PROJECTS OF LIMITED
FEDERAL ASSISTANCE.—An action by the Administrator to approve,
permit, finance, or otherwise authorize any airport project that
is undertaken by the sponsor, owner, or operator of a public-use
airport shall be presumed to be covered by a categorical exclusion
under FAA Order 1050.1F (or any successor document), if such
project—

(1) receives less than $6,000,000 (as adjusted annually by
the Administrator to reflect any increases in the Consumer
Price Index prepared by the Department of Labor) of Federal
funds or funds from charges collected under section 40117 of
title 49, United States Code; or

(2) has a total estimated cost of not more than $35,000,000
(as adjusted annually by the Administrator to reflect any
increases in the Consumer Price Index prepared by the
Department of Labor) and Federal funds comprising less than
15 percent of the total estimated project cost.

(b) CATEGORICAL EXCLUSION IN EMERGENCIES.—An action by
the Administrator to approve, permit, finance, or otherwise
authorize an airport project that is undertaken by the sponsor,
owner, or operator of a public-use airport shall be presumed to be

covered by a categorical exclusion under FAA Order 1050.1F (or any successor document), if such project is—

(1) for the repair or reconstruction of any airport facility, runway, taxiway, or similar structure that is in operation or under construction when damaged by an emergency declared by the Governor of the State with concurrence of the Administrator or for a disaster or emergency declared by the President pursuant to the Robert T. Stafford Disaster Relief and Emergency Assistance Act (42 U.S.C. 5121 et seq.);

(2) in the same location with the same capacity, dimensions, and design as the original airport facility, runway, taxiway, or similar structure as before the declaration described in this section; and

(3) commenced within a 2-year period beginning on the date of a declaration described in this section.

(c) EXTRAORDINARY CIRCUMSTANCES.—The presumption that an action is covered by a categorical exclusion under subsections (a) and (b) shall not apply if the Administrator determines that extraordinary circumstances exist with respect to such action.

(d) RULE OF CONSTRUCTION.—Nothing in this section shall be construed to impact any aviation safety authority of the Administrator.

(e) DEFINITIONS.—In this section:

(1) CATEGORICAL EXCLUSION.—The term "categorical exclusion" has the meaning given such term in section 1508.1(d) of title 40, Code of Federal Regulations.

(2) PUBLIC-USE AIRPORT; SPONSOR.—The terms "public-use airport" and "sponsor" have the meanings given such terms in section 47102 of title 49, United States Code.

* * * * * * *

SEC. 792. AIRCRAFT NOISE ADVISORY COMMITTEE.

(a) ESTABLISHMENT.—Not later than 180 days after the date of enactment of this Act, the Administrator shall establish an Aircraft Noise Advisory Committee (in this section referred to as the "Advisory Committee") to advise the Administrator on issues facing the aviation community that are related to aircraft noise exposure and existing FAA noise policies and regulations.

(b) MEMBERSHIP.—The Administrator shall appoint the members of the Advisory Committee, which shall be comprised of—

(1) at least 1 representative of each of—

(A) engine manufacturers;

(B) air carriers;

(C) airport owners or operators;

(D) aircraft manufacturers;

(E) advanced air mobility manufacturers or operators; and

(F) institutions of higher education; and

(2) representatives of airport-adjacent communities from geographically diverse regions.

(c) DUTIES.—The duties of the Advisory Committee shall include—

(1) the evaluation of existing research on aircraft noise impacts and annoyance;

(2) the assessment of alternative noise metrics that could be used to supplement or replace the existing Day Night Level standard, in consultation with the National Academies;

(3) the evaluation of the current 65-decibel exposure threshold, including the impact to land use compatibility around airports if such threshold was lowered;

(4) the evaluation of current noise mitigation strategies and the community engagement efforts by the FAA with respect to changes in airspace utilization, such as the integration of new entrants and usage of performance-based navigation; and

(5) other duties determined appropriate by the Administrator.

(d) REPORTS.—

(1) IN GENERAL.—Not later than 1 year after the date of establishment of the Advisory Committee, the Advisory Committee shall submit to the Administrator a report on any recommended changes to current aviation noise policies.

(2) REPORT TO CONGRESS.—Not later than 180 days after the date the Administrator receives the report under paragraph (1), the Administrator shall submit to the appropriate committees of Congress a report containing the

SEC. 793. [49 U.S.C. 40101 note] COMMUNITY
COLLABORATION PROGRAM.

FAA Reauthorization Act of 2024

recommendations made by the Advisory Committee.

(e) CONGRESSIONAL BRIEFING.—Not later than 30 days after submission of the report under paragraph (2), the Administrator shall brief the appropriate committees of Congress on how the Administrator plans to implement recommendations contained in the report and, for each recommendation that the Administrator does not plan to implement, the reason of the Administrator for not implementing the recommendation.

(f) CONSULTATION.—The Advisory Committee shall consult with other relevant Federal agencies, including the National Aeronautics and Space Administration, in carrying out the duties described in section (c).

SEC. 793. [49 U.S.C. 40101 note] COMMUNITY COLLABORATION PROGRAM.

(a) ESTABLISHMENT.—The Administrator shall continue existing community engagement activities under the designation of a Community Collaboration Program (in this section referred to as the "Program").

(b) RESPONSIBILITIES.—

(1) IN GENERAL.—In carrying out the Program, the Administrator shall facilitate and harmonize, as appropriate, policies and procedures carried out by various offices of the FAA pertaining to community engagement relating to—

(A) airport planning and development;

(B) noise and environmental policy;

(C) NextGen implementation;

(D) air traffic route changes;

(E) integration of new and emerging entrants; and

(F) other topics with respect to which community engagement is critical to program success.

(2) SPECIFIED RESPONSIBILITIES.—In carrying out the Program, the Administrator shall be responsible for—

(A) updating the internal guidance of the FAA for community engagement based on—

(i) best practices of other Federal agencies and external organizations with expertise in community engagement;

SEC. 793. [49 U.S.C. 40101 note] COMMUNITY
COLLABORATION PROGRAM.

FAA Reauthorization Act of 2

(ii) interviews with impacted residents; and

(iii) recommendations solicited from individuals and local government officials in communities adversely impacted by aircraft noise;

(B) coordinating with the Air Traffic Organization on community engagement efforts related to air traffic procedure changes to ensure that impacted communities are consulted in a meaningful way;

(C) coordination with Regional Ombudsmen of the FAA;

(D) oversight, streamlining, and increasing the responsiveness of the noise complaint process of the FAA by—

(i) centralizing noise complaint data and improving data collection methodologies;

(ii) ensuring such Regional Ombudsmen are consulted in local air traffic procedure development decisions; and

(iii) collecting feedback from such Regional Ombudsmen to inform national policymaking efforts;

(E) timely implementation of the recommendations, as appropriate, made by the Comptroller General to the Secretary contained in the report titled "Aircraft Noise: FAA Could Improve Outreach Through Enhanced Noise Metrics, Communication, and Support to Communities", issued in September 2021 (GAO-21-103933) to improve the outreach of the FAA to local communities impacted by aircraft noise, including—

(i) any recommendations to—

(I) identify appropriate supplemental metrics for assessing noise impacts and circumstances for their use to aid in the internal assessment of the FAA of noise impacts related to proposed flight path changes;

(II) update guidance to incorporate additional tools to more clearly convey expected impacts, such as other noise metrics and visualization tools; and

SEC. 794. [49 U.S.C. 47501 note] INFORMATION
SHARING REQUIREMENT.

FAA Reauthorization Act of 2024

(III) improve guidance to airports and communities on effectively engaging with the FAA; and

(ii) any other recommendations included in the report that would assist the FAA in improving outreach to communities affected by aircraft noise;

(F) ensuring engagement with local community groups as appropriate in conducting the other responsibilities described in this section; and

(G) other responsibilities as considered appropriate by the Administrator.

(c) BRIEFING.—Not later than 2 years after the Administrator implements the recommendations described in subsection (b)(2)(E), the Administrator shall brief the appropriate committees of Congress describing—

(1) the implementation of each such recommendation;

(2) how any recommended actions are assisting the Administrator in improving outreach to communities affected by aircraft noise and other community engagement concerns; and

(3) any challenges or barriers that limit or prevent the ability of the Administrator to take such actions.

(d) RULE OF CONSTRUCTION.—Nothing in this section shall be construed to require the Administrator to alter the organizational structure of the FAA nor change the reporting structure of any employee.

SEC. 794. [49 U.S.C. 47501 note] INFORMATION SHARING REQUIREMENT.

(a) IN GENERAL.—Not later than 2 years after the date of enactment of this Act, the Secretary, acting through the Administrator, shall establish a mechanism to make helicopter noise complaint data accessible to the FAA, to helicopter operators operating in the Washington, DC area, and to the public on a website of the FAA, based on the recommendation of the Government Accountability Office in the report titled "Aircraft Noise: Better Information Sharing Could Improve Responses to Washington, D.C. Area Helicopter Noise Concerns", published on January 7, 2021 (GAO-21-200).

SEC. 805. [49 U.S.C. 44703 note] TIMELY
RESOLUTION OF INVESTIGATIONS.

FAA Reauthorization Act of 2

(b) COOPERATION.—Any helicopter operator operating in the
Washington, DC area shall, to the extent practicable, provide
helicopter noise complaint data to the FAA through the mechanism
established under subsection (a).

(c) DEFINITIONS.—In this section:

(1) HELICOPTER NOISE COMPLAINT DATA.—The term
"helicopter noise complaint data"—

(A) means general data relating to a complaint made
by an individual about helicopter noise in the Washington,
DC area and may include—

(i) the location and description of the event that is
the subject of the complaint;

(ii) the start and end time of such event;

(iii) a description of the aircraft that is the subject
of the complaint; and

(iv) the airport name associated with such event;
and

(B) does not include the personally identifiable
information of the individual who submitted the complaint.

(2) WASHINGTON, DC AREA.—The term "Washington, DC
area" means the area inside of a 30-mile radius surrounding
Ronald Reagan Washington National Airport.

* * * * * * *

TITLE VIII—GENERAL AVIATION

* * * * * * *

SEC. 805. [49 U.S.C. 44703 note] TIMELY RESOLUTION OF
INVESTIGATIONS.

(a) IN GENERAL.—Not later than 2 years after the date of
issuance of a letter of investigation to any person, as required by
section 2(b) of the Pilot's Bill of Rights (49 U.S.C. 44703 note), the
Administrator shall—

(1) make a determination regarding such investigation and
pursue subsequent action; or

(2) close such investigation.

(b) EXTENSION.—

(1) IN GENERAL.—If, upon review of the facts and status of an investigation described in subsection (a), the Administrator determines that the time provided to make a final determination or close such investigation is insufficient, the Administrator shall approve an extension of such investigation for 2 years.

(2) ADDITIONAL EXTENSIONS.—The Administrator may approve consecutive extensions under paragraph (1).

(c) DELEGATION.—The Administrator may not delegate the authority to approve an extension described in subsection (b) to anyone other than the leadership of the Administration as described in section 106(b) of title 49, United States Code.

SEC. 806. [49 U.S.C. 44703 note] ALL MAKES AND MODELS AUTHORIZATION.

(a) IN GENERAL.—

(1) UNLIMITED LETTER OF AUTHORIZATION.—Not later than 1 year after the date of enactment of this Act, the Administrator shall take such action as may be necessary to allow for the issuance of letters of authorizations to airmen with the authorization for—

(A) all types and makes of experimental high-performance single engine piston powered aircraft; and

(B) all types and makes of experimental high-performance multiengine piston powered aircraft.

(2) REQUIREMENTS.—An individual who holds a letter of authorization and applies for an authorization described in paragraph (1)(A) or (1)(B)—

(A) shall be given an all-makes and models authorization of—

(i) experimental single-engine piston powered authorized aircraft; or

(ii) experimental multiengine piston powered authorized aircraft;

(B) shall hold the appropriate category and class rating for the authorized aircraft;

(C) shall hold 3 experimental aircraft authorizations

in aircraft of the same category and class rating for the authorization sought; and

(D) may become qualified in additional experimental aircraft by completing aircraft-specific ground and flight training.

(b) RULE OF CONSTRUCTION.—Nothing in this section may be construed to disallow an individual from being given both an authorization described in paragraph (1)(A) and an authorization described in paragraph (1)(B).

(c) FAILURE TO COMPLY.—

(1) IN GENERAL.—If the Administrator fails to implement subsection (a) within the time period prescribed in such subsection, the Administrator shall brief the appropriate committees of Congress on the status of the implementation of such subsection on a monthly basis until the implementation is complete.

(2) NO DELEGATION.—The Administrator may not delegate the briefing described in paragraph (1).

* * * * * * *

SEC. 808. ADS-B OUT EQUIPAGE STUDY; VEHICLE-TO-VEHICLE LINK PROGRAM.

* * * * * * *

(b) [49 U.S.C. 40101 note] VEHICLE-TO-VEHICLE LINK PROGRAM.—Not later than 270 days after the date of enactment of this Act, the Administrator, in coordination with the Administrator of the National Aeronautics and Space Administration and the Chair of the Federal Communications Commission, shall establish an interagency coordination program to advance vehicle-to-vehicle link initiatives that—

(1) enable the real-time digital exchange of key information between nearby aircraft; and

(2) are not reliant on ground infrastructure or air-to-ground communication links.

SEC. 809. [49 U.S.C. 44701 note] ENSURING SAFE LANDINGS DURING OFF-AIRPORT OPERATIONS.

The Administrator shall not apply section 91.119 of title 14,

Code of Federal Regulations, in any manner that requires a pilot to continue a landing that is unsafe.

* * * * * * *

SEC. 811. [49 U.S.C. 40103 note] AIRSHOW SAFETY TEAM.

(a) IN GENERAL.—Not later than 180 days after the date of enactment of this Act, the Administrator may, as determined necessary by the Administration, coordinate with the General Aviation Joint Safety Committee to establish an Airshow Safety Team focused on airshow and aerial event safety.

(b) OBJECTIVE.—The objective of the Airshow Safety Team described in subsection (a) shall be to—

(1) serve as a mechanism for Federal Government and industry cooperation, communication, and coordination on airshow and aerial event safety; and

(2) reduce airshow and aerial event accidents and incidents through non-regulatory, proactive safety strategies.

(c) ACTIVITIES.—In carrying out the objectives pursuant to subsection (b), the Airshow Safety Team shall, at a minimum—

(1) perform an analysis of airshow and aerial event accidents and incidents in conjunction with the Safety Analysis Team;

(2) publish and update every 2 years after initial publication an Airshow Safety Plan that incorporates consensus based and data driven mitigation measures and non-regulatory safety strategies to improve and promote safety of the public, performers, and airport personnel; and

(3) engage the airshow and aerial event community to—

(A) communicate non-regulatory, proactive safety strategies identified by the Airshow Safety Plan to mitigate incidents; and

(B) discuss best practices to uphold and maintain safety at events.

(d) MEMBERSHIP.—The Administrator may request the Airshow Safety Team be comprised of at least 10 individuals, each of whom shall have knowledge or a background in the planning, execution, operation, or management of an airshow or aerial event.

SEC. 814. [49 U.S.C. 44701 note] LETTER OF
DEVIATION AUTHORITY.

FAA Reauthorization Act of 2

(e) MEETINGS.—The Airshow Safety Team shall meet at least twice a year at the direction of the co-chairs of the General Aviation Joint Safety Committee.

(f) CONSTRUCTION.—Nothing in this section shall be construed to require an amendment to the charter of the General Aviation Joint Safety Committee.

* * * * * * *

SEC. 814. [49 U.S.C. 44701 note] LETTER OF DEVIATION AUTHORITY.

(a) IN GENERAL.—A flight instructor, registered owner, lessor, or lessee of a covered aircraft shall not be required to obtain a letter of deviation authority from the Administrator to allow, conduct, or receive flight training, checking, and testing in such aircraft if—

(1) the flight instructor is not providing both the training and the aircraft;

(2) no person advertises or broadly offers the aircraft as available for flight training, checking, or testing; and

(3) no person receives compensation for use of the aircraft for a specific flight during which flight training, checking, or testing was received, other than expenses for owning, operating, and maintaining the aircraft.

(b) COVERED AIRCRAFT DEFINED.—In this section, the term "covered aircraft" means—

(1) an experimental category aircraft;

(2) a limited category aircraft; and

(3) a primary category aircraft.

* * * * * * *

SEC. 818. [49 U.S.C. 41108 note] PART 135 AIR CARRIER CERTIFICATE BACKLOG.

(a) IN GENERAL.—The Administrator shall take such actions as may be necessary to achieve the goal of reducing the backlog of air carrier certificate applications under part 135 of title 14, Code of Federal Regulations, to—

(1) not later than 1 year after the date of enactment of this Act, maintain an average application acceptance or rejection

time of less than 60 days; and

(2) not later than 2 years after the date of enactment of this Act, maintain an average application acceptance or rejection time of less than 30 days.

(b) MEASURES.—In meeting the goal under subsection (a), the Administrator may—

(1) assign, as appropriate, additional personnel or support staff, including on a temporary basis, to review, adjudicate, and approve applications;

(2) improve and expand promotion of existing applicant resources which could improve the quality of applications submitted to decrease the need for Administration applicant coordination and communications; and

(3) take into consideration any third-party entity that assisted in the preparation of an application for an air carrier certificate under part 135 of title 14, Code of Federal Regulations.

(c) CONGRESSIONAL BRIEFING.—Beginning 6 months after the date of enactment of this Act, and not less than every 6 months thereafter until the Administrator complies with the requirements under subsection (a)(2), the Administrator shall provide a briefing to appropriate committees of Congress on the status of the backlog of air carrier certificate applications under part 135 of title 14, Code of Federal Regulations, any measures the Administrator has put in place under subsection (b).

* * * * * * *

SEC. 826. [49 U.S.C. 44703 note] PUBLIC AIRCRAFT FLIGHT TIME LOGGING ELIGIBILITY.

(a) FORESTRY AND FIRE PROTECTION FLIGHT TIME LOGGING.—

(1) IN GENERAL.—Notwithstanding any other provision of law, aircraft under the direct operational control of forestry and fire protection agencies are eligible to log pilot flight times, if the flight time was acquired by the pilot while engaged on an official forestry or fire protection flight, in the same manner as aircraft under the direct operational control of a Federal, State, county, or municipal law enforcement agency.

(2) RETROACTIVE APPLICATION.—Paragraph (1) shall be

applied as if enacted on October 5, 2018.

(b) REGULATIONS.—Not later than 180 days after the date of enactment of this Act, the Administrator shall make such regulatory changes as are necessary to conform to the requirements of this section.

SEC. 827. [49 U.S.C. 44714 note] EAGLE INITIATIVE.

(a) EAGLE INITIATIVE.—

(1) IN GENERAL.—The Administrator shall continue to partner with industry and other Federal Government stakeholders in carrying out the Eliminate Aviation Gasoline Lead Emissions Initiative (in this section referred to as the "EAGLE Initiative") through the end of 2030.

(2) FAA RESPONSIBILITIES.—In collaborating with industry and other Government stakeholders to carry out the EAGLE Initiative, the Administrator shall take such actions as may be necessary under the authority of the Administrator to facilitate—

(A) the safe elimination of the use of leaded aviation gasoline by piston-engine aircraft by the end of 2030 without adversely affecting the safe and efficient operation of the piston-engine aircraft fleet;

(B) the approval of the use of unleaded alternatives to leaded aviation gasoline for use in all piston-engine aircraft types and piston-engine models;

(C) the implementation of the requirements of section 47107(a)(22) of title 49, United States Code, as added by this Act, as such requirements relate to the continued availability of aviation gasoline;

(D) efforts to make unleaded aviation gasoline that is approved for use in piston-engine aircraft and engines widely available for purchase and use at airports in the National Plan of Integrated Airport Systems; and

(E) the development of a transition plan to safely enable the transition of the piston-engine general aviation aircraft fleet to unleaded aviation gasoline by 2030, to the extent practicable.

(3) ACTIVITIES.—In carrying out the responsibilities of the Administrator pursuant to paragraph (2), the Administrator

shall, at a minimum—

(A) maintain a fleet authorization process for the efficient approval or authorization of eligible piston-engine aircraft and engine models to operate safely using qualified unleaded aviation gasolines;

(B) review, update, and prioritize, as soon as practicable, certification processes and projects, as necessary, for aircraft engines and modifications to such engines to operate with unleaded aviation gasoline;

(C) seek to facilitate programs that accelerate the creation, evaluation, qualification, deployment, and use of unleaded aviation gasolines;

(D) carry out, in partnership with the general aviation community, an ongoing campaign for training and educating aircraft owners and operators on how to safely transition to unleaded aviation gasoline;

(E) evaluate aircraft and aircraft engines to ensure that such aircraft and aircraft engines can safely operate with unleaded aviation gasoline candidates during cold weather conditions; and

(F) facilitate the development of agency policies and processes, as appropriate, to support the deployment of necessary infrastructure at airports to enable the distribution and storage of unleaded aviation gasolines.

(4) CONSULTATION AND COLLABORATION WITH RELEVANT STAKEHOLDERS.—In carrying out the EAGLE Initiative, the Administrator shall continue to consult and collaborate, as appropriate, with relevant stakeholders, including—

(A) general aviation aircraft engine, aircraft propulsion, and aircraft airframe manufacturers;

(B) general aviation aircraft users, aircraft owners, aircraft pilots, and aircraft operators;

(C) airports and fixed-base operators;

(D) State, local, and Tribal aviation officials;

(E) representatives of the petroleum industry, including developers, refiners, producers, and distributors of unleaded aviation gasolines; and

(F) air carriers and commercial operators operating

under part 135 of title 14, Code of Federal Regulations.

(5) REPORT TO CONGRESS.—

(A) INITIAL REPORT.—Not later than 1 year after the date of enactment of this Act, the Administrator shall submit to the appropriate committees of Congress a report that—

(i) contains an updated strategic plan for maintaining a fleet authorization process for the efficient approval and authorization of eligible piston-engine aircraft and engine models to operate using unleaded aviation gasolines in a manner that ensures safety;

(ii) describes the structure and involvement of all FAA offices that have responsibilities described in paragraph (2); and

(iii) identifies policy initiatives, regulatory initiatives, or legislative initiatives needed to improve and enhance the timely and safe transition to unleaded aviation gasoline for the piston-engine aircraft fleet.

(B) ANNUAL BRIEFING.—Not later than 1 year after the date on which the Administrator submits the initial report under subparagraph (A), and annually thereafter through 2030, the Administrator shall brief the appropriate committees of Congress on activities and progress of the EAGLE Initiative.

(C) SUNSET.—Subparagraph (B) shall cease to be effective after December 31, 2030.

(b) TRANSITION PLAN TO UNLEADED AVIATION GASOLINE.—

(1) IN GENERAL.—In developing the transition plan under subsection (a)(2)(E), the Administrator may, at a minimum, assess the following:

(A) Efforts undertaken by the EAGLE Initiative, including progress towards—

(i) safely eliminating the use of leaded aviation gasoline by piston-engine aircraft by the end of 2030 without adversely affecting the safe and efficient operation of the piston-engine aircraft fleet;

(ii) approving the use of unleaded alternatives to

leaded aviation gasoline for use in all piston-engine aircraft types and piston-engine models; and

(iii) facilitating efforts to make approved unleaded aviation gasoline that is approved for use in piston-engine aircraft and engines widely available at airports for purchase and use in the National Plan of Integrated Airport Systems.

(B) The evaluation and development of necessary airport infrastructure, including fuel storage and dispensing facilities, to support the distribution and storage of unleaded aviation gasoline.

(C) The establishment of best practices for piston-engine aircraft owners and operators, airport operators and personnel, aircraft maintenance technicians, and other appropriate personnel for protecting against exposure to lead containment when—

(i) conducting fueling operations;

(ii) disposing of inspected gasoline samples;

(iii) performing aircraft maintenance; and

(iv) conducting engine run-ups.

(D) Efforts to address supply chain and other logistical barriers inhibiting the timely distribution of unleaded aviation gasoline to airports.

(E) Outreach efforts to educate and update piston-engine aircraft owners and operators, airport operators, and other members of the general aviation community on the potential benefits, availability, and safety of unleaded aviation gasoline.

(2) PUBLICATION; GUIDANCE.—Upon completion of developing such transition plan, the Administrator shall—

(A) make the plan available to the public on an appropriate website of the FAA; and

(B) provide guidance supporting the implementation of the transition plan.

(3) COLLABORATION WITH EAGLE INITIATIVE.—In supporting the development of such transition plan and issuing associated guidance pertaining to the implementation of such transition plan, the Administrator shall consult and collaborate with

individuals carrying out the EAGLE Initiative.

(4) UNLEADED AVIATION GASOLINE COMMUNICATION MATERIALS.—The Administrator may collaborate with individuals carrying out the EAGLE Initiative to jointly develop and continuously update websites, brochures, and other communication materials associated with such transition plan to clearly convey the availability of unleaded aviation gasoline at airports.

(5) BRIEFING TO CONGRESS.—Not later than 60 days after the publication of such transition plan, the Administrator shall brief the appropriate committees of Congress on such transition plan and any agency efforts or actions pertaining to the implementation of such transition plan.

(6) SAVINGS CLAUSE.—Nothing in this section shall be construed to delay or alter the ongoing work of the EAGLE Initiative established by the Administrator in 2022.

* * * * * * *

SEC. 830. [49 U.S.C. 40101 note] CHARITABLE FLIGHT FUEL REIMBURSEMENT EXEMPTIONS.

(a) IN GENERAL.—

(1) VALIDITY OF EXEMPTION.—Except as otherwise provided in this subsection, an exemption from section 61.113(c) of title 14, Code of Federal Regulations, that is granted by the Administrator for the purpose of allowing a volunteer pilot to accept reimbursement from a volunteer pilot organization for the fuel costs and airport fees attributed to a flight operation to provide charitable transportation pursuant to section 821 of the FAA Modernization and Reform Act of 2012 (49 U.S.C. 40101 note) shall be valid for 5 years.

(2) FAILING TO ADHERE.—If the Administrator finds an exemption holder under paragraph (1) or a volunteer pilot fails to adhere to the conditions and limitations of the exemption described under such paragraph, the Administrator may rescind or suspend the exemption.

(3) NO LONGER QUALIFYING.—If the Administrator finds that such exemption holder no longer qualifies as a volunteer pilot organization, the Administrator shall rescind such exemption.

(4) FORGOING EXEMPTION.—If such exemption holder informs the Administrator that such holder no longer plans to exercise the authority granted by such exemption, the Administrator may rescind such exemption.

(b) ADDITIONAL REQUIREMENTS.—

(1) IN GENERAL.—A volunteer pilot organization may impose additional safety requirements on a volunteer pilot without—

(A) being considered—

(i) an air carrier (as such term is defined in section 40102 of title 49, United States Code); or

(ii) a commercial operator (as such term is defined in section 1.1 of title 14, Code of Federal Regulations); or

(B) constituting common carriage.

(2) SAVINGS CLAUSE.—Nothing in this subsection may be construed to limit or otherwise affect the authority of the Administrator to regulate, as appropriate, a flight operation associated with a volunteer pilot organization that constitutes a commercial operation or common carriage.

(c) REISSUANCE OF EXISTING EXEMPTIONS.—In reissuing an expiring exemption described in subsection (a) that was originally issued prior to the date of enactment of this Act, the Administrator shall ensure that the reissued exemption—

(1) accounts for the provisions of this section and section 821 of the FAA Modernization and Reform Act of 2012 (49 U.S.C. 40101 note); and

(2) is otherwise substantially similar to the previously issued exemption.

(d) STATUTORY CONSTRUCTION.—Nothing in this section shall be construed to—

(1) affect the authority of the Administrator to exempt a pilot (exercising the private pilot privileges) from any restriction on receiving reimbursement for the fuel costs and airport fees attributed to a flight operation to provide charitable transportation; or

(2) impose or authorize the imposition of any additional requirements by the Administrator on a flight that is arranged

SEC. 832. [49 U.S.C. 44740 note] FLIGHT
INSTRUCTION OR TESTING.

FAA Reauthorization Act of 2

by a volunteer pilot organization in which the volunteer pilot—

(A) is not reimbursed the fuel costs and airport fees attributed to a flight operation to provide charitable flights; or

(B) pays a pro rata share of expenses as described in section 61.113(c) of title 14, Code of Federal Regulations.

(e) DEFINITIONS.—In this section:

(1) VOLUNTEER PILOT.—The term "volunteer pilot" means a person who—

(A) acts as a pilot in command of a flight operation to provide charitable transportation pursuant to section 821 of the FAA Modernization and Reform Act of 2012 (49 U.S.C. 40101 note); and

(B) holds a private pilot certificate, commercial pilot certificate, or an airline transportation pilot certificate issued under part 61 of title 14, Code of Federal Regulations.

(2) VOLUNTEER PILOT ORGANIZATION.—The term "volunteer pilot organization" has the meaning given such term in section 821(c) of the FAA Modernization and Reform Act of 2012 (49 U.S.C. 40101 note).

* * * * * * *

SEC. 832. [49 U.S.C. 44740 note] FLIGHT INSTRUCTION OR TESTING.

(a) AUTHORIZED ADDITIONAL PILOTS.—An individual acting as an authorized additional pilot during Phase I flight testing of aircraft holding an experimental airworthiness certificate, in accordance with section 21.191 of title 14, Code of Federal Regulations, and meeting the requirements set forth in FAA regulations and policy in effect as of the date of enactment of this Act, shall not be deemed to be operating an aircraft carrying persons or property for compensation or hire.

(b) USE OF AIRCRAFT.—An individual who uses, causes to use, or authorizes to use aircraft for flights conducted under subsection (a) shall not be deemed to be operating an aircraft carrying persons or property for compensation or hire.

(c) REVISION OF RULES.—The Administrator shall, as necessary, issue, revise, or repeal the rules, regulations, guidance, or procedures of the FAA to conform to the requirements of this section.

SEC. 833. [49 U.S.C. 44703 note] NATIONAL COORDINATION AND OVERSIGHT OF DESIGNATED PILOT EXAMINERS.

(a) IN GENERAL.—The Administrator shall establish an office to provide oversight and facilitate national coordination of designated pilot examiners appointed under section 183.23 of title 14, Code of Federal Regulations.

(b) RESPONSIBILITIES.—The office described in subsection (a) shall be responsible for the following:

(1) Oversight of designated pilot examiners appointed under section 183.23 of title 14, Code of Federal Regulations.

(2) Coordinating with other offices, as appropriate, to support the standardization of policy, guidance, and regulations across the FAA pertaining to the selection, training, duties, and deployment of designated pilot examiners appointed under section 183.23 of title 14, Code of Federal Regulations, including evaluating the consistency by which such examiners apply Administration policies, orders, and guidance.

(3) Evaluating the consistency by which such examiners apply FAA policies, orders, and guidance.

(4) Coordinating placement and deployment of such examiners across regions based on demand for examinations from the pilot community.

(5) Developing a code of conduct for such examiners.

(6) Deploying a survey system to track the performance and merit of such examiners.

(7) Facilitating an industry partnership to create a formal mentorship program for such examiners.

(c) COORDINATION.—In carrying out the responsibilities listed in subsection (b), the Administrator shall ensure the office—

(1) coordinates on an ongoing basis with flight standards district offices, designated pilot examiner managing specialists, and aviation industry stakeholders, including representatives of the general aviation community; and

(2) considers whether to implement the final recommendations report issued by the Designated Pilot

Examiner Reforms Working Group and accepted by the Aviation Rulemaking Advisory Committee on June 17, 2021.

* * * * * * *

TITLE IX—NEW ENTRANTS AND AEROSPACE INNOVATION

Subtitle A—Unmanned Aircraft Systems

SEC. 901. [49 U.S.C. 44502 note] DEFINITIONS.

Except as otherwise provided, the definitions contained in section 44801 of title 49, United States Code, apply to this subtitle.

* * * * * * *

SEC. 905. [49 U.S.C. 44505 note] RADAR DATA PILOT PROGRAM.

(a) SENSITIVE RADAR DATA FEED PILOT PROGRAM.—Not later than 270 days after the date of enactment of this Act, the Administrator, in coordination with the Secretary of Defense, and other heads of relevant Federal agencies, shall establish a pilot program to make airspace data feeds containing controlled unclassified information available to qualified users (as determined by the Administrator), consistent with subsection (b).

(b) AUTHORIZATION.—In carrying out subsection (a), the Administrator, in coordination with the Secretary of Defense and other heads of relevant Federal agencies, shall establish a process to authorize qualified users to receive airspace data feeds containing controlled unclassified information related to air traffic within the national airspace system and use such information in an agreed upon manner to—

(1) provide and enable—

(A) air traffic management services; and

(B) unmanned aircraft system traffic management services; or

(2) to test technologies that may enable or enhance the provision of the services described in paragraph (1).

SEC. 908. [49 U.S.C. 44802 note] PART 107
WAIVER IMPROVEMENTS.

FAA Reauthorization Act of 2024

(c) CONSULTATION.—In establishing the process described in subsection (b), the Administrator shall consult with representatives of the unmanned aircraft systems industry and related technical groups to identify an efficient, secure, and effective format and method for providing data described in this section.

(d) BRIEFING.—Not later than 90 days after establishing the pilot program under subsection (a), and annually thereafter through 2028, the Administrator shall brief the appropriate committees of Congress on the findings of the pilot program established under this section.

(e) SUNSET.—This section shall cease to be effective on October 1, 2028.

* * * * * * *

SEC. 908. [49 U.S.C. 44802 note] PART 107 WAIVER IMPROVEMENTS.

(a) IN GENERAL.—The Administrator shall adopt a performance- and risk-based approach in reviewing requests for certificates of waiver under section 107.200 of title 14, Code of Federal Regulations.

(b) STANDARDIZATION OF WAIVER APPLICATION.—

(1) IN GENERAL.—In carrying out subsection (a), the Administrator shall improve the process to submit requests for certificates of waiver described in subsection (a).

(2) FORMAT.—In carrying out paragraph (1), the Administrator may not require the use of open-ended descriptive prompts that are required to be filled out by an applicant, except to provide applicants the ability to provide the FAA with information for an unusual or irregular operation.

(3) DATA.—

(A) IN GENERAL.—In carrying out paragraph (1), the Administrator shall leverage data gathered from previous requests for certificates of waivers.

(B) CONSIDERATIONS.—In carrying out subparagraph (A), the Administrator shall safely use—

(i) big data analytics; and

(ii) machine learning.

(c) CONSIDERATION OF PROPERTY ACCESS.—

SEC. 908. [49 U.S.C. 44802 note] PART 107
WAIVER IMPROVEMENTS.

FAA Reauthorization Act of 2

(1) IN GENERAL.—In determining whether to issue a certificate of waiver under section 107.200 of title 14, Code of Federal Regulations, the Administrator shall—

(A) consider whether the waiver applicant has control over access to all real property on the ground within the area of operation; and

(B) recognize and account for the safety enhancements of such controlled access.

(2) RULE OF CONSTRUCTION.—Nothing in this subsection shall be construed to influence the extent to which the Administrator considers a lack of control over access to all real property on the ground within an area of operation as affecting the safety of an operation intended to be conducted under such certificate of waiver.

(d) PUBLIC AVAILABILITY OF WAIVERS.—

(1) IN GENERAL.—The Administrator shall publish all certificates of waiver issued under section 107.200 of title 14, Code of Federal Regulations, on the website of the FAA, including, with respect to each issued certificate of waiver—

(A) the terms, conditions, and limitations; and

(B) the class of airspace and any restrictions related to operating near airports or heliports.

(2) PUBLICATION.—In carrying out paragraph (1), the Administrator shall ensure that published information is made available in a manner that prevents inappropriate disclosure of proprietary information.

(e) PRECEDENTIAL USE OF PREVIOUSLY APPROVED WAIVERS.—

(1) WAIVER APPROVAL PRECEDENT.—If the Administrator determines, using criteria for a particular waiver, that an application for a certificate of waiver issued under section 107.200 of title 14, Code of Federal Regulations, is substantially similar (or is comprised of elements that are substantially similar) to an application for a certificate of waiver that the Administrator has previously approved, the Administrator may streamline, as appropriate, the approval of applications for such a particular waiver.

(2) RULE OF CONSTRUCTION.—Nothing in paragraph (1) shall be construed to preclude an applicant for a certificate

of waiver from applying to modify a condition or remove a limitation of such certificate.

(f) MODIFICATION OF WAIVERS.—

(1) IN GENERAL.—The Administrator shall establish an expedited review process for a request to modify or renew certificates of waiver previously issued under section 107.200 of title 14, Code of Federal Regulations, as appropriate.

(2) USE OF REVIEW PROCESS.—The review process established under paragraph (1) shall be used to modify or renew certificates of waiver that cover operations that are substantially similar in all material facts to operations covered under a previously issued certificate of waiver.

SEC. 909. [49 U.S.C. 44801 note] ENVIRONMENTAL REVIEW AND NOISE CERTIFICATION.

(a) NATIONAL ENVIRONMENTAL POLICY ACT GUIDANCE.—Not later than 180 days after the date of enactment of this Act, the Administrator shall publish unmanned aircraft system-specific environmental review guidance and implementation procedures and, thereafter, revise such guidance and procedures as appropriate to carry out the requirements of this section.

(b) PRIORITIZATION.—The guidance and procedures established by the Administrator under subsection (a) shall include processes that allow for the prioritization of project applications and activities that—

(1) offset or limit the impacts of non-zero emission activities;

(2) offset or limit the release of environmental pollutants to soil or water; or

(3) demonstrate other factors that benefit human safety or the environment, as determined by the Administrator.

(c) PROGRAMMATIC LEVEL APPROACH TO NEPA REVIEW.—Not later than 180 days after the date of enactment of this Act, the Administrator shall examine and integrate programmatic-level approaches to the requirements of the National Environmental Policy Act of 1969 (42 U.S.C. 4321 et seq.) by which the Administrator can—

(1) leverage an environmental review for unmanned aircraft operations within a defined geographic region,

including within and over commercial sites, industrial sites, or other sites closed or restricted to the public; and

(2) leverage an environmental assessment or environmental impact statement for nationwide programmatic approaches for large scale distributed unmanned aircraft operations.

(d) DEVELOPING 1 OR MORE CATEGORICAL EXCLUSIONS.—

(1) IN GENERAL.—The Administrator shall engage in periodic consultations with the Council on Environmental Quality to identify actions that are appropriate for a new categorical exclusion and shall incorporate such actions in FAA Order 1050.1F (or successor order) as considered appropriate by the Administrator to more easily allow for safe commercial operations of unmanned aircraft.

(2) PRIOR OPERATIONS.—The Administrator shall review existing categorical exclusions for applicability to unmanned aircraft operations in accordance with the National Environmental Policy Act of 1969 (42 U.S.C. 4321 et seq.) and subchapter A of chapter V of title 40, Code of Federal Regulations.

(e) BRIEFING.—Not later than 90 days after the date of enactment of this Act, the Administrator shall brief the appropriate committees of Congress on the plan of the Administrator to implement subsection (a).

(f) NONAPPLICATION OF NOISE CERTIFICATION REQUIREMENTS PENDING STANDARDS DEVELOPMENT.—

(1) IN GENERAL.—Notwithstanding the requirements of section 44715 of title 49, United States Code, the Administrator shall—

(A) waive the determination of compliance with part 36 of title 14, Code of Federal Regulations, for an applicant seeking unmanned aircraft type and airworthiness certifications; and

(B) not deny, withhold, or delay such certifications due to the absence of a noise certification basis under such part, if the Administrator has developed appropriate noise measurement procedures for unmanned aircraft and the Administrator has received from the applicant the noise measurement results based on such procedures.

(2) DURATION.—The nonapplication of the noise certification requirements under paragraph (1) shall continue until the Administrator finalizes the noise certification requirements for unmanned aircraft in part 36 of title 14, Code of Federal Regulations, or another part of title 14 of such Code, as required under paragraph (3).

(3) ASSOCIATED UAS CERTIFICATION STANDARDS.—

(A) DEVELOPMENT OF CRITERIA.—Not later than 18 months after the date of enactment of this Act, the Administrator shall develop and establish substantive criteria and standard metrics to determine whether to approve an unmanned aircraft pursuant to part 36 of title 14, Code of Federal Regulations.

(B) SUBSTANTIVE CRITERIA AND STANDARD METRICS.—In establishing the substantive criteria and standard metrics under subparagraph (A), the Administrator shall include criteria and metrics related to the noise impacts of an unmanned aircraft.

(C) PUBLICATION.—The Administrator shall publish in the Federal Register and post on the website of the FAA the criteria and metrics established under subparagraph (A).

(g) CONCURRENT REVIEWS.—If the Administrator determines that the design, construction, maintenance and operational sustainability, airworthiness approval, or operational approval of an unmanned aircraft require environmental assessments, including under the requirements of the National Environmental Policy Act of 1969 (42 U.S.C. 4321 et seq.), the Administrator shall, to the maximum extent practicable, conduct such reviews and analyses concurrently.

(h) THIRD-PARTY SUPPORT.—In implementing subsection (a), the Administrator shall allow for the engagement of approved specialized third parties, as appropriate, to support an applicant's preparation of, or the Administration's preparation and review of, documentation relating to the requirements of the National Environmental Policy Act of 1969 (42 U.S.C. 4321 et seq.) to ensure streamlined timelines for complex reviews.

(i) RULE OF CONSTRUCTION.—Nothing in this section shall be construed as prohibiting, restricting, or otherwise limiting the authority of the Administrator from implementing or complying with the requirements of the National Environmental Policy Act of 1969 (42 U.S.C. 4321 et seq.) and any related requirements to ensure the protection of the environment and aviation safety.

SEC. 910. UNMANNED AIRCRAFT SYSTEM USE IN WILDFIRE RESPONSE.

(a) UNMANNED AIRCRAFT SYSTEMS IN WILDFIRE RESPONSE.—

(1) IN GENERAL.—Not later than 18 months after the date of enactment of this Act, the Administrator, in coordination with the Chief of the Forest Service, the Administrator of the National Aeronautics and Space Administration, and any other Federal entity (or a contracted unmanned aircraft system operator of a Federal entity) the Administrator considers appropriate, shall develop a plan for the use of unmanned aircraft systems by public entities in wildfire response efforts, including wildfire detection, mitigation, and suppression.

(2) PLAN CONTENTS.—The plan developed under paragraph (1) shall include recommendations to—

(A) identify and designate areas of public land with high potential for wildfires in which public entities may conduct unmanned aircraft system operations beyond visual line of sight as part of wildfire response efforts, including wildfire detection, mitigation, and suppression;

(B) develop a process to facilitate the safe and efficient operation of unmanned aircraft systems beyond the visual line of sight in wildfire response efforts in areas designated under subparagraph (A), including a waiver process under section 91.113 or section 107.31 of title 14, Code of Federal Regulations, for public entities that use unmanned aircraft systems for aerial wildfire detection, mitigation, and suppression; and

(C) improve coordination between the relevant Federal agencies and public entities on the use of unmanned aircraft systems in wildfire response efforts.

(3) PLAN SUBMISSION.—Upon completion of the plan under paragraph (1), the Administrator shall submit such plan to, and provide a briefing for, the appropriate committees of Congress and the Committee on Science, Space, and Technology of the House of Representatives.

(4) PUBLICATION.—Upon submission of the plan under paragraph (1), the Administrator shall publish such plan on a publicly available website of the FAA.

(b) APPLICABILITY.—The plan developed under this section shall cover only unmanned aircraft systems that are—

(1) operated by, or on behalf of, a public entity;

(2) operated in airspace covered by a wildfire-related temporary flight restriction under section 91.137 of title 14, Code of Federal Regulations; and

(3) under the operational control of, or otherwise are being operationally coordinated by, an authorized aviation coordinator responsible for coordinating disaster response aircraft within the airspace covered by such temporary flight restriction.

(c) INTERAGENCY COORDINATION.—Not later than 180 days after the date of enactment of this Act, the Administrator shall seek to enter into the necessary agreements to provide a liaison of the Administration to the National Interagency Fire Center to facilitate the implementation of the plan developed under this section and the use of manned and unmanned aircraft in wildfire response efforts, including wildfire detection, mitigation, and suppression.

(d) SAVINGS CLAUSE.—Nothing in this section shall be construed to confer upon the Administrator the authorities of the Administrator of the Federal Emergency Management Agency under section 611 of the Robert T. Stafford Disaster Relief and Emergency Assistance Act (42 U.S.C. 5196).

(e) DEFINITIONS.—In this section:

(1) PUBLIC ENTITY.—The term "public entity" means—

(A) a Federal agency;

(B) a State government;

(C) a local government;

(D) a Tribal Government; and

(E) a territorial government.

(2) PUBLIC LAND.—The term "public land" has the meaning given such term in section 205 of the Sikes Act (16 U.S.C. 670k).

(3) WILDFIRE.—The term "wildfire" has the meaning given that term in section 2 of the Emergency Wildfire Suppression

Act (42 U.S.C. 1856m).

SEC. 911. [49 U.S.C. 44502 note] PILOT PROGRAM FOR UAS INSPECTIONS OF FAA INFRASTRUCTURE.

(a) IN GENERAL.—Not later than 180 days after the date of enactment of this Act, the Secretary shall initiate a pilot program to supplement inspection and oversight activities of the Department of Transportation with unmanned aircraft systems to increase employee safety, enhance data collection, increase the accuracy of inspections, reduce costs, and for other purposes the Secretary considers to be appropriate.

(b) GROUND-BASED AVIATION INFRASTRUCTURE.—In participating in the program under subsection (a), the Administrator shall evaluate the use of unmanned aircraft systems to inspect ground-based aviation infrastructure that may require visual inspection in hard-to-reach areas, including—

(1) navigational aids;

(2) air traffic control towers;

(3) radar facilities;

(4) communication facilities; and

(5) other air traffic control facilities.

(c) COORDINATION.—In carrying out subsection (b), the Administrator shall consult with the labor union certified under section 7111 of title 5, United States Code, to represent personnel responsible for the inspection of the ground-based aviation infrastructure.

(d) BRIEFING.—Not later than 2 years after the date of enactment of this Act, and annually thereafter until the termination of the pilot program under this section, the Secretary shall provide to the appropriate committees of Congress a briefing on the status and results of the pilot program established under subsection (a), including—

(1) cost savings;

(2) a description of how unmanned aircraft systems were used to supplement existing inspection, data collection, or oversight activities of Department employees, including the number of operations and types of activities performed;

(3) efficiency or safety improvements, if any, associated

with the use of unmanned aircraft systems to supplement
conventional inspection, data collection, or oversight activities;

(4) the fleet of unmanned aircraft systems maintained by
the Department for the program, or an overview of the services
used as part of the pilot program; and

(5) recommendations for improving the use or efficacy of
unmanned aircraft systems to supplement the Department's
inspection, data collection, or oversight activities.

(e) SUNSET AND INCORPORATION INTO STANDARD PRACTICE.—

(1) SUNSET.—The pilot program established under
subsection (a) and the briefing requirement under subsection
(d) shall terminate on the date that is 4 years after the date of
enactment of this Act.

(2) INCORPORATION INTO STANDARD PRACTICE.—Upon
termination of the pilot program under this section, the
Secretary shall assess the results and determine whether to
permanently incorporate the use of unmanned aircraft systems
into the regular inspection, data collection, and oversight
activities of the Department.

(3) REPORT TO CONGRESS.—Not later than 9 months after
the termination of the pilot program under paragraph (1), the
Secretary shall submit to the appropriate committees of
Congress a report on the final results of the pilot program and
the actions taken by the Administrator under paragraph (2).

SEC. 912. [49 U.S.C. 44802 note] DRONE INFRASTRUCTURE
INSPECTION GRANT PROGRAM.

(a) AUTHORITY.—Not later than 270 days after the date of
enactment of this Act, the Secretary shall establish an unmanned
aircraft system infrastructure inspection grant program to provide
grants to governmental entities to facilitate the use of small
unmanned aircraft systems to support more efficient inspection,
operation, construction, maintenance, and repair of an element of
critical infrastructure to improve worker safety related to projects.

(b) USE OF GRANT AMOUNTS.—A governmental entity may use
a grant provided under this section to—

(1) purchase or lease small unmanned aircraft systems;

(2) support the operational capabilities of small unmanned
aircraft systems used by the governmental entity;

(3) contract for services performed using a small unmanned aircraft system in circumstances in which the governmental entity does not have the resources or expertise to safely carry out or assist in carrying out the activities described under subsection (a); and

(4) support the program management capability of the governmental entity to use or contract the use of a small unmanned aircraft system, as described in paragraph (3).

(c) APPLICATION.—To be eligible to receive a grant under this section, a governmental entity shall submit to the Secretary an application at such time, in such form, and containing such information as the Secretary may require, including an assurance that the governmental entity or any contractor of the governmental entity, will comply with relevant Federal regulations.

(d) SELECTION OF APPLICANTS.—In selecting an application for a grant under this section, the Secretary shall prioritize applications that propose to—

(1) carry out a project in a variety of communities, including urban, suburban, rural, Tribal, or any other type of community; and

(2) address a safety risk in the inspection, operation, construction, maintenance, or repair of an element of critical infrastructure.

(e) RULE OF CONSTRUCTION.—Nothing in this section shall be construed to interfere with an agreement between a governmental entity and a labor union, including the requirements of section 5333(b) of title 49, United States Code.

(f) REPORT TO CONGRESS.—Not later than 2 years after the first grant is provided under this section, the Secretary shall submit to the appropriate committees of Congress a report that evaluates the program carried out under this section that includes—

(1) a description of the number of grants provided under this section;

(2) the amount of each grant provided under this section;

(3) the activities carried out with a grant provided under this section; and

(4) the effectiveness of such activities in meeting the objectives described in subsection (a).

(g) FUNDING.—

(1) FEDERAL SHARE.—

(A) IN GENERAL.—Except as provided in subparagraph (B), the Federal share of the cost of a project carried out using a grant provided under this section shall not exceed 50 percent of the total project cost.

(B) WAIVER.—The Secretary may increase the Federal share under subparagraph (A) to up to 75 percent for a project carried out using a grant provided under this section by a governmental entity if such entity—

(i) submits a written application to the Secretary requesting an increase in the Federal share; and

(ii) demonstrates that the additional assistance is necessary to facilitate the acceptance and full use of a grant under this section, such as alleviating economic hardship, meeting additional workforce needs, or any other uses that the Secretary determines to be appropriate.

(2) AUTHORIZATION OF APPROPRIATIONS.—Out of amounts authorized to be appropriated under section 106(k) of title 49, United States Code, the following amounts are authorized to carry out this section:

(A) $12,000,000 for fiscal year 2025.

(B) $12,000,000 for fiscal year 2026.

(C) $12,000,000 for fiscal year 2027.

(D) $12,000,000 for fiscal year 2028.

(h) DEFINITIONS.—In this section:

(1) CRITICAL INFRASTRUCTURE.—The term "critical infrastructure" has the meaning given such term in subsection (e) of the Critical Infrastructures Protection Act of 2001 (42 U.S.C. 5195c(e)).

(2) ELEMENT OF CRITICAL INFRASTRUCTURE.—The term "element of critical infrastructure" means a critical infrastructure facility or asset, including public bridges, tunnels, roads, highways, dams, electric grid, water infrastructure, communication systems, pipelines, or other related facilities or assets, as determined by the Secretary.

(3) GOVERNMENTAL ENTITY.—The term "governmental

entity" means—

(A) a State, the District of Columbia, the Commonwealth of Puerto Rico, a territory of the United States, or a political subdivision thereof;

(B) a unit of local government;

(C) a Tribal government;

(D) a metropolitan planning organization; or

(E) a consortia of more than 1 of the entities described in subparagraphs (A) through (D).

(4) PROJECT.—The term "project" means a project for the inspection, operation, construction, maintenance, or repair of an element of critical infrastructure, including mitigating environmental hazards to such infrastructure.

SEC. 913. [49 U.S.C. 40101 note] DRONE EDUCATION AND WORKFORCE TRAINING GRANT PROGRAM.

(a) AUTHORITY.—Not later than 180 days after the date of enactment of this Act, the Secretary of Transportation shall establish a drone education and training grant program to make grants to educational institutions for workforce training for small unmanned aircraft systems.

(b) USE OF GRANT AMOUNTS.—Amounts from a grant under this section shall be used in furtherance of activities authorized under section 631 and 632 of the FAA Reauthorization Act of 2018 (49 U.S.C. 40101 note).

(c) ELIGIBILITY.—To be eligible to receive a grant under this section, an educational institution shall submit an application to the Secretary at such time, in such form, and containing such information as the Secretary may require.

(d) AUTHORIZATION OF APPROPRIATIONS.—Out of amounts authorized to be appropriated under section 106(k) of title 49, United States Code, the Secretary shall make available to carry out this section $5,000,000 for each of fiscal years 2025 through 2028.

(e) EDUCATIONAL INSTITUTION DEFINED.—In this section, the term "educational institution" means an institution of higher education (as such term is defined in section 101 of the Higher Education Act of 1965 (20 U.S.C. 1001)) that participates in a program authorized under sections 631 and 632 of the FAA

Reauthorization Act of 2018 (49 U.S.C. 40101 note).

* * * * * * *

SEC. 915. TERMINATION OF ADVANCED AVIATION ADVISORY COMMITTEE.

The Secretary may not renew the charter of the Advanced Aviation Advisory Committee (chartered by the Secretary on June 10, 2022).

SEC. 916. [49 U.S.C. 44801 note] UNMANNED AND AUTONOMOUS FLIGHT ADVISORY COMMITTEE.

(a) IN GENERAL.—Not later than 1 year after the termination of the Advanced Aviation Advisory Committee pursuant to section 915, the Administrator shall establish an Unmanned and Autonomous Flight Advisory Committee (in this section referred to as the "Advisory Committee").

(b) DUTIES.—The Advisory Committee shall provide the Administrator advice on policy- and technical-level issues related to unmanned and autonomous aviation operations and activities, including, at a minimum, the following:

(1) The safe integration of unmanned aircraft systems and autonomous flight operations into the national airspace system, including feedback on—

(A) the certification and operational standards of highly automated aircraft, unmanned aircraft, and associated elements of such aircraft;

(B) coordination of procedures for operations in controlled and uncontrolled airspace; and

(C) communication protocols.

(2) The use cases of unmanned aircraft systems, including evaluating and assessing the potential benefits of using unmanned aircraft systems.

(3) The development of processes and methodologies to address safety concerns related to the operation of unmanned aircraft systems, including risk assessments and mitigation strategies.

(4) Unmanned aircraft system training, education, and workforce development programs, including evaluating

aeronautical knowledge gaps in the unmanned aircraft system workforce, assessing the workforce needs of unmanned aircraft system operations, and establishing a strong pipeline to ensure a robust unmanned aircraft system workforce.

(5) The analysis of unmanned aircraft system data and trends.

(6) Unmanned aircraft system infrastructure, including the use of existing aviation infrastructure and the development of necessary infrastructure.

(c) MEMBERSHIP.—

(1) IN GENERAL.—The Advisory Committee shall be composed of not more than 12 members.

(2) REPRESENTATIVES.—The Advisory Committee shall include at least 1 representative of each of the following:

(A) Commercial operators of unmanned aircraft systems.

(B) Unmanned aircraft system manufacturers.

(C) Counter-UAS manufacturers.

(D) FAA-approved unmanned aircraft system service suppliers.

(E) Unmanned aircraft system test ranges under section 44803 of title 49, United States Code.

(F) An unmanned aircraft system physical infrastructure network provider.

(G) Community advocates.

(H) Certified labor organizations representing commercial airline pilots, air traffic control specialists employed by the Administration, certified aircraft maintenance technicians, certified aircraft dispatchers, or aviation safety inspectors.

(I) Academia or a relevant research organization.

(3) OBSERVERS.—The Administrator may invite appropriate representatives of other Federal agencies to observe or provide input on the work of the Advisory Committee, but shall not allow such representatives to participate in any decision-making of the Advisory Committee.

(d) REPORTING.—

(1) IN GENERAL.—The Advisory Committee shall submit to the Administrator an annual report of the activities, findings, and recommendations of the Committee.

(2) CONGRESSIONAL REPORTING.—The Administrator shall submit to the appropriate committees of Congress the reports required under paragraph (1).

(e) PROHIBITION.—The Administrator may not task the Advisory Committee established under this section with a review or the development of recommendations relating to operations conducted under part 121 of title 14, Code of Federal Regulations.

SEC. 917. NEXTGEN ADVISORY COMMITTEE MEMBERSHIP EXPANSION.

(a) IN GENERAL.—Not later than 90 days after the date of enactment of this Act, the Secretary shall take such actions as may be necessary to expand the membership of the NextGen Advisory Committee (chartered by the Secretary on June 15, 2022) to include 1 representative from the unmanned aircraft system industry and 1 representative from the powered-lift industry.

(b) QUALIFICATIONS.—The representatives required under subsection (a) shall have the following qualifications, as applicable:

(1) Demonstrated expertise in the design, manufacturing, or operation of unmanned aircraft systems and powered-lift aircraft.

(2) Demonstrated experience in the development or implementation of unmanned aircraft system and powered-lift aircraft policies and procedures.

(3) Demonstrated commitment to advancing the safe integration of unmanned aircraft systems and powered-lift aircraft into the national airspace system.

SEC. 918. INTERAGENCY COORDINATION.

(a) SENSE OF CONGRESS.—It is the sense of Congress that—

(1) the purpose of the joint Department of Defense-Federal Aviation Administration executive committee (in this section referred to as the "Executive Committee") on conflict and dispute resolution as described in section 1036(b) of the Duncan Hunter National Defense Authorization Act for Fiscal Year 2009 (Public Law 110-417) is to resolve disputes on the matters

of policy and procedures between the Department of Defense and the Federal Aviation Administration relating to airspace, aircraft certifications, aircrew training, and other issues, including the access of unmanned aerial systems of the Department of Defense to the national airspace system;

(2) by mutual agreement of Executive Committee leadership, operating with the best of intentions, the current scope of activities and membership of the Executive Committee has exceeded the original intent of, and tasking to, the Executive Committee; and

(3) the expansion described in paragraph (2) has resulted in an imbalance in the oversight of certain Federal entities in matters concerning civil aviation safety and security.

(b) CHARTER.—

(1) CHARTER REVISION.—Not later than 45 days after the date of enactment of this Act, the Administrator shall seek to revise the charter of the Executive Committee to reflect the scope, objectives, membership, and activities described in section 1036(b) of the Duncan Hunter National Defense Authorization Act for Fiscal Year 2009 (Public Law 110-417) in order to achieve the increasing, and ultimately routine, access of unmanned aircraft systems of the Department of Defense into the national airspace system.

(2) SUNSET.—Not earlier than 2 years after the date of enactment of this Act, the Administrator shall seek to sunset the activities of the Executive Committee by joint agreement of the Administrator and the Secretary of Defense.

* * * * * * *

SEC. 920. EXTENSION OF BEYOND PROGRAM.

(a) FAA BEYOND PROGRAM EXTENSION.—The Administrator shall extend the BEYOND program of the FAA as in effect on the day before the date of enactment of this Act (in this section referred to as the "Program") and the existing agreements with State, local, and Tribal governments entered into under the Program until the date on which the Administrator determines the Program is no longer necessary or useful.

(b) FAA BEYOND PROGRAM EXPANSION.—

(1) IN GENERAL.—The Administrator shall consider expanding the Program to include additional State, local, and Tribal governments to test and evaluate the use of new and emerging aviation concepts and technologies to evaluate and inform FAA policies, rulemaking, and guidance related to the safe integration of such concepts and technologies into the national airspace system.

(2) SCOPE.—If the Administrator determines the Program should be expanded, the Administrator shall address additional factors in the Program, including—

(A) increasing automation in civil aircraft, including unmanned aircraft systems and new or emerging aviation technologies;

(B) operations of such systems and technologies, including beyond visual line of sight; and

(C) the societal and economic impacts of such operations.

(3) ADDITIONAL WAIVER AUTHORITY.—In carrying out an expansion of the Program, the Administrator may waive the requirements of section 44711 of title 49, United States Code, including related regulations, under any BEYOND program agreement to the extent consistent with aviation safety.

* * * * * * *

SEC. 924. FAA COMPREHENSIVE PLAN ON UAS AUTOMATION.

(a) COMPREHENSIVE PLAN.—The Administrator shall establish a comprehensive plan for the integration of autonomous unmanned aircraft systems into the national airspace system.

(b) COMPREHENSIVE PLAN CONTENTS.—In establishing the comprehensive plan under subsection (a), the Administrator shall—

(1) identify FAA processes and regulations that need to change to accommodate the increasingly automated role of a remote operator of an unmanned aircraft system; and

(2) identify how the Administrator intends to authorize operations ranging from low risk automated operations to increasingly complex automated operations of such systems.

(c) COORDINATION.—In establishing the comprehensive plan under subsection (a), the Administrator shall consult with—

(1) the National Aeronautics and Space Administration;

(2) the Department of Defense;

(3) manufacturers of autonomous unmanned aircraft systems;

(4) operators of autonomous unmanned aircraft systems; and

(5) other stakeholders with knowledge of automation in aviation, the human-computer interface, and aviation safety, as determined appropriate by the Administrator.

(d) SUBMISSION.—Not later than 1 year after the date of enactment of this Act, the Administrator shall submit to the appropriate committees of Congress, the subcommittee on Transportation, Housing and Urban Development, and Related Agencies of the Committee on Appropriations of the Senate and the subcommittee on Transportation, Housing and Urban Development, and Related Agencies of the Committee on Appropriations of the House of Representatives the plan established under subsection (a).

* * * * * * *

SEC. 931. [49 U.S.C. 44801 note] ACCEPTABLE LEVELS OF RISK AND RISK ASSESSMENT METHODOLOGY.

(a) IN GENERAL.—Not later than 180 days after the date of enactment of this Act, the Administrator shall develop a risk assessment methodology that allows for the determination of acceptable levels of risk for unmanned aircraft system operations, including operations beyond visual line of sight, conducted—

(1) under waivers issued to part 107 of title 14, Code of Federal Regulations;

(2) pursuant to section 44807 of title 49, United States Code; or

(3) pursuant to other applicable regulations, as appropriate.

(b) RISK ASSESSMENT METHODOLOGY CONSIDERATIONS.—In establishing the risk assessment methodology under this section, the Administrator shall ensure alignment with the considerations included in the order issued by the FAA titled "UAS Safety Risk Management Policy" (FAA Order 8040.6A), and any subsequent amendments to such order, as the Administrator considers

SEC. 932. [49 U.S.C. 44802 note] THIRD-PARTY
SERVICE APPROVALS.

FAA Reauthorization Act of 2024

appropriate.

(c) PUBLICATION.—The Administrator shall make the risk assessment methodology established under this section available to the public on an appropriate website of the Administration and update such methodology as necessary.

SEC. 932. [49 U.S.C. 44802 note] THIRD-PARTY SERVICE APPROVALS.

(a) APPROVAL PROCESS.—Not later than 1 year after the date of enactment of this Act, the Administrator shall establish procedures, which may include a rulemaking, to approve third-party service suppliers, including third-party service suppliers of unmanned aircraft system traffic management, to support the safe integration and commercial operation of unmanned aircraft systems.

(b) ACCEPTANCE OF STANDARDS.—In establishing the approval process required under subsection (a), the Administrator shall ensure that, to the maximum extent practicable, industry consensus standards, such as ASTM International Standard F3548-21, titled "UAS Traffic Management (UTM) UAS Service Supplier (USS) Interoperability", are included as an acceptable means of compliance for third-party services.

(c) APPROVALS.—In establishing the approval process required under subsection (a), the Administrator shall—

(1) define and implement criteria and conditions for the approval and oversight of third-party service suppliers that—

(A) could have a direct or indirect impact on air traffic services in the national airspace system; and

(B) require FAA oversight; and

(2) establish procedures by which unmanned aircraft systems can use the capabilities and services of third-party service suppliers to support operations.

(d) HARMONIZATION.—In carrying out this section, the Administrator shall seek to harmonize, to the extent practicable and advisable, any requirements and guidance for the development, use, and operation of third-party capabilities and services, including UTM, with similar requirements and guidance of other civil aviation authorities.

(e) COORDINATION.—In carrying out this section, the Administrator shall consider any relevant information provided by the Administrator of the National Aeronautics and Space Administration regarding research and development efforts the National Aeronautics and Space Administration may have conducted related to the use of UTM providers.

(f) THIRD-PARTY SERVICE SUPPLIER DEFINED.—In this section, the term "third-party service supplier" means an entity other than the FAA that provides a distributed service that affects the safety or efficiency of the national airspace system, including UAS service suppliers, supplemental data service providers, and infrastructure providers, such as providers of ground-based surveillance, command-and-control, and information exchange to another party.

(g) RULES OF CONSTRUCTION.—

(1) BEYOND VISUAL LINE OF SIGHT OPERATIONS.—Nothing in this section shall be construed to prevent or prohibit beyond visual line of sight operations of unmanned aircraft systems, or other types of operations, through the use of technologies other than third-party capabilities and services.

(2) AIRSPACE.—Nothing in this section shall be construed to alter the authorities provided under section 40103 of title 49, United States Code.

SEC. 933. [49 U.S.C. 44801 note] SPECIAL AUTHORITY FOR TRANSPORT OF HAZARDOUS MATERIALS BY COMMERCIAL PACKAGE DELIVERY UNMANNED AIRCRAFT SYSTEMS.

(a) IN GENERAL.—Notwithstanding any other Federal requirement or restriction related to the transportation of hazardous materials on aircraft, the Secretary shall, beginning not later than 180 days after enactment of this section, use a risk-based approach to establish the operational requirements, standards, or special permits necessary to approve or authorize an air carrier to transport hazardous materials by unmanned aircraft systems providing common carriage under part 135 of title 14, Code of Federal Regulations, or under successor authorities, as applicable, based on the weight, amount, and type of hazardous material being transported and the characteristics of the operations subject to such requirements, standards, or special purposes.

(b) REQUIREMENTS.—In carrying out subsection (a), the Secretary shall consider, at a minimum—

(1) the safety of the public and users of the national

airspace system;

(2) efficiencies of allowing the safe transportation of hazardous materials by unmanned aircraft systems and whether such transportation complies with the hazardous materials regulations under subchapter C of chapter I of title 49, Code of Federal Regulations, including any changes to such regulations issued pursuant to this section;

(3) the risk profile of the transportation of hazardous materials by unmanned aircraft systems, taking into consideration the risk associated with differing weights, quantities, and packing group classifications of hazardous materials;

(4) mitigations to the risk of the hazardous materials being transported, based on the weight, amount, and type of materials being transported and the characteristics of the operation, including operational and aircraft-based mitigations; and

(5) the altitude at which unmanned aircraft operations are conducted.

(c) SAFETY RISK ASSESSMENTS.—The Secretary may require unmanned aircraft systems operators to submit a safety risk assessment acceptable to the Administrator, as part of the operator certification process, in order for such operators to perform the carriage of hazardous materials as authorized under this section.

(d) CONFORMITY OF HAZARDOUS MATERIALS REGULATIONS.—The Secretary shall make such changes as are necessary to conform the hazardous materials regulations under parts 173 and 175 of title 49, Code of Federal Regulations, to this section. Such changes shall be made concurrently with the activities described in subsection (a).

(e) STAKEHOLDER INPUT ON CHANGES TO THE HAZARDOUS MATERIALS REGULATIONS.—

(1) IMPLEMENTATION.—Not later than 180 days of the date of enactment of this Act, the Secretary shall hold a public meeting to obtain input on changes necessary to implement this section.

(2) PERIODIC UPDATES.—The Secretary shall—

(A) periodically review, as necessary, amounts of hazardous materials allowed to be carried by unmanned aircraft systems pursuant to this section; and

(B) determine whether such amounts should be revised, based on operational and safety data, without negatively impacting overall aviation safety.

(f) SAVINGS CLAUSE.—Nothing in this section shall be construed to—

(1) limit the authority of the Secretary, the Administrator, or the Administrator of the Pipeline and Hazardous Materials Safety Administration from implementing requirements to ensure the safe carriage of hazardous materials by aircraft; and

(2) confer upon the Administrator the authorities of the Administrator of the Pipeline and Hazardous Materials Safety Administration under part 175 of title 49, Code of Federal Regulations, and chapter 51 of title 49, United States Code.

(g) DEFINITION OF HAZARDOUS MATERIALS.—In this section, the term "hazardous materials" has the meaning given such term in section 5102 of title 49, United States Code.

SEC. 934. [49 U.S.C. 44801 note] OPERATIONS OVER HIGH SEAS.

(a) IN GENERAL.—To the extent permitted by treaty obligations of the United States, including the Convention on International Civil Aviation (in this section referred to as "ICAO"), the Administrator shall work with other civil aviation authorities to establish and implement operational approval processes to permit unmanned aircraft systems to operate over the high seas within flight information regions for which the United States is responsible for operational control.

(b) CONSULTATION.—In establishing and implementing the operational approval process under subsection (a), the Administrator shall consult with appropriate stakeholders, including industry stakeholders.

(c) ICAO ACTIVITIES.—Not later than 6 months after the date of enactment of this Act, the Administrator shall engage ICAO through the submission of a working paper, panel proposal, or other appropriate mechanism to clarify the permissibility of unmanned aircraft systems to operate over the high seas.

(d) REVIEW.—Not later than 6 months after the date of enactment of this Act, the Administrator shall review whether, and to what extent, ICAO member states are approving the operation of unmanned aircraft systems over the high seas and brief the appropriate committees of Congress regarding the findings of such review.

* * * * * * *

SEC. 936. [49 U.S.C. 44801 note] COVERED DRONE PROHIBITION.

(a) PROHIBITIONS.—The Secretary is prohibited from—

(1) entering into, extending, or renewing a contract or awarding a grant—

(A) for the operation, procurement, or contracting action with respect to a covered unmanned aircraft system; or

(B) to an entity that operates (as determined by the Administrator) a covered unmanned aircraft system in the performance of such contract;

(2) issuing a grant to a covered foreign entity for any project related to covered unmanned aircraft systems; and

(3) operating a covered unmanned aircraft system.

(b) EXEMPTIONS.—The Secretary is exempt from any prohibitions under subsection (a) if the grant, operation, procurement, or contracting action is for the purposes of testing, researching, evaluating, analyzing, or training related to—

(1) unmanned aircraft detection systems and counter-UAS systems, including activities conducted—

(A) under the Alliance for System Safety of UAS through Research Excellence Center of Excellence of the FAA; or

(B) by the unmanned aircraft system test ranges designated under section 44803 of title 49, United States Code;

(2) the safe, secure, or efficient operation of the national airspace system or maintenance of public safety;

(3) the safe integration of advanced aviation technologies into the national airspace system, including activities carried out under the Alliance for System Safety of UAS through Research Excellence Center of Excellence of the FAA;

(4) in coordination with other relevant Federal agencies,

determining security threats of covered unmanned aircraft systems; and

(5) intelligence, electronic warfare, and information warfare operations.

(c) WAIVERS.—The Secretary may waive any restrictions under subsection (a) on a case-by-case basis by notifying the appropriate committees of Congress in writing, not later than 15 days after waiving such restrictions, that the procurement or other activity is in the public interest.

(d) REPLACEMENT OF CERTAIN UNMANNED AIRCRAFT SYSTEMS.—

(1) IN GENERAL.—The Secretary shall take such actions as are necessary to replace any covered unmanned aircraft system that is owned or operated by the Department of Transportation as of the date of enactment of this Act with an unmanned aircraft system manufactured in the United States or an allied country (as such term is defined in section 2350f(d)(1) of title 10, United States Code) if the capabilities of such covered unmanned aircraft system are consequential to the work of the Department or the mission of the Department.

(2) FUNDING.—There is authorized to be appropriated to the Secretary $5,000,000 to carry out this subsection.

(e) EFFECTIVE DATES.—

(1) OPERATIONS.—The prohibitions under paragraphs (1) and (3) of subsection (a) shall be in effect on the date of enactment of this Act.

(2) GRANTS.—The prohibitions under paragraphs (1) and (2) of subsection (a) shall—

(A) not apply to grants awarded before the date of enactment of this Act; and

(B) apply to grants awarded after the date of enactment of this Act.

(f) APPLICATION OF PROHIBITIONS.—The prohibitions under subsection (a) are applicable to all offices and programs of the Department of Transportation, including—

(1) aviation research grant programs;

(2) aviation workforce development programs established under section 625 of the FAA Reauthorization Act of 2018 (49

U.S.C. 40101 note);

(3) FAA Air Transportation Centers of Excellence;

(4) programs established under sections 631 and 632 of the
FAA Reauthorization Act of 2018 (49 U.S.C. 40101 note); and

(5) the airport improvement program under subchapter I of
chapter 471 of title 49, United States Code.

(g) RULE OF CONSTRUCTION.—Nothing in this section shall
prevent a State, local, Tribal, or territorial governmental agency
from procuring or operating a covered unmanned aircraft system
purchased with non-Federal funding.

(h) DEFINITIONS.—In this section:

(1) COVERED FOREIGN COUNTRY.—The term "covered
foreign country" means any of the following:

(A) The People's Republic of China.

(B) The Russian Federation.

(C) The Islamic Republic of Iran.

(D) The Democratic People's Republic of Korea.

(E) The Bolivarian Republic of Venezuela.

(F) The Republic of Cuba.

(G) Any other country the Secretary determines
necessary.

(2) COVERED FOREIGN ENTITY.—The term "covered foreign
entity" means—

(A) an entity included on the list developed and
maintained by the Federal Acquisition Security Council
and published in the System for Award Management;

(B) an entity included on the Consolidated Screening
List or Entity List as designated by the Secretary of
Commerce;

(C) an entity that is domiciled in, or under the
influence or control of, a covered foreign country; or

(D) an entity that is a subsidiary or affiliate of an
entity described under subparagraphs (A) through (C).

(3) COVERED UNMANNED AIRCRAFT SYSTEM.—The term
"covered unmanned aircraft system" means—

(A) a small unmanned aircraft, an unmanned aircraft,

and unmanned aircraft system, or the associated elements of such aircraft and aircraft systems related to the collection and transmission of sensitive information (consisting of communication links and the components that control the unmanned aircraft) that enable the operator to operate the aircraft in the National Airspace System which is manufactured or assembled by a covered foreign entity; and

(B) an unmanned aircraft detection system or counter-UAS system that is manufactured or assembled by a covered foreign entity.

SEC. 937. [49 U.S.C. 44803 note] EXPANDING USE OF INNOVATIVE TECHNOLOGIES IN THE GULF OF MEXICO.

(a) IN GENERAL.—The Administrator shall prioritize the authorization of an eligible UAS test range sponsor partnering with an eligible airport authority to achieve the goals specified in subsection (b).

(b) GOALS.—The goals of a partnership authorized pursuant to subsection (a) shall be to test the operations of innovative technologies in both commercial and non-commercial applications, consistent with existing law, to—

(1) identify challenges associated with aviation operations over large bodies of water;

(2) provide transportation of cargo and passengers to offshore energy infrastructure;

(3) assess the impacts of operations in saltwater environments;

(4) identify the challenges of integrating such technologies in complex airspace, including with commercial rotorcraft; and

(5) identify the differences between coordinating with Federal air traffic control towers and towers operated under the FAA Contract Tower Program.

(c) BRIEFING TO CONGRESS.—The Administrator shall provide an annual briefing to the appropriate committees of Congress on the status of the partnership authorized under this section, including detailing any barriers to the commercialization of innovative technologies in the Gulf of Mexico.

(d) DEFINITIONS.—In this section:

(1) ELIGIBLE AIRPORT AUTHORITY.—The term "eligible airport authority" means an AIP-eligible airport authority that is—

(A) located in a state bordering the Gulf of Mexico which does not already contain a UAS Test Range;

(B) has an air traffic control tower operated under the FAA Contract Tower Program;

(C) is located within 60 miles of a port; and

(D) does not have any scheduled passenger airline service as of the date of the enactment of this Act.

(2) INNOVATIVE TECHNOLOGIES.—The term "innovative technologies" means unmanned aircraft systems and powered-lift aircraft.

(3) UAS.—The term "UAS" means an unmanned aircraft system.

Subtitle B—Advanced Air Mobility

SEC. 951. [49 U.S.C. 40101 note] DEFINITIONS.
In this subtitle:

(1) ADVANCED AIR MOBILITY.—The terms "advanced air mobility" and "AAM" mean a transportation system that is comprised of urban air mobility and regional air mobility using manned or unmanned aircraft.

(2) POWERED-LIFT AIRCRAFT.—The term ""powered-lift aircraft"" has the meaning given the term ""powered-lift"" in section 1.1 of title 14, Code of Federal Regulations.

(3) REGIONAL AIR MOBILITY.—The term ""regional air mobility"" means the movement of passengers or property by air between 2 points using an airworthy aircraft that—

(A) has advanced technologies, such as distributed propulsion, vertical takeoff and landing, powered lift, nontraditional power systems, or autonomous technologies;

(B) has a maximum takeoff weight of greater than 1,320 pounds; and

(C) is not urban air mobility.

(4) URBAN AIR MOBILITY.—The term ""urban air mobility""

means the movement of passengers or property by air between
2 points in different cities or 2 points within the same city using
an airworthy aircraft that—

(A) has advanced technologies, such as distributed
propulsion, vertical takeoff and landing, powered lift,
nontraditional power systems, or autonomous technologies;
and

(B) has a maximum takeoff weight of greater than
1,320 pounds.

(5) VERTIPORT.—The term ""vertiport"" means an area of
land, water, or a structure used or intended to be used to
support the landing, takeoff, taxiing, parking, and storage of
powered-lift aircraft or other aircraft that vertiport design and
performance standards established by the Administrator can
accommodate.

SEC. 952. [49 U.S.C. 40101 note] SENSE OF CONGRESS ON FAA
LEADERSHIP IN ADVANCED AIR MOBILITY.

It is the sense of Congress that—

(1) the United States should take actions to become a global
leader in advanced air mobility;

(2) as such a global leader, the FAA should—

(A) prioritize work on the type certification of powered-
lift aircraft;

(B) publish, in line with stated deadlines, rulemakings
and policy necessary to enable commercial operations, such
as the Special Federal Aviation Regulation of the FAA
titled "Integration of Powered-Lift: Pilot Certification and
Operations; Miscellaneous Amendments Related to
Rotorcraft and Airplanes", issued on June 14, 2023
(2120-AL72);

(C) work with global partners to promote acceptance of
advanced air mobility products; and

(D) leverage the existing aviation system to the
greatest extent possible to support advanced air mobility
operations; and

(3) the FAA should work with manufacturers, prospective
operators of powered-lift aircraft, and other relevant
stakeholders to enable the safe entry of such aircraft into the

national airspace system.

SEC. 953. [49 U.S.C. 40101 note] APPLICATION OF NATIONAL ENVIRONMENTAL POLICY ACT CATEGORICAL EXCLUSIONS FOR VERTIPORT PROJECTS.

In considering the environmental impacts of a proposed vertiport project on an airport for purposes of compliance with the National Environmental Policy Act of 1969 (42 U.S.C. 4321 et seq.), the Administrator shall—

(1) apply any applicable categorical exclusions in accordance with the National Environmental Policy Act of 1969 (42 U.S.C. 4321 et seq.) and subchapter A of chapter V of title 40, Code of Federal Regulations; and

(2) after consultation with the Council on Environmental Quality, take steps to establish additional categorical exclusions, as appropriate, for vertiports on an airport, in accordance with the National Environmental Policy Act of 1969 (42 U.S.C. 4321 et seq.) and subchapter A of chapter V of title 40, Code of Federal Regulations.

* * * * * * *

SEC. 955. [49 U.S.C. 40101 note] RULES FOR OPERATION OF POWERED-LIFT AIRCRAFT.

(a) SFAR RULEMAKING.—

(1) IN GENERAL.—Not later than 7 months after the date of enactment of this Act, the Administrator shall publish a final rule for the Special Federal Aviation Regulation of the FAA titled "Integration of Powered-Lift: Pilot Certification and Operations; Miscellaneous Amendments Related to Rotorcraft and Airplanes", issued on June 14, 2023 (2120-AL72), establishing procedures for certifying pilots of powered-lift aircraft and providing operational rules for powered-lift aircraft capable of transporting passengers and cargo.

(2) REQUIREMENTS.—With respect to any powered-lift aircraft type certificated by the Administrator, the regulations established under paragraph (1) shall—

(A) provide a practical pathway for pilot qualification and operations;

(B) establish performance-based requirements for

SEC. 955. [49 U.S.C. 40101 note] RULES FOR
OPERATION OF POWERED-LIFT AIRCRAFT.

FAA Reauthorization Act of 2

energy reserves and other range- and endurance-related requirements that reflect the capabilities and intended operations of the aircraft;

(C) provide for a combination of pilot training requirements, including simulators, to ensure the safe operation of powered-lift aircraft; and

(D) to the maximum extent practicable, align powered-lift pilot qualifications with section 2.1.1.4 of Annex 1 to the Convention on International Civil Aviation published by the International Civil Aviation Organization.

(3) CONSIDERATIONS.—In developing the regulations required under paragraph (1), the Administrator shall—

(A) consider whether to grant an individual with an existing commercial airplane (single- or multi-engine) or helicopter pilot certificate the authority to serve as pilot-in-command of a powered-lift aircraft in commercial operation following the completion of an FAA-approved pilot type rating for such type of aircraft;

(B) consult with the Secretary of Defense with regard to—

(i) the Agility Prime program of the United States Air Force;

(ii) powered-lift aircraft evaluated and deployed for military purposes, including the F-35B program; and

(iii) the commonalities and differences between powered-lift aircraft types and the handling qualities of such aircraft; and

(C) consider the adoption of the recommendations for powered-lift operations, as appropriate, contained in document 10103 of the International Civil Aviation Organization titled "Guidance on the Implementation of ICAO Standards and Recommended Practices for Tilt-rotors", published in 2019.

(b) INTERIM APPLICATION OF RULES AND PRIVILEGES IN LIEU OF RULEMAKING.—

(1) IN GENERAL.—Beginning 16 months after the date of enactment of this Act, if a final rule has not been published

SEC. 955. [49 U.S.C. 40101 note] RULES FOR
OPERATION OF POWERED-LIFT AIRCRAFT.

FAA Reauthorization Act of 2024

pursuant to subsection (a)—

 (A) the rules in effect on the date that is 16 months after the date of enactment of this Act that apply to the operation and the operator of rotorcraft or fixed-wing aircraft under subchapters F, G, H, and I of chapter 1 of title 14, Code of Federal Regulations, shall be—

  (i) deemed to apply to—

   (I) the operation of a powered-lift aircraft in the national airspace system; and

   (II) the operator of such a powered-lift aircraft; and

  (ii) applicable, as determined by the operator of an airworthy powered-lift aircraft in consultation with the Administrator, and consistent with sections 91.3 and 91.13 of title 14, Code of Federal Regulations; and

 (B) upon the completion of a type rating for a specific powered-lift aircraft, airmen that hold a pilot or instructor certification with airplane category ratings in any class or rotorcraft category ratings in the helicopter class shall be deemed to have privileges of a powered-lift rating for such specific powered-lift aircraft.

(2) TERMINATION OF INTERIM RULES AND PRIVILEGES.—This subsection shall cease to have effect 1 month after the effective date of a final rule issued pursuant to subsection (a).

(c) POWERED-LIFT AIRCRAFT AVIATION RULEMAKING COMMITTEE.—

(1) IN GENERAL.—Not later than 3 years after the date on which the Administrator issues the first certificate to commercially operate a powered-lift aircraft, the Administrator shall establish an aviation rulemaking committee (in this section referred to as the "Committee") to provide the Administrator with specific findings and recommendations for, at a minimum, the creation of a standard pathway for the—

 (A) performance-based certification of powered-lift aircraft;

 (B) certification of airmen capable of serving as pilot-in-command of a powered-lift aircraft; and

 (C) operation of powered-lift aircraft in commercial

SEC. 955. [49 U.S.C. 40101 note] RULES FOR
OPERATION OF POWERED-LIFT AIRCRAFT.

FAA Reauthorization Act of 2(

service and air transportation.

(2) CONSIDERATIONS.—In providing findings and recommendations under paragraph (1), the Committee shall consider the following:

(A) Outcome-driven safety objectives to spur innovation and technology adoption and promote the development of performance-based regulations.

(B) Lessons and insights learned from previously published special conditions and other Federal Register notices of airworthiness criteria for powered-lift aircraft.

(C) To the maximum extent practicable, aligning powered-lift pilot qualifications with section 2.1.1.4 of Annex 1 to the Convention on International Civil Aviation published by the International Civil Aviation Organization.

(D) The adoption of the recommendations contained in document 10103 of the International Civil Aviation Organization titled "Guidance on the Implementation of ICAO Standards and Recommended Practices for Tilt-rotors", published in 2019, as appropriate.

(E) Practical pathways for pilot qualification and operations.

(F) Performance-based requirements for energy reserves and other range- and endurance-related designs and technologies that reflect the capabilities and intended operations of the aircraft.

(G) A combination of pilot training requirements, including simulators, to ensure the safe operation of powered-lift aircraft.

(3) REPORT.—The Committee shall submit to the Administrator a report detailing the findings and recommendations of the Committee.

(d) POWERED-LIFT AIRCRAFT RULEMAKING.—

(1) IN GENERAL.—Not later than 270 days after the date on which the Committee submits the report under subsection (c)(3), the Administrator shall initiate a rulemaking to implement the findings and recommendations of the Committee, as determined appropriate by the Administrator.

(2) REQUIREMENTS.—In developing the rulemaking under

SEC. 956. [49 U.S.C. 40101 note] ADVANCED
PROPULSION SYSTEMS REGULATIONS.

FAA Reauthorization Act of 2024

paragraph (1), the Administrator shall—

(A) consult with the Secretary of Defense with regard to methods for pilots to gain proficiency and earn the necessary ratings required to act as a pilot-in-command of powered-lift aircraft;

(B) consider and plan for unmanned and remotely piloted powered-lift aircraft, and the associated elements of such aircraft, through the promulgation of performance-based regulations;

(C) consider any information and experience gained from operations and efforts that occur as a result of the Special Federal Aviation Regulation of the FAA titled "Integration of Powered-Lift: Pilot Certification and Operations; Miscellaneous Amendments Related to Rotorcraft and Airplanes", issued on June 14, 2023 (2120-AL72);

(D) consider whether to grant an individual with an existing commercial airplane (single- or multi-engine) or helicopter pilot certificate the authority to serve as pilot-in-command of a powered-lift aircraft in commercial operation following the completion of an FAA-approved pilot type rating for such type of aircraft;

(E) work to harmonize the certification and operational requirements of the FAA with those of civil aviation authorities with bilateral safety agreements in place with the United States, to the extent such harmonization does not negatively impact domestic manufacturers and operators; and

(F) consider and plan for the use of alternative fuel types and propulsion methods, including reviewing the performance-based nature of parts 33 and 35 of title 14, Code of Federal Regulations, and any related recommendations provided to the Administrator by the aviation rulemaking advisory committee described in section 956.

SEC. 956. [49 U.S.C. 40101 note] ADVANCED PROPULSION SYSTEMS REGULATIONS.

(a) IN GENERAL.—Not later than 3 years after the date of

SEC. 957. [49 U.S.C. 40101 note] POWERED-
LIFT AIRCRAFT ENTRY INTO SERVICE.

FAA Reauthorization Act of 2

enactment of this Act, the Administrator shall task the Aviation Rulemaking Advisory Committee (in this section referred to as the "Committee") to provide the Administrator with specific findings and recommendations for regulations related to the certification and installation of—

(1) electric engines and propellers;

(2) hybrid electric engines and propulsion systems;

(3) hydrogen fuel cells;

(4) hydrogen combustion engines or propulsion systems; and

(5) other new or novel propulsion mechanisms and methods as determined appropriate by the Administrator.

(b) CONSIDERATIONS.—In carrying out subsection (a), the Committee shall consider, at a minimum, the following:

(1) Outcome-driven safety objectives to spur innovation and technology adoption, and promote the development of performance-based regulations.

(2) Lessons and insights learned from previously published special conditions and other published airworthiness criteria for novel engines, propellers, and aircraft.

(3) The requirements of part 33 and part 35 of title 14, Code of Federal Regulations, any boundaries of applicability for standalone engine type certificates (including highly integrated systems), and the use of technical standards order authorizations.

(c) REPORT.—Not later than 1 year after providing findings and recommendations under subsection (a), the Committee shall submit to the Administrator and the appropriate committees of Congress a report containing such findings and recommendations.

(d) BRIEFING.—Not later than 180 days after the date on which the Committee submits the report under subsection (c), the Administrator shall brief the appropriate committees of Congress regarding plans of the FAA in response to the findings and recommendations contained in the report.

SEC. 957. [49 U.S.C. 40101 note] POWERED-LIFT AIRCRAFT ENTRY INTO SERVICE.

(a) IN GENERAL.—The Administrator shall, in consultation with exclusive bargaining representatives of air traffic controllers certified under section 7111 of title 5, United States Code, and any relevant stakeholder as determined appropriate by the Administrator, take such actions as may be necessary to safely integrate powered-lift aircraft into the national airspace system, including in controlled airspace, and learn from any efforts to adopt and update related policy and guidance.

(b) AIR TRAFFIC POLICIES FOR ENTRY INTO SERVICE.—Not later than 40 months after the date of enactment of this Act, the Administrator shall update air traffic orders and policies, to the extent necessary, and address air traffic control system challenges in order to allow for—

(1) the use of existing air traffic procedures, where determined to be safe by the Administrator, by powered-lift aircraft; and

(2) the approval of letters of agreement between air traffic control system facilities and powered-lift operators and infrastructure operators to minimize the amount of active coordination required for safe recurring powered-lift aircraft operations, as appropriate.

(c) LONG-TERM AIR TRAFFIC POLICIES.—Beginning 40 months after the date of enactment of this Act, the Administrator shall—

(1) continue to update air traffic orders and policies to support the operation of powered-lift aircraft;

(2) to the extent necessary, develop powered-lift specific procedures for airports, heliports, and vertiports;

(3) evaluate the human factors impacts on controllers associated with managing powered-lift aircraft operations, consider the impact of additional operations on air traffic controller staffing, and make necessary changes to staffing, procedures, regulations, and orders; and

(4) consider the use of third-party service providers to manage increased operations in controlled airspace to support, supplement, and enhance the work of air traffic controllers.

SEC. 958. [49 U.S.C. 40101 note] INFRASTRUCTURE SUPPORTING VERTICAL FLIGHT.

(a) UPDATE TO DESIGN STANDARDS.—The Administrator shall—

(1) not later than December 31, 2024, publish an update to

SEC. 959. [49 U.S.C. 40101 note] CHARTING OF
AVIATION INFRASTRUCTURE.

FAA Reauthorization Act of 2

the memorandum of the FAA titled "Engineering Brief No. 105,
Vertiport Design", issued on September 21, 2022 (EB No. 105);

(2) not later than December 31, 2025, publish a
performance-based vertiport design advisory circular; and

(3) begin the work necessary to update the advisory
circular of the FAA titled "Heliport Design" (Advisory Circular
150/5390) in order to provide performance-based guidance for
heliport design, including consideration of alternative fuel and
propulsion mechanisms.

(b) ENGINEERING BRIEF SUNSET.—Upon the publication of an
advisory circular pursuant to subsection (a)(2), the Administrator
shall cancel the memorandum described in subsection (a)(1).

(c) DUAL USE FACILITIES.—The Administrator shall establish
a mechanism by which owners and operators of aviation
infrastructure can safely accommodate, or file a notice to
accommodate, powered-lift aircraft if such infrastructure meets the
safety requirements or guidance of the FAA for such aircraft.

(d) GUIDANCE, FORMS, AND PLANNING.—The Administrator
shall—

(1) not later than 18 months after the date of enactment
of this Act, ensure airport district offices of the FAA have
sufficient guidance and policy direction regarding the use and
applicability of heliport and vertiport design standards of the
FAA, and update such guidance routinely;

(2) determine if updates to FAA Form 7460 and Form 7480
are necessary and update such forms, as appropriate; and

(3) ensure that the methodology and underlying data
sources of the Terminal Area Forecast of the FAA include
commercial operations conducted by aircraft regardless of
propulsion type or fuel type.

SEC. 959. [49 U.S.C. 40101 note] CHARTING OF AVIATION
INFRASTRUCTURE.

The Administrator shall increase efforts to update and keep
current the Airport Master Record of the FAA, including by
establishing a streamlined process by which the owners and
operators of public and private aviation facilities with
nontemporary, nonintermittent operations are encouraged to keep
the information on such facilities current.

SEC. 961. [49 U.S.C. 40101 note] CENTER FOR ADVANCED AVIATION TECHNOLOGIES.

FAA Reauthorization Act of 2024

* * * * * * *

SEC. 961. [49 U.S.C. 40101 note] CENTER FOR ADVANCED AVIATION TECHNOLOGIES.

(a) PLAN.—Not later than 90 days after the date of enactment of this Act, the Administrator shall develop a plan to establish a Center for Advanced Aviation Technologies to support the testing and advancement of new and emerging aviation technologies.

(b) CONSULTATION.—In developing the plan under subsection (a), the Administrator may consult with the Advanced Air Mobility Working Group established in the Advanced Air Mobility Coordination and Leadership Act (Public Law 117-203), as amended by this Act, and the interagency working group established in section 1042 of this Act.

(c) CONSIDERATIONS.—In developing the plan under subsection (a), the Administrator shall consider as roles and responsibilities for the Center for Advanced Aviation Technologies—

(1) developing an airspace laboratory and flight demonstration zones to facilitate the safe integration of advanced air mobility aircraft into the national airspace system, with at least 1 such zone to be established within the same geographic region as the Center for Advanced Aviation Technologies and that also has aviation manufacturers with relevant expertise, such as powered-lift;

(2) establishing testing corridors for the purposes of validating air traffic requirements for advanced air mobility operations, operational procedures, and performance requirements, with at least 1 such corridor to be established within the same geographic region as the Center for Advanced Aviation Technologies;

(3) developing and facilitating technology partnerships with, and between, industry, academia, and other government agencies, and supporting such partnerships;

(4) identifying new and emerging aviation technologies, innovative aviation concepts, and relevant aviation services, including advanced air mobility, powered-lift aircraft, and other advanced aviation technologies, as determined appropriate by the Administrator; and

(5) any other duties, as determined appropriate by the

SEC. 961. [49 U.S.C. 40101 note] CENTER FOR
ADVANCED AVIATION TECHNOLOGIES.

FAA Reauthorization Act of 2[

Administrator.

(d) SUBMISSION TO CONGRESS.—Not later than 1 year after the date of enactment of this Act, the Administrator shall submit to the Committee on Transportation and Infrastructure and the Committee on Science, Space, and Technology of the House of Representatives and the Committee on Commerce, Science, and Transportation of the Senate the plan developed under subsection (a).

(e) CENTER.—Not later than September 30, 2026, the Administrator shall establish the Center for Advanced Aviation Technologies in accordance with the plan developed under subsection (a). In choosing the location for the Center for Advanced Aviation Technologies, the Administrator shall give preference to a community or region with a strong aeronautical presence, specifically the presence of—

(1) a large commercial airport or large air logistics center;

(2) aviation manufacturing with expertise in advanced aviation technologies, such as powered-lift;

(3) existing FAA facilities or offices, such as a Center, Institute, certificate management office, or a regional headquarters;

(4) airspace utilized for advanced aviation technology testing activity, and capable of supporting a wide range of use cases;

(5) proximity to both rural and urban communities;

(6) State, local, or Tribal governments;

(7) programs to support public-private partnerships for advanced aviation technologies; and

(8) academic institutions that offer programs relating to advanced aviation technologies engineering.

(f) AUTHORIZATION.—Out of amounts made available under section 106(k) of title 49, United States Code, $35,000,000 for each of fiscal years 2025 through 2028 is authorized to carry out this section.

(g) INTERACTION WITH OTHER ENTITIES.—The Administrator, in carrying out this section, shall, to the maximum extent practicable, leverage the research and testing capacity and capabilities of the Center of Excellence for Unmanned Aircraft

SEC. 1009. [49 U.S.C. 44701 note] HIGH-SPEED
FLIGHT TESTING.

FAA Reauthorization Act of 2024

Systems and, as appropriate, the unmanned aircraft test ranges established in section 44803 of title 49, United States Code.

(h) SAVINGS CLAUSES.—Nothing in this section shall be construed to interfere with any of the following activities:

(1) The ongoing activities of the unmanned aircraft test ranges established in section 44803 of title 49, United States Code, to the maximum extent practicable.

(2) The ongoing activities of the William J. Hughes Technical Center for Advanced Aerospace, to the maximum extent practicable.

(3) The ongoing activities of the Center of Excellence for Unmanned Aircraft Systems, to the maximum extent practicable.

(4) The ongoing activities of the Mike Monroney Aeronautical Center, to the maximum extent practicable.

TITLE X—RESEARCH AND DEVELOPMENT

Subtitle A—General Provisions

* * * * * * *

SEC. 1009. [49 U.S.C. 44701 note] HIGH-SPEED FLIGHT TESTING.

(a) IN GENERAL.—The Administrator, in consultation with the Administrator of NASA, shall establish procedures for the exclusive purposes of developmental and airworthiness testing and demonstration flights, which may include the establishment of high-speed testing corridors in the national airspace system—

(1) with respect to manufacturers and operators of high-speed aircraft that conduct flights operating with supersonic speed, not later than 1 year after the date of enactment of this Act; and

(2) with respect to manufacturers and operators of high-speed aircraft that conduct flights operating with hypersonic speed, not later than 2 years after the date of enactment of this Act.

(b) AREAS OF TESTING AND DEMONSTRATION.—The

SEC. 1009. [49 U.S.C. 44701 note] HIGH-SPEED FLIGHT TESTING.

FAA Reauthorization Act of 2◊

Administrator shall take action, as appropriate, to ensure flight testing and demonstration flights occur in areas where such flights will not interfere with the safety of other aircraft or the efficient use of airspace in the national airspace system.

(c) CONSIDERATIONS.—In carrying out subsection (a), the Administrator shall consider—

(1) sections 91.817 and 91.818 of title 14, Code of Federal Regulations;

(2) applications for special flight authorizations for flights operating at supersonic or hypersonic speed, as described in section 91.818 of such title;

(3) the environmental impacts of developmental and airworthiness testing operations;

(4) requiring applicants to include specification of proposed flight areas;

(5) the authorization of flights to and from airports in Class D airspace within 10 nautical miles of oceanic coastline;

(6) developing the vertical limits at or above the altitude necessary for safe supersonic and hypersonic operations;

(7) proponent-provided data regarding the design and operational analysis of the aircraft, as well as data regarding sonic boom overpressures;

(8) the safety of the uninvolved public; and

(9) community outreach, education, and engagement.

(d) CONSULTATION.—Not later than 1 year after the date of enactment of this Act, the Administrator, in consultation with the Environmental Protection Agency and other stakeholders, shall assess and report to the covered committees of Congress on a means for supporting continued compliance with the National Environmental Policy Act of 1969 (42 U.S.C. 4321 et seq.). The Administrator shall seek to enter into an agreement with an appropriate federally funded research and development center, or other independent nonprofit organization that recommends long term solutions for maintaining compliance with such Act for 1 or more over-land or near-land hypersonic and supersonic test areas as established by the Administrator.

(e) DEFINITIONS.—In this section:

(1) HIGH-SPEED AIRCRAFT.—The term "high-speed aircraft"

SEC. 1018. [49 U.S.C. 44504 note] NEXT
GENERATION RADIO ALTIMETERS.

FAA Reauthorization Act of 2024

means an aircraft operating at speeds in excess of Mach 1,
including supersonic and hypersonic aircraft.

(2) HYPERSONIC.—The term "hypersonic" means flights
operating at speeds that exceed Mach 5.

(3) SUPERSONIC.—The term "supersonic" means flights
operating at speeds in excess of Mach 1 but less than Mach 5.

* * * * * * *

SEC. 1018. [49 U.S.C. 44504 note] NEXT GENERATION RADIO
ALTIMETERS.

(a) IN GENERAL.—Not later than 60 days after the date of
enactment of this Act, the Administrator, in coordination with the
aviation and commercial wireless industries, the National
Telecommunications and Information Administration, the Federal
Communications Commission, and other relevant government
stakeholders, shall carry out an accelerated research and
development program to inform the development and testing of
the standards and technology necessary to ensure appropriate FAA
certification actions and industry production that meets the
installation requirements for next generation radio altimeters
across all necessary aircraft by January 1, 2028.

(b) GRANT PROGRAM.—Subject to the availability of
appropriations, the Administrator may award grants for the
purposes of research and development, testing, and other activities
necessary to ensure that next generation radio altimeter technology
is developed, tested, certified, and installed on necessary aircraft by
2028, including through public-private partnership grants (which
shall include protections for necessary intellectual property with
respect to any private sector entity testing, certifying, or producing
next generation radio altimeters under the program carried out
under this section) with industry to ensure the accelerated
production and installation by January 1, 2028.

(c) REVIEW AND REPORT.—Not later than 180 days after the
enactment of this Act, the Administrator shall submit to the covered
committees of Congress and the Committee on Transportation and
Infrastructure of the House of Representatives a report on the steps
the Administrator has taken as of the date on which such report
is submitted and any actions the Administrator plans to take,
including as part of the program carried out under this section, to

SEC. 1019. [49 U.S.C. 44504 note] HYDROGEN
AVIATION STRATEGY.

FAA Reauthorization Act of 2

ensure that next generation radio altimeter technology is developed, tested, certified, and installed by 2028.

(d) RULE OF CONSTRUCTION.—Nothing in this section shall be construed to apply to efforts to retrofit the existing supply of altimeters in place as of the date of enactment of this Act.

SEC. 1019. [49 U.S.C. 44504 note] HYDROGEN AVIATION STRATEGY.

(a) FAA AND DEPARTMENT OF ENERGY LEADERSHIP ON USING HYDROGEN TO PROPEL COMMERCIAL AIRCRAFT.—The Secretary, acting through the Administrator and jointly with the Secretary of Energy, shall exercise leadership in and shall conduct research and development activities relating to enabling the safe use of hydrogen in civil aviation, including the safe and efficient use and sourcing of hydrogen to propel commercial aircraft.

(b) RESEARCH STRATEGY.—Not later than 1 year after the date of enactment of this Act, the Administrator, in consultation with the Administrator of NASA and other relevant Federal agencies, shall complete the development of a research and development strategy on the safe use of hydrogen in civil aviation.

(c) CONSIDERATIONS.—The strategy developed under subsection (b) shall consider the following:

(1) The feasibility, opportunities, challenges, and pathways toward the potential and safe uses of hydrogen in civil aviation.

(2) The use of hydrogen in addition to electric propulsion to propel commercial aircraft and any related operational efficiencies.

(d) EXERCISE OF LEADERSHIP.—The Secretary, the Administrator, and the Secretary of Energy shall carry out the research activities consistent with the strategy in subsection (b), and that may include the following:

(1) Establishing positions and goals for the safe use of hydrogen in civil aviation, including to propel commercial aircraft.

(2) Understanding of the qualification of hydrogen aviation fuel, the safe transition to such fuel for aircraft, the advancement of certification efforts for such fuel, and risk mitigation measures for the use of such fuel in aircraft systems, including propulsion and storage systems.

(3) Through grant, contract, or interagency agreements,

SEC. 1019. [49 U.S.C. 44504 note] HYDROGEN
AVIATION STRATEGY.

FAA Reauthorization Act of 2024

carrying out research and development to understand the
contribution that the use of hydrogen would have on civil
aviation, including hydrogen as an input for conventional jet
fuel, hydrogen fuel cells as a source of electric propulsion,
sustainable aviation fuel, and power to liquids or synthetic
fuel, and researching ways of accelerating the introduction of
hydrogen-propelled aircraft.

(4) Reviewing grant eligibility requirements, loans, loan
guarantees, and other policies and requirements of the FAA
and the Department of Energy to identify ways to increase the
safe and efficient use of hydrogen in civil aviation.

(5) Considering the needs of the aerospace industry,
aviation suppliers, hydrogen producers, airlines, airport
sponsors, fixed base operators, and other stakeholders in
creating policies that enable the safe use of hydrogen in civil
aviation.

(6) Coordinating with NASA, and obtaining input from
the aerospace industry, aviation suppliers, hydrogen producers,
airlines, airport sponsors, fixed base operators, academia and
other stakeholders regarding—

(A) the safe and efficient use of hydrogen in civil
aviation, including—

(i) updating or modifying existing policies on such
use;

(ii) assessing barriers to, and benefits of, the
introduction of hydrogen in civil aviation, including
aircraft propelled by hydrogen;

(iii) the operational differences between aircraft
propelled by hydrogen and aircraft propelled with
other types of fuels; and

(iv) public, economic, and noise benefits of the
operation of commercial aircraft propelled by hydrogen
and associated aerospace industry activity; and

(B) other issues identified by the Secretary, the
Administrator, the Secretary of Energy, or the advisory
committee established under paragraph (7) that must be
addressed in order to enable the safe and efficient use of
hydrogen in civil aviation.

(7) Establish an advisory committee composed of

representatives of NASA, the aerospace industry, aviation suppliers, hydrogen producers, airlines, airport sponsors, fixed base operators, and other stakeholders to advise the Secretary, the Administrator, and the Secretary of Energy on the activities carried out under this subsection.

(e) INTERNATIONAL LEADERSHIP.—The Secretary, the Administrator, and the Secretary of Energy, in the appropriate international forums, shall take actions that—

(1) demonstrate global leadership in carrying out the activities required by subsections (a) and (b);

(2) consider the needs of the aerospace industry, aviation suppliers, hydrogen producers, airlines, airport sponsors, fixed base operators, and other stakeholders identified under subsection (b);

(3) consider the needs of fuel cell manufacturers; and

(4) seek to advance the competitiveness of the United States in the safe use of hydrogen in civil aviation.

(f) REPORT TO CONGRESS.—Not later than 3 years after the date of enactment of this Act, the Secretary, acting through the Administrator and jointly with the Secretary of Energy, shall submit to the covered committees of Congress and the Committee on Transportation and Infrastructure of the House of Representatives a report detailing—

(1) the actions of the Secretary, the Administrator, and the Secretary of Energy to exercise leadership in conducting research relating to the safe and efficient use of hydrogen in civil aviation;

(2) the planned, proposed, and anticipated actions to update or modify existing policies related to the safe and efficient use of hydrogen in civil aviation, based on the results of the research and development carried out under this section, including such actions identified as a result of consultation with, and feedback from, the aerospace industry, aviation suppliers, hydrogen producers, airlines, airport sponsors, fixed base operators, academia and other stakeholders identified under subsection (b); and

(3) a proposed timeline for any such actions pursuant to paragraph (2).

SEC. 1032. [49 U.S.C. 44504 note] HYDROGEN
AVIATION STRATEGY.

FAA Reauthorization Act of 2024

* * * * * * *

SEC. 1032. LIMITATION.

(a) PROHIBITED ACTIVITIES.—None of the funds authorized in this title may be used to conduct research, develop, design, plan, promulgate, implement, or execute a policy, program, order, or contract of any kind with the Chinese Communist Party or any entity that is domiciled in China or under the influence of China unless such activities are specifically authorized by a law enacted after the date of enactment of this Act.

(b) EXEMPTION.—The Administrator is exempt from the prohibitions under subsection (a) if the prohibited activities are executed for the purposes of testing, research, evaluating, analyzing, or training related to—

(1) counter-unmanned aircraft detection and mitigation systems, including activities conducted—

(A) under the Center of Excellence for Unmanned Aircraft Systems of the FAA; or

(B) by the test ranges designated under section 44803 of title 49, United States Code;

(2) the safe, secure, or efficient operation of the national airspace system or maintenance of public safety;

(3) the safe integration of advanced aviation technologies into the national airspace system, including activities carried out by the Center of Excellence for Unmanned Aircraft Systems of the FAA;

(4) in coordination with other relevant Federal agencies, determining security threats of unmanned aircraft systems; and

(5) intelligence, electronic warfare, and information warfare operations.

(c) WAIVERS.—

(1) PUBLIC INTEREST DETERMINATION.—The Administrator may waive any prohibitions under subsection (a) on a case-by-case basis if the Administrator determines that activities described in subsection (a) are in the public interest.

(2) NOTIFICATION.—If the Administrator provides a waiver under paragraph (1), the Administrator shall notify the covered

SEC. 1042. [49 U.S.C. 40101 note]
INTERAGENCY WORKING GROUP.

FAA Reauthorization Act of 2(

committees of Congress in writing not later than 15 days after exercising such waiver.

Subtitle B—Unmanned Aircraft Systems and Advanced Air Mobility

* * * * * * *

SEC. 1042. [49 U.S.C. 40101 note] INTERAGENCY WORKING GROUP.

(a) DESIGNATION.—

(1) IN GENERAL.—The National Science and Technology Council shall establish or designate an interagency working group on advanced air mobility and unmanned aircraft systems to coordinate Federal research, development, deployment, testing, and education activities to enable advanced air mobility and unmanned aircraft systems.

(2) MEMBERSHIP.—The interagency working group shall be comprised of senior representatives from NASA, the Department of Transportation, the National Oceanic and Atmospheric Administration, the National Science Foundation, the National Institute of Standards and Technology, Department of Homeland Security, and such other Federal agencies as appropriate.

(b) DUTIES.—The interagency working group shall—

(1) develop a strategic research plan to guide Federal research to enable advanced air mobility and unmanned aircraft systems and oversee implementation of the plan;

(2) oversee the development of—

(A) an assessment of the current state of United States competitiveness and leadership in advanced air mobility and unmanned aircraft systems, including the scope and scale of United States investments in relevant research and development; and

(B) strategies to strengthen and secure the domestic supply chain for advanced air mobility systems and unmanned aircraft systems;

(3) facilitate communication and outreach opportunities with academia, industry, professional societies, State, local,

Tribal, and Federal governments, and other stakeholders;

(4) facilitate partnerships to leverage knowledge and resources from industry, State, local, Tribal, and Federal governments, National Laboratories, unmanned aircraft systems test range (as defined in section 44801 of title 49, United States Code), academic institutions, and others;

(5) coordinate with the advanced air mobility working group established under section 2 of the Advanced Air Mobility Coordination and Leadership Act (Public Law 117-203) and heads of other Federal departments and agencies to avoid duplication of research and other activities to ensure that the activities carried out by the interagency working group are complementary to those being undertaken by other interagency efforts; and

(6) coordinate with the National Security Council and other authorized agency coordinating bodies on the assessment of risks affecting the existing Federal unmanned aircraft systems fleet and outlining potential steps to mitigate such risks.

(c) REPORT TO CONGRESS.—Not later than 1 year after the date of enactment of this Act, and every 2 years thereafter until December 31, 2028, the interagency working group shall transmit to the covered committees of Congress a report that includes a summary of federally funded advanced air mobility and unmanned aircraft systems research, development, deployment, and testing activities, including the budget for each of the activities described in this paragraph.

(d) RULE OF CONSTRUCTION.—The interagency working group shall not be construed to conflict with or duplicate the work of the interagency working group established under the advanced air mobility working group established by the Advanced Air Mobility Coordination and Leadership Act (Public Law 117-203).

SEC. 1043. [49 U.S.C. 40101 note] STRATEGIC RESEARCH PLAN.

(a) IN GENERAL.—Not later than 2 years after the date of enactment of this Act, the interagency working group shall develop and periodically update, as appropriate, a strategic plan for Federal research, development, deployment, and testing of advanced air mobility systems and unmanned aircraft systems.

(b) CONSIDERATIONS.—In developing the plan required under

subsection (a), the interagency working group shall consider and use—

(1) information, reports, and studies on advanced air mobility and unmanned aircraft systems that have identified research, development, deployment, and testing needed;

(2) information set forth in the national aviation research plan developed under section 44501(c) of title 49, United States Code; and

(3) recommendations made by the National Academies in the review of the plan under subsection (d).

(c) CONTENTS OF THE PLAN.—In developing the plan required under subsection (a), the interagency working group shall—

(1) determine and prioritize areas of advanced air mobility and unmanned aircraft systems research, development, demonstration, and testing requiring Federal Government leadership and investment;

(2) establish, for the 10-year period beginning in the calendar year the plan is submitted, the goals and priorities for Federal research, development, and testing which will—

(A) support the development of advanced air mobility technologies and the development of an advanced air mobility research, innovation, and manufacturing ecosystem;

(B) take into account sustained, consistent, and coordinated support for advanced air mobility and unmanned aircraft systems research, development, and demonstration, including through grants, cooperative agreements, testbeds, and testing facilities;

(C) apply lessons learned from unmanned aircraft systems research, development, demonstration, and testing to advanced air mobility systems;

(D) inform the development of voluntary consensus technical standards and best practices for the development and use of advanced air mobility and unmanned aircraft systems;

(E) support education and training activities at all levels to prepare the United States workforce to use and interact with advanced air mobility systems and unmanned aircraft systems;

(F) support partnerships to leverage knowledge and
resources from industry, State, local, Tribal, and Federal
governments, the National Laboratories, Center of
Excellence for Unmanned Aircraft Systems Research of the
FAA, unmanned aircraft systems test ranges (as defined
in section 44801 of title 49, United States Code), academic
institutions, labor organizations, and others to advance
research activities;

(G) leverage existing Federal investments; and

(H) promote hardware interoperability and open-
source systems;

(3) support research and other activities on the impacts
of advanced air mobility and unmanned aircraft systems on
national security, safety, economic, legal, workforce, and other
appropriate societal issues;

(4) reduce barriers to transferring research findings,
capabilities, and new technologies related to advanced air
mobility and unmanned aircraft systems into operation for the
benefit of society and United States competitiveness;

(5) in consultation with the Council of Economic Advisers,
measure and track the contributions of unmanned aircraft
systems and advanced air mobility to United States economic
growth and other societal indicators; and

(6) identify relevant research and development programs
and make recommendations for the coordination of relevant
activities of the Federal agencies and set forth the role of each
Federal agency in implementing the plan.

(d) NATIONAL ACADEMIES OF SCIENCES, ENGINEERING, AND
MEDICINE EVALUATION.—The Administrator shall seek to enter into
an agreement with the National Academies to review the plan every
5 years.

(e) PUBLIC PARTICIPATION.—In developing the plan under
subsection (a), the interagency working group shall consult with
representatives of stakeholder groups, which may include
academia, research institutions, and State, industry, and labor
organizations. Not later than 90 days before the plan, or any
revision thereof, is submitted to Congress, the plan shall be
published in the Federal Register for a public comment period of not

less than 60 days.

(f) REPORTS TO CONGRESS ON THE STRATEGIC RESEARCH
PLAN.—

(1) PROGRESS REPORT.—Not later than 1 year after the
date of enactment of this Act, the interagency working group
described in section 1042 of this Act shall transmit to the
covered committees of Congress a report that describes the
progress in developing the plan required under this section.

(2) INITIAL REPORT.—Not later than 2 years after the date
of enactment of this Act, the interagency working group shall
transmit to the covered committees of Congress the strategic
research plan developed under this section.

(3) BIENNIAL REPORT.—Not later than 1 year after the
transmission of the initial report under paragraph (2) and every
2 years thereafter until December 31, 2033, the interagency
working group shall transmit to the covered committees of
Congress a report that includes an analysis of the progress
made towards achieving the goals and priorities for the
strategic research plan.

SEC. 1044. [49 U.S.C. 40101 note] FEDERAL AVIATION
ADMINISTRATION UNMANNED AIRCRAFT SYSTEM AND ADVANCED
AIR MOBILITY RESEARCH AND DEVELOPMENT.

(a) IN GENERAL.—Consistent with the research plan in section
1043, the Administrator, in coordination with the Administrator
of NASA and other Federal agencies, shall carry out and support
research, development, testing, and demonstration activities and
technology transfer, and activities to facilitate the transition of such
technologies into application to enable advanced air mobility and
unmanned aircraft systems and to facilitate the safe integration
of advanced air mobility and unmanned aircraft systems into the
national airspace system, in areas including—

(1) beyond visual-line-of-sight operations;

(2) command and control link technologies;

(3) development and integration of unmanned aircraft
system traffic management into the national airspace system;

(4) noise and other societal and environmental impacts;

(5) informing the development of an industry consensus
vehicle-to-vehicle standard;

(6) safety, including collisions between advanced air mobility and unmanned aircraft systems of various sizes, traveling at various speeds, and various other crewed aircraft or various parts of other crewed aircraft of various sizes and traveling at various speeds; and

(7) detect-and-avoid capabilities.

(b) DUPLICATIVE RESEARCH AND DEVELOPMENT ACTIVITIES.—The Administrator shall ensure that research and development and other activities conducted under this section do not duplicate other Federal activities related to the integration of unmanned aviation systems or advanced air mobility.

(c) LESSONS LEARNED.—The Administrator shall apply lessons learned from unmanned aircraft systems research, development, demonstration, and testing to advanced air mobility systems.

(d) RESEARCH ON APPROACHES TO EVALUATING RISK.—The Administrator shall conduct research on approaches to evaluating risk in emerging vehicles, technologies, and operations for unmanned aircraft systems and advanced air mobility systems. Such research shall include—

(1) defining quantitative metrics, including metrics that may support the Administrator in making determinations, and research to inform the development of requirements, as practicable, for the operations of certain unmanned aircraft systems, as described under section 44807 of title 49, United States Code;

(2) developing risk-based processes and criteria to inform the development of regulations and certification of complex operations, to include autonomous beyond-visual-line-of-sight operations, of unmanned aircraft systems of various sizes and weights, and advanced air mobility systems; and

(3) considering the utility of performance standards to make determinations under section 44807 of title 49, United States Code.

(e) REPORT.—Not later than 9 months after the date of enactment of this Act, the Administrator shall submit to the covered committees of Congress a report on the actions taken by the Administrator to implement provisions under this section that includes—

(1) a summary of the costs and results of research under

subsection (a)(6);

(2) a description of plans for and progress toward the implementation of research and development under subsection (d);

(3) a description of the progress of the FAA in using research and development to inform FAA certification guidance and regulations of—

(A) large unmanned aircraft systems, including those weighing more than 55 pounds; and

(B) extended autonomous and remotely piloted operations beyond visual line of sight in controlled and uncontrolled airspace; and

(4) a current plan for full operational capability of unmanned aircraft systems traffic management, as described in section 376 the FAA Reauthorization Act of 2018 (49 U.S.C. 44802 note).

(f) PARALLEL EFFORTS.—

(1) IN GENERAL.—Research and development activities under this section may be conducted concurrently with the deployment of technologies outlined in (a) and in carrying out the this title and title IX.

(2) RULE OF CONSTRUCTION.—Nothing in this section shall be construed to delay appropriate actions to deploy the technologies outlined in subsection (a), including the deployment of beyond visual-line-of-sight operations of unmanned aircraft systems, or delay the Administrator in carrying out this title and title IX, or limit FAA use of existing risk methodologies to make determinations pursuant to section 44807 of title 49, United States Code, prior to completion of relevant research and development activities.

(3) PRACTICES AND REGULATIONS.—The Administrator shall, to the maximum extent practicable, use the results of research and development activities conducted under this section to inform decisions on whether and how to maintain or update existing regulations and practices, or whether to establish new practices or regulations.

* * * * * * *

TITLE XI—MISCELLANEOUS

* * * * * * *

SEC. 1102. TRANSPORTATION OF ORGANS.

(a) IN GENERAL.—Not later than 90 days after the date of enactment of this Act, the Secretary, in consultation with the Administrator, shall convene a working group (in this section referred to as the "working group") to assist in developing best practices for transportation of an organ in the cabin of an aircraft operating under part 121 of title 14, Code of Federal Regulations, and to identify regulations that hinder such transportation, if applicable.

(b) COMPOSITION.—The working group shall be comprised of representatives from the following:

(1) Air carriers operating under part 121 of title 14, Code of Federal Regulations.

(2) Organ procurement organizations.

(3) Organ transplant hospitals.

(4) Flight attendants.

(5) Other relevant Federal agencies involved in organ transportation or air travel.

(c) CONSIDERATIONS.—In establishing the best practices described in subsection (a), the working group shall consider—

(1) a safe, standardized process for acceptance, handling, management, and transportation of an organ in the cabin of such aircraft; and

(2) protocols to ensure the safe and timely transport of an organ in the cabin of such aircraft, including through connecting flights.

(d) RECOMMENDATIONS.—Not later than 1 year after the convening of the working group, such working group shall submit to the Secretary a report containing recommendations for the best practices described in subsection (a).

(e) DEFINITION OF ORGAN.—In this section, the term "organ"—

(1) has the meaning given such term in section 121.2 of title 42, Code of Federal Regulations; and

(2) includes—

(A) organ-related tissue;

(B) bone marrow; and

(C) human cells, tissues, or cellular or tissue-based products (as such term is defined in section 1271.3(d) of title 21, Code of Federal Regulations).

SEC. 1103. [49 U.S.C. 40101 note] ACCEPTANCE OF DIGITAL DRIVER'S LICENSE AND IDENTIFICATION CARDS.

The Administrator shall take such actions as may be necessary to accept, in any instance where an individual is required to submit government-issued identification to the Administrator, a digital or mobile driver's license or identification card issued to such individual by a State.

SEC. 1104. QUASQUICENTENNIAL OF AVIATION.

(a) FINDINGS.—Congress finds the following:

(1) December 17, 2028, is the 125th anniversary of the first successful manned, free, controlled, and sustained flight by an aircraft.

(2) The first flight by Orville and Wilbur Wright in Kitty Hawk, North Carolina, is a defining moment in the history of the United States and the world.

(3) The Wright brothers' achievement is a testament to their ingenuity, perseverance, and commitment to innovation, which has inspired generations of aviators and scientists alike.

(4) The advent of aviation and the air transportation industry has fundamentally transformed the United States and the world for the better.

(5) The 125th anniversary of the Wright brothers' first flight is worthy of recognition and celebration to honor their legacy and to inspire a new generation of Americans as aviation reaches an inflection point of innovation and change.

(b) SENSE OF CONGRESS.—It is the sense of Congress that the Secretary, the Administrator, and the heads of other appropriate Federal agencies should facilitate and participate in local, national, and international observances and activities that commemorate and celebrate the 125th anniversary of powered flight.

SEC. 1105. [49 U.S.C. 44714 note] LIMITATIONS
FOR CERTAIN CARGO AIRCRAFT.

FAA Reauthorization Act of 2024

SEC. 1105. [49 U.S.C. 44714 note] LIMITATIONS FOR CERTAIN CARGO AIRCRAFT.

(a) IN GENERAL.—The standards adopted by the Administrator of the Environmental Protection Agency in part 1030 of title 40, Code of Federal Regulations, and the requirements in part 38 of title 14, Code of Federal Regulations, that were finalized by the Administrator of the FAA under the final rule titled "Airplane Fuel Efficiency Certification", and published on February 16, 2024 (89 Fed. Reg. 12634) in part 38 of title 14, Code of Federal Regulations, shall not apply to any covered airplane before the date that is 5 years after January 1, 2028.

(b) OPERATIONAL LIMITATION.—The Administrator shall limit to domestic use or international operations, consistent with relevant international agreements and standards, the operation of any covered airplane that—

(1) does not meet the standards and requirements described in subsection (a); and

(2) received an original certificate of airworthiness issued by the Administrator on or after January 1, 2028.

(c) DEFINITIONS.—In this section:

(1) COVERED AIRPLANE.—The term "covered airplane" means an airplane that—

(A) is a subsonic jet that is a purpose-built freighter;

(B) has a maximum takeoff mass greater than 180,000 kilograms but not greater than 240,000 kilograms; and

(C) has a type design certificated prior to January 1, 2023.

(2) PURPOSE-BUILT FREIGHTER.—The term "purpose-built freighter" means any airplane that—

(A) was configured to carry cargo rather than passengers prior to receiving an original certificate of airworthiness; and

(B) is configured to carry cargo rather than passengers.

SEC. 1106. [49 U.S.C. 106 note] PROHIBITION ON MANDATES.

(a) PROHIBITION ON MANDATES.—The Administrator may not require any contractor to mandate that employees of such contractor obtain a COVID-19 vaccine or enforce any condition

SEC. 1109. [49 U.S.C. 44504 note] FAA
LEADERSHIP IN HYDROGEN AVIATION.

FAA Reauthorization Act of 2●

regarding the COVID-19 vaccination status of employees of a contractor.

(b) PROHIBITION ON IMPLEMENTATION.—The Administrator may not implement or enforce any requirement that—

(1) employees of air carriers be vaccinated against COVID-19;

(2) employees of the FAA be vaccinated against COVID-19; or

(3) passengers of air carriers be vaccinated against COVID-19 or wear a mask as a result of a COVID-19 related public health measure.

* * * * * * *

SEC. 1109. [49 U.S.C. 44504 note] FAA LEADERSHIP IN HYDROGEN AVIATION.

(a) IN GENERAL.—The Administrator shall exercise leadership in the development of Federal regulations, standards, best practices, and guidance relating to the safe and efficient certification of the use of hydrogen in civil aviation, including the certification of hydrogen-powered commercial aircraft.

(b) EXERCISE OF LEADERSHIP.—In carrying out subsection (a), the Administrator shall—

(1) develop a viable path for the certification of the safe use of hydrogen in civil aviation, including hydrogen-powered aircraft, that considers existing frameworks, modifying an existing framework, or developing new standards, best practices, or guidance to complement the existing frameworks, as appropriate;

(2) review certification regulations, guidance, and other requirements of the FAA to identify ways to safely and efficiently certify hydrogen-powered commercial aircraft;

(3) consider the needs of the aerospace industry, aviation suppliers, hydrogen producers, airlines, airport sponsors, fixed base operators, and other stakeholders when developing regulations and standards that enable the safe certification and deployment of the use of hydrogen in civil aviation, including hydrogen-powered commercial aircraft, in the national airspace system; and

(4) obtain the input of the aerospace industry, aviation suppliers, hydrogen producers, airlines, airport sponsors, fixed base operators, academia, research institutions, and other stakeholders regarding—

(A) an appropriate regulatory framework and timeline for permitting the safe and efficient use of hydrogen in civil aviation, including the deployment and operation of hydrogen-powered commercial aircraft in the United States, which may include updating or modifying existing regulations;

(B) how to accelerate the resolution of issues related to data, standards development, and related regulations necessary to facilitate the safe and efficient certification of the use of hydrogen in civil aviation, including hydrogen-powered commercial aircraft; and

(C) other issues identified and determined appropriate by the Administrator or the advisory committee established under section 1019(d)(7) to be addressed to enable the safe and efficient use of hydrogen in civil aviation, including the deployment and operation of hydrogen-powered commercial aircraft.

* * * * * * *

SEC. 1115. CERTIFICATES OF AUTHORIZATION OR WAIVER.

(a) [49 U.S.C. 40103 note] REQUIRED COORDINATION.—

(1) IN GENERAL.—On an annual basis, the Administrator shall convene a meeting with representatives of FAA-approved air shows, the general aviation community, stadiums and other large outdoor events and venues or organizations that run such events, the Department of Homeland Security, and the Department of Justice—

(A) to identify scheduling conflicts between FAA-approved air shows and large outdoor events and venues where—

(i) flight restrictions will be imposed pursuant to section 521 of division F of the Consolidated Appropriations Act, 2004 (49 U.S.C. 40103 note); or

(ii) any other restriction will be imposed pursuant

to FAA Flight Data Center Notice to Airmen 4/3621 (or any successor notice to airmen); and

(B) in instances where a scheduling conflict between events is identified or is found to be likely to occur, develop appropriate operational and communication procedures to ensure for the safety and security of both events.

(2) SCHEDULING CONFLICT.—If the Administrator or any other stakeholder party to the required annual coordination required in paragraph (1) identifies a scheduling conflict outside of the annual meeting at any point prior to the scheduling conflict, the Administrator shall work with impacted stakeholders to develop appropriate operational and communication procedures to ensure for the safety and security of both events.

* * * * * * *

TITLE XII—NATIONAL TRANSPORTATION SAFETY BOARD

* * * * * * *

SEC. 1217. [49 U.S.C. 1114 note] ELECTRONIC AVAILABILITY OF PUBLIC DOCKET RECORDS.

(a) IN GENERAL.—Not later than 24 months after the date of enactment of this Act, the National Transportation Safety Board shall make all records included in the public docket of an accident or incident investigation conducted by the Board (or the public docket of a study, report, or other product issued by the Board) electronically available in a publicly accessible database on a website of the Board, regardless of the date on which such public docket or record was created.

(b) DATABASE.—In carrying out subsection (a), the Board may utilize the multimodal accident database management system established pursuant to section 1108 of the FAA Reauthorization Act of 2018 (49 U.S.C. 1119 note) or such other publicly available database as the Board determines appropriate.

(c) BRIEFINGS.—The Board shall provide the appropriate committees of Congress an annual briefing on the implementation of this section until requirements of subsection (a) are fulfilled. Such briefings shall include—

(1) the number of public dockets that have been made electronically available pursuant to this section; and

(2) the number of public dockets that were unable to be made electronically available, including all reasons for such inability.

(d) DEFINITIONS.—In this section, the terms "public docket" and "record" have the same meanings given such terms in section 801.3 of title 49, Code of Federal Regulations, as in effect on the date of enactment of this Act.

* * * * * * *

POPULAR TITLE NAMES

POPULAR TITLE NAMES

Act of June 29, 1940--(Washington Airports)
    54 stat. 686
Act of October 31, 1945
    Chapter 443 of 79th Congress
    59 Stat. 553
Act of September 7, 1950--(Washington Airports)
    Chapter 905 of 81st Congress 64
    Stat. 770
Air Transportation Safety and System Stabilization Act
    Pub. L. 107 42, Sept. 22, 2001,
    115 Stat. 230 (49 U.S.C. 40101 note)
Aircraft Certification, Safety, and Accountability Act
    Pub. L. 116 260, div. V, title I, Dec. 27, 2020,
    134 Stat. 2309
    Short title, see 49 U.S.C. 40101 note
Airline Safety and Federal Aviation Administration Extension Act of 2010
    Pub. L. 111 216, Aug. 1, 2010,
    124 Stat. 2348
    Short title, see 49 U.S.C. 40101 note
Airport and Airway Improvement Act of 1982
    Pub. L. 97 248, title V, Sept. 3, 1982,
    96 Stat. 671
Airport Security Improvement Act of 2000
    Pub. L. 106 528, Nov. 22, 2000, 1
    14 Stat. 2517
    Short title, see 49 U.S.C. 40101 note
Atomic Energy Defense Act
    Pub. L. 107 314, div. D, as added Pub. L. 108 136, div. C, title XXXI, § 3141(b), Nov. 24, 2003,
    117 Stat. 1753 (50 U.S.C. 2501 et seq.)
    Short title, see 50 U.S.C. 2501 note
Aviation and Transportation Security Act
    Pub. L. 107 71, Nov. 19, 2001, 1
    15 Stat. 597
    Short title, see 49 U.S.C. 40101 note
Aviation Medical Assistance Act of 1998

Pub. L. 105 170, Apr. 24, 1998,
112 Stat. 47 (49 U.S.C. 44701 note)
Bob Stump National Defense Authorization Act for Fiscal Year 2003
Pub. L. 107 314, Dec. 2, 2002,
116 Stat. 2458
Cape Town Treaty Implementation Act of 2004
Pub. L. 108 297, Aug. 9, 2004,
118 Stat. 1095
Short title, see 49 U.S.C. 40101 note
Clean Air Act
July 14, 1955, ch. 360,
69 Stat. 322 (42 U.S.C. 7401 et seq.)
Short title, see 42 U.S.C. 7401 note
Consolidated Appropriations Act, 2021
Pub. L. 116 260, Dec. 27, 2020,
134 Stat. 1182
Consolidated Appropriations Resolution, 2003
Pub. L. 108 7, Feb. 20, 2003,
117 Stat. 11
Death on the High Seas Act
Title 46, chapter 303 (§ 30301 et seq.) Mar. 30, 1920, ch. 111,
41 Stat. 537
Short title, see 46 U.S.C. 30301
Department of Housing and Urban Development Appropriations Act, 2006
Pub. L. 109 115, div. A, title III, Nov. 30, 2005,
119 Stat. 2440
Department of Transportation and Related Agencies Appropriations Act, 2000
Pub. L. 106 69, Oct. 9, 1999,
113 Stat. 986
European Union Emissions Trading Scheme Prohibition Act of 2011
Pub. L. 112 200, Nov. 27, 2012,
126 Stat. 1477 (49 U.S.C. 40101 note)
FAA Extension, Safety, and Security Act of 2016
Pub. L. 114 190, July 15, 2016, 1
30 Stat. 615
Short title, see 49 U.S.C. 40101 note
FAA Modernization and Reform Act of 2012
Pub. L. 112 95, Feb. 14, 2012,
126 Stat. 11
Short title, see 49 U.S.C. 40101 note
FAA Reauthorization Act of 2018
Pub. L. 115 254, Oct. 5, 2018,
132 Stat. 3186
Short title, see 49 U.S.C. 40101 note
Fairness for Pilots Act

Pub. L. 115-254, div. B, title III, subtitle C (Secs. 391-396), Oct. 5, 2018,132 Stat. 3323
Short title, see 49 U.S.C. 40101 note

FAA Reauthorization Act of 2024
Pub. L. 118 63, May 16, 2024,
138 Stat. 1025
Short title, see 49 U.S.C. 40101 note

Federal Airport Act
May 13, 1946, ch. 251,
60 Stat. 170

Federal Aviation Act of 1958
Pub. L. 85 726, Aug. 23, 1958,
72 Stat. 731

Federal Aviation Reauthorization Act of 1996
Pub. L. 104 264, Oct. 9, 1996,
110 Stat. 3213
Short title, see 49 U.S.C. 40101 note

General Aviation Revitalization Act of 1994
Pub. L. 103 298, Aug. 17, 1994,
108 Stat. 1552 (49 U.S.C. 40101 note)

Homeland Security Act of 2002
Pub. L. 107 296, Nov. 25, 2002,
116 Stat. 2135 (6 U.S.C. 101 et seq.)
Short title, see 6 U.S.C. 101 note

Implementing Recommendations of the 9/11 Commission Act of 2007
Pub. L. 110 53, Aug. 3, 2007,
121 Stat. 266
Short title, see 6 U.S.C. 101 note

Intelligence Reform and Terrorism Prevention Act of 2004
Pub. L. 108 458, Dec. 17, 2004,
118 Stat. 3638
Short title, see 50 U.S.C. 3001 note

International Air Transportation Competition Act of 1979
Pub. L. 96 192, Feb. 15, 1980,
94 Stat. 35

International Security and Development Cooperation Act of 1985
Pub. L. 99 83, Aug. 8, 1985,
99 Stat. 190
Short title, see 22 U.S.C. 2151 note

John S. McCain National Defense Authorization Act for Fiscal Year 2019
Pub. L. 115 232, Aug. 13, 2018,
132 Stat. 1636

MAP 21 Also known as *Moving Ahead for Progress in the 21st Century Act*
Pub. L. 112 141, July 6, 2012,
126 Stat. 405

Short title, see 23 U.S.C. 101 note

Moving Ahead for Progress in the 21st Century Act also known as *MAP 21*
Pub. L. 112 141, July 6, 2012, 126 Stat. 405
Short title, see 23 U.S.C. 101 note

Narcotics Control Trade Act
Pub. L. 93 618, title VIII, as added Pub. L. 99 570, title IX, § 9001, Oct. 27, 1986,
100 Stat. 3207 164 (19 U.S.C. 2491 et seq.)
Short title, see 19 U.S.C. 2491

National Defense Authorization Act for Fiscal Year 2016
Pub. L. 114 92, Nov. 25, 2015,
129 Stat. 726

National Defense Authorization Act for Fiscal Year 2017
Pub. L. 114 328, Dec. 23, 2016,
130 Stat. 2000

National Emission Standards Act
July 14, 1955, ch. 360, title II, as added Pub. L. 89 272, Title I, § 101(8), Oct. 20,
1965,
79 Stat. 992
Short title, see 42 .S.C. 7401 note

National Parks Air Tour Management Act of 2000
Pub. L. 106 181, title VIII, Apr. 5, 2000,
114 Stat. 185
Short title, see 49 U.S.C. 40128 note

National Transportation Safety Board Amendments Act of 2000
Pub. L. 106 424, Nov. 1, 2000,
114 Stat. 1883
Short title, see 49 U.S.C. 1101 note

National Transportation Safety Board Reauthorization Act of 2003
Pub. L. 108 168, Dec. 6, 2003,
117 Stat. 2032
Short title, see 49 U.S.C. 1101 note134 Stat. 1182

National Transportation Safety Board Reauthorization Act of 2006
Pub. L. 109 443, Dec. 21, 2006,
120 Stat. 3297
Short title, see 49 U.S.C. 1101 note

NOTAM Improvement Act of 2023
Pub. L. 118 4, June 3,,2023, 137 Stat. 7
Short title, see 49,U.S.C. 40101 note

Railway Labor Act
May 20, 1926, ch. 347, 44 Stat. 577
(45 U.S.C. 151 et seq.)
Short title, see 45,U.S.C. 151

Safe, Accountable, Flexible, Efficient Transportation, Equity Act: A Legacy for Users
Also known as *SAFETEA LU*
Pub. L. 109 59, Aug. 10, 2005,

119 Stat. 1144

Short title, see 23 U.S.C. 101 note

SAFETEA LU Also known as *Safe, Accountable, Flexible, Efficient Transportation Equity Act: A Legacy for Users*

Pub. L. 109 59, Aug. 10, 2005,

119 Stat. 1144

Short title, see 23 U.S.C. 101 note

September 11th Victim Compensation Fund of 2001

Pub. L. 107 42, title IV, Sept. 22, 2001,

115 Stat. 237 (49 U.S.C. 40101 note)

TICKETS Act Also known as the *Transparency Improvements and Compensation to Keep Every Ticketholder Safe Act of 2018*

Pub. L. 115-254, div. B, title IV, Sec. 425, Oct. 5, 2018,

132 Stat. 3338 (49 U.S.C. note prec. 42301)

Trade Act of 1974

Pub. L. 93 618, Jan. 3, 1975,

88 Stat. 1978 (19 U.S.C. 2101 et seq.)

Short title, see 19 U.S.C. 2101

Transparency Improvements and Compensation to Keep Every Ticketholder Safe Act of 2018 Also known as the *TICKETS Act*

Pub. L. 115-254, div. B, title IV, Sec. 425, Oct. 5, 2018,

132 Stat. 3338 (49 U.S.C. note prec. 42301)

Trust Fund Code of 1981

Aug. 16, 1954, ch. 736, § 1(d) [Internal Revenue Title, subtitle I], as added Pub. L. 97 119, title I, § 103(a), Dec. 29, 1981,

95 Stat. 1636 (26 U.S.C. 9500 et seq.)

Vision 100 Century of Aviation Reauthorization Act

Pub. L. 108 176, Dec. 12, 2003,

117 Stat. 2490

Short title, see 49 U.S.C. 40101 note

Wendell H. Ford Aviation Investment and Reform Act for the 21st Century

Pub. L. 106 181, Apr. 5, 2000,

114 Stat. 61

Short title, see 49 U.S.C. 40101 note

INDEX

Index

A

ADS-B - 259, 456
Advanced Materials Center of
   Excellence - 140, 210
advisory committee - 192,
   255–256, 259–260, 264–265,
   278–280, 284, 289, 345, 350,
   366, 381–384, 395–397, 399,
   404, 411–412, 415–416, 447,
   449–451, 468, 481–483,
   501–502, 511, 525
   Air Carrier Access Act - 280,
      395–397
   aviation consumer protection -
      380
   *Safety Oversight and
      certification* - 192, 264
   *Safety Oversight and
      Certification Advisory
      Committee* - 192, 264
   *Safety Oversight and
      Certification Advisory
      Committee* - 192, 264
   Transportation Statistics - 256,
      289, 379–382
aeronautics - 27, 41–42, 143, 166,
   233, 451, 456, 474, 486, 488
air ambulance - 300
air carrier - 16, 41–42, 61, 144,
   161, 164, 183–184, 187,
   199–200, 217, 254, 256, 259,
   279–283, 285, 288–289, 291,
   294–295, 299, 304, 307–308,
   315–316, 318–319, 326,
   333–339, 342–343, 345–346,
   357, 361, 371–373, 379–382,
   385–390, 392, 394–401, 410,
   414, 421, 424, 450, 458–459,
   461, 465, 488, 521, 524
air carrier operating - 343, 361,
   372–373

air commerce - 70, 303, 344
air navigation facility - 70
air show - 525
air tour - 255, 318–328, 534
air traffic control - 77–78, 85–86,
   256–257, 265, 283, 285, 312,
   314, 339–341, 350, 360,
   374–380, 406, 408–410, 413,
   419–423, 476, 482, 494–495, 503
air traffic control system - 77,
   265, 285, 339–340, 375–376,
   379–380, 503
Air Traffic Control System
   Command Center - 380
Air Traffic Organization - 273,
   376, 382, 452
air transportation - 1, 7, 39, 41,
   150, 198, 205–206, 262, 266,
   280, 282, 300, 380–381, 400,
   493, 500, 522, 531, 533, 540
air transportation safety - 531
Aircraft certification - 1, 8, 137,
   139–140, 142–144, 149–150,
   159, 166, 170–171, 173, 175,
   177, 180, 184, 195, 200, 270,
   278, 283, 287, 292, 294, 301,
   310, 368–370, 484, 531, 544
Aircraft Certification Service -
   143–144, 149–150, 166,
   170–171, 173, 175, 177, 195,
   294, 310, 370
aircraft manufacturer - 73
aircraft manufacturers - 45,
   198, 293, 304, 307–308, 342,
   346, 382, 386, 398, 450
Airline transport pilot - 154,
   158, 255, 335, 338
airlines - 3, 41, 185, 187, 192,
   307, 511–512, 524–525
airman - 85–86, 185–186, 213,
   239, 242–249, 255, 288–289,
   339, 344–348, 350–352,
   355–356, 359, 365–366, 455,